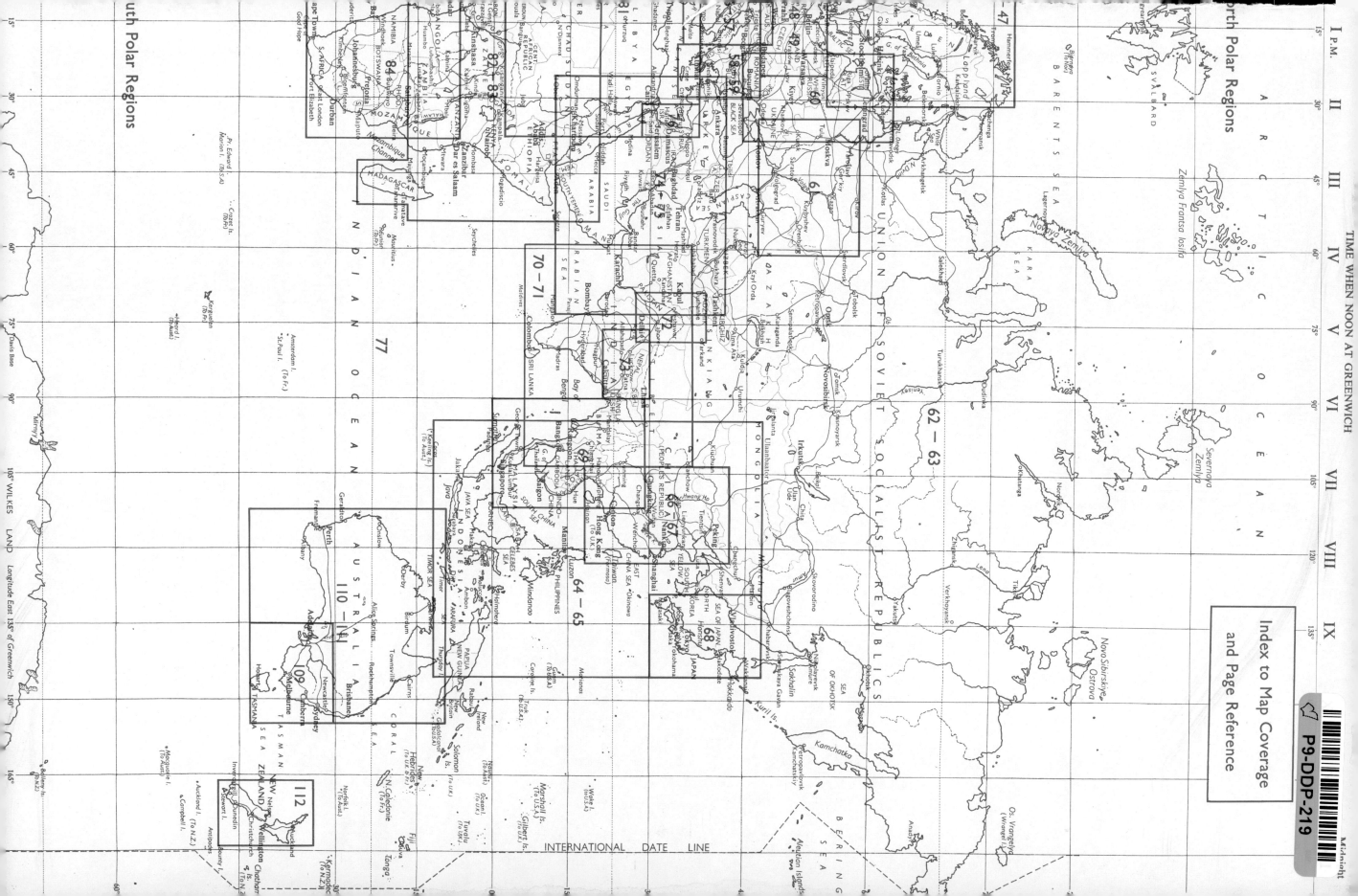

THE
WORLD ATLAS

JOHN C. BARTHOLOMEW, M.A., F.R.S.E.

DIRECTOR, THE GEOGRAPHICAL INSTITUTE, EDINBURGH

ELEVENTH EDITION

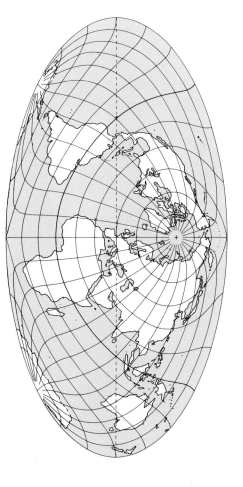

JOHN BARTHOLOMEW & SON LTD

EDINBURGH

1977

As Edinburgh World Atlas
First Edition – 1954
Eighth Edition – 1973

As The World Atlas
Ninth Edition – 1974
Tenth Edition – 1975
Eleventh Edition – 1977

© 1977 JOHN BARTHOLOMEW & SON LTD
PRINTED IN GREAT BRITAIN
AT THE GEOGRAPHICAL INSTITUTE, EDINBURGH
ISBN 0 85152 780 9
6666

FOREWORD

THIS Atlas, planned originally for academic purposes, has become so popular among general readers throughout the world, on account of its fresh scientific approach to many world problems, that it is now issued as a library and general reference atlas under the present modified title.

A humanistic viewpoint is given to all continental areas by showing density of population along with its vegetational, climatic and physical backgrounds. Special introductory maps show racial distinctions along with mineral and agricultural resources of the world.

Students of cartography will find matter of interest in the new projections employed. These to the number of four are designed to show more realistic relations of the inhabited land masses, as in the *Nordic* Projection on pages 22-23, which reveals the proximity of the Soviet Union to the United States; another, the *Regional* on pages 14-15, claims to show conformal properties (truth to shape) in the best manner possible; while another, the *Atlantis* on page 11, is ideal for displaying world air communications centred on the Atlantic Ocean.

Place-names are spelt on the most rational system possible, viz., to conform with the local usage of the country in question; traditional or English forms are given in brackets where these are of sufficient importance.

A new form of co-ordinate system for the ready location of positions has been introduced and is explained on page 1; being related to time, it is known as the "Hour System".

THE GEOGRAPHICAL INSTITUTE,
EDINBURGH, July 1954.

JOHN BARTHOLOMEW.

PREFACE TO SEVENTH EDITION

Recent strides in the advancement of our knowledge of the earth and its resources are reflected in a series of new world maps illustrating structure, seismology, relief, continental drift, minerals, energy, food and soils. The British Isles likewise have a comparable series of new maps.

In conformity with the metrication of units of measurement, all temperature maps have been redrawn in degrees Celsius (°C) and spot heights have been altered from feet to metres.

EDINBURGH, September 1970.

JOHN C. BARTHOLOMEW

CONTENTS

The contraction "M" is used to denote scale of map in millionths.

PAGE

Page	Entry	Scale
1	GEOGRAPHICAL CO-ORDINATES	
2–3	GEOGRAPHICAL TERMS	
4	CLIMATIC TABLES	
5	STATES AND POPULATION	
6	WORLD EXPLORATION (Old World)	
7	WORLD EXPLORATION (New World)	
8–9	MAP PROJECTIONS	
10	MAP PROJECTIONS (modern)	
11	WORLD AIRWAYS	
12	ASTRONOMICAL CHARTS	

THE WORLD

Page	Entry	Scale
13	(a) STRUCTURE	1:130 M.
	(b) SEISMOLOGY	1:130 M.
14–15	PHYSIOGRAPHY	1:90 M.
	Drainage Regions, Continental Drift	
16–17	TEMPERATURE AND AIR MOVEMENTS	
	Air Pressure and Winds, January, July	
	Temperature, January, July	
	Air Masses and Fronts	
	Storm Tracks	
	Temperature Extremes	
	Amount of Cloud	
18–19	RAINFALL AND OCEANOGRAPHY	
	Climatic Regions	
	Length of Growing Seasons	
20–21	ECONOMIC RESOURCES	
	Minerals Food	
	Energy Soils	
22–23	ETHNOLOGY	1:140 M.
	Cephalic Index, Religions	
24–25	STATES OF THE WORLD	
	Changes of Sovereignty	
	Time Zones	
26	NORTH POLAR REGIONS	1:30 M.
	Temperature, January, July	
27	SOUTH POLAR REGIONS	1:30 M.
	Temperature, January, July	

EURASIA

Page	Entry	Scale
28	VEGETATION	1:45 M.
	Rainfall, January, July	
29	POPULATION	1:45 M.
	Temperature, January, July	
30–31	EURASIA	1:30 M.
	Races	

EUROPE

Page	Entry	Scale
32–33	EUROPE	1:15 M.
34	NORTH-WEST EUROPE	1:10 M.
35	BRITISH ISLES	1:6 M.
	Geology	
	Structure and	
	Land Use	
36	Climate	
	Population	
	Energy	
	Industry	
37	NORTH ENGLAND	1:8 M.
	Isle of Man	1:1¼ M.
38–39	SOUTH ENGLAND AND WALES	1:1¼ M.
	Channel Islands	
40–41	SCOTLAND	1:1¼ M.
	Shetland, Fair Isle, St Kilda	
42–43	IRELAND	1:1¼ M.
	Population	
44	THE LOW COUNTRIES	1:1¼ M.
45	SWITZERLAND	1:1¼ M.
46–47	SCANDINAVIA AND THE BALTIC	1:4½ M.
	Iceland, The Faeroes	
48–49	GERMANY, POLAND & CZECHOSLOVAKIA	1:3 M.
50–51	CENTRAL EUROPE & MEDITERRANEAN	1:10 M.
52–53	IBERIAN PENINSULA	1:3 M.
54–55	FRANCE AND NORTH ALGERIA	1:3 M.
	Corsica	

PAGE

EUROPE—continued

Page	Entry	Scale
56–57	ITALY AND THE ADRIATIC	1:3 M.
58–59	THE BALKANS AND LOWER DANUBE	1:3 M.
60	EUROPEAN RUSSIA	1:6 M.
61	VOLGA BASIN	1:6 M.

ASIA

Page	Entry	Scale
62–63	SOVIET UNION	1:17½ M.
64–65	THE FAR EAST	1:15 M.
66–67	EAST CHINA	1:6 M.
68	JAPAN	1:6 M.
69	INDO-CHINA	1:10 M.
	Singapore	
70–71	INDIA, PAKISTAN AND SRI LANKA	1:10 M.
	Races, Population, Religions	
72	PUNJAB AND KASHMIR	1:4 M.
73	PLAIN OF THE GANGES	1:4 M.
74–75	THE MIDDLE EAST	1:10 M.
76	THE LEVANT COAST	1:2½ M.
77	INDIAN OCEAN	1:40 M.
	Islands	

AFRICA

Page	Entry	Scale
78	VEGETATION	1:35 M.
	Rainfall, January, July	
79	POPULATION	1:35 M.
	Temperature, January, July	
80–81	NORTH-WEST AFRICA	1:12½ M.
	Azores (Açores), Cape Verde Is.	
82–83	CENTRAL AND EAST AFRICA	1:12½ M.
	Ascension, St Helena, Madagascar	
84	SOUTH AFRICA	1:12½ M.
	The Cape, Witwatersrand	

NORTH AMERICA

Page	Entry	Scale
85	ATLANTIC OCEAN	1:48 M.
86	VEGETATION	1:34 M.
	Rainfall, January, July	
87	POPULATION	1:34 M.
	Temperature, January, July	
88–89	CANADA	1:12½ M.
90	GULF OF ST LAWRENCE	1:5 M.
91	GREAT LAKES	1:5 M.
92	PACIFIC COAST	1:5 M.
93	NORTH CENTRAL STATES	1:5 M.
94–95	MIDDLE WEST STATES	1:5 M.
96	MIDDLE ATLANTIC STATES	1:2½ M.
97	SOUTHERN STATES	1:5 M.
98–99	UNITED STATES OF AMERICA	1:12½ M.
	Hawaiian Is., San Francisco,	
	Alaska, New York	
100	MEXICO	1:10 M.
101	THE CARIBBEAN	1:10 M.
	The Panama Canal	

SOUTH AMERICA

Page	Entry	Scale
102	VEGETATION	1:32 M.
	Rainfall, January, July	
103	ARGENTINA AND CHILE	1:12½ M.
	South America Population	
104–105	BRAZIL & NORTH ANDEAN STATES	1:12½ M.
	South America Temperature, Jan., July	

AUSTRALASIA

Page	Entry	Scale
106–107	PACIFIC OCEAN	1:45 M.
	Islands	
108	VEGETATION	1:28 M.
	Temperature, January, July	
	Rainfall, January, July	
109	SOUTH-EAST AUSTRALIA	1:5 M.
	Tasmania	
110–111	AUSTRALIA	1:12½ M.
	Population	
112	NEW ZEALAND	1:5 M.
	Population	

INDEX OF GEOGRAPHICAL NAMES

GEOGRAPHICAL CO-ORDINATES

THE most ancient function of geography has probably been to describe the location of places on the earth's surface. Thus it cameabout that early Greek philosophers, absorbed in conjectures as to the size and shape of the world they lived in, hit on the method of measuring its estimated circumference by 360 degrees to the circle. Any locality could then be determined by reference to a prime meridian and the number of degrees from the Equator. This method was adopted by Claudius Ptolemy of Alexandria in his tables and maps; and with modifications is much the same as the system of latitude and longitude in use to-day. That it should have survived so long is testimony of its efficiency, especially for navigational purposes. For more ordinary use, however, it is surprising that a simpler and more easily quoted system has not been adopted. True, there have been attempts in that direction. The circle has been divided into 100, which would help if all maps were so printed. More noteworthy are the systems of Military and National Grids, which served an essential purpose during both World Wars. For civilian and international use, however, these grids stand at great disadvantage. Being imposed in right-angled pattern on a particular projection of limited area, they are not suitable for extending to other areas. For instance, a grid planned for Great Britain on Transverse Mercator's Projection would not at the same time be suitable for Germany. Moreover, unless the grid were printed on all maps in common use it would be of little service to the man-in-the-street.

To avoid these disadvantages, therefore, the system used in this atlas has been devised. It has the merit of being international. It is related to the World Grid, based on Greenwich, and can thus be used on any map, if necessary without being specially so printed. It avoids the confusing factor of reading east and west of a prime meridian. Its formula is compact and simple to understand. Finally, it is capable of infinite precision by the use of decimal subdivision.

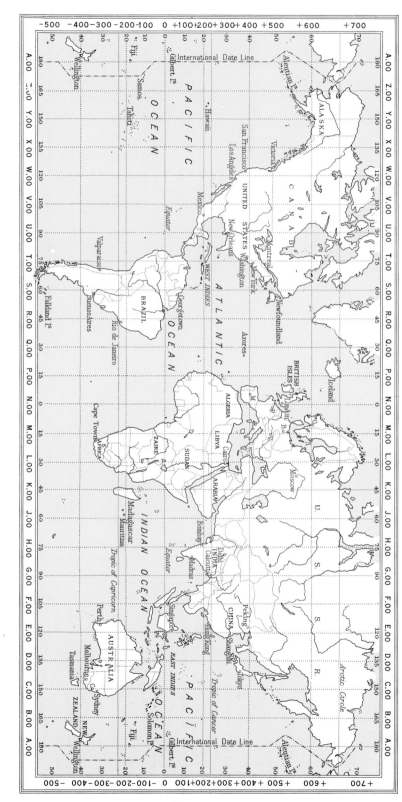

RULES FOR USE OF "HOUR" CO-ORDINATES

1. The World is divided into twenty-four hour zones, each of 15° longitude and denoted by a letter of the alphabet, omitting I and O which may be confused with numerals. Starting point of the A zone is the meridian 180° E. of Greenwich, associated with the International Date Line. All readings are made East to West, i.e., with transit of the Sun, Greenwich being N.

2. Every hour zone of 15° is subdivided longitudinally, i.e., by Westings into 90 units, reading likewise East to West. For greater precision these may be divided into further decimal parts. The units are marked in the top and bottom borders of each map.

   It will be found that 60 units Westing = 10° of longitude

06	,,	,,	= 1°
01	,,	,,	= 10'
001	,,	,,	= 1'
0001	,,	,,	= 6"

3. In the co-ordinate of latitude the quadrant from Equator to Pole is divided into 90 parts, each of which is then subdivided into 10 units.

   It will be found that 100 units Northing = 10° of latitude

010	,,	,,	= 1°
001	,,	,,	= 6'
0001	,,	,,	= 36"

   The coupling sign + or − marks this co-ordinate, meaning North or South respectively from the Equator. These Northing or Southing units are marked on the East and West sides of the Atlas maps. Further decimal subdivisions may also be used.

4. The complete co-ordinate is given by the hour figure or Westing, followed by the latitude figure or Northing,

   thus M 89 + 522 = Cambridge, England
   and T 12 + 389 = Washington, D.C.

   As the hour letter and the + or − are both treated as if they were decimal points, it is important to include the initial 0's so that all readings less than 10 should be written 05, 001, or as the case may be.

5. Readings apply to the space between the last digit given and the next digit; but, where greater precision on a larger scale is required, as in the case of the annexed One-Inch section of the English Lake District readings may be made to several places of decimals. Here the Church at Grasmere becomes N 1813 + 5456.

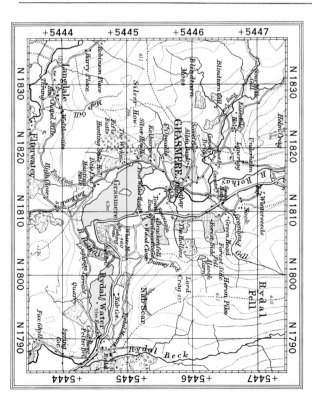

6. The above system, as used in this Atlas, is intended to assist travellers, writers, or scientific and commercial interests in their work. Free permission is accordingly given by the author for its use anywhere without restriction. It may be described as Bartholomew's Hour System of Geographical Co-ordinates.

GEOGRAPHICAL TERMS

Abad *(Persian)*, town.
Aborigines, the earliest inhabitants of a country.
Ada *(Turkish)*, island.
Aiguille *(French)*, needle; applied to certain pinnacle-shaped mountain peaks.
Ain, Bir *(Arabic)*, a well or spring.
Ainu, a race inhabiting N. Hokkaido and S. Sakhalin.
Air Mass, an extensive body of air, moving or stationary, having throughout similar characteristics of temperature and humidity.
Akaba *(Arabic)*, pass.
Alf, älv, elf, elv *(Swedish* and *Norse)*, river.
Alluvium, fine sand or silt deposited, largely during flood periods, by streams and rivers.
Anticline, an arch of strata on both sides of which the rocks dip downwards.
Anticyclone, a high pressure system occuring in the zone of the "Westerlies", usually accompanied by fine weather. Wind tends to move outwards in clockwise direction in the Northern Hemisphere, anticlockwise in the Southern.
Antipodes, that part of the earth diametrically opposite to our feet, on the same meridian, but with latitude and seasons reversed, *e.g.* New Zealand is the antipodes of Great Britain.
Arctic Circle, constituted by the parallel 66°32′ N., separating North Temperate and North Frigid Zones. North of this at mid-summer the sun does not set during the 24 hours, while at mid-winter it does not rise. In the Southern Hemisphere the same conditions apply S. of the **Antarctic Circle**, 66°32′ S.
Artesian Well, a water supply obtained by tapping porous rock strata from which the water rises by natural pressure. Derived from Artois in France.
Atolls, circular coral reefs enclosing a central lagoon connected with the outside sea by an opening. Found mostly in the Pacific Ocean.
Avalanches, masses of loosened snow and ice mixed with earth and stone, precipitated with destructive force down mountain sides.
Axis, the imaginary line running from pole to pole through the centre of and on which the earth revolves.
Aztecs, the highly civilised dominant race in Mexico at the time of the Spanish invasion in 1519.
Bahia *(Portuguese* and *Spanish)*, bay.
Bahr *(Arabic)*, sea, lake, river.
Bal, Bally, Baile *(Celtic)*, town, village.
Ban *(Siamese)*, village.
Bandar, Nagar, Pura *(Indian)*, town.
Bantu, *i.e.*, "people"; correlated races of Africa between lat. 5° N. and 25° S. They include Xhosas and Zulus.
Bar, gravel, sand or mud deposited across the mouth of a river by currents or wave action; often impedes navigation.
Bas *(French)*, low, low-lying.
Basin, area of land drained by a river, and its tributaries.
Basin of Inland Drainage, an area of land which has no surface drainage outlet to the sea.
Basques, an ancient race with a distinct language inhabiting N.E. Spain and S.W. France, on the shores of the Bay of Biscay.
Basutos, a branch of the Bantu race occupying Lesotho.
Batang *(Malay)*, river.
Beaches, Raised, small platforms of land, formerly sea shore, now left dry through a rise of the land level.
Beaufort Scale, a scale of 13 symbols used in weather maps to portray the force of the wind from calm to more than 120 kilometres per hour.
Bedouins, nomadic tribes of Arabia and North Africa.
Beled *(Arabic)*, country, village.
Ben, Beinn *(Celtic)*, mountain.
Bender *(Persian)*, harbour, landing-place.
Black Earth, fertile soil in S. Russia and parts of Romania and Hungary on which heavy grain crops are grown.
Boers, descendants of the early Dutch colonists in South Africa.
Bora, a cold, dry, northerly wind, blowing in winter and spring along the Dalmatian coast of the Adriatic Sea.
Bore or **Eagre**, a tidal wave arising in the estuaries of certain rivers.
Boulder Clay, a glacial deposit, consisting of boulders of various sizes embedded in finer material, laid down under a glacier or ice cap and often found to great depths in glaciated valleys.
Brdo *(Czech.)*, a hill.
Brunn *(German)*, a spring, well.
Bugt, Bukt *(Danish* and *Swedish)*, a bay.
Buran, snow blizzards of winter occuring in Russia and Siberia.
Burun *(Turkish)*, a headland, promontory.
Bush, The, interior uncultivated scrubland.
Bushmen, or in Afrikaans **Boesmanne** an aboriginal Negrito nomadic race of south central Africa, now mostly in the Kalahari desert.
Butte *(French* and *Amer.)*, an isolated hill or peak.
Cabo *(Portoguese* and *Spanish)*, a cape.
Campo *(Italian* and *Spanish)*, a plain.
Campos, grasslands of S.E. Brazil.
Canon or Canyon *(Spanish)*, a deep gorge or ravine with lofty sides. Formed by rapid erosion of the softer strata in a dry region, *e.g.*, Colorado Canon.
Catingas, open forest lands on the plateaux of Eastern Brazil, north of 15° S. Drier and warmer than the adjoining **Cerrados**; they contain cactus, mimosa and other types of dry vegetation.
Cephalic Index, the shape of the head expressed by a number which is obtained by giving the breadth of the head as a percentage of its length.
Cerrados, semi-dry plateaux of S.E. Brazil covered with grass and trees of stunted growth.
Chart, map of the sea for use of navigators.
Chinook, a warm, dry west wind blowing down the east slopes of the Rocky Mountains.
Chotts, *see* Shotts.
Chow *(Chinese)*, town of the second rank.
Chrebet *(Russian)*, a chain; mountain range.
Cidade *(Portuguese)*, town.
Cima, Pizzo *(Italian)*, mountain peak.
Cirrus Clouds, very lofty (eight to ten kilometres high) fibrous looking clouds, associated with fine weather.
Città *(Italian)*, town, city.
Ciudad *(Spanish)*, city, town.
Climate, the generalisation of day to day weather conditions.
Col *(French)*, **Colle** *(Italian)*, a pass or neck.
Cold Front, the sloping boundary between an advancing mass of cold air and warmer air under which the cold air forms a wedge.
Continental Shelf, a sea-covered platform extending from the coast-line of all continents. It varies in width and the edge is usually marked by the isobath for 200 metres.
Contour, a line on a map joining all points which are situated at the same height above sea-level.
Cordillera *(Spanish)*, mountain range.
Crater, the cup-shaped cavity forming the mouth of a volcano.
Creek *(Amer.)*, a stream or small river.
Crevasse, rent or fissure in a glacier or ice sheet.
Cumulus Clouds, massive rounded clouds (approx. 1500 metres high), associated with hot weather and rising air-currents.
Cycle of Erosion, the development of the landscape by the various processes of denudation from the youthful stage, after a period of instability and mountain building, through maturity till the surface is reduced to a peneplane.
Cyclone, a low pressure system, or **depression**, generally associated with stormy or wet weather. Winds tend to blow inwards in anti-clockwise direction in N. Hemisphere; clockwise in South.
Daban *(Mongolian)*, a pass.
Dagh *(Turkish)*, mountain.
Dake, Take *(Japanese)*, mountain.
Dal *(Norwegian, Swedish)*, valley.
Darya *(Persian)*, sea, stream, river.
Date Line, this follows approximately the 180° meridian from Greenwich, and marks the point where according to international convention the day begins. A ship crossing this line eastwards goes back a day, while westward it goes forward a day.
Declineation, the deviation of the compass needle from True North.
Delta, a triangular or finger-shaped tract of mud and detritus deposited by a river at its mouth when it no longer has sufficient speed to keep them in suspension.
Denudation, the slow process of laying bare and levelling down the physical features of the earth's surface by natural forces.
Depression, a localised and mobile low pressure system occuring in the zone of the "Westerlies" associated with rain and stormy weather.
Derbend *(Persian, Turkish)*, pass.
Desert, a barren area of land, practically devoid of rainfall or vegetation.
Dip, the angle between the downward slope of a stratum of rock and the horizontal.
Dogger Bank, important fishing ground in North Sea, depth varies from 11 to 36 metres.
Doldrums, nautical term for a region of calms and baffling winds near the equator between the N.E. and S.E. Trade Winds.
Dolina *(Slav.)*, a large hollow or basin caused by the dissolving of limestone. Cultivated if not occupied by a pond.
Donga *(Afrikaans)*, ravine, gulley.
Dorp *(Dutch)*, **Dorf** *(German)*, village.
Dunes, mounds formed by wind-blown sand; capable of considerable advances over level ground unless arrested by the planting of suitable vegetation.
Earthquake, disturbance of the earth's surface generally occuring along faults or lines of weakness in the earth's crust. Sometimes cause great destruction, especially on alluvial ground.
Eiland *(Dutch)*' island.
Ennis *(Irish)*, island.
Equator, imaginary line circumscribing the globe midway between the poles and at its greatest circumference (40 074.72 km). It constitutes the zero from which latitudes N. and S. are calculated.
Equinox, one of the two periods of the year when day and night are of equal duration owing to the sun's crossing the Equator. 20th March and 22nd September.
Erosion, the wearing away of surface features of the earth by the action of wind, water or ice.
Escarpment, the steep face of a hill or range which on the other side slopes gently downwards *e.g.*, Cotswold and Chiltern escarpments.
Eskimos or **Esquimaux**, an aboriginal race inhabiting the Arctic coasts of America, especially of Greenland and Alaska. They live chiefly by fishing.
Estuary, the lower reaches of a river affected by the tides.
Falu *(Hungarian)*, village.
Fault, a break or crack in the earth's surface.
Fell *(Norwegian*, **Fjeld**; *Swedish*, **Fjäll**), mountain.
Fen *(Anglo-Saxon)*, swampy or boggy land.
Fiume *(Italian)*, river.
Fjord, old glacial valley filled by the sea. Sides often steepened by faulting.
Flood Plain, the generally flat area in the bottom of a valley which is covered by water when the river draining it is in flood.
Föhn, a dry warm wind in the valleys of the Alps, blowing in winter from the south.
Fork, the junction of two streams or rivers of approximately the same size.
Fu *(Chinese)*, town of importance.
Ganga *(Indian)*, river.
Gap, *see* **Pass.**
Gawa, Kawa *(Japanese)*, river.
Gebel, Jebel *(Arabic)*, rock, mountain.
Geysers, intermittent spouting hot springs associated with volcanic activity as in Iceland.
Glaciers, rivers of ice originating in snowfields, and moving slowly down valleys until they melt, or on reaching the sea break off as icebergs.
Gol, Song *(Mongolian)*, river.
Gora *(Slav.)*, mountain.
Gorod, Grad *(Slav.)*, town.
Gran Chaco, "the great hunting place", is an extensive area between Argentina, Bolivia and Paraguay consisting for the most part of swampy plains with varied vegetation; rich in animal and bird life.
Grand Banks, submarine banks situated south-east of Newfoundland. One of the best cod fishing grounds in the world.
Great Circle, a circle on the earth's surface whose plane passes through the centre of the earth.
Great Circle Route, shortest distance between two points on the earth, hence used for preference by shipping and air services.
Growing Season, that part of the year during which plant growth is possible. The main factors limiting the length of the period are the occurence of killing frosts and drought.
Guba *(Russian)*, bay.
Gulch *(Amer.)*, a narrow, deep ravine.
Gulf Stream, great warm water current originating in the Gulf of Mexico and flowing across the Atlantic to North-West Europe.
Gunung *(Malay)*, mountain.
Hachures, closely drawn lines sometimes used on maps to denote ground relief. They should follow the direction of slope and vary in intensity with the gradient.
Haf *(Swedish)*, sea.
Hai, Hu *(Chinese)*, sea or lake.
Hamn *(Swedish)*, harbour.
Harmattan, a hot dry wind laden with clouds of reddish dust from the desert blowing over the Guinea Lands in December, January and February. It is an extension of the N.E. Trade wind.
Havn *(Danish)*' harbour.
Havre *(French)*, harbour, port.
Hegy *(Hungarian)*, mountain.
Height of Land *(Amer.)*, a watershed or divide.
Hinterland, region inland from a coast. Often deciding factor in location or growth of a port.
Ho *(Chinese)*, river.
Hoek *(Dutch)*, cape.
Höhe *(German)*, height, hill.
Horse Latitudes, regions of calms and variable winds between 25° and 40° N. and S. on the polar margins of the Trade Winds.
Horst, a block of rock left upstanding by the down faulting of rocks on either side. Exact opposite of rift valley.
Hottentots, an indigenous race in western South Africa.
Hsi *(Chinese)*, west.
Hsien *(Chinese)*, town of the third class.
Humidity, the amount of water vapour in the air. Relative Humidity is percentage of moisture contained as compared with that contained in air completely saturated at the given temperature.
Hurricane or **Typhoon**, a violent and destructive tropical cyclone which occasionally blows in the Gulf of Mexico and the China Seas (where it is known as Typhoon) in August, September or October.
Icebergs, detached masses of ice floating in the Polar Seas, carried along by ocean currents. Originate from glaciers, terminating in the sea. Danger to navigation in Atlantic.
Inch, Innis *(Celtic)*, island.

Irmak (*Turkish*), river.
Isla (*Spanish*), **Isola** (*Italian*), island.
Isobars, lines connecting points having the same barometric pressure at a given time.
Isobaths, lines connecting points of the ocean of equal depths.
Isobytes, lines connecting points with equal rainfall over given period.
Isotherms, lines connecting points of equal temperature at a given time.
Jaur, Javr, Järvi (*Finnish*), lake.
Jesero (*Serbian*), lake.
Joch (*German*), mountain ridge; pass.
Joki (*Finnish*), river.
Jug (*Serbian*), **Yug** (*Russian*), south.
Kahil (*Arabic*), desert.
Kampong (*Malay*), village.
Karroo, terraced plains between the mountains in South Africa. Desert in dry season, but develop vegetation in wet season and are used as sheep pasture.
Karst, the porous limestone region of the Dinaric Alps north-east of Adriatic Sea. Also applied to similar types of country in other lands where the river system disappears underground.
Kato (*Greek*), under.
Khamsin (*Arabic*, "Fifty"), name given to Sirocco in Lower Egypt where it blows for fifty days between April and June.
Kiang (*Chinese*), river.
Koppie (*S. African*), a small hill.
Kraal, a native dwelling in South Africa.
Kuh (*Persian*), mountain.
Kul (*Turkish*), lake.
Kum or **Qum** (*Turkish*), sand.
La (*Tibetan*), pass.
Lac (*French*), **Lacul** (*Romanian*), lake.
Lago (*Italian, Portuguese, Spanish*), lake.
Lande (*French*), heath or waste land.
Latitude, the angular distance of a place N. or S. of the equator measured on its meridian. Each degree represents sixty geographical or nautical miles equal to 69.172 statute miles (111.319 km).
Levante (*Italian*), east.
Levees, embankments, natural or artificial, erected along the banks of rivers and built, as on the Mississippi, to prevent flooding.
Llanos, grasslands of the N.W. Orinoco Basin.
Loch, Lough (*Celtic*), lake.
Loess, a post glacial wind-blown soil of great fertility: found in N. European Plain and in the Hwang Ho Valley of China.
Long Forties, a portion of the North Sea, so known to fishermen because the depth of water approximates 40 fathoms (73 metres).
Longitude, the angular distance of any place on the globe eastward or westward from a standard meridian, as in Great Britain that of Greenwich. Each degree of longitude represents 4 minutes of time, so that 15° of longitude represent an hour.
Magyars, native name of Hungarians.
Mallee, type of Australian scrub growing in the Murray-Darling and other areas. It is characterised by low-growing eucalyptus and other gum trees.
Maoris, the aboriginal inhabitants of New Zealand.
Marais (*French*), marsh.
Mean Annual Rainfall, the average amount of rain which falls in a year. The average is deduced from observations taken over a considerable period.
Meander, the winding about of a river in its flood plain when it has reached its base line of erosion but still has energy for further corrosion.
Medine (*French*), town.
Mer (*French*), **Meer** (*German*), sea.
Meridian, an imaginary line represented by a portion of a circle passing through the earth's two poles and on which all places have noon at the same time.
Miasto (*Polish*), village.
Mile (geographical) = 1 minute of latitude, or 6080 feet (1.15 statute miles)(1.9 kilometres).
Millibar, a standard unit of barometric pressure. Average pressure is approximately 1013 millibars or 76 cms of mercury.
Mistral, a violent, dry, cold wind blowing in winter down the Rhône Valley which acts as a funnel when a depression lies over the Mediterranean.
Monsoon, seasonal winds blowing over the S.E. half of Asia. General direction October to March from N.E., April to September from S.W.
Mont (*French*), **Monte** (*Italian*), mount.
Monte, a type of deciduous hardwood forest situ-

ated in the higher portions of the **Gran Chaco**, moister than **Cerrados**.
Montagna (*Italian*), mountain range.
Moraine, the waste material deposited by a glacier.
Morye (*Russian*), sea.
Muang (*Siamese*), town.
Myo (*Burmese*), town.
Nagar (*Indian*), town.
Nahr (*Arabic*), river.
Nan (*Siamese*), south.
Nan (*Chinese*), south.
Näs (*Scandinavian*), cape.
Natural Scale, see Representative Fraction.
Neap-Tides, period of lowest tide-range, when sun and moon are at right angles, as seen from the earth.
Negeri (*Malay*), town.
Nejd (*Arabic*), high plain.
Nimbus, dark water-laden rain cloud.
Nor (*Mongol.*), lake.
Nos (*Russian*), cape.
Oasis, fertile spot in a desert owing its existence to a spring or well.
Occluded Front, a line along which warm air of the atmosphere has been raised from the earth's surface by the junction of cold and warm fronts.
Ola (*Mongolian*), mountain range.
Oxbow Lake, remains of a pronounced meander which has been short circuited by the river cutting through its neck. They occur on a river like the Mississippi.
Ozero (*Russian*), lake.
Pack Ice, sea ice which has drifted from its original position. It takes the form of floes of various sizes and can be either loosely or tightly packed together.
Pampa (*Argentina*), dreary expanse of treeless grass plain, and salt steppe, lat. 30° to 40° S., between the Andes and the Atlantic Ocean.
Pampero, a cold south-westerly wind that sweeps over the pampas in Central South America.
Pass, a depression or **Gap** in a mountain range which serves as way for communication between the lands on either side.
Peneplane, the almost level surface which, if the normal course of denudation is undisturbed, results from the erosion of a landscape by running water. The gradient of a river draining a peneplane is just great enough for the flow of water to be maintained.
Pizzo (*Italian*), peak.
Plain, an area of flat or undulating ground usually at low level.
Planina (*Bulg., Serb.*), mountain range.
Plateau, an area of relatively flat ground at considerable altitude, sometimes called a Tableland.
Polder, land recovered from the sea in Holland, and protected by dykes from being again flooded.
Ponente (*Italian*), evening, west.
Pont, Ponte (*French, Span., Italian*), bridge.
Potomos (*Greek*), river.
Prairie, a series of grassy plains stretching eastwards from the Rocky Mountains in Canada and U.S.A.
Primeval Forest, a forest which has not been interfered with by man and is allowed to remain in its natural state.
Pristan (*Russian*), port, harbour.
Projection, is the process of transferring the outline of the features on the earth's spherical surface on to a flat surface, thus constituting a map.
Pueblo (*Spanish*), village.
Pulau (*Malay*), island.
Puna, a high plateau between the E. and W. Andes in Bolivia and Peru.
Pur, Pura (*Indian*), town.
Ras (*Arabic*), cape.
Reef, a ridge of rock or coral generally covered by sea, but exposed at low tide.
Representative Fraction, a fraction representing a distance of unit lengths on a map over its corresponding length on the earth's surface.
Ria, river valley drowned by the sea owing to a fall in the land level.
Rieka (*Slav.*), river.
Rift Valley, valley with steep walls caused by the sinking of land between two parallel geological faults.
Rio (*Portuguese, Spanish*), river.
River Capture, process by which one river having more rapid powers of erosion than another cuts into the head waters of the latter and steals certain of its tributaries.
Riviera, narrow strip of sea coast between Toulon

and Spezia, noted for mild climate in winter.
Roaring Forties, nautical name of steady northwesterly winds between lat. 40° and 60° S. Equivalent to Westerlies of N. Hemisphere.
Ross (*Celtic*), promontory.
Saki (*Japanese*), cape.
Sargasso Sea, an area of calms and floating seaweed in the N. Atlantic, east of the Bahamas and the Antilles Current.
Savannas, grasslands of the sub-tropics.
Sea Level, the mean level of the sea between high and low tide.
Selo (*Russian*), village.
Selva (*Portuguese*), forest. The name of Selvas is given to the vast rain forests of the Amazon basin.
Shan (*Chinese*), mountain range.
Shotts (*Arabic*), salt marshy lakes of N. Algeria and Tunisia.
Sierra (*Spanish*), **Serra** (*Portuguese*), mountain range.
Silt, material, finer than sand, which is often carried in suspension by rivers and deposited by them, on flood plains and deltas, when the river has lost the force required to hold the load.
Sirocco, a hot southerly wind blowing off Africa in Southern Mediterranean Countries.
Sjö (*Swedish*), lake.
Slieve (*Irish*), mountain.
Snow Line, the lower limit in altitude of the region which is never free from snow.
Spring Tides, period of highest tides at new or at full moon time, *i.e.* when sun and moon are pulling in line with the earth.
Stad, Stadt (*Dutch, Swedish, German*), town.
Steppe, large expanses of grassland as in European Russia and S.W. Siberia.
Strath (*Celtic*), broad valley of a river.
Stratus, cloud in the form of a level or horizontal sheet.
Sudd, large floating islands of vegetable matter which impede navigation on the Upper White Nile.
Syd (*Danish-Norwegian*), south.
Sziget (*Hungarian*), island.
Taiga, coniferous forest belt south of the Tundra, chiefly used for hunting.
Tanjong (*Malay*), cape.
Tind (*Norwegian*), peak.
Trade Winds, regular steady winds in the tropics, between latitudes 30° N. and 30° S. blowing to the equator, from N.E. in N. Hemisphere and S.E. in Southern.
Tributary, a river or stream which flows into and thus becomes part of a larger river.
Tropics, the parallels 23½° N., **Tropic of Cancer**, and 23½° S., **Tropic of Capricorn**, are "turning points" in the apparent seasonal movements of the sun. On June 22nd at noon it is vertically over all points on the Northern Tropic, on December 22nd at noon it is vertically over all points on the Southern Tropic.
Tundra, treeless plains along Arctic and Antarctic coasts; hard frozen in winter, and only partly thawed in summer; scanty vegetation of lichens and mosses.
Tung (*Chinese*), east.
Ula (*Mongol.*), mountain.
Vatn (*Norwegian*), lake.
Veld, grassy plain in South Africa.
Volcano, a vent in the earth's crust through which molten rock, ashes and steam are ejected from the hot interior.
Wadi, Oued (*Arabic*), a water-course.
Wallace's Line, an imaginary line dividing the characteristic flora and fauna of Asia from that of Australasia. It passes between the islands of Bali and Lombok, thence through the Strait of Macassar between Borneo and Celebes and south of the Philippine Islands. Named after Alfred Russel Wallace the noted scientist.
Warm Front, the sloping boundary in the atmosphere between an advancing mass of warm air and colder air over which the warm air rises.
Watershed, the land-form separating head streams of two river systems. Also known as **waterparting** or **divide**.
Westerlies, predominantly westerly winds in the northern and southern hemispheres N. of 30° N. and S. of 30° S.
Zee (*Dutch*), sea.

CLIMATIC TABLES

A selection of characteristic stations in different parts of the world, giving Mean Temperature in degrees Celsius (°C), and Mean Rainfall in millimetres for each month of the year.

Climatic Type	Station	Lat.	Alt in m.		Jan.	Feb.	Mar.	April	May	June	July	Aug.	Sept.	Oct.	Nov.	Dec.	Year
SUB-POLAR	Nome, Alaska	64.30N	7	°C	-17.1	-14.6	-13.2	-8.2	1.3	7.1	10.1	9.7	5.1	-1.7	-9.8	-14.3	-3.8
				mm	25	28	23	15	23	30	74	76	58	38	25	28	445
	North Cape, Norway	71.6N	6	°C	-3.6	-4.2	-3.4	-0.3	2.8	6.8	9.9	10.0	6.6	2.1	-1.1	-2.9	1.9
				mm	58	61	58	46	48	46	66	58	84	76	74	66	747
WEST MARITIME	Stanley Harbour, Falkland Is.	51.41s	2	°C	9.7	9.8	8.6	6.7	4.7	3.1	2.6	3.0	4.1	5.3	6.8	8.3	6.1
				mm	71	58	56	61	76	61	56	53	33	38	53	71	686
	Ben Nevis, Scotland	56.48N	1344	°C	-4.4	-4.6	-4.5	-2.3	0.7	4.2	4.7	4.4	3.3	-0.8	-2.0	-3.9	-0.5
				mm	480	340	391	221	196	193	279	348	394	386	399	478	4105
	Christchurch, N.Z.	43.31s	6	°C	16.3	15.9	14.5	11.9	8.8	6.4	5.9	6.8	9.4	11.7	13.6	15.7	11.4
				mm	56	46	53	51	66	71	46	46	41	41	46	51	640
	Edinburgh, Scotland	55.55N	80	°C	3.9	4.2	5.2	7.4	10.1	13.2	14.8	14.6	12.6	9.2	6.3	4.4	8.8
				mm	56	41	48	36	51	48	69	79	51	66	53	53	635
	Paris, France	48.50N	50	°C	2.5	3.9	6.2	9.7	13.4	16.9	18.6	18.0	15.0	10.3	6.0	4.1	10.3
				mm	36	36	36	43	53	53	51	48	51	53	48	41	528
	Valdivia, Chile	39.46s	43	°C	15.3	14.9	13.7	11.9	10.8	9.2	8.9	9.1	9.6	10.6	11.8	13.7	11.4
				mm	74	81	163	236	389	445	391	343	185	127	112	122	2667
	Valentia, Ireland	51.56N	9	°C	6.9	6.8	7.2	8.9	11.1	13.7	14.9	14.9	13.7	10.8	8.6	7.5	10.4
				mm	140	132	114	94	79	81	97	122	104	142	140	165	1415
	Victoria, B.C.	48.24N	26	°C	3.8	4.6	6.3	8.8	11.6	13.9	15.7	15.4	13.3	10.2	6.9	5.1	9.6
				mm	117	81	64	41	30	23	10	15	46	64	112	147	787
SEMI-CONTINENTAL	Chicago, Illinois	41.53N	251	°C	-3.6	-2.8	2.6	8.6	14.7	20.0	23.3	22.7	19.1	12.7	5.3	-0.9	10.1
				mm	53	53	66	74	91	84	86	76	79	64	61	53	841
	Nashville, Tennessee	36.10N	175	°C	3.8	4.9	9.7	14.9	20.2	24.4	26.1	25.3	22.2	15.8	9.4	5.1	15.2
				mm	119	107	130	112	97	107	104	89	89	61	94	99	1204
	Warsaw, Poland	52.13N	119	°C	-3.1	-1.9	1.8	7.9	14.1	17.2	18.8	17.5	13.5	7.9	2.2	-1.2	7.9
				mm	27	25	33	41	51	61	79	66	46	41	38	36	478
COLD CONTINENTAL	Moscow, U.S.S.R.	55.50N	146	°C	-10.8	-9.2	-4.3	3.4	11.8	15.6	18.0	15.8	9.7	3.7	-2.8	-7.9	3.6
				mm	33	30	36	36	46	66	79	79	53	41	46	36	599
	Verkhoyansk, U.S.S.R.	67.33N	101	°C	-50.5	-44.0	-31.0	-13.3	1.6	13.1	15.6	10.0	1.9	-15.0	-36.5	-46.4	-16.2
				mm	5	5	5	5	13	23	28	25	13	8	8	5	99
	Winnipeg, Manitoba	49.53N	232	°C	-17.5	-16.8	-9.8	3.5	11.3	16.8	19.1	17.7	12.1	4.8	-5.9	-14.5	1.4
				mm	23	18	30	36	51	79	69	56	56	36	28	23	513
EAST MARITIME	Miyako, Japan	39.38N	30	°C	-0.6	-0.3	2.6	8.2	12.3	16.0	19.9	22.1	18.5	12.6	7.2	2.2	10.0
				mm	69	66	89	99	119	127	135	178	216	170	81	64	1412
	St John's, Newfoundland	47.34N	38	°C	-4.7	-5.3	-2.4	1.6	6.1	10.6	15.2	15.4	12.1	7.4	2.8	-1.7	4.8
				mm	137	127	117	109	91	91	97	97	137	137	152	137	1382
PRAIRIE STEPPE	Bahia Blanca, Argentina	38.43s	15	°C	23.2	22.2	19.4	15.3	11.5	8.4	8.1	9.4	12.2	14.9	18.6	21.7	15.4
				mm	41	38	48	56	43	28	20	20	61	56	71	51	533
	Calgary, Alberta	51.2N	1033	°C	-10.9	-9.2	-3.7	4.6	9.5	13.5	16.2	15.2	10.4	5.4	-2.4	-7.0	3.4
				mm	18	18	23	41	56	79	53	48	41	20	18	15	401
	Semipalatinsk, U.S.S.R.	50.26N	180	°C	-17.5	-16.8	-9.8	5.5	14.0	20.0	22.2	19.6	12.7	3.4	-6.6	-14.4	2.5
				mm	13	15	15	20	23	33	28	25	15	15	18	20	185
MANCHURIAN	Peking, China	39.55N	40	°C	-4.7	-1.5	5.0	13.7	19.9	24.5	26.0	24.7	19.8	12.5	3.6	-2.6	11.7
				mm	3	5	10	15	36	76	239	160	66	15	8	3	632
HUMID TEMPERATE	Brisbane, Australia	27.28s	42	°C	25.1	24.7	23.5	21.3	18.1	15.7	14.7	15.8	18.5	21.0	23.1	24.7	20.5
				mm	160	157	142	91	71	66	58	53	53	66	94	122	1135
	Charleston, S. Carolina	32.47N	15	°C	9.9	10.7	14.2	17.7	22.3	25.6	27.0	26.7	24.6	19.4	14.3	10.6	18.6
				mm	74	84	86	74	86	127	178	168	127	91	61	73	1229
	Wuhan, China	30.35N	36	°C	3.8	4.5	9.6	16.2	21.7	25.7	28.6	28.5	24.4	18.2	12.1	6.3	16.6
				mm	41	56	91	132	152	180	168	97	61	91	25	19	1113
MEDITERRANEAN	Adelaide, Australia	34.55s	43	°C	23.3	23.3	21.1	17.8	14.3	11.9	10.8	12.1	13.9	16.6	19.4	21.7	17.2
				mm	20	15	28	46	71	71	66	61	46	46	25	20	521
	Athens, Greece	37.58N	107	°C	9.1	9.7	11.3	14.8	19.1	23.5	26.7	26.4	22.9	18.9	14.1	11.2	17.4
				mm	53	43	41	28	23	15	5	8	18	48	56	56	394
	Gibraltar	36.6N	15	°C	12.8	13.3	14.1	15.9	18.2	20.8	23.0	23.8	22.2	18.7	15.8	13.4	17.6
				mm	130	107	122	69	43	13	3	3	36	84	163	124	897
	Marseilles, France	43.18N	75	°C	6.9	7.9	10.0	12.8	16.3	19.7	22.2	21.3	19.4	14.8	10.6	7.6	14.1
				mm	41	38	48	56	43	28	18	20	61	97	71	53	574
	Sacramento, California	38.35N	22	°C	8.1	10.2	12.6	14.7	18.0	21.6	23.9	23.0	21.6	16.0	11.6	8.4	15.6
				mm	97	71	71	38	15	5	0	0	5	20	48	97	472
SEMI-ARID	Alice Springs, Australia	23.38s	587	°C	28.5	27.8	24.8	20.1	15.4	12.4	11.4	14.7	18.6	22.9	26.1	27.9	20.9
				mm	46	43	30	20	18	15	10	10	10	18	25	41	284
	Denver, Colorado	39.45N	1613	°C	-1.2	-0.2	3.8	8.6	13.7	19.6	22.3	21.6	16.9	10.3	4.0	-0.2	9.9
				mm	18	13	25	53	61	36	46	36	25	25	15	13	363
	Kabul, Afghanistan	34.35N	1905	°C	-0.7	2.1	8.2	14.9	20.0	22.3	24.8	24.2	20.4	14.6	4.7	0.4	13.9
				mm	28	33	66	84	18	5	5	5	3	8	13	18	284
	Karachi, Pakistan	24.51N	4	°C	18.5	20.2	23.9	27.3	29.3	30.4	28.6	27.8	27.0	26.7	23.3	19.7	25.3
				mm	10	10	8	3	3	18	81	43	13	3	3	5	188
	Madrid, Spain	40.24N	655	°C	4.6	6.5	8.7	12.2	16.1	20.8	25.1	24.8	19.6	13.4	8.4	5.0	13.7
				mm	33	41	41	46	43	33	10	13	38	46	51	41	422
	Tombouctou, Mali	16.37N	250	°C	21.9	23.1	28.4	33.1	34.7	34.3	31.8	30.3	31.8	31.6	27.1	23.8	29.1
				mm	0	0	0	3	8	23	71	81	38	10	0	0	229
DESERT	Esfahān, Iran	32.40N	1773	°C	1.2	5.3	9.4	15.6	20.7	25.2	27.8	25.6	22.4	16.1	9.1	4.4	15.2
				mm	18	18	23	20	13	3	0	0	0	8	15	13	114
	Swakopmund, S.W. Africa	22.40s	6	°C	17.0	17.4	17.4	15.9	15.5	14.7	13.6	12.7	13.4	14.0	14.8	16.4	15.2
				mm	0	3	5	3	0	0	0	0	0	0	0	5	18
	Yuma, Arizona	32.45N	43	°C	12.6	15.1	18.1	21.2	24.9	29.3	32.7	32.3	28.8	22.4	16.1	13.2	22.3
				mm	13	10	10	3	5	0	5	13	8	5	8	10	84
DRY TROPICAL	Bombay, India	18.55N	11	°C	24.2	24.3	26.4	28.4	29.9	28.9	27.4	27.1	27.2	28.0	27.0	25.2	27.0
				mm	3	3	3	0	18	523	693	406	300	61	10	3	2017
	Cuyaba, Brazil	15.36s	165	°C	27.2	27.1	27.1	26.8	25.3	24.1	24.4	25.7	27.6	27.8	27.6	28.4	26.4
				mm	251	211	211	102	53	8	5	10	51	114	152	206	1389
	Darwin, N. Australia	12.28s	30	°C	28.9	28.6	28.9	28.9	27.7	26.1	25.2	26.3	28.1	29.6	29.9	29.5	28.1
				mm	404	330	257	104	18	3	3	3	13	56	122	262	1570
WET TROPICAL	Manila, Philippines	14.35N	14	°C	24.8	25.3	26.6	28.1	28.6	27.8	27.1	27.1	26.8	26.6	25.8	25.1	26.5
				mm	20	10	18	33	114	234	439	406	363	170	122	103	2032
	Veracruz, Mexico	19.10N	15	°C	21.9	22.9	23.8	26.1	27.2	27.5	27.6	27.7	27.2	24.7	23.8	21.6	25.2
				mm	10	15	15	20	33	318	376	226	295	170	173	76	1727
	Georgetown, Guyana	6.50N	23	°C	25.8	25.8	26.1	26.4	26.3	26.0	26.1	26.5	27.3	27.3	26.9	26.1	26.4
				mm	201	117	183	152	282	297	251	165	79	170	170	186	2253
	Lagos, Nigeria	6.27N	8	°C	27.2	27.9	28.5	28.1	27.7	26.3	26.3	25.4	25.8	26.4	27.4	27.5	26.9
				mm	28	53	94	147	267	472	272	71	135	196	66	20	1819
	Singapore	1.24N	3	°C	25.7	26.1	26.8	27.1	27.5	27.3	27.2	27.0	26.9	26.7	26.3	25.9	26.7
				mm	216	155	165	175	183	173	170	196	178	208	254	287	2360
MOUNTAIN	Bogota, Colombia	4.36N	2661	°C	14.2	14.4	14.8	14.7	14.6	14.5	14.0	13.9	13.9	14.4	14.6	14.5	14.4
				mm	58	61	104	145	114	61	51	56	61	163	117	66	1057
	Darjeeling, India	27.3N	2248	°C	4.5	5.3	9.7	13.4	14.6	15.5	16.4	16.1	15.2	12.9	8.8	5.4	11.5
				mm	20	28	51	104	198	615	805	660	465	135	20	5	3094
	Johannesburg, S. Africa	26.11s	1806	°C	19.2	18.6	17.4	15.4	12.4	10.4	10.3	13.3	15.2	17.0	18.4	18.4	15.3
				mm	157	132	112	43	20	13	13	25	25	66	127	137	843
	Mexico City, Mexico	19.26N	2278	°C	12.3	13.8	15.8	17.9	18.3	17.7	16.9	16.7	16.2	15.0	13.6	11.9	15.5
				mm	5	5	15	25	48	99	104	119	104	46	13	5	587

STATES AND POPULATIONS

	area (sq. km)	POPULATION
AFGHANISTAN -	657 500	17 600 000
ALBANIA -	28 748	2 170 000
ALGERIA -	2 381 730	14 600 000
ANDORRA -	453	20 000
ANGOLA -	1 246 700	5 673 000
ARGENTINA -	2 778 412	24 000 000
AUSTRALIA -	7 686 900	12 959 000
Australian Capital Terr. -	2 432	158 000
New South Wales -	801 432	4 463 000
Northern Territory -	1 347 515	93 000
Queensland -	1 727 520	1 869 000
South Australia -	984 381	1 186 000
Tasmania -	68 332	392 200
Victoria -	227 620	3 546 000
Western Australia -	2 527 623	1 053 000
AUSTRIA -	83 849	7 456 000
BAHAMAS, THE -	11 400	171 000
BAHRAIN -	598	216 000
BANGLADESH -	142 776	75 000 000
BARBADOS -	430	238 141
BELGIUM -	30 513	9 676 000
BELIZE -	22 963	126 000
BENIN -	112 600	2 800 000
BERMUDA -	53	55 000
BHUTAN -	46 600	1 000 000
BOLIVIA -	1 098 580	5 100 000
BOTSWANA -	600 000	700 000
BRAZIL -	8 511 965	98 000 000
BRUNEI -	5 765	142 000
BULGARIA -	110 912	8 490 000
BURMA -	678 034	28 870 000
BURUNDI -	27 834	3 800 000
CAMBODIA -	181 305	7 200 000
CAMEROUN -	475 500	6 200 000
CANADA -	9 976 169	21 568 000
Alberta -	661 188	1 627 900
British Columbia -	948 600	2 184 000
Manitoba -	650 090	988 200
New Brunswick -	73 437	634 600
Newfoundland -	404 519	522 100
Northwest Territories -	3 379 689	34 800
Nova Scotia -	55 490	789 000
Ontario -	1 068 587	7 703 000
Prince Edward Island -	5 657	111 600
Quebec -	1 540 677	6 027 800
Saskatchewan -	651 903	926 200
Yukon -	536 327	18 400
CAPE VERDE ISLANDS -	4 033	272 000
CENT. AFRICAN REP. -	623 018	1 520 000
CHAD -	1 284 000	3 710 000
CHILE -	756 945	10 000 000
CHINA -	9 560 975	750 000 000
Inner Mongolia -	450 000	9 000 000
Sinkiang -	1 646 790	8 000 000
Tibet -	1 221 600	1 250 000
COLOMBIA -	1 138 914	22 500 000
CONGO -	342 000	1 000 000
COSTA RICA -	50 900	1 800 000
CUBA -	114 524	8 553 395
CYPRUS -	9 255	600 000
CZECHOSLOVAKIA -	127 870	14 362 000
DENMARK -	43 069	4 976 000
DOMINICAN REP. -	48 442	4 200 000
ECUADOR -	281 341	6 500 000
EGYPT -	1 000 253	34 700 000
EL SALVADOR -	21 393	3 700 000
EQUATORIAL GUINEA -	28 051	290 000
ETHIOPIA -	1 221 900	26 000 000
FAEROES -	1 373	38 000
FALKLAND ISLANDS -	11 961	2 105
FIJI -	18 272	533 000
FINLAND -	337 032	4 706 000
FRANCE -	549 430	51 600 000
FRENCH GUIANA -	91 000	51 000
FRENCH TERR. OF AFARS & ISSAS -	23 000	81 000
GABON -	267 000	500 000
GAMBIA, THE -	11 295	364 000
EAST GERMANY -	108 173	17 042 000
WEST GERMANY -	248 533	61 682 000
GHANA -	238 539	9 600 000
GIBRALTAR -	6	26 833
GILBERT IS. & TUVALU -	886	56 000
GREECE -	131 944	9 000 000
GREENLAND -	2 175 600	47 000
GUATEMALA -	108 889	5 500 000
GUINEA -	245 857	3 920 000
GUINEA-BISSAU -	36 125	560 000
GUYANA -	214 970	700 000
HAITI -	27 750	5 000 000
HONDURAS -	112 088	2 700 000
HONG KONG -	1 032	4 078 000
HUNGARY -	93 030	10 415 000
ICELAND -	103 000	200 000
INDIA -	3 268 000	564 008 000
INDONESIA -	1 904 334	129 000 000
IRAN -	1 648 180	30 550 000
IRAQ -	438 446	9 800 000
IRELAND, Rep. of -	68 893	3 000 000
ISRAEL -	20 700	3 080 000
ITALY -	301 224	55 000 000
IVORY COAST -	322 463	4 500 000
JAMAICA -	11 525	2 040 000
JAPAN -	372 077	106 958 000
JORDAN -	97 740	2 467 000
KENYA -	582 600	11 800 000
KOREA, NORTH -	127 158	14 500 000
KOREA, SOUTH -	98 431	33 400 000
KUWAIT -	16 000	800 000
LAOS -	236 800	2 962 000
LEBANON -	10 400	2 855 000
LESOTHO -	30 340	1 200 000
LIBERIA -	111 000	1 300 000
LIBYA -	1 759 540	2 100 000
LIECHTENSTEIN -	160	21 350
LUXEMBOURG -	2 586	345 000
MADAGASCAR -	594 180	7 655 000
MALAWI -	126 338	4 530 000
MALAYSIA -	333 507	10 800 000
MALI -	1 240 000	5 300 000
MALTA -	316	326 000
MAURITANIA -	1 030 700	1 400 000
MAURITIUS -	1 865	836 000
MEXICO -	1 967 183	52 500 000
MONACO -	15	23 000
MONGOLIA -	1 565 000	1 290 000
MOROCCO -	458 730	15 700 000
MOZAMBIQUE -	784 961	8 234 000
NEPAL -	141 400	11 500 000
NETHERLANDS -	40 893	13 270 000
NETHERLANDS ANTILLES -	1 019	225 000
NEW HEBRIDES -	14 760	84 000
NEW ZEALAND -	268 680	2 900 000
NICARAGUA -	148 000	2 210 000
NIGER -	1 267 000	4 200 000
NIGERIA -	923 773	58 000 000
NORWAY -	324 219	3 918 000
OMAN -	212 000	660 000
PAKISTAN -	803 994	58 000 000
PANAMA -	75 650	1 500 000
PANAMA CANAL ZONE -	1 676	50 000
PAPUA-NEW GUINEA -	461 700	2 467 000
PARAGUAY -	406 752	2 500 000
PERU -	1 285 215	14 400 000
PHILIPPINES -	299 400	40 600 000
POLAND -	312 700	32 900 000
PORTUGAL -	92 082	9 700 000
PUERTO RICO -	8 891	2 770 000
QATAR -	22 000	80 000
RHODESIA -	390 622	5 780 000
ROMANIA -	237 500	20 600 000
RWANDA -	26 330	3 800 000
SAN MARINO -	61	19 000
SAUDI ARABIA -	2 263 600	7 200 000
SENEGAL -	197 161	3 925 000
SIERRA LEONE -	73 326	2 550 000
SIKKIM -	7 298	205 000
SOLOMON IS. -	29 785	163 000
SOMALI REPUBLIC -	637 660	2 790 000
SOUTH AFRICA, Rep. of -	1 221 042	22 700 000
Cape of Good Hope -	721 004	5 363 000
Natal -	86 967	2 980 000
Orange Free State -	129 153	1 387 000
Transvaal -	283 918	6 273 000
SOUTH-WEST AFRICA (Namibia) -	824 295	630 000
SPAIN -	504 748	34 600 000
SRI LANKA -	65 610	13 033 000
SUDAN -	2 505 813	16 700 000
SURINAM -	17 400	385 000
SWAZILAND -	173 400	408 000
SWEDEN -	449 793	8 127 000
SWITZERLAND -	41 288	6 270 000
SYRIA -	185 680	6 600 000
TAIWAN -	35 961	14 990 000
TANZANIA -	939 700	14 000 000
THAILAND -	514 000	38 000 000
TOGO -	56 000	2 004 711
TRINIDAD & TOBAGO -	5 128	1 070 000
TUNISIA -	164 150	5 300 000
TURKEY -	780 576	37 010 000
UGANDA -	236 037	9 764 000
UNION OF SOVIET SOCIALIST REPS. -	22 400 000	246 300 000
Armenian S.S.R. -	29 759	2 600 000
Azerbaijan S.S.R. -	86 853	5 300 000
Byelorussian S.S.R. -	207 588	9 100 000
Estonian S.S.R. -	45 092	1 357 000
Georgian S.S.R. -	69 670	4 800 000
Kazakh S.S.R. -	2 717 000	13 500 000
Kirghiz S.S.R. -	198 652	3 100 000
Latvian S.S.R. -	64 000	2 365 000
Lithuanian S.S.R. -	65 190	3 129 000
Moldavian S.S.R. -	33 800	3 700 000
Russian S.F.S.R. -	17 077 962	130 000 000
Tadzhik S.S.R. -	143 072	3 100 000
Turkmen S.S.R. -	487 956	2 300 000
Ukrainian S.S.R. -	604 000	47 900 000
Uzbek S.S.R. -	447 000	12 500 000
UNITED ARAB EMIRATES -	83 660	180 000
UNITED KINGDOM OF GT. BRITAIN & N. IRELAND -	244 030	55 356 000
England and Wales -	151 126	48 604 000
Scotland -	78 749	5 224 000
Northern Ireland -	14 147	1 528 000
Channel Islands -	195	125 240
Isle of Man -	588	49 743
UNITED STATES OF AMERICA -	9 363 353	209 000 000
Alabama -	133 167	3 444 165
Alaska -	1 518 800	302 173
Arizona -	295 022	1 772 482
Arkansas -	137 539	1 923 295
California -	411 012	19 953 134
Colorado -	269 998	2 207 259
Connecticut -	12 973	3 032 217
Delaware -	5 328	548 104
District of Columbia -	174	756 510
Florida -	151 670	6 789 443
Georgia -	152 488	4 589 575
Hawaii -	16 705	769 913
Idaho -	216 412	713 008
Illinois -	146 075	11 113 976
Indiana -	93 993	5 193 669
Iowa -	145 791	2 825 041
Kansas -	213 063	2 249 071
Kentucky -	104 623	3 219 311
Louisiana -	125 674	3 643 180
Maine -	86 027	993 663
Maryland -	27 394	3 922 399
Massachusetts -	21 386	5 689 170
Michigan -	150 779	8 875 083
Minnesota -	217 735	3 805 069
Mississippi -	123 584	2 216 912
Missouri -	180 486	4 677 399
Montana -	381 084	694 409
Nebraska -	200 017	1 483 791
Nevada -	286 296	488 738
New Hampshire -	24 097	737 681
New Jersey -	20 295	7 168 164
New Mexico -	315 113	1 016 000
New York -	128 401	18 241 266
North Carolina -	136 197	5 082 059
North Dakota -	183 022	617 716
Ohio -	106 765	10 652 017
Oklahoma -	181 090	2 559 253
Oregon -	251 180	2 091 385
Pennsylvania -	117 412	11 793 909
Rhode Island -	3 144	949 723
South Carolina -	80 432	2 590 516
South Dakota -	199 551	666 257
Tennessee -	109 412	3 924 164
Texas -	692 403	11 196 730
Utah -	219 932	1 059 273
Vermont -	24 887	444 732
Virginia -	105 816	4 648 494
Washington -	176 617	3 409 169
West Virginia -	62 629	1 744 237
Wisconsin -	145 438	4 417 933
Wyoming -	253 597	332 416
UPPER VOLTA -	274 122	5 600 000
URUGUAY -	186 926	3 000 000
VATICAN CITY -	0.44	1 000
VENEZUELA -	912 050	11 000 000
VIETNAM -	329 650	41 000 000
YEMEN -	195 000	5 750 000
YEMEN, SOUTH -	160 300	1 280 000
YUGOSLAVIA -	255 804	20 800 000
ZAIRE -	2 345 409	22 800 000
ZAMBIA -	752 262	4 500 000

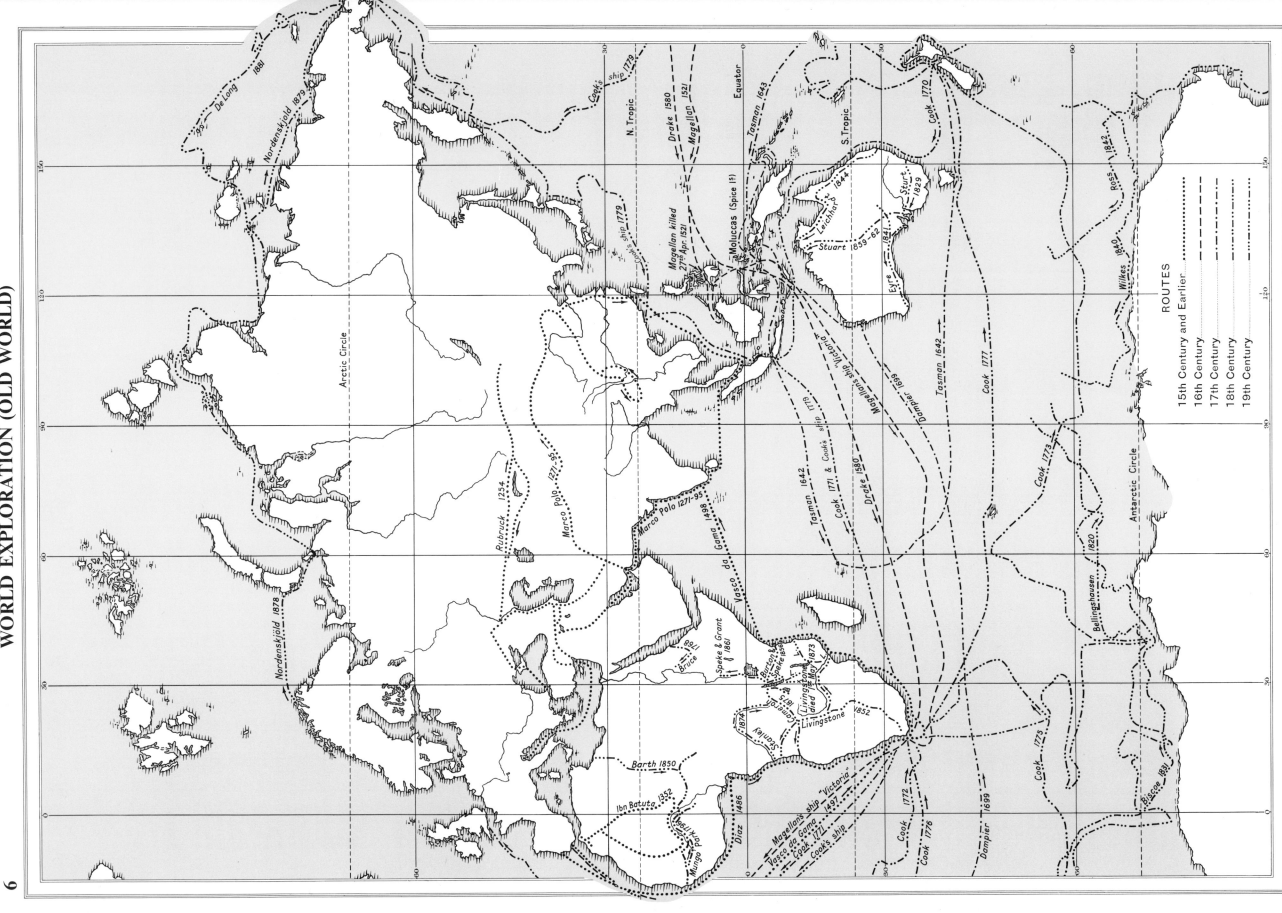

WORLD EXPLORATION (OLD WORLD)

ROUTES

15th Century and Earlier
16th Century
17th Century
18th Century
19th Century

MERCATOR'S PROJECTION

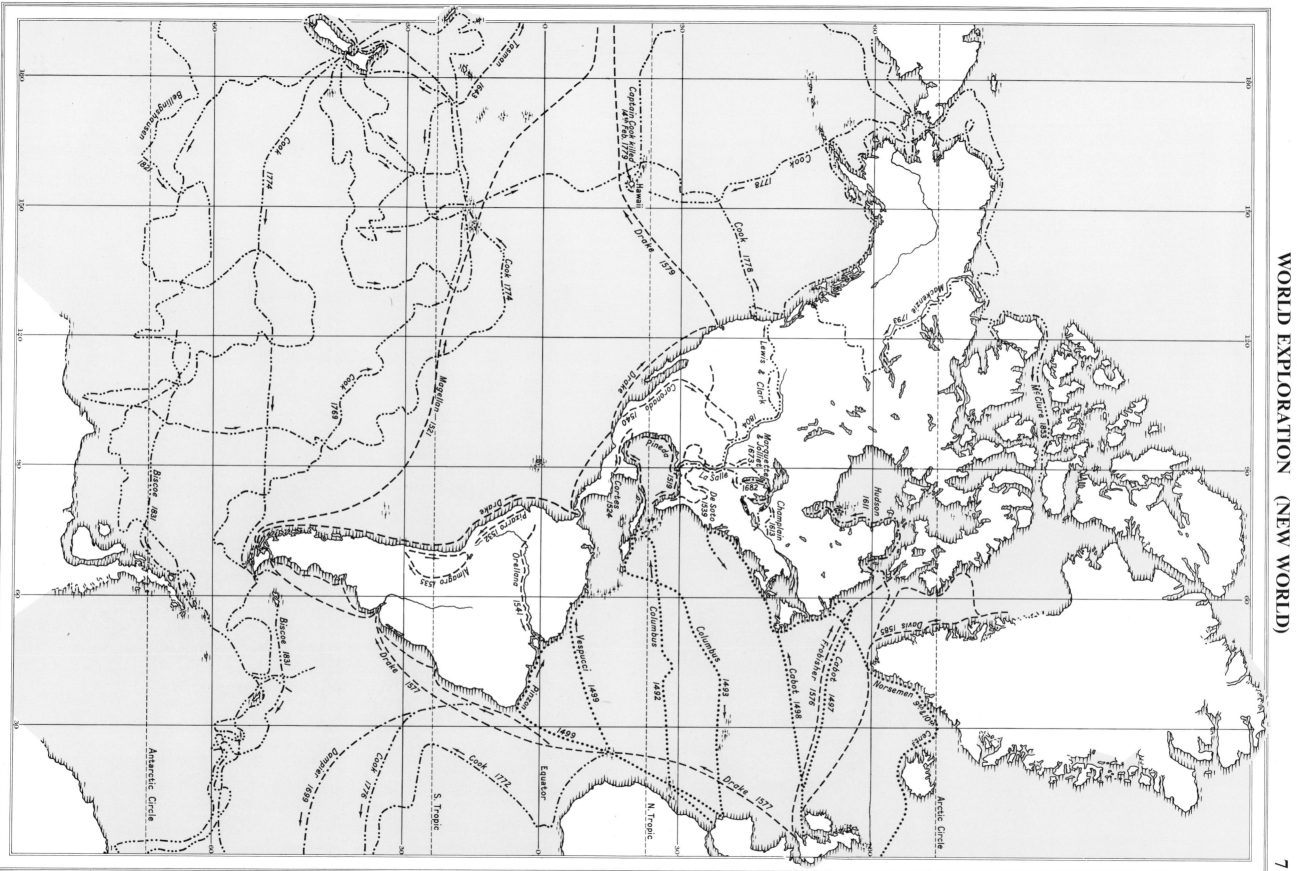

WORLD EXPLORATION (NEW WORLD)

7

Captain Cook killed 14th Feb. 1779

Hawaii

Cook 1778

Cook 1778

Mackenzie 1793

Drake 1579

Cook 1774

Cook 1774

Magellan 1521

Cook 1769

Bellingshausen 1821

Biscoe 1831

Drake

Drake

Pizarro 1532

Almagro 1535

Orellana 1541

Pinzón 1519

Cortés 1524

De Soto 1539

Coronado 1540

Lewis & Clark 1804

Marquette & Jolliet 1673

La Salle 1682

Champlain 1613

Hudson 1611

McClure 1853

Biscoe 1831

Drake 1577

Pinzón

Vespucci 1499

Columbus 1499

Columbus 1492

Columbus 1493

Cabot 1498

Cabot 1497

Frobisher 1576

Davis 1585

Norsemen 1000

Cartier

Dampier 1699

Cook 1776

Cook 1772

Drake 1577

Antarctic Circle

S. Tropic

Equator

N. Tropic

Arctic Circle

MAP PROJECTIONS

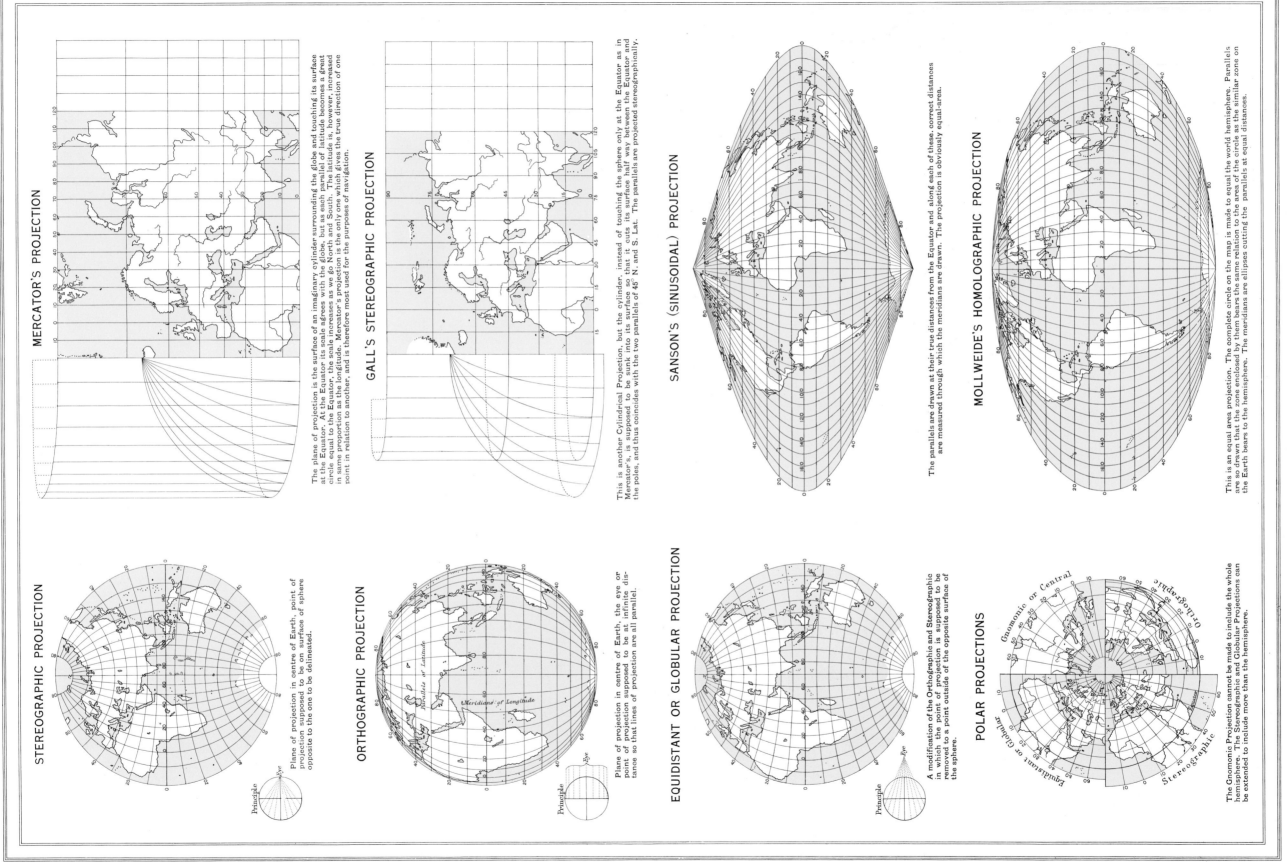

MERCATOR'S PROJECTION

The plane of projection is the surface of an imaginary cylinder surrounding the globe and touching its surface at the Equator. At the Equator its scale agrees with the globe, but as each parallel of latitude becomes a great circle equal to the Equator, the scale increases as we go North and South. The latitude is, however, increased in same proportion as the longitude. Mercator's projection is the only one which gives the true direction of one point in relation to another, and is therefore most used for the purposes of navigation.

GALL'S STEREOGRAPHIC PROJECTION

This is another Cylindrical Projection, but the cylinder, instead of touching the sphere only at the Equator as in Mercator's, is supposed to be sunk into its surface so that it cuts its surface half way between the Equator and the poles, and thus coincides with the two parallels of 45° N. and S. Lat. The parallels are projected stereographically.

SANSON'S (SINUSOIDAL) PROJECTION

The parallels are drawn at their true distances from the Equator and along each of these, correct distances are measured through which the meridians are drawn. The projection is obviously equal-area.

MOLLWEIDE'S HOMOLOGRAPHIC PROJECTION

This is an equal area projection. The complete circle on the map is made to equal the world hemisphere. Parallels are so drawn that the zone enclosed by them bears the same relation to the area of the circle as the similar zone on the Earth bears to the hemispheres. The meridians are ellipses cutting the parallels at equal distances.

STEREOGRAPHIC PROJECTION

Plane of projection in centre of Earth, point of projection supposed to be on surface of sphere opposite to the one to be delineated.

ORTHOGRAPHIC PROJECTION

Plane of projection in centre of Earth, the eye or point of projection supposed to be at infinite distance so that lines of projection are all parallel.

EQUIDISTANT OR GLOBULAR PROJECTION

A modification of the Orthographic and Stereographic in which the point of projection is supposed to be removed to a point outside of the opposite surface of the sphere.

POLAR PROJECTIONS

The Gnomonic Projection cannot be made to coincide the whole hemisphere. The Stereographic and Globular Projections can be extended to include more than the hemisphere.

MAP PROJECTIONS

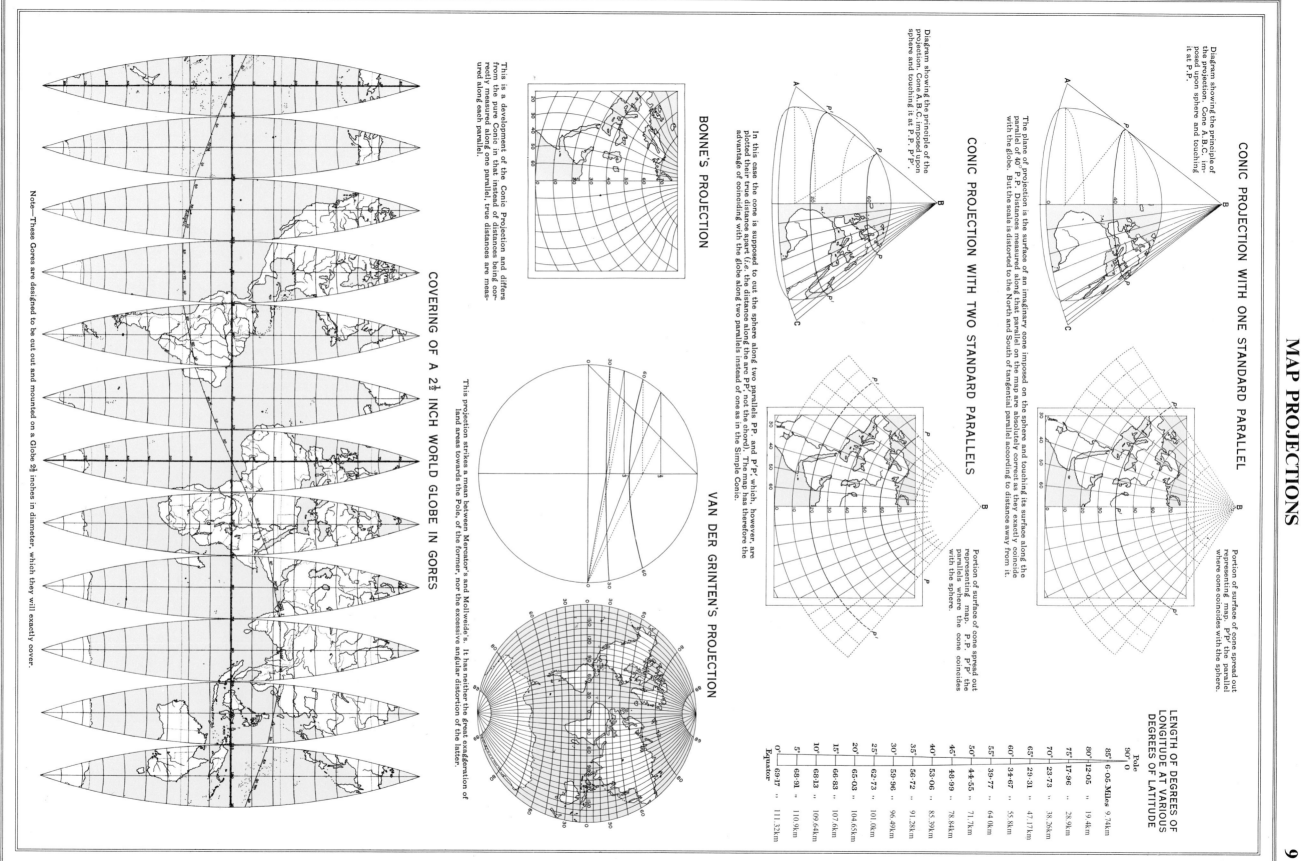

CONIC PROJECTION WITH ONE STANDARD PARALLEL

Diagram showing the principle of the projection. Cone A.B.C. imposed upon sphere and touching it at P.P.

The plane of projection is the surface of an imaginary cone imposed on the sphere and touching its surface along the parallel of 40° P.P. Distances measured along that parallel on the map are absolutely correct as they exactly coincide with the globe. But the scale is distorted to the North and South of tangential parallel according to distance away from it.

Portion of cone spread out representing map. P'P' the parallel where cone coincides with the sphere.

CONIC PROJECTION WITH TWO STANDARD PARALLELS

In this case the cone is supposed to cut the sphere along two parallels PP, and P'P', which, however, are plotted their true distance apart (i.e. the distance along the arc P.P. not the chord). The map has therefore the advantage of coinciding with the globe along two parallels instead of one as in the Simple Conic.

Portion of surface of cone representing map. P.P. P'P' the parallels where the cone coincides with the sphere.

BONNE'S PROJECTION

This is a development of the Conic Projection and differs from the pure Conic in that instead of distances being correctly measured along one parallel, true distances are measured along each parallel.

VAN DER GRINTEN'S PROJECTION

This projection strikes a mean between Mercator's and Mollweide's. It has neither the great exaggeration of land areas towards the Pole, of the former, nor the excessive angular distortion of the latter.

COVERING OF A 2½ INCH WORLD GLOBE IN GORES

This is a development of the pure Conic projection. Cone A.B.C. imposed upon sphere and touching it at P.P. P'P'.

Note—These Gores are designed to be cut out and mounted on a Globe 2½ inches in diameter, which they will exactly cover.

© John Bartholomew & Son Ltd, Edinburgh

LENGTH OF DEGREES OF LONGITUDE AT VARIOUS DEGREES OF LATITUDE

Pole 90°	0
85°	6·05 Miles 9·74km
80°	12·05 " 19·4km
75°	17·96 " 28·9km
70°	23·73 " 38·26km
65°	29·31 " 47·17km
60°	34·67 " 55·8km
55°	39·77 " 64·0km
50°	44·55 " 71·7km
45°	48·99 " 78·84km
40°	53·06 " 85·39km
35°	56·72 " 91·28km
30°	59·96 " 96·49km
25°	62·73 " 101·0km
20°	65·03 " 104·65km
15°	66·83 " 107·6km
10°	68·13 " 109·64km
5°	68·91 " 110·9km
Equator 0°	69·17 " 111·32km

9

MAP PROJECTIONS

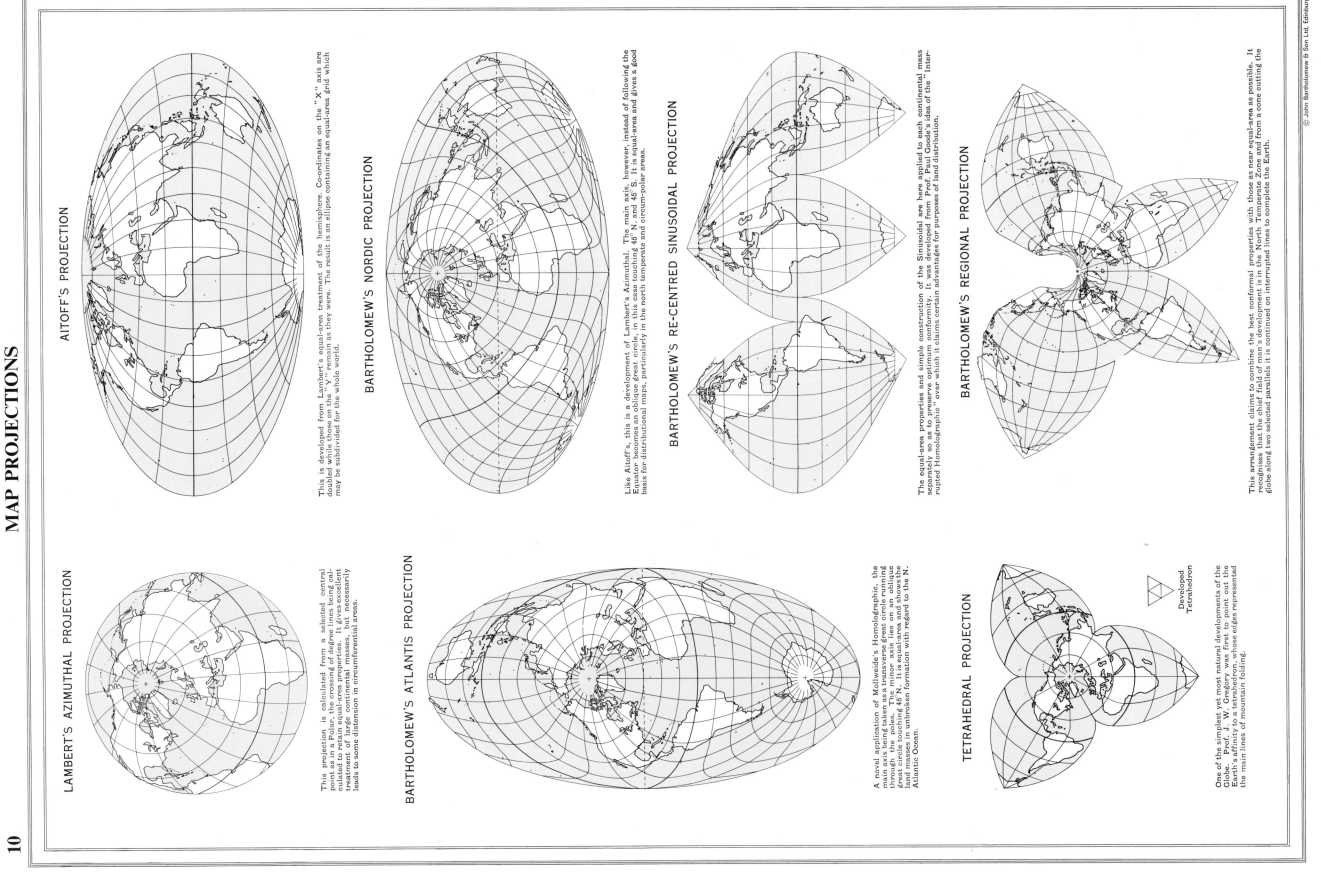

AITOFF'S PROJECTION

This is developed from Lambert's equal-area treatment of the hemisphere. Co-ordinates on the "X" axis are doubled while those on the "Y" remain as they were. The result is an ellipse containing an equal-area grid which may be subdivided for the whole world.

BARTHOLOMEW'S NORDIC PROJECTION

Like Aitoff's, this is a development of Lambert's Azimuthal. The main axis, however, instead of following the Equator becomes an oblique great circle, in this case touching 45° N. and 45° S. It is equal-area and gives a good basis for distributional maps, particularly in the north temperate and circum-polar areas.

BARTHOLOMEW'S RE-CENTRED SINUSOIDAL PROJECTION

The equal-area properties and simple construction of the Sinusoidal are here applied to each continental mass separately so as to preserve optimum conformity. It was developed from Prof. Paul Goode's idea of the "Interrupted Homolographic" over which it claims certain advantages for purposes of land distribution.

BARTHOLOMEW'S REGIONAL PROJECTION

This arrangement claims to combine the best conformal properties with those as near equal-area as possible. It recognises that the chief field of man's development is in the North Temperate Zone and from a cone cutting the globe along two selected parallels it is continued on interrupted lines to complete the Earth.

LAMBERT'S AZIMUTHAL PROJECTION

This projection is calculated from a selected central point as in a Polar, the crossing of degree lines being calculated to retain equal-area properties. It gives excellent treatment of large continental masses, but necessarily leads to some distension in circumferential areas.

BARTHOLOMEW'S ATLANTIS PROJECTION

A novel application of Mollweide's Homolographic, the main axis being taken as a transverse great circle running through the poles. The minor axis lies on an oblique great circle touching 45° N. It is equal-area and shows the land masses in unbroken formation with regard to the N. Atlantic Ocean.

TETRAHEDRAL PROJECTION

Developed Tetrahedron

One of the simplest yet most natural developments of the Globe. Prof. J. W. Gregory was first to point out the Earth's affinity to a tetrahedron, whose edges represented the main lines of mountain folding.

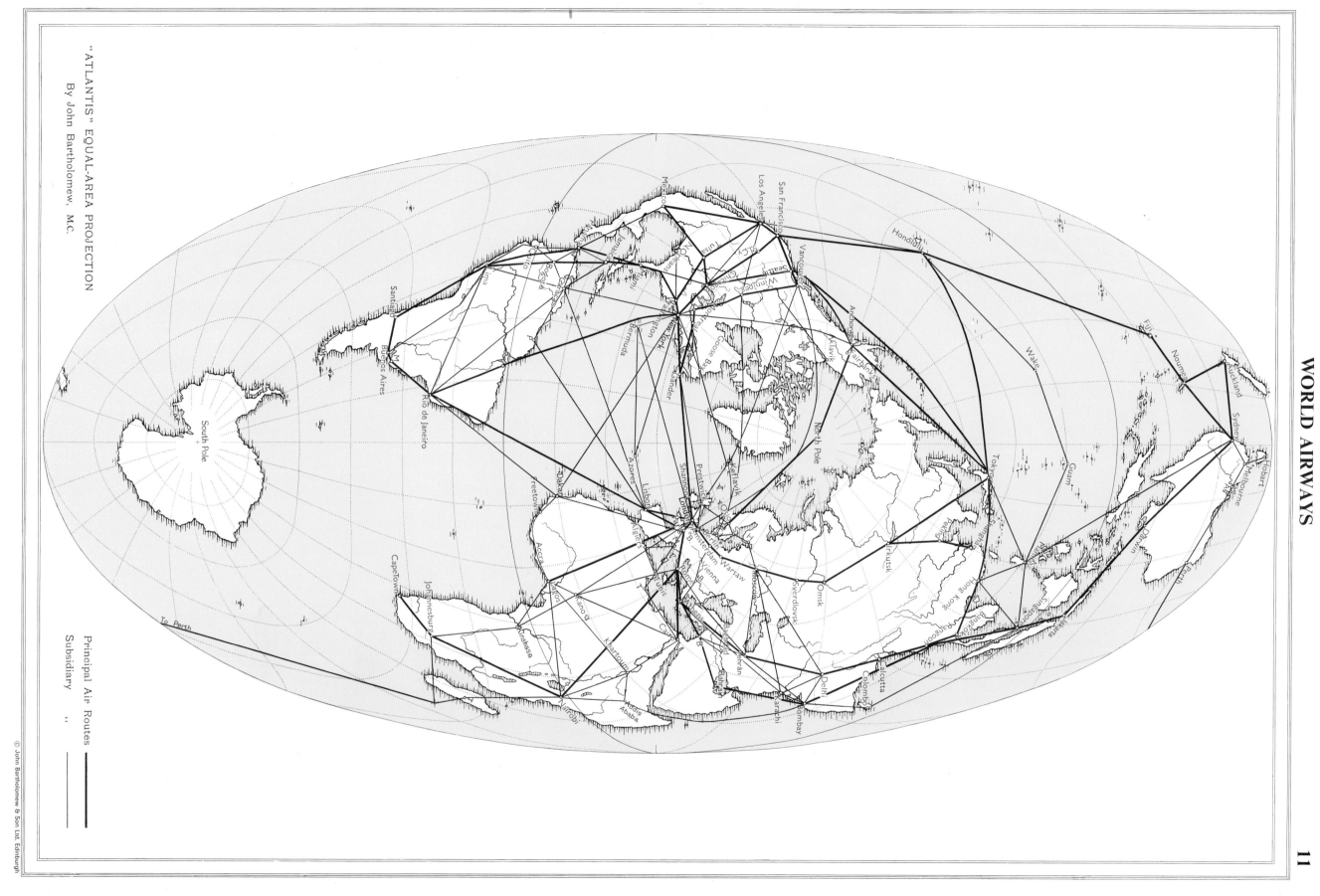

"ATLANTIS" EQUAL-AREA PROJECTION
By John Bartholomew, M.C.

1:120M

Principal Air Routes ——————
Subsidiary ''

ASTRONOMICAL GEOGRAPHY

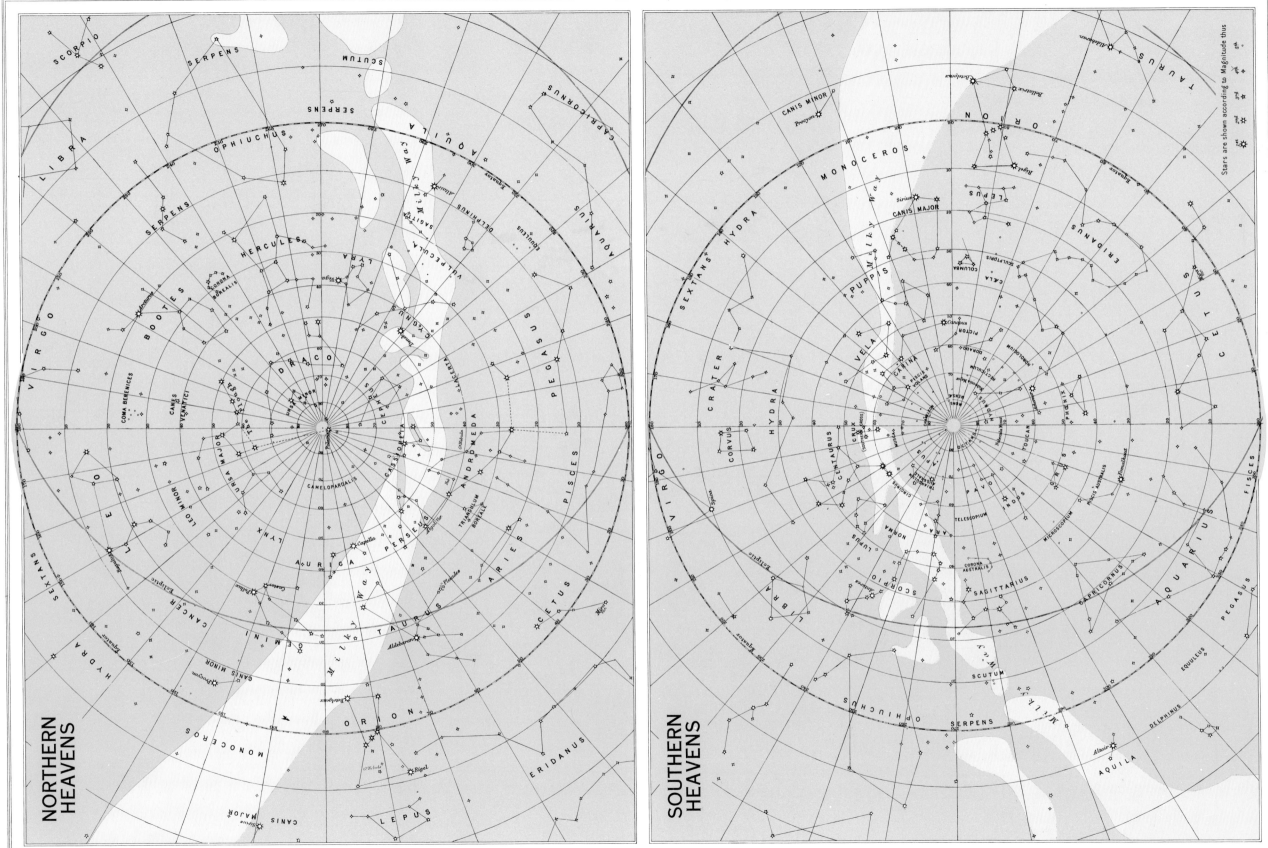

NORTHERN HEAVENS

SOUTHERN HEAVENS

Stars are shown according to Magnitude thus

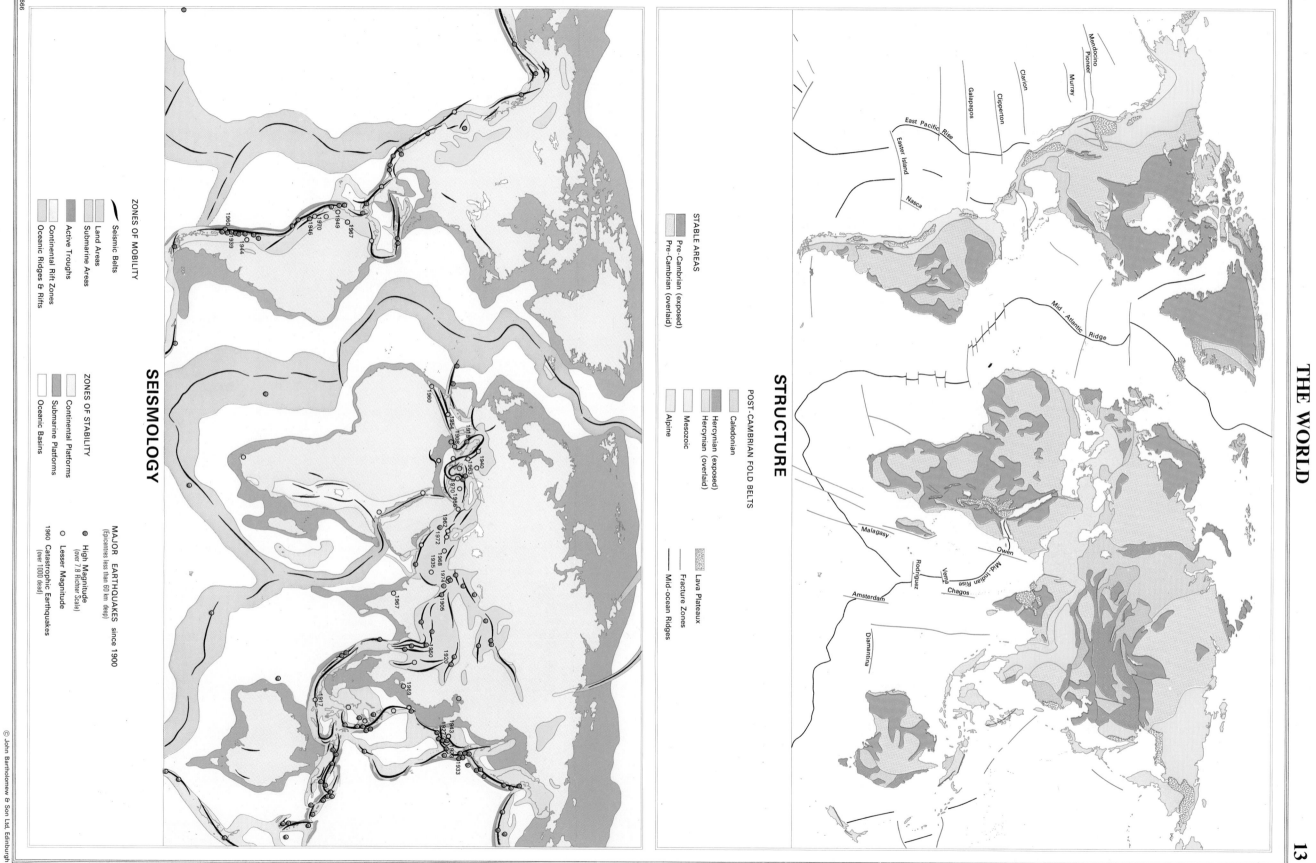

STRUCTURE

POST-CAMBRIAN FOLD BELTS

Caledonian

Hercynian (exposed)

Hercynian (overlaid)

Mesozoic

Alpine

STABLE AREAS

Pre-Cambrian (exposed)

Pre-Cambrian (overlaid)

Lava Plateaux

Fracture Zones

Mid-ocean Ridges

SEISMOLOGY

ZONES OF MOBILITY

Seismic Belts

Land Areas

Submarine Areas

Active Troughs

Continental Rift Zones

Oceanic Ridges & Rifts

ZONES OF STABILITY

Continental Platforms

Submarine Platforms

Oceanic Basins

MAJOR EARTHQUAKES since 1900
(Epicentres less than 60 km deep)

High Magnitude
(over 7.8 Richter Scale)

Lesser Magnitude

1960 Catastrophic Earthquakes
(over 1000 dead)

1:140M

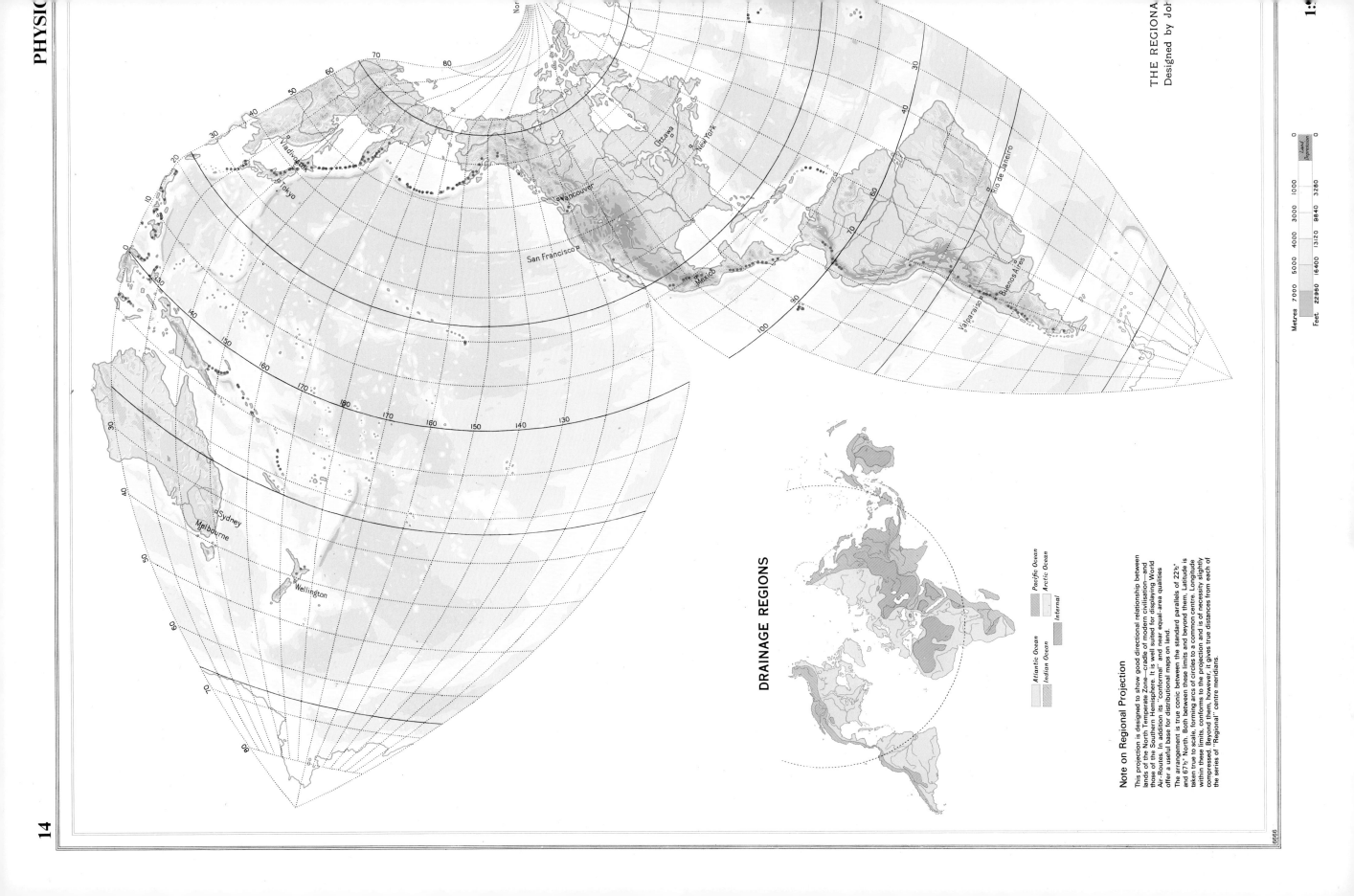

Vladivostok
Tokyo
Vancouver
Ottawa
New York
San Francisco
Mexico
Rio de Janeiro
Valparaiso
Buenos Aires
Sydney
Melbourne
Wellington

THE REGIONA
Designed by Joh

Metres 7000 5000 4000 3000 1000 0

Feet. 22960 16400 13120 9840 3280 0

Land
Depression

DRAINAGE REGIONS

Atlantic Ocean | Pacific Ocean
Indian Ocean | Arctic Ocean
| Internal

Note on Regional Projection

This projection is designed to show good directional relationship between
lands of the North Temperate Zone—cradle of modern civilisation—and
those of the Southern Hemisphere. It is well suited for displaying World
Air-Routes. In addition its "conformal" and near equal-area qualities
offer a useful base for distributional maps on land.

The arrangement is true conic between the standard parallels of 22½°
and 67½° North. Both between these limits and beyond them, Latitude is
taken true to scale, forming arcs of circles to a common centre. Longitude
within these limits, conforms to the projection and is of necessity slightly
compressed. Beyond them, however, it gives true distances from each of
the series of "Regional" centre meridians.

6666

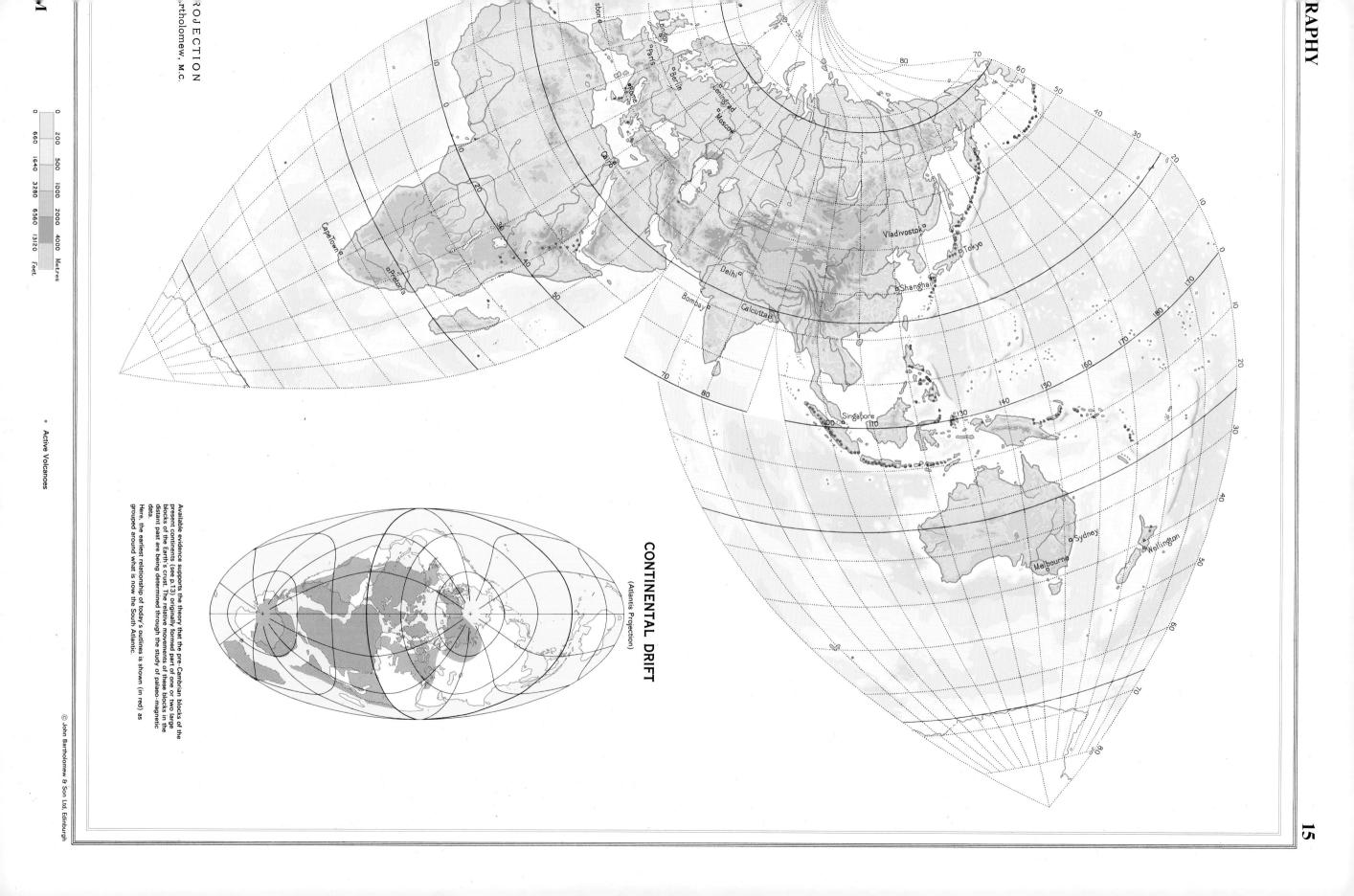

PROJECTION

rtholomew, M.C.

0
200
500
1000
2000
4000 Metres

0
660
1640
3280
6560
13120 Feet

• Active Volcanoes

CONTINENTAL DRIFT
(Atlantis Projection)

Available evidence supports the theory that the pre-Cambrian blocks of the
present continents (see p.13) originally formed part of one or two large
blocks of the Earth's crust. The relative movements of these blocks in the
distant past are being determined through the study of palaeo-magnetic
data.
Here, the earliest relationship of today's outlines is shown (in red) as
grouped around what is now the South Atlantic.

© John Bartholomew & Son Ltd, Edinburgh

Capetown
Pretoria
Paris
Rome
Berlin
Leningrad
Moscow
Cairo
Delhi
Bombay
Calcutta
Vladivostok
Tokyo
Shanghai
Singapore
Sydney
Melbourne
Wellington

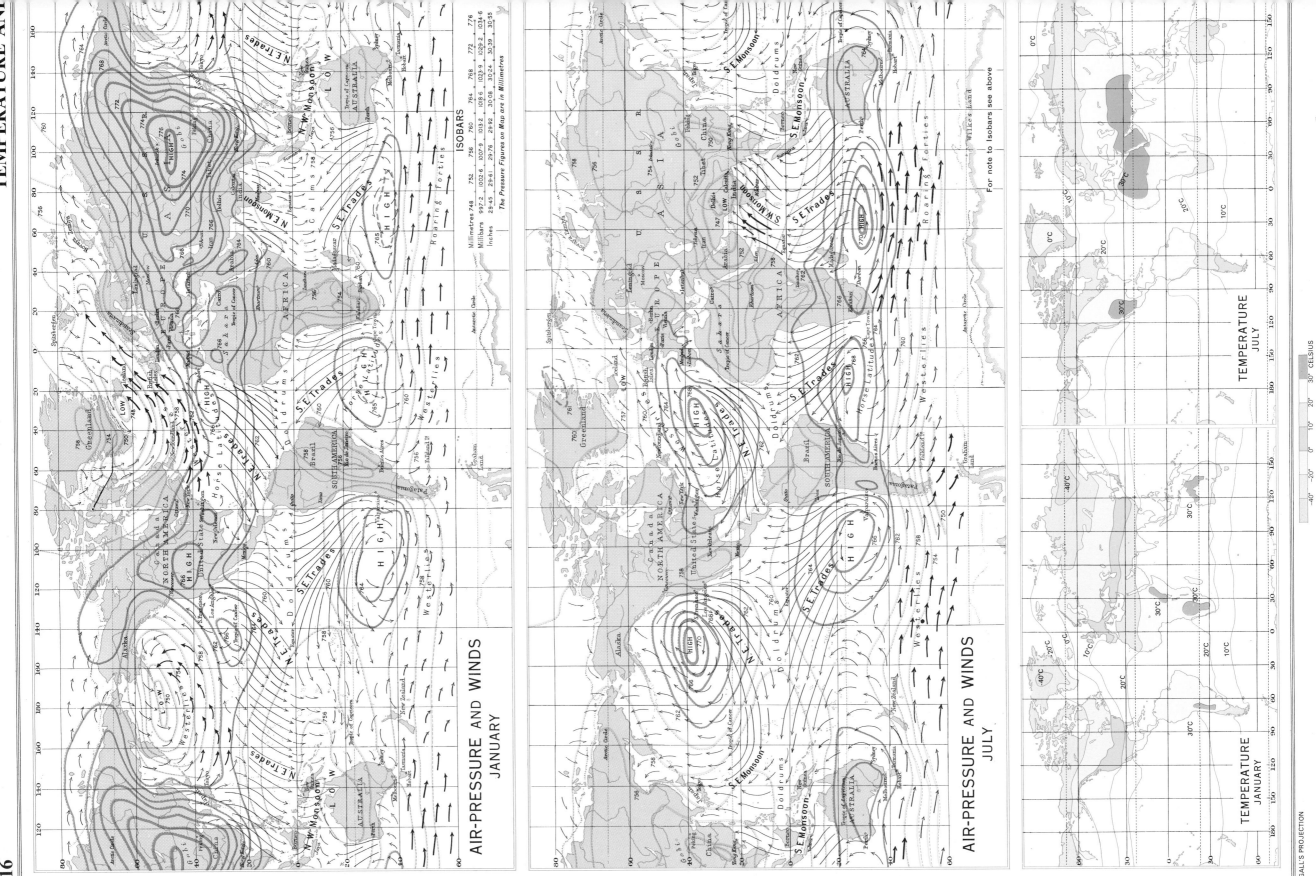

AIR-PRESSURE AND WINDS
JANUARY

ISOBARS

Millimetres	748	752	756	760	764	768	772	776
Millibars	997·2	1002·6	1007·9	1013·2	1018·6	1023·9	1029·2	1034·6
Inches	29·45	29·61	29·76	29·92	30·08	30·24	30·39	30·55

The Pressure Figures on Map are in Millimetres

AIR-PRESSURE AND WINDS
JULY

For note to Isobars see above

TEMPERATURE
JULY

TEMPERATURE
JANUARY

°CELSIUS

| -40° | -20° | 0° | 10° | 20° | 30° |

GALL'S PROJECTION

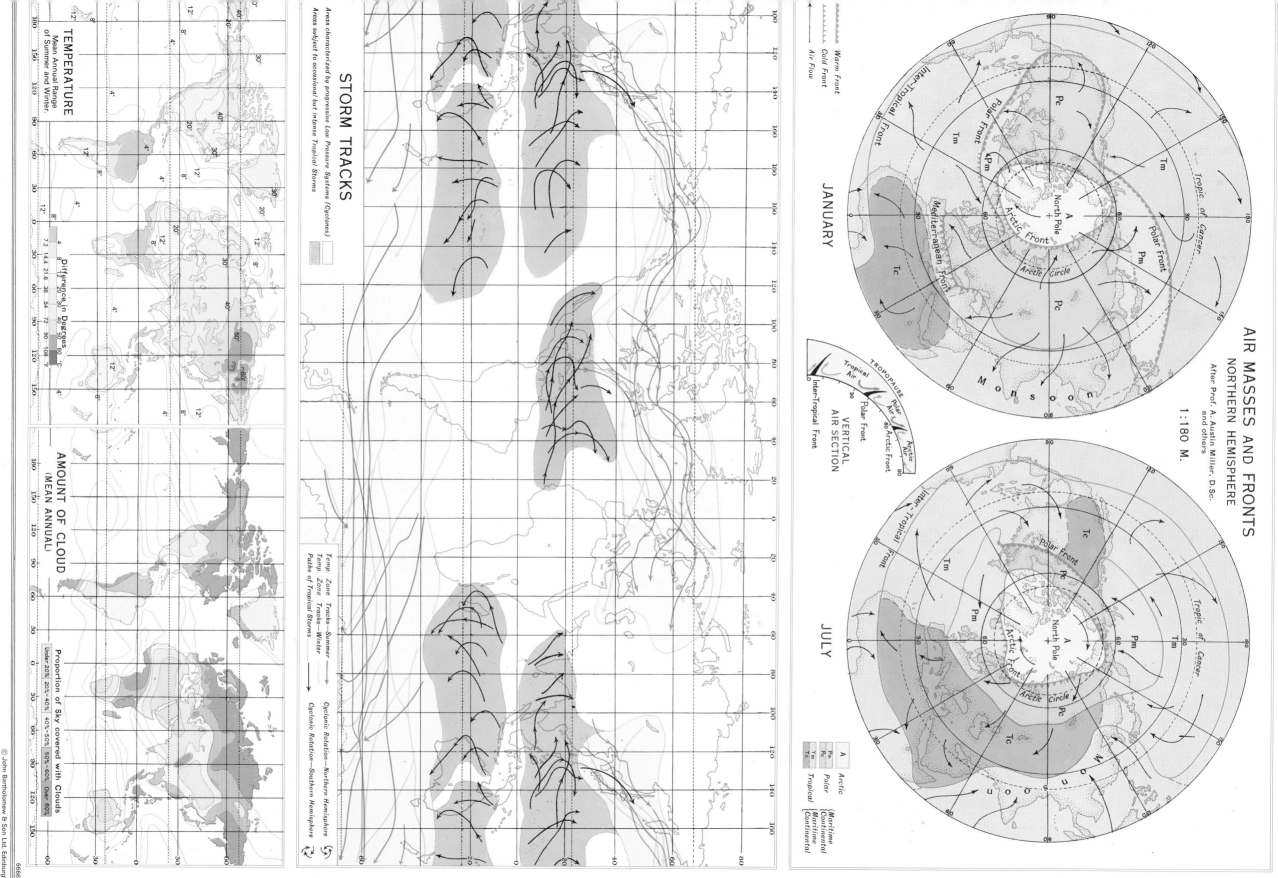

AIR MASSES AND FRONTS
NORTHERN HEMISPHERE
After Prof. A. Austin Miller, D.Sc.
and others
1:180 M.

JANUARY

JULY

VERTICAL
AIR SECTION

Warm Front
Cold Front
Air Flow

STORM TRACKS

Areas characterized by progressive Low Pressure Systems (Cyclones)

Areas subject to occasional but intense Tropical Storms

Temp. Zone Tracks—Summer
Temp. Zone Tracks—Winter
Paths of Tropical Storms

Cyclonic Rotation—Northern Hemisphere
Cyclonic Rotation—Southern Hemisphere

TEMPERATURE
Mean Annual Range
of Summer and Winter.

Difference in Degrees

AMOUNT OF CLOUD
(MEAN ANNUAL)

Proportion of Sky covered with Clouds
Under 20% 20%-40% 40%-50% 50%-60% Over 60%

A   Arctic
Pm Pc   Polar   {Maritime
                   {Continental
Tm Tc   Tropical {Maritime
                   {Continental

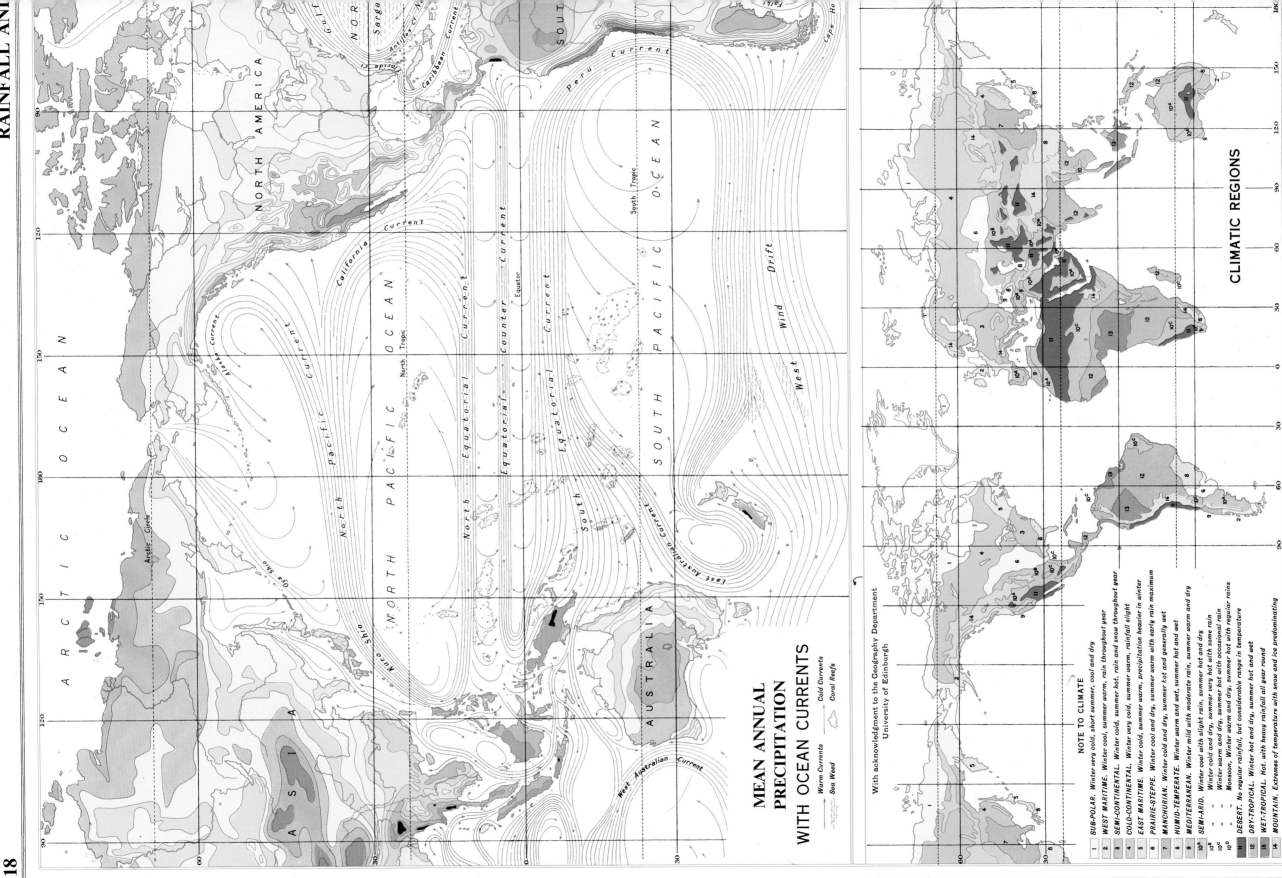

NORTH AMERICA

ARCTIC OCEAN

NORTH PACIFIC OCEAN

SOUTH PACIFIC OCEAN

ASIA

AUSTRALIA

Arctic Circle

North Tropic

Equator

South Tropic

Gulf Current
Antilles Current
Caribbean Current
Peru Current
California Current
Alaska Current
North Pacific Current
North Equatorial Current
Equatorial Counter Current
South Equatorial Current
South Pacific Current
West Wind Drift
East Australian Current
West Australian Current
Kuro Shio
Oya Shio

**MEAN ANNUAL
PRECIPITATION
WITH OCEAN CURRENTS**

→ Warm Currents
— Cold Currents
Sea Weed
Coral Reefs

With acknowledgment to the Geography Department
University of Edinburgh

CLIMATIC REGIONS

NOTE TO CLIMATE

1 SUB-POLAR. Winter very cold, short summer, cool and dry
2 WEST MARITIME. Winter cool, summer warm, rain throughout year
3 SEMI-CONTINENTAL. Winter cold, summer hot, rain and snow throughout year
4 COLD-CONTINENTAL. Winter very cold, summer warm, rainfall slight
5 EAST MARITIME. Winter cold, summer warm, precipitation heavier in winter
6 PRAIRIE-STEPPE. Winter cold and dry, summer warm with early rain maximum
7 MANCHURIAN. Winter cold and dry, summer warm and generally wet
8 MEDITERRANEAN. Winter mild with moderate rain, summer warm and dry
9 SEMI-ARID. Winter cool with slight rain, summer hot and dry
10ᴬ Winter cold and dry, summer very hot with some rain
10ᴮ Winter warm and dry, summer hot with occasional rain
10ᴰ Monsoon. Winter warm and dry, summer hot with regular rains
11 DESERT. No regular rainfall, but considerable range in temperature
12 DRY-TROPICAL. Winter hot and dry, summer hot and wet
13 WET-TROPICAL. Hot, with heavy rainfall all year round
14 MOUNTAIN. Extremes of temperature with snow and ice predominating

GALL'S PROJECTION

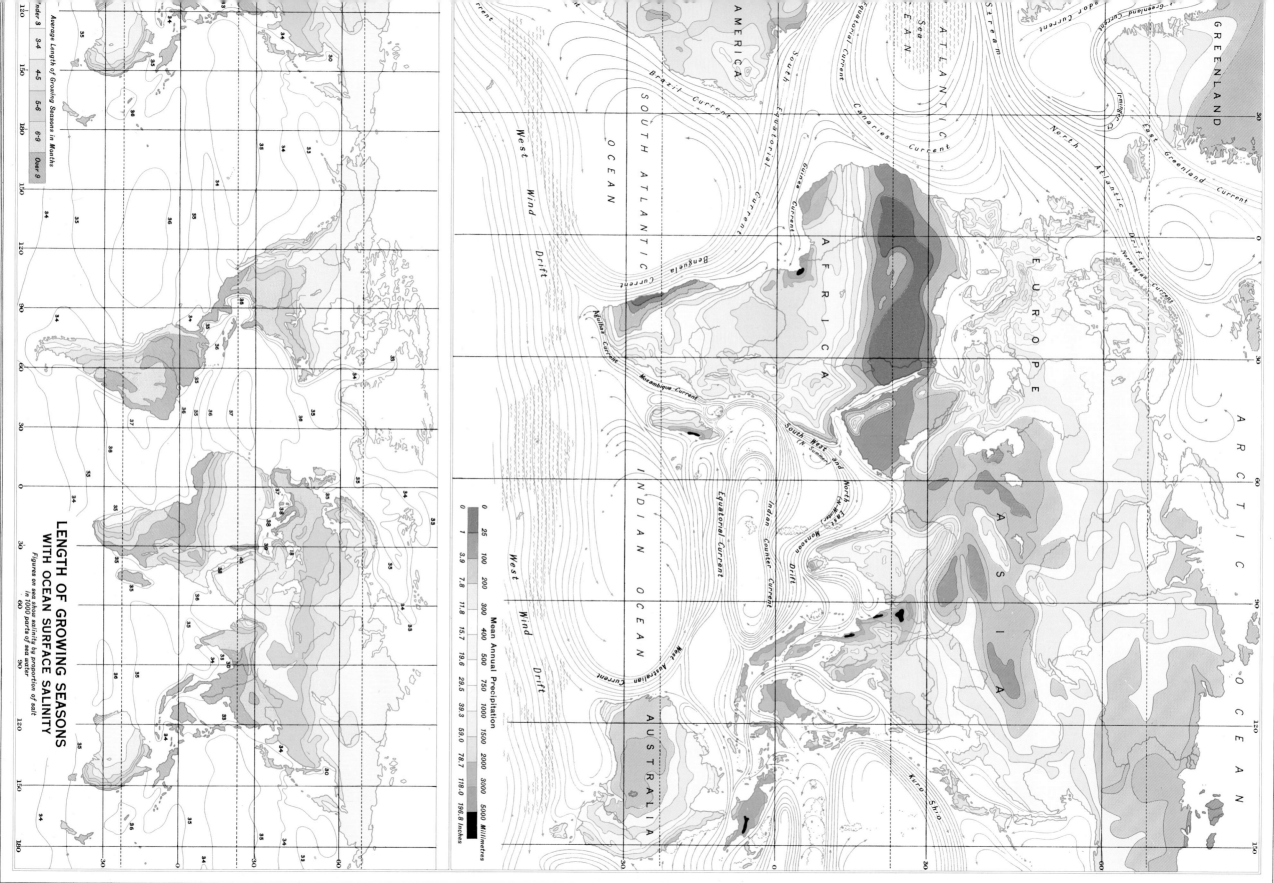

**LENGTH OF GROWING SEASONS
WITH OCEAN SURFACE SALINITY**

*Figures on sea show salinity by proportion of salt
in 1000 parts of sea water*

Average Length of Growing Seasons in Months

Under 3	3-4	4-5	5-6	6-9	Over 9

Mean Annual Precipitation

0	25	100	200	300	400	500	750	1000	1500	2000	3000	5000 Millimetres
0	1	3.9	7.8	11.8	15.7	19.6	29.5	39.3	59.0	78.7	118.0	196.8 Inches

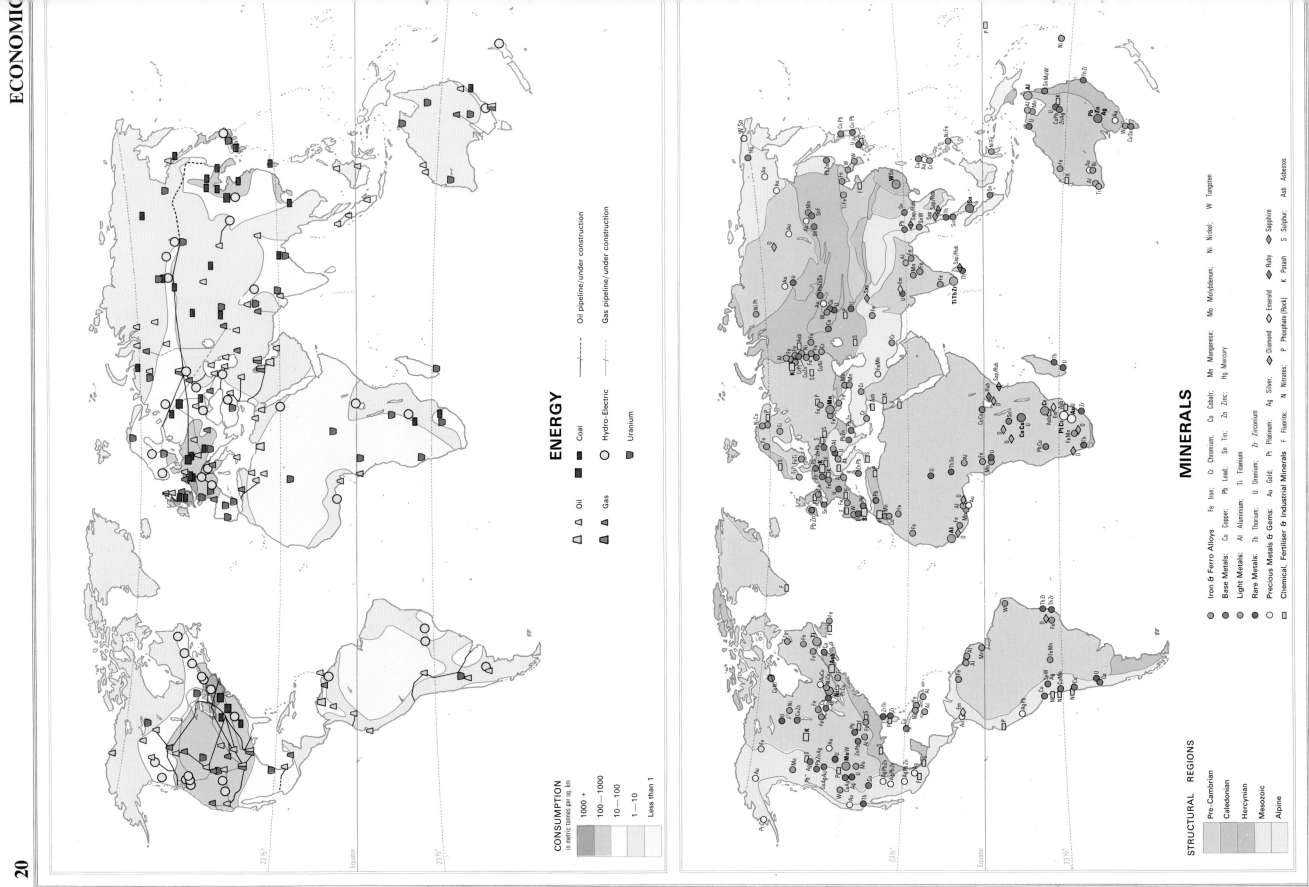

ENERGY

CONSUMPTION
in metric tonnes per sq. km

1000 +
100 — 1000
10 — 100
1 — 10
Less than 1

△ ◺ Oil
▲ ◣ Gas
■ ◼ Coal
○ Hydro-Electric
◧ Uranium

Oil pipeline/under construction
Gas pipeline/under construction

MINERALS

1:135M

Iron & Ferro Alloys   Fe Iron;   Cr Chromium;   Co Cobalt;   Mn Manganese;   Mo Molybdenum;   Ni Nickel;   W Tungsten
Base Metals: Cu Copper;   Pb Lead;   Sn Tin;   Zn Zinc;   Hg Mercury
Light Metals: Al Aluminium;   Ti Titanium
Rare Metals: Th Thorium;   U Uranium;   Zr Zirconium
Precious Metals & Gems: Au Gold;   Pt Platinum;   Ag Silver;   ◇ Diamond   ◇ Emerald   ◆ Ruby   ◆ Sapphire
Chemical, Fertiliser & Industrial Minerals   F Fluorite;   N Nitrates;   K Potash;   P Phosphate (Rock);   S Sulphur;   Asb Asbestos

STRUCTURAL REGIONS

Pre-Cambrian
Caledonian
Hercynian
Mesozoic
Alpine

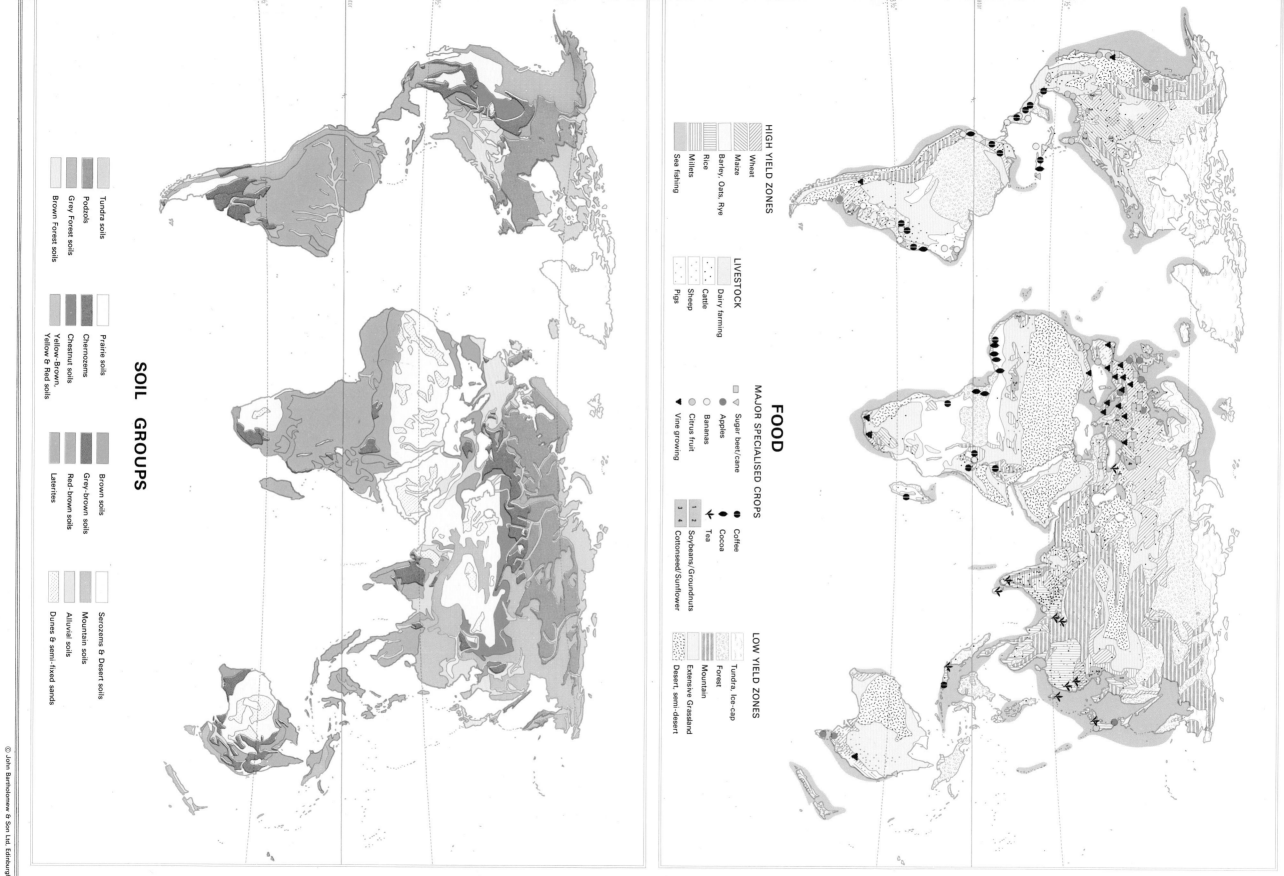

1:135M

SOIL GROUPS

Tundra soils
Podzols
Grey Forest soils
Brown Forest soils

Prairie soils
Chernozems
Chestnut soils
Yellow-Brown,
Yellow & Red soils

Brown soils
Grey-brown soils
Red-brown soils
Laterites

Serozems & Desert soils
Mountain soils
Alluvial soils
Dunes & semi-fixed sands

HIGH YIELD ZONES

Wheat
Maize
Barley, Oats, Rye
Rice
Millets
Sea fishing

LIVESTOCK

Dairy farming
Cattle
Sheep
Pigs

FOOD

MAJOR SPECIALISED CROPS

Sugar beet/cane
Apples
Bananas
Citrus fruit
Vine growing

Coffee
Cocoa
Tea
Soybeans/Groundnuts
Cottonseed/Sunflower

1 2
3 4

LOW YIELD ZONES

Tundra, Ice-cap
Forest
Mountain
Extensive Grassland
Desert, semi-desert

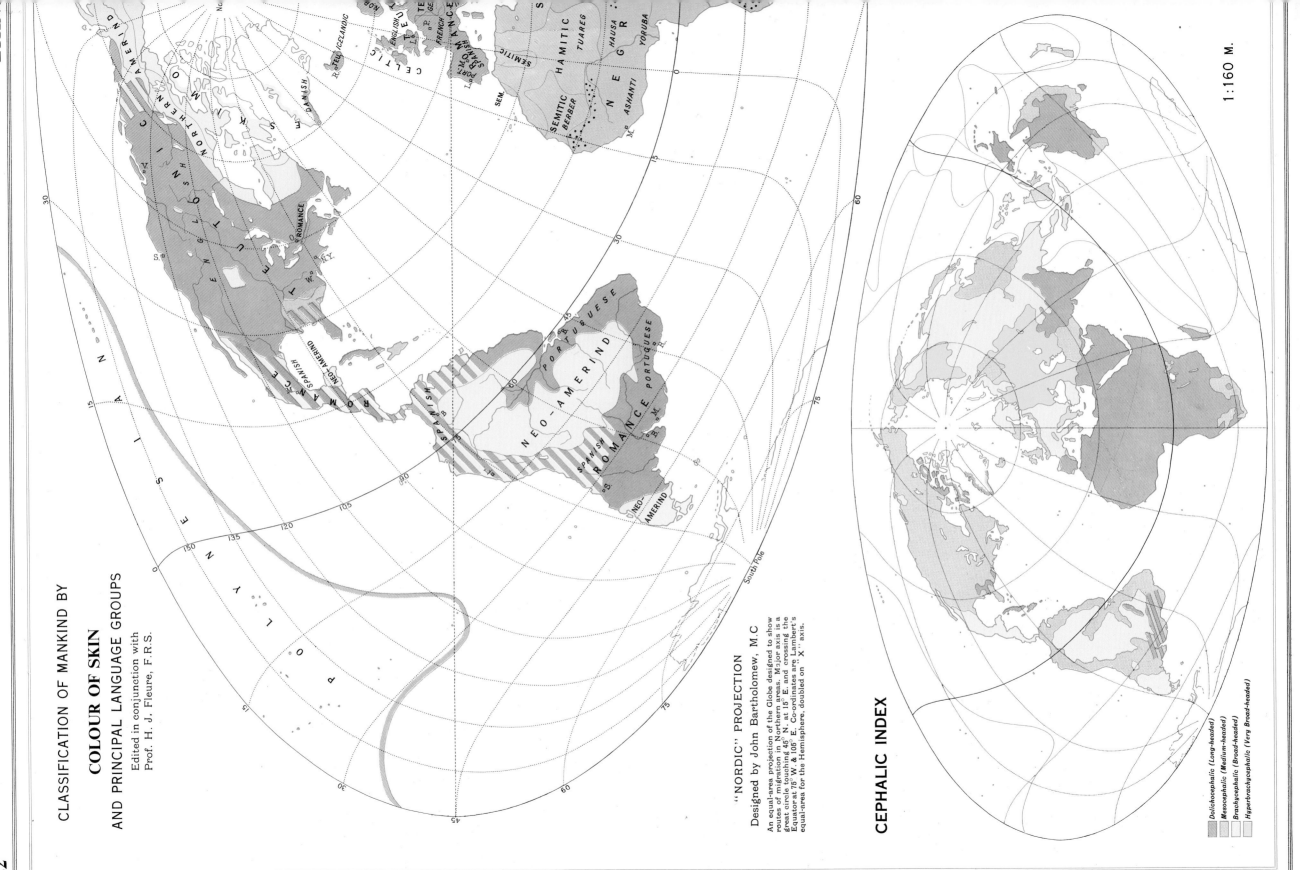

CLASSIFICATION OF MANKIND BY

COLOUR OF SKIN

AND PRINCIPAL LANGUAGE GROUPS

Edited in conjunction with
Prof. H. J. Fleure, F.R.S.

1:160 M.

"NORDIC" PROJECTION

Designed by John Bartholomew, M.C

An equal-area projection of the Globe designed to show
routes of migration in Northern areas. Major axis is a
great circle touching 46° N. at 15° E. and crossing the
Equator at 75° W. & 105° E. Co-ordinates are Lambert's
equal-area for the Hemisphere, doubled on "X" axis.

CEPHALIC INDEX

Dolichocephalic (Long-headed)
Mesocephalic (Medium-headed)
Brachycephalic (Broad-headed)
Hyperbrachycephalic (Very Broad-headed)

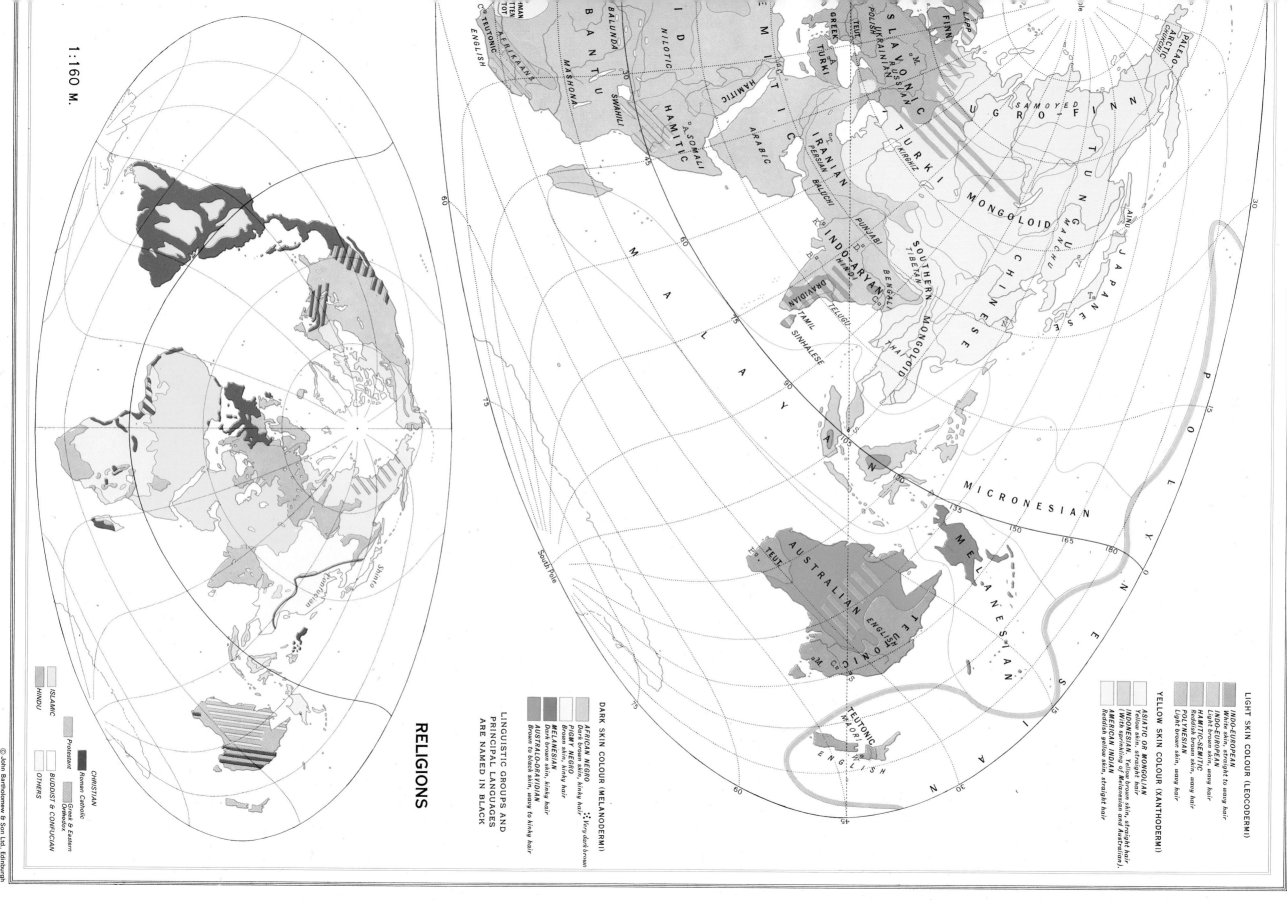

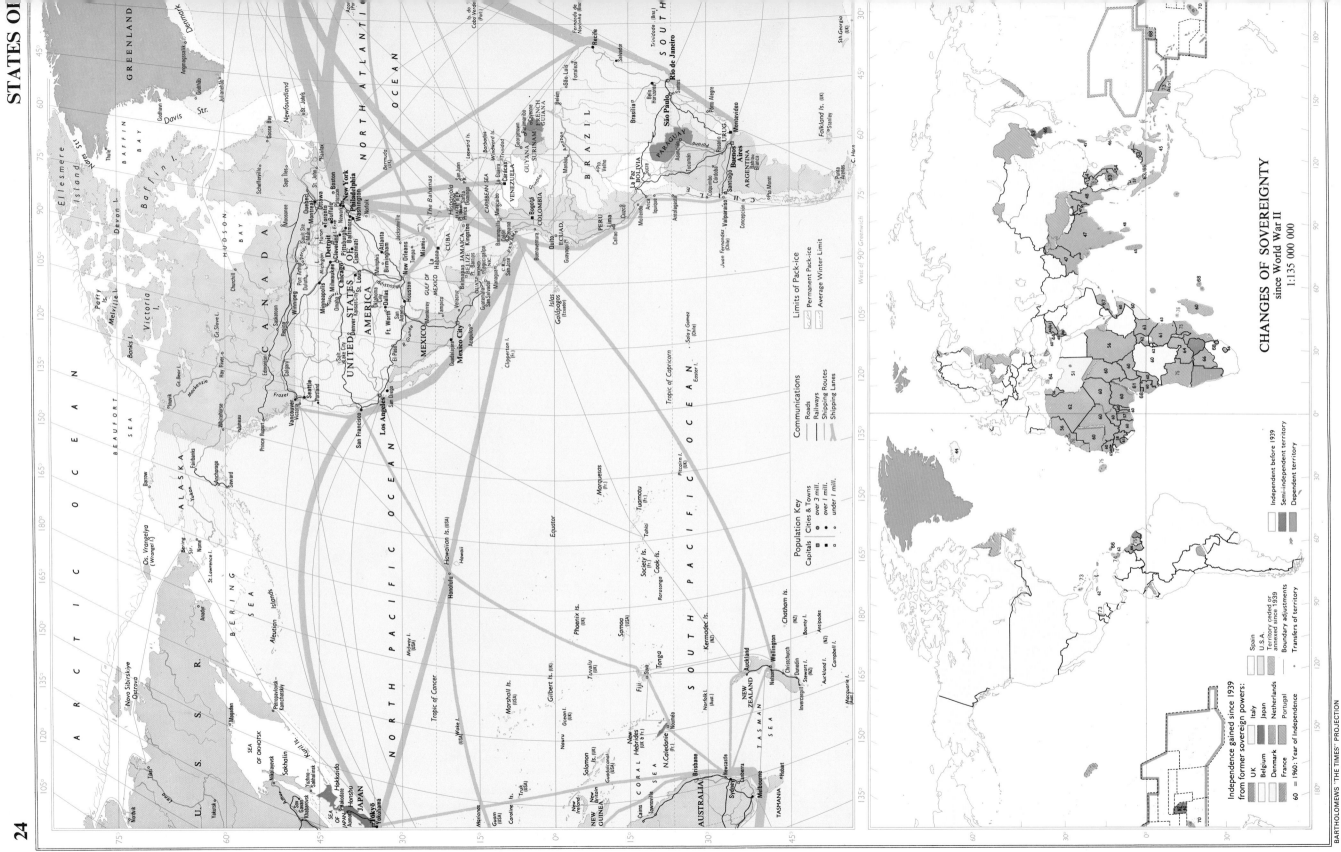

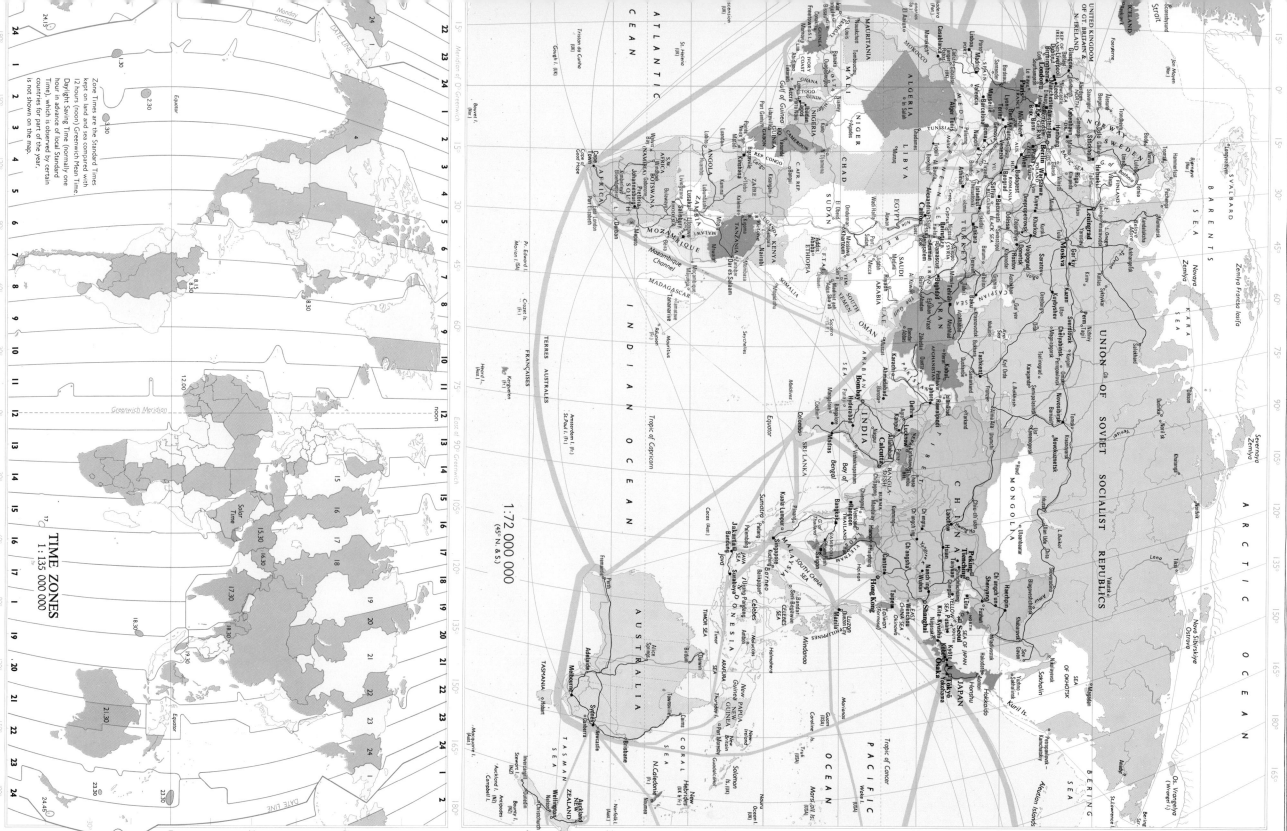

1:72 000 000
(45° N. & S.)

TIME ZONES
1:135 000 000

Zone Times are the Standard Times
kept on land and sea compared with
12 hours (noon) Greenwich Mean Time.
Daylight Saving Time (normally one
hour in advance of local Standard
Time), which is observed by certain
countries for part of the year,
is not shown on the map.

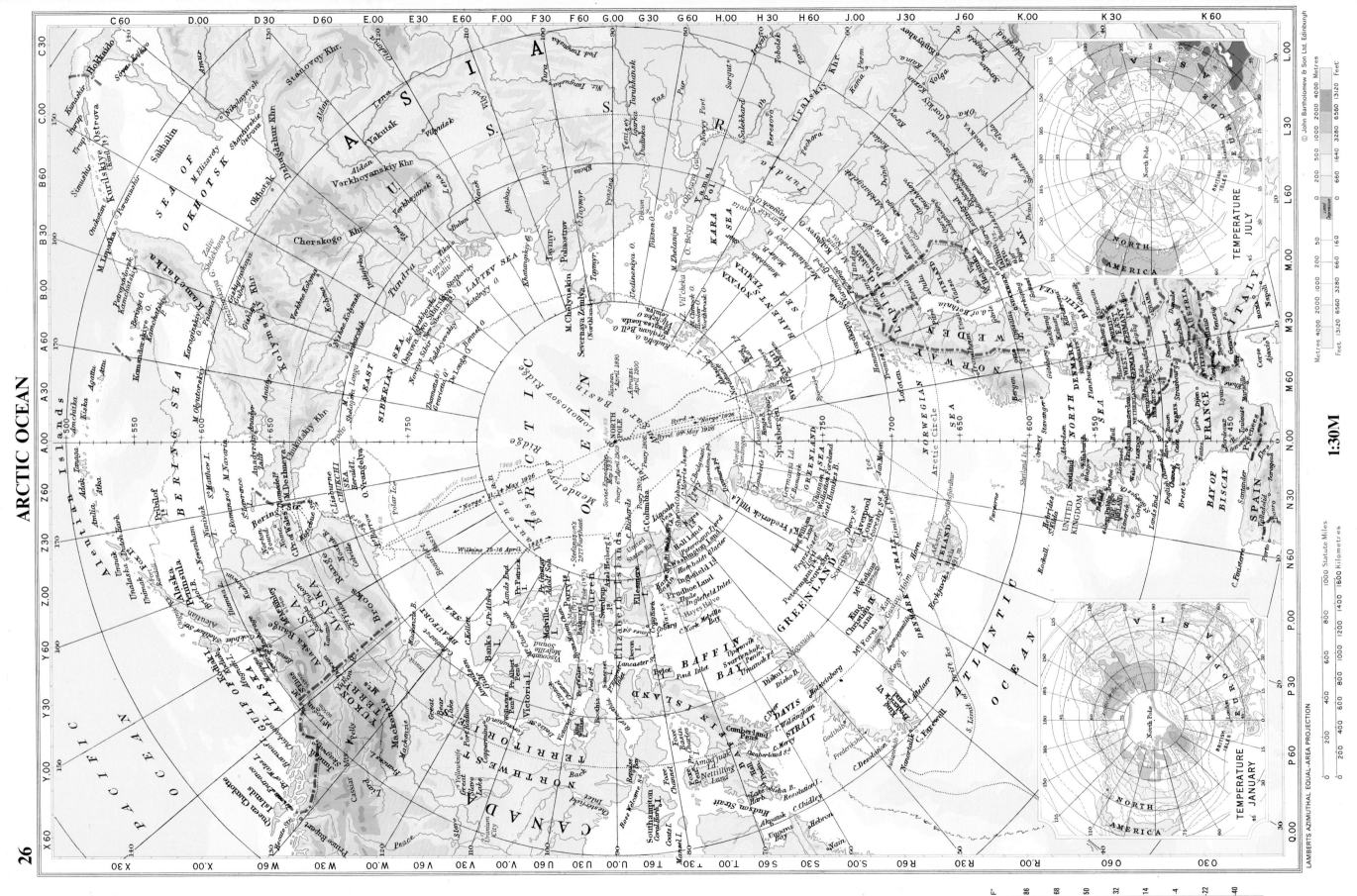

ARCTIC OCEAN

1:30M

26

LAMBERTS AZIMUTHAL EQUAL-AREA PROJECTION

© John Bartholomew & Son Ltd. Edinburgh

TEMPERATURE JULY

TEMPERATURE JANUARY

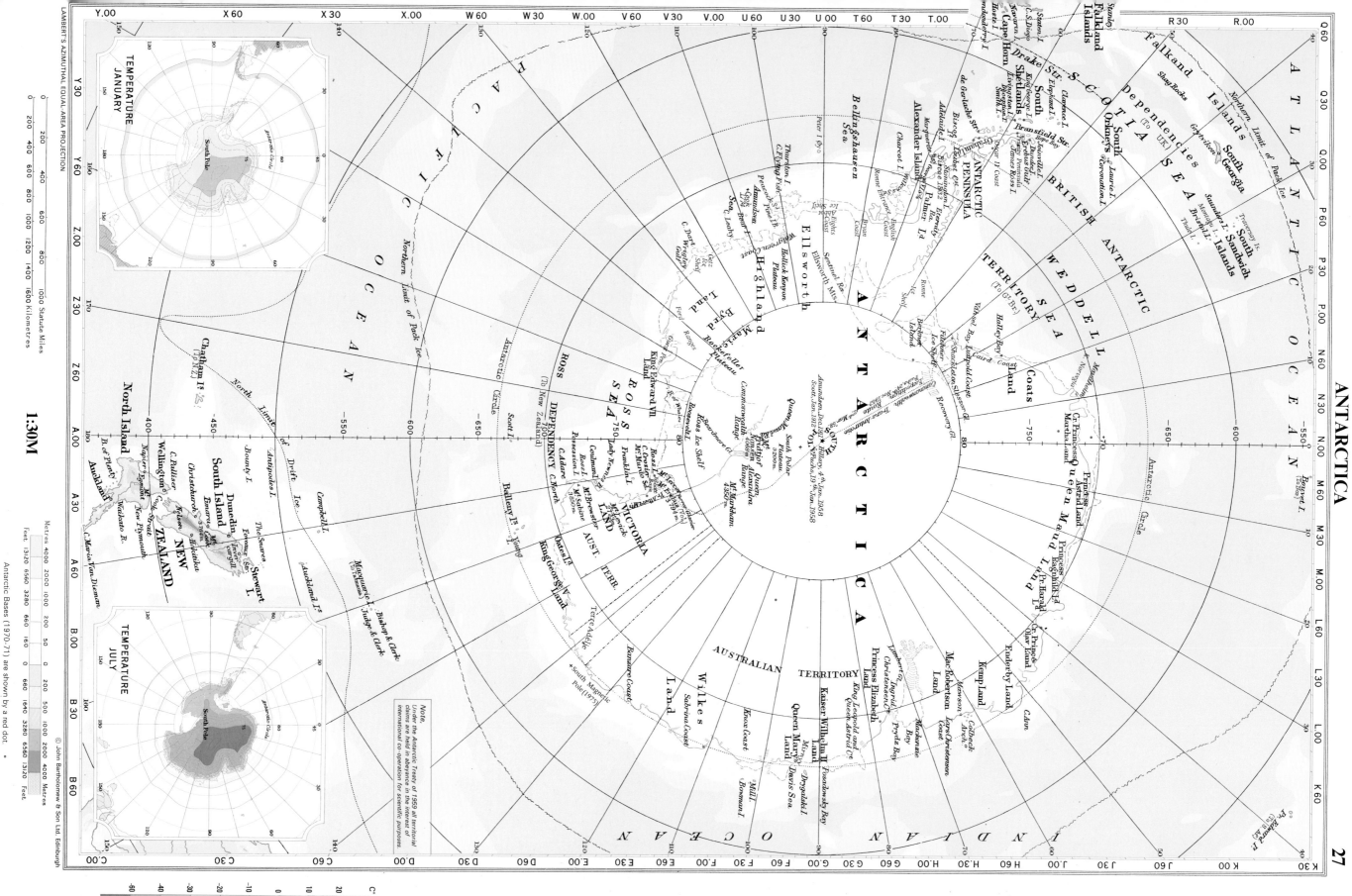

ANTARCTICA

27

TEMPERATURE JANUARY

TEMPERATURE JULY

LAMBERT'S AZIMUTHAL EQUAL-AREA PROJECTION

1:30M

Statute Miles

Kilometres

Antarctic Bases (1970-71) are shown by a red dot.

Note:
Under the Antarctic Treaty of 1959 all territorial claims are held in abeyance in the interest of international co-operation for scientific purposes

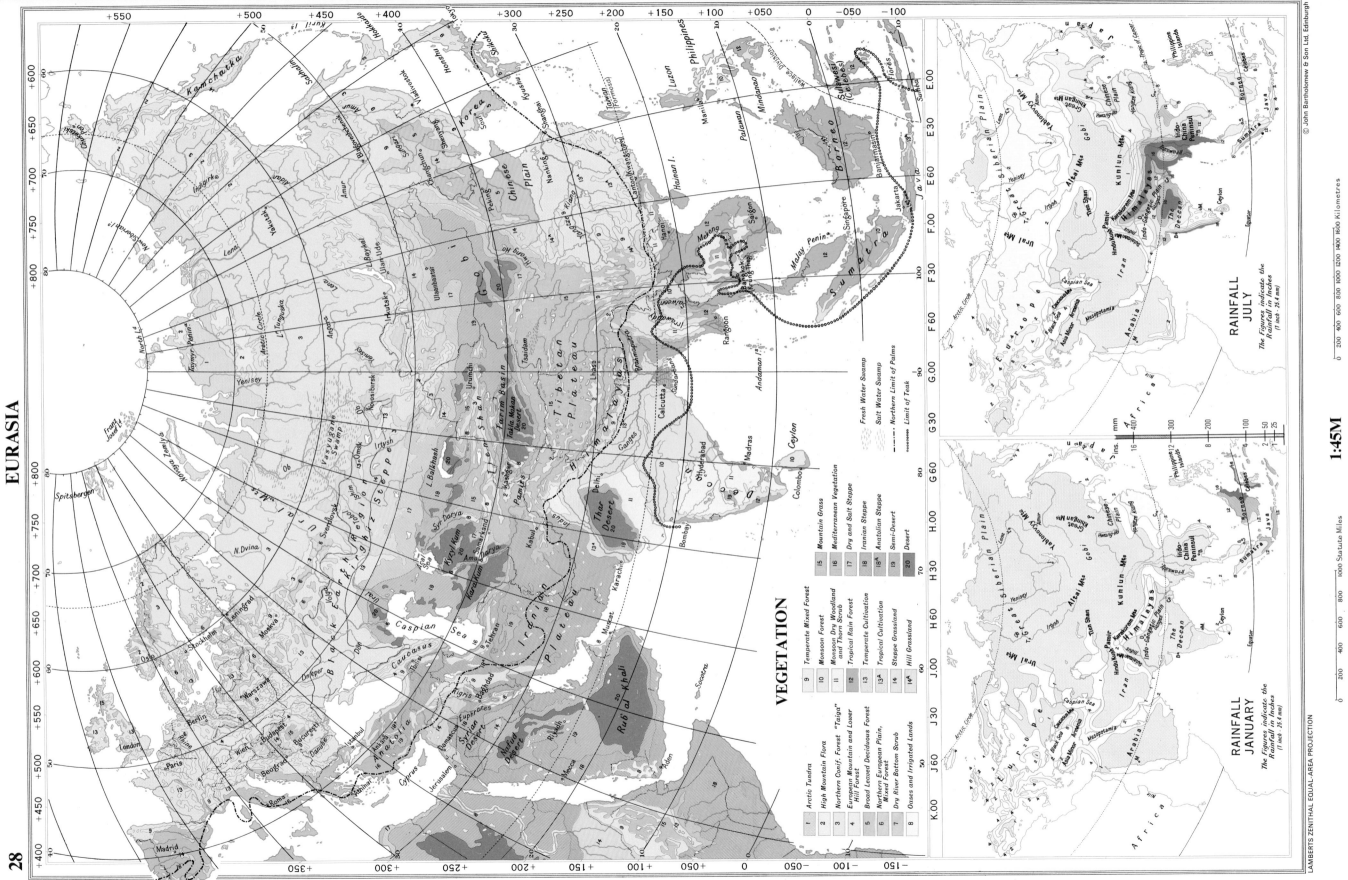

EURASIA

28

VEGETATION

1	Arctic Tundra	
2	High Mountain Flora	
3	Northern Conif. Forest "Taiga"	
4	European Mountain and Lower Hill Forest	
5	Broad Leaved Deciduous Forest	
6	Northern European Plain, Mixed Forest	
7	Dry River Bottom Scrub	
8	Oases and Irrigated Lands	
9	Temperate Mixed Forest	15 Mountain Grass
10	Monsoon Forest	16 Mediterranean Vegetation
11	Monsoon Dry Woodland and Thorn Scrub	17 Dry and Salt Steppe
12	Tropical Rain Forest	18 Iranian Steppe
13	Temperate Cultivation	18A Anatolian Steppe
13A	Tropical Cultivation	19 Semi-Desert
14	Steppe Grassland	20 Desert
14A	Hill Grassland	

Fresh Water Swamp

Salt Water Swamp

Northern Limit of Palms

Limit of Teak

RAINFALL JULY

The Figures indicate the Rainfall in Inches (1 inch · 25.4 mm)

RAINFALL JANUARY

The Figures indicate the Rainfall in Inches (1 inch · 25.4 mm)

1:45M

LAMBERTS ZENITHAL EQUAL-AREA PROJECTION

© John Bartholomew & Son Ltd. Edinburgh

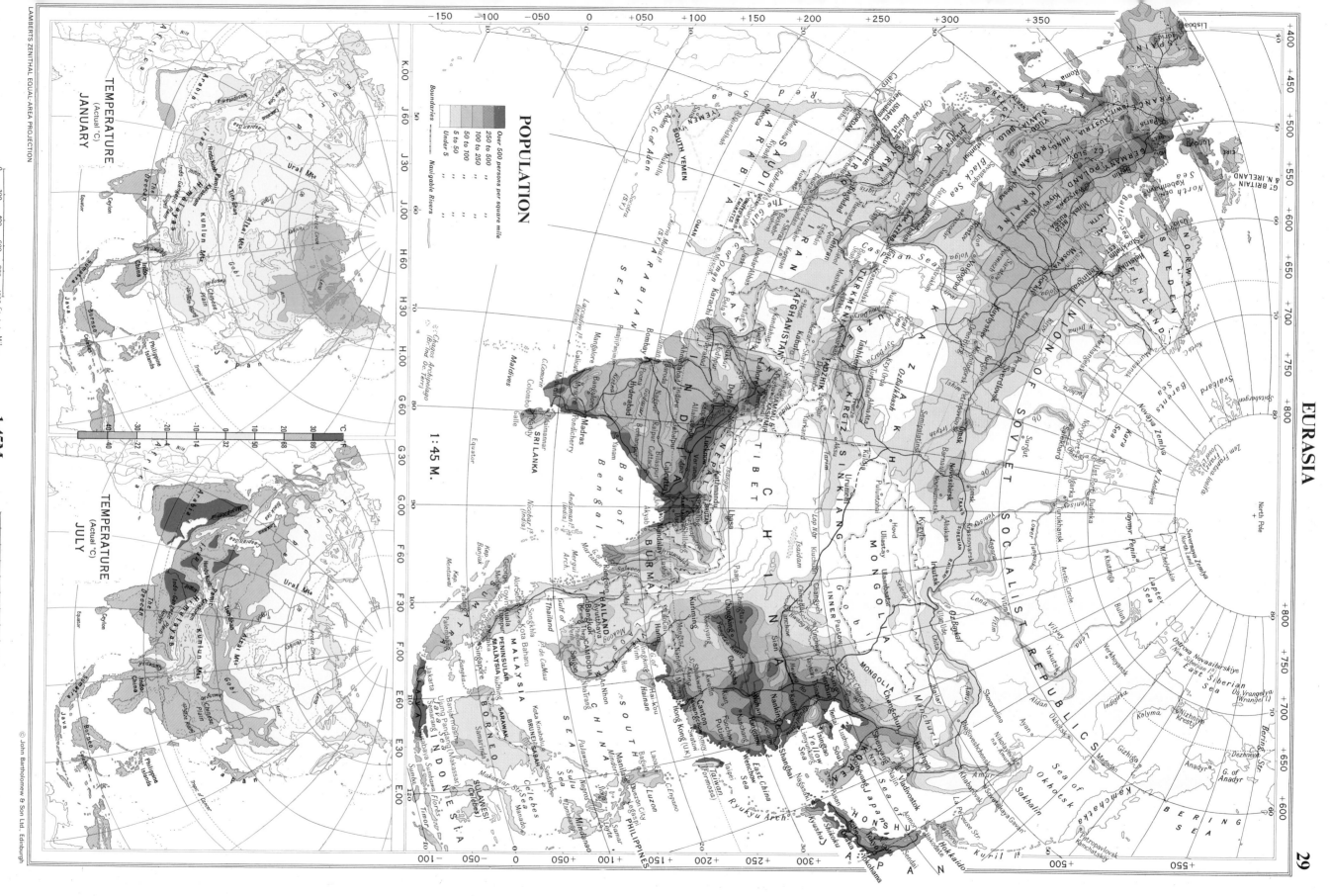

TEMPERATURE
(Actual °C)
JANUARY

TEMPERATURE
(Actual °C)
JULY

1:45M

1:45M

1:45 M.

POPULATION

Over 500 persons per square mile
250 to 500
100 to 250 "
50 to 100 "
5 to 50 "
Under 5 "

Boundaries
Navigable Rivers

LAMBERTS ZENITHAL EQUAL AREA PROJECTION

© John Bartholomew & Son Ltd. Edinburgh

2

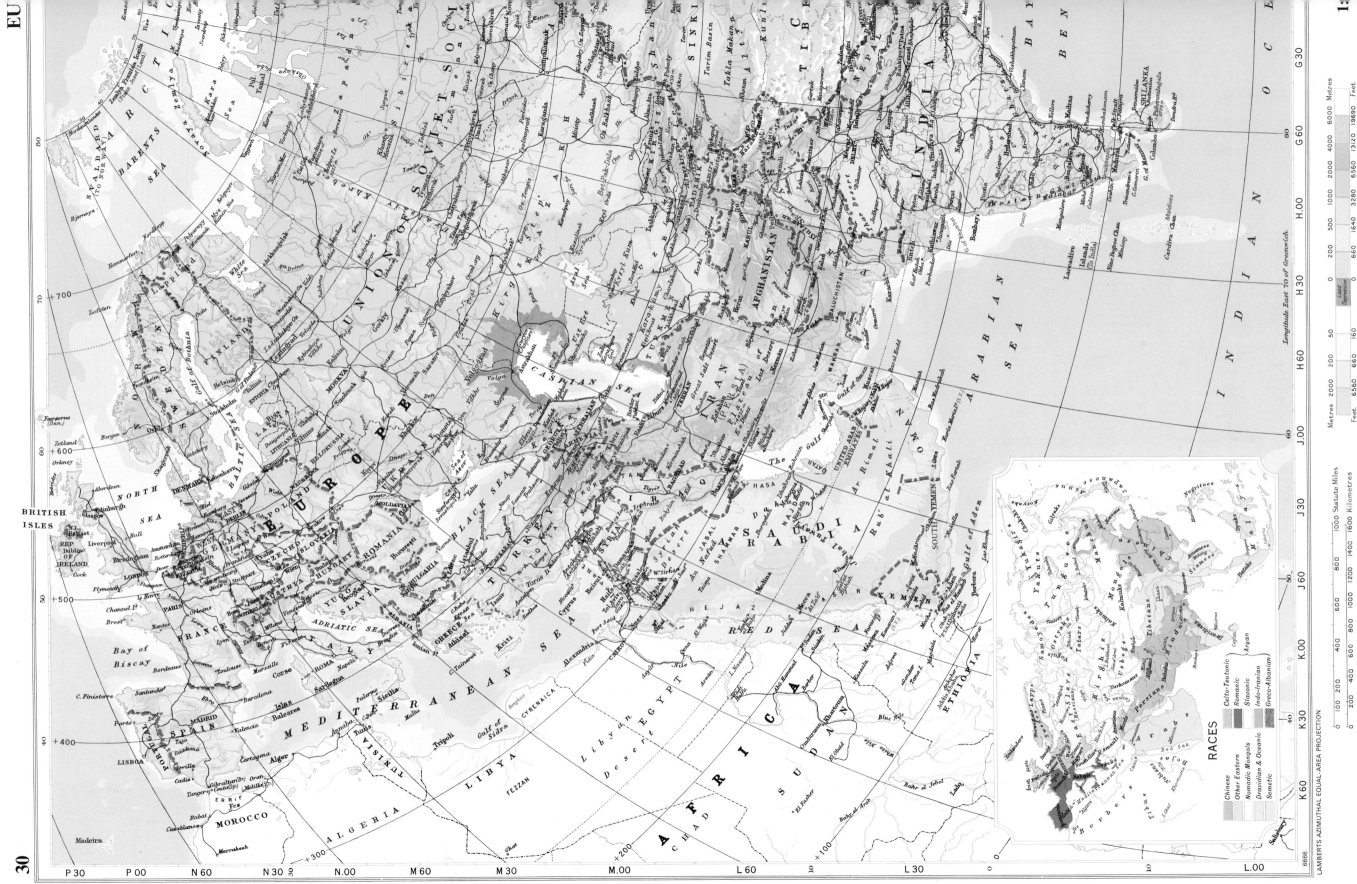

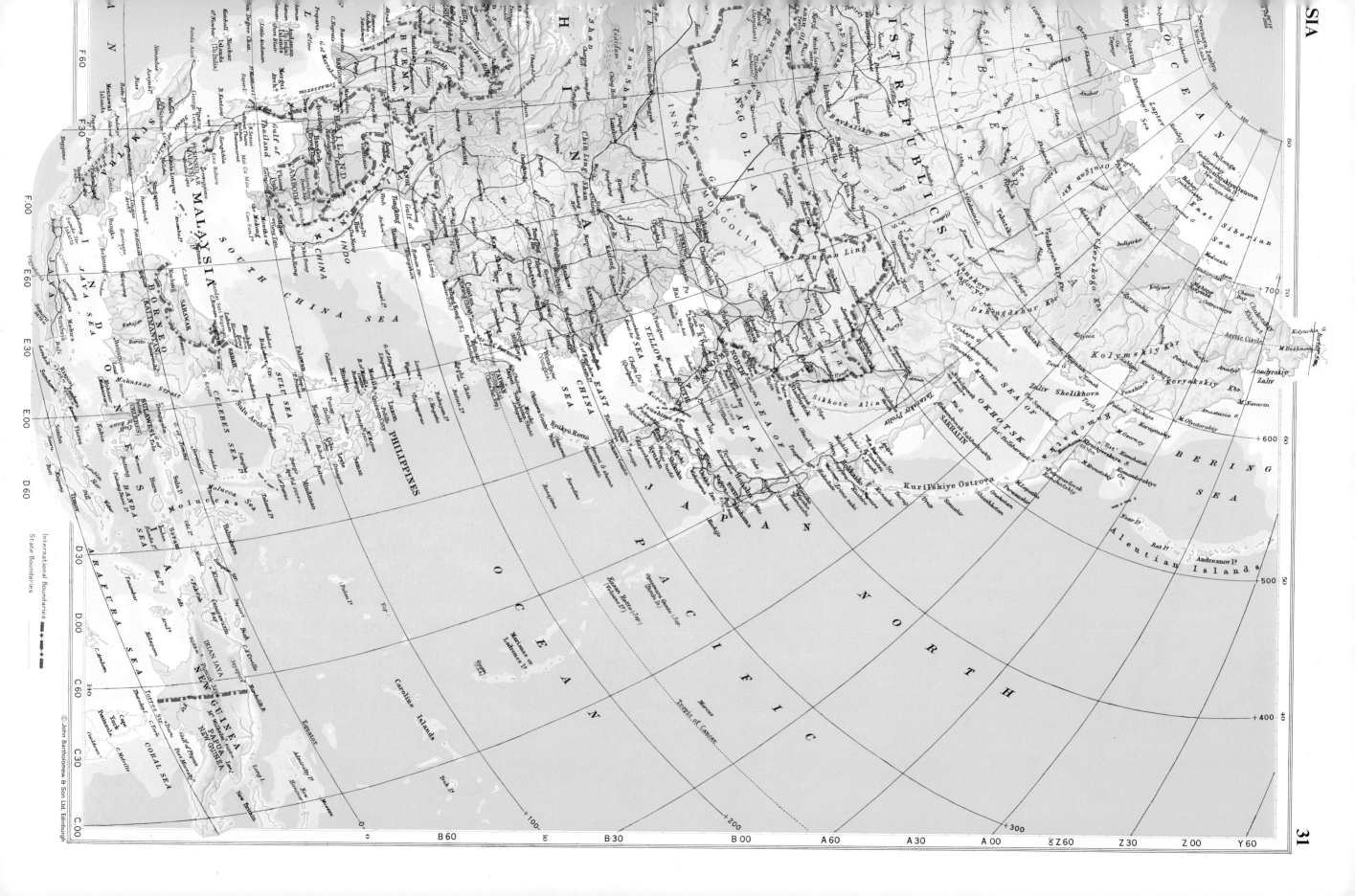

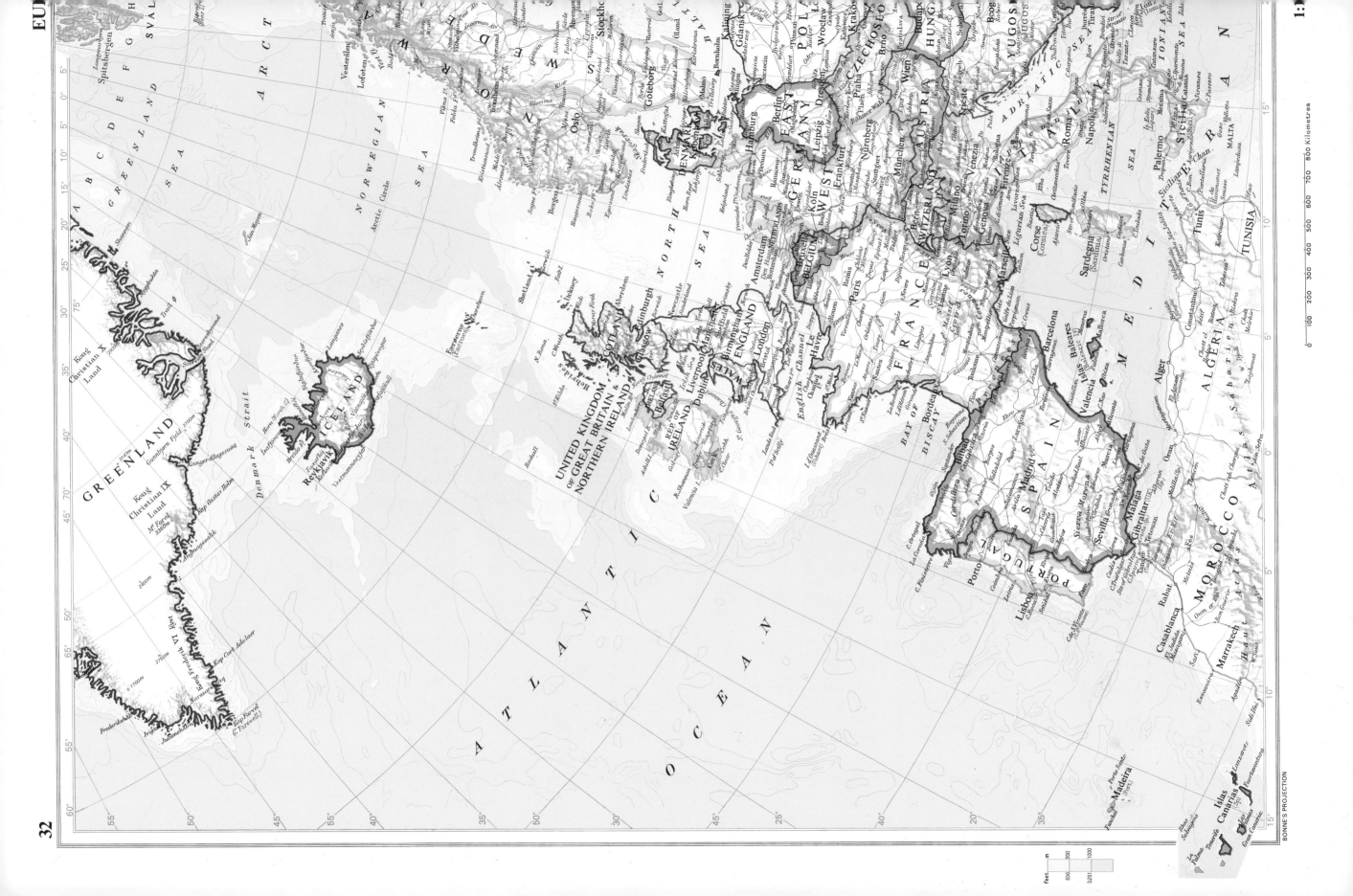

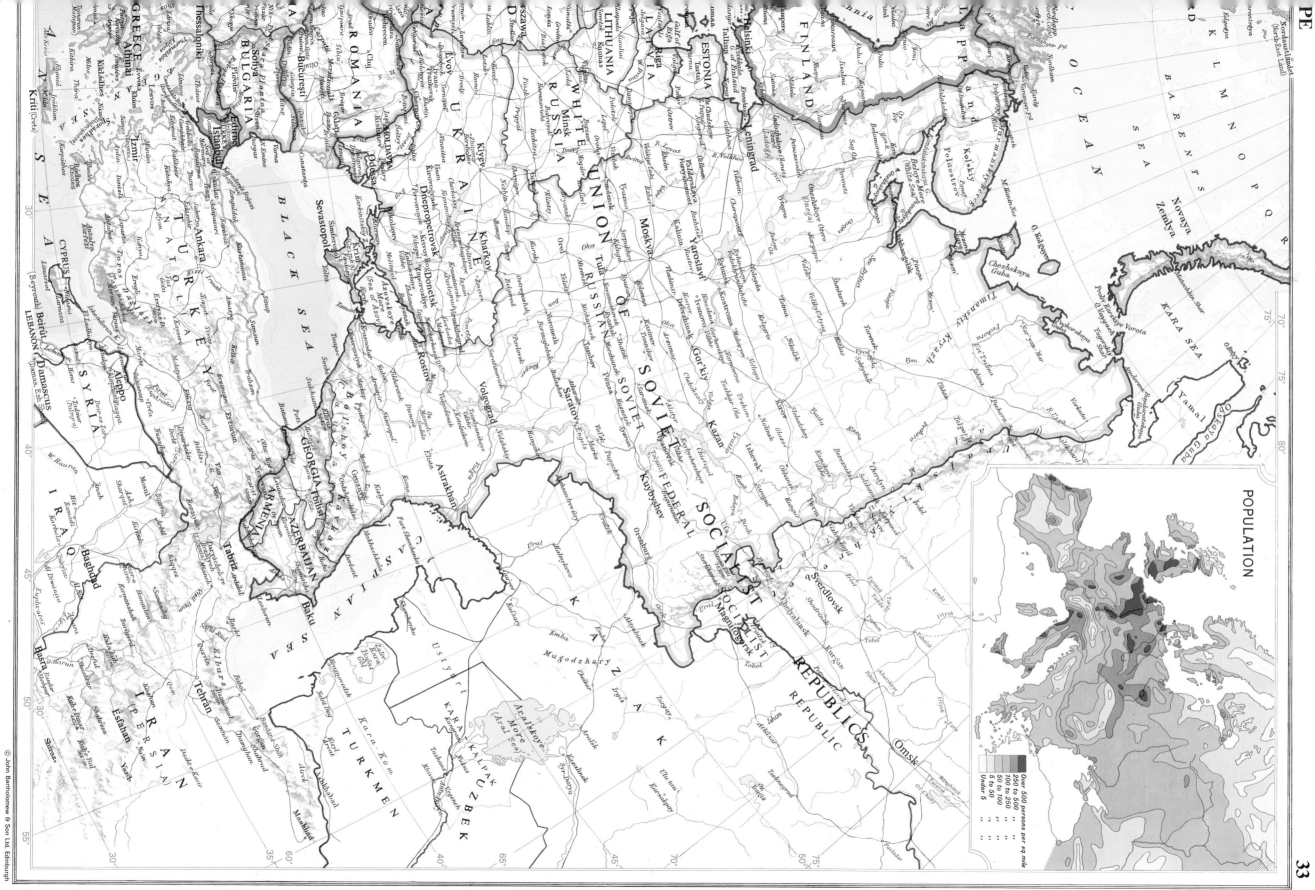

POPULATION

| Over 500 persons per sq. mile |
| 250 to 500 " " " " |
| 100 to 250 " " " " |
| 50 to 100 " " " " |
| 5 to 50 " " " " |
| Under 5 " " " " |

© John Bartholomew & Son Ltd, Edinburgh

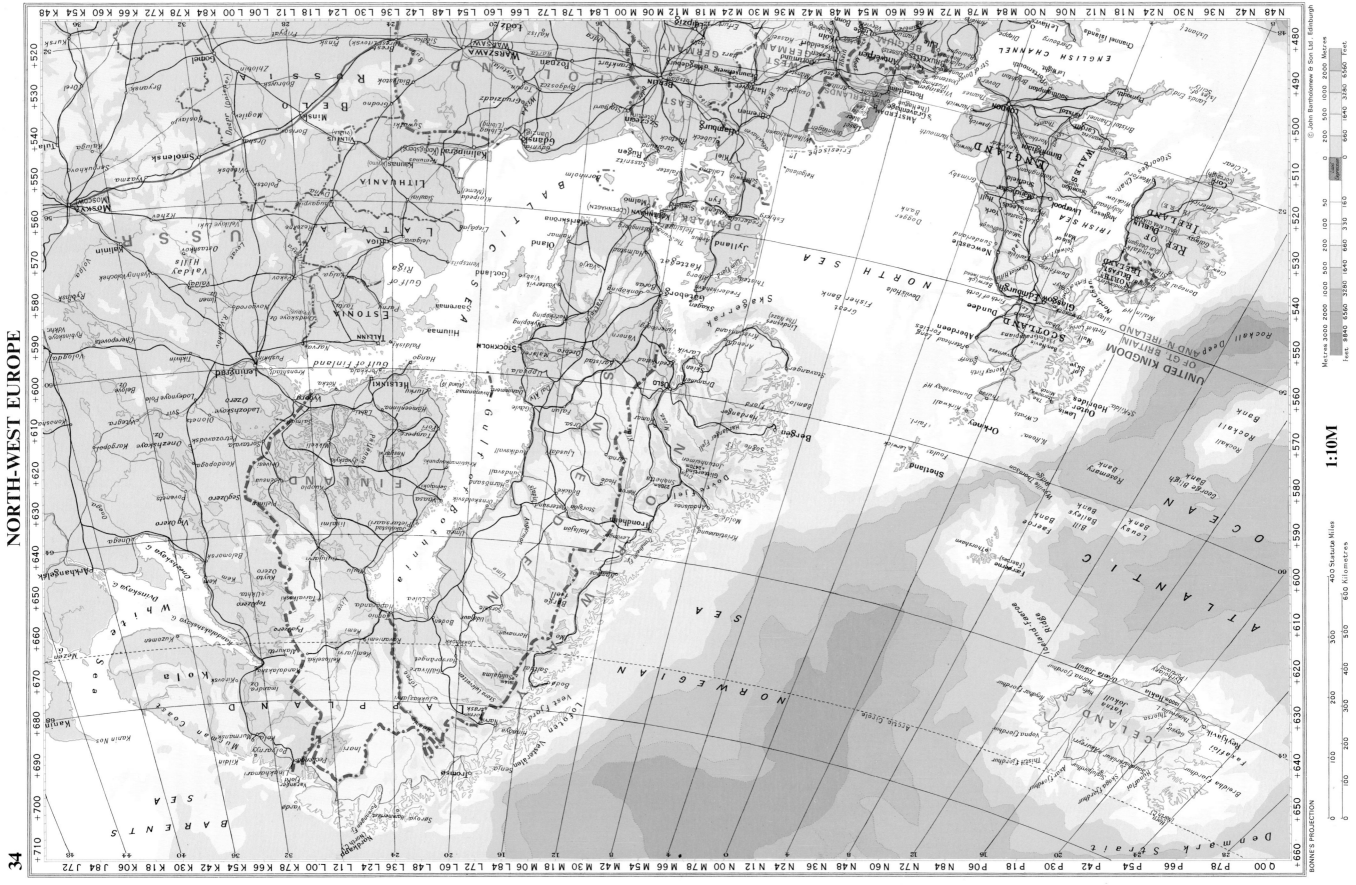

1:10M

BONNE'S PROJECTION

© John Bartholomew & Son Ltd. Edinburgh

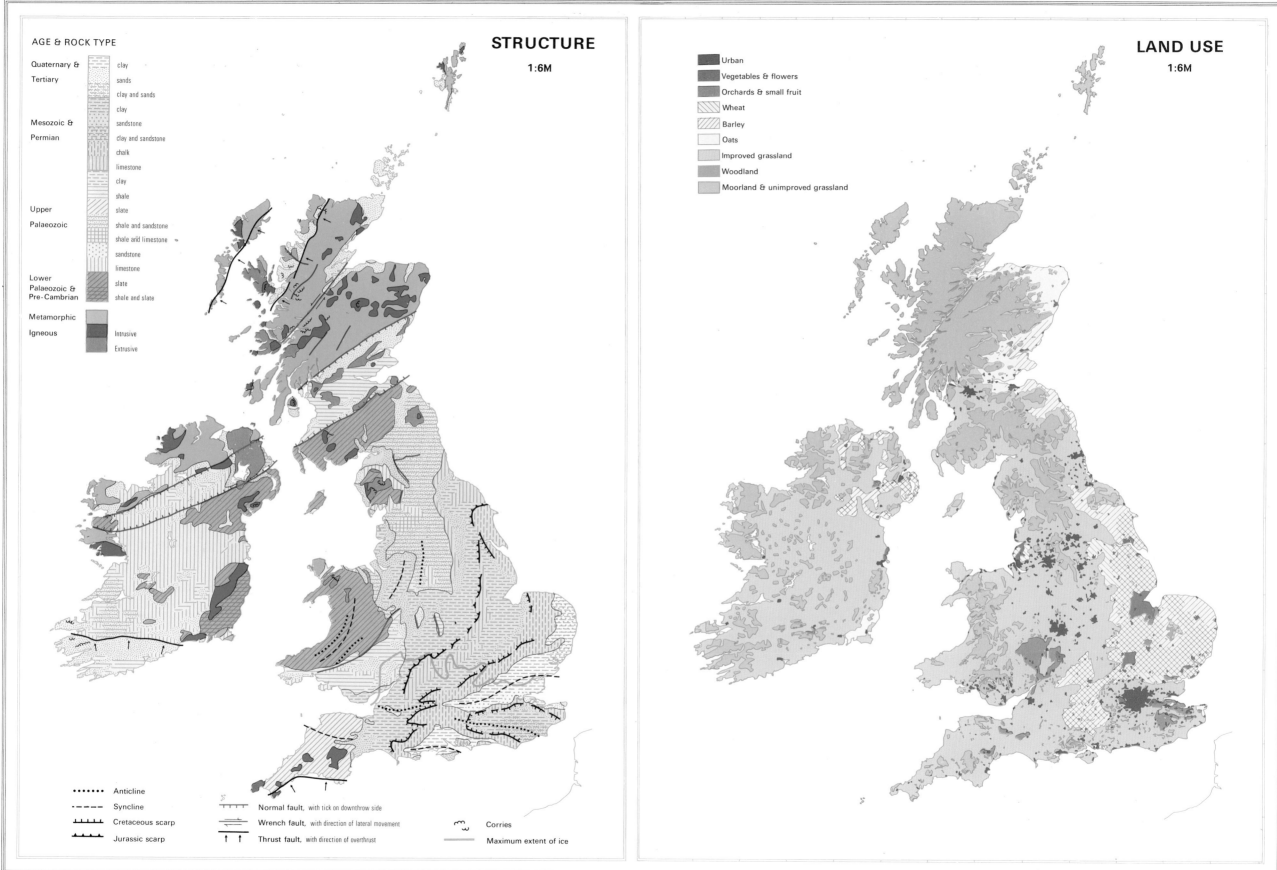

STRUCTURE

1:6M

AGE & ROCK TYPE

Quaternary &
Tertiary
- clay
- sands
- clay and sands

Mesozoic &
Permian
- clay
- sandstone
- clay and sandstone
- chalk
- limestone
- clay

Upper
Palaeozoic
- shale
- slate
- shale and sandstone
- shale and limestone
- sandstone
- limestone

Lower
Palaeozoic &
Pre-Cambrian
- slate
- shale and slate

Metamorphic

Igneous
- Intrusive
- Extrusive

••••••• Anticline
– – – – Syncline
Cretaceous scarp
Jurassic scarp

Normal fault, with tick on downthrow side
Wrench fault, with direction of lateral movement
Thrust fault, with direction of overthrust

Corries
Maximum extent of ice

LAND USE

1:6M

Urban
Vegetables & flowers
Orchards & small fruit
Wheat
Barley
Oats
Improved grassland
Woodland
Moorland & unimproved grassland

BRITISH ISLES

35

BRITISH ISLES

36

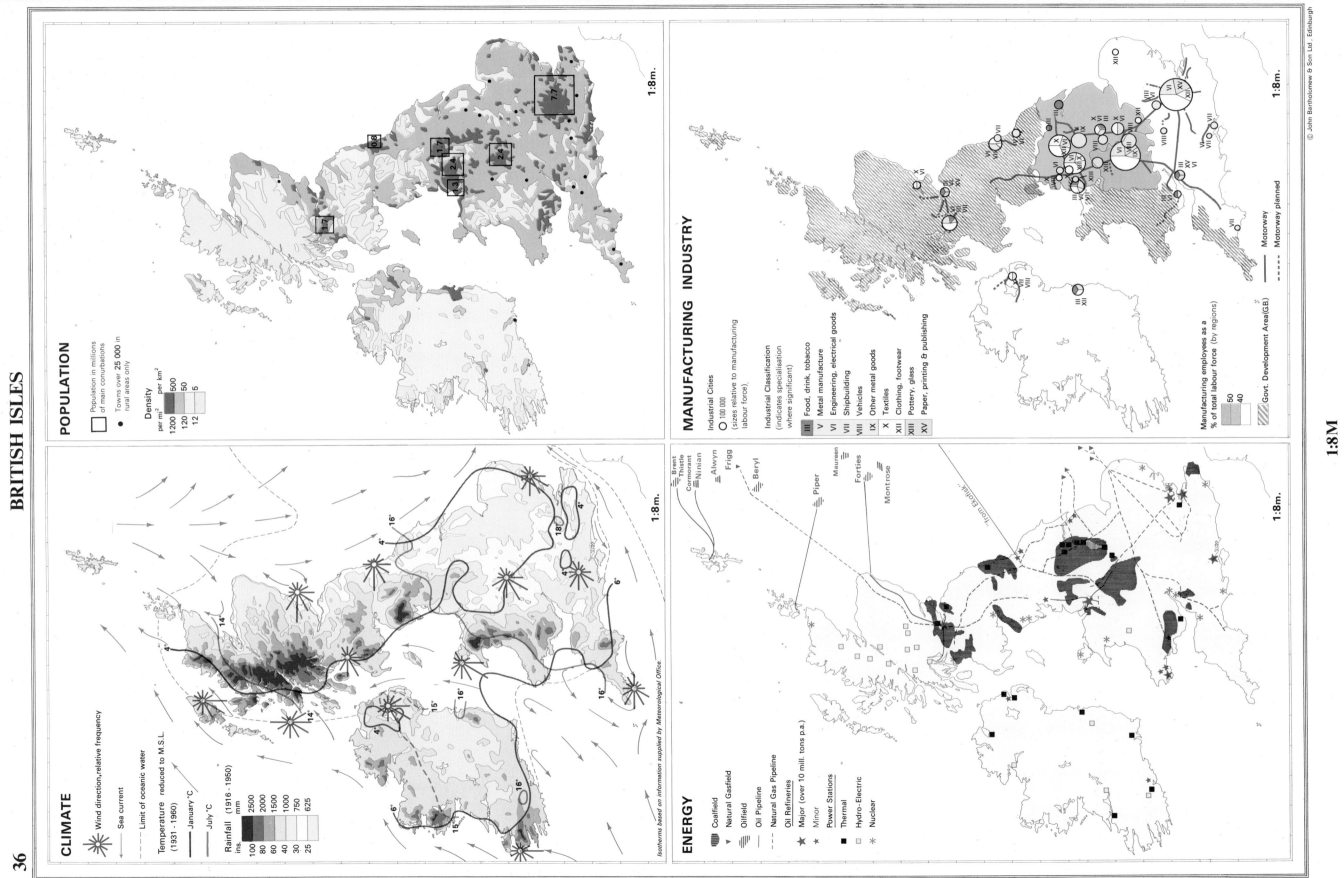

POPULATION

Population in millions of main conurbations

Towns over 25 000 in rural areas only

Density

per mi²	per km²
1200	500
120	50
12	5

1:8 m.

CLIMATE

Wind direction, relative frequency

Sea current

Limit of oceanic water

Temperature reduced to M.S.L. (1931 - 1960)

January °C

July °C

Rainfall (1916 - 1950)

ins.	mm
100	2500
80	2000
60	1500
40	1000
30	750
25	625

Isotherms based on information supplied by Meteorological Office.

1:8 m.

MANUFACTURING INDUSTRY

Industrial Cities

○ 100 000 (sizes relative to manufacturing labour force)

Industrial Classification (indicates specialisation where significant)

III	Food, drink, tobacco
V	Metal manufacture
VI	Engineering, electrical goods
VII	Shipbuilding
VIII	Vehicles
IX	Other metal goods
X	Textiles
XII	Clothing, footwear
XIII	Pottery, glass
XV	Paper, printing & publishing

Manufacturing employees as a % of total labour force (by regions)

50	
40	

Govt. Development Area (G.B.)

Motorway

Motorway planned

1:8M

ENERGY

Coalfield

▼ Natural Gasfield

Oilfield

Oil Pipeline

Natural Gas Pipeline

Oil Refineries

★ Major (over 10 mill. tons p.a.)

✱ Minor

Power Stations

■ Thermal

□ Hydro-Electric

✳ Nuclear

Brent
Thistle
Cormorant
Ninian

Alwyn
Frigg

Beryl

Piper

Maureen

Forties

Montrose

"from Ekofisk"

1:8 m.

© John Bartholomew & Son Ltd. Edinburgh

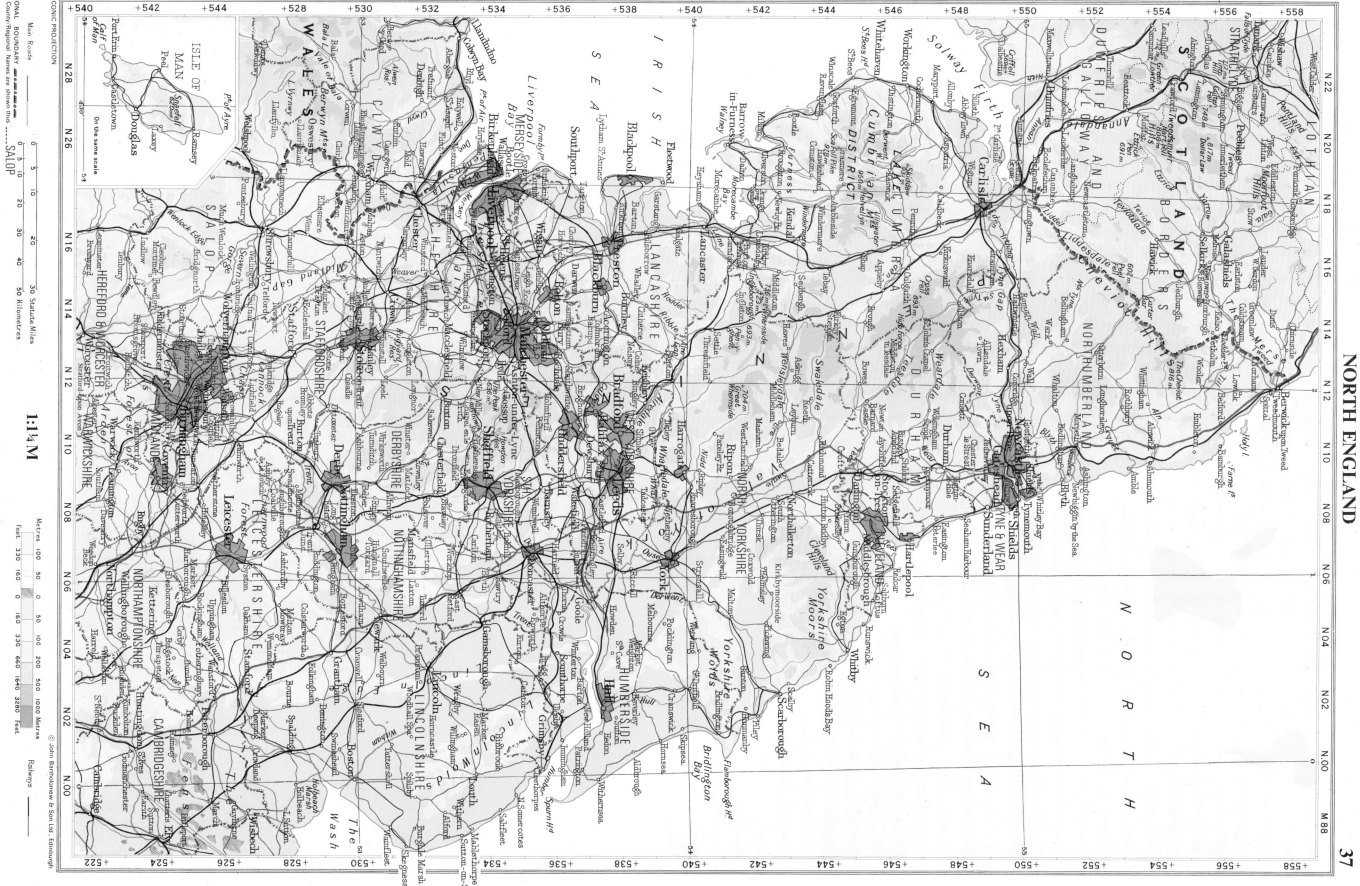

1:1¼ M

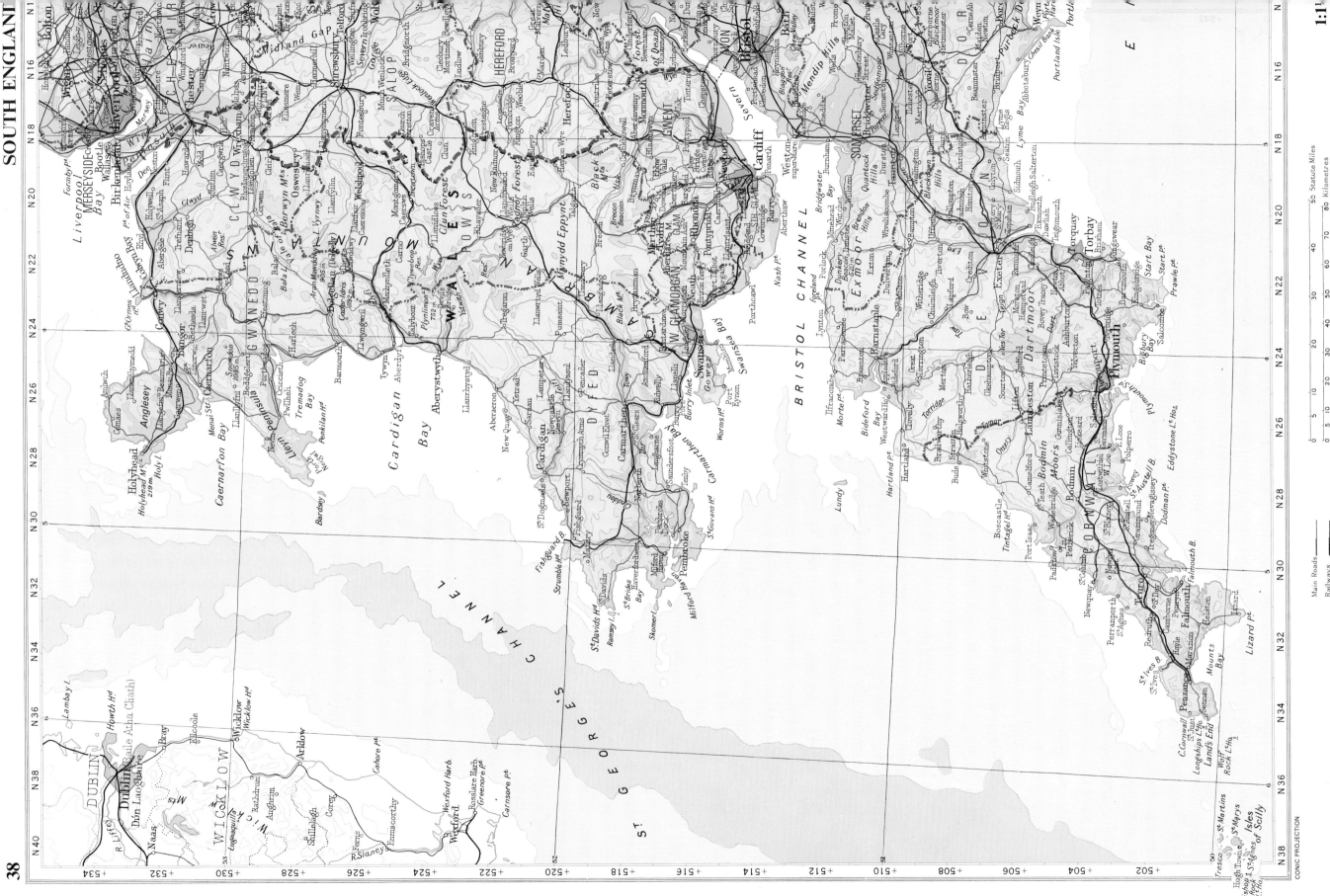

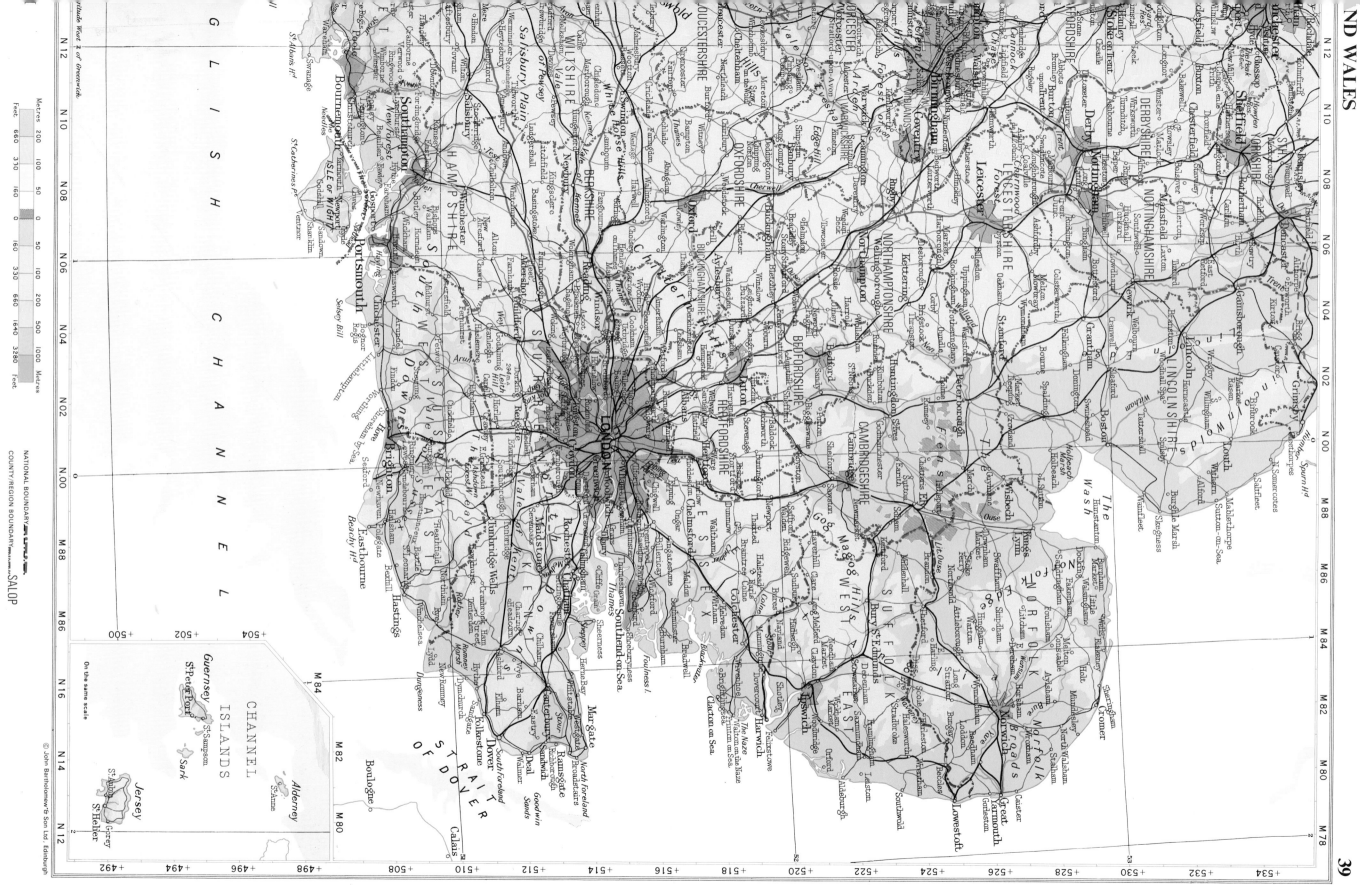

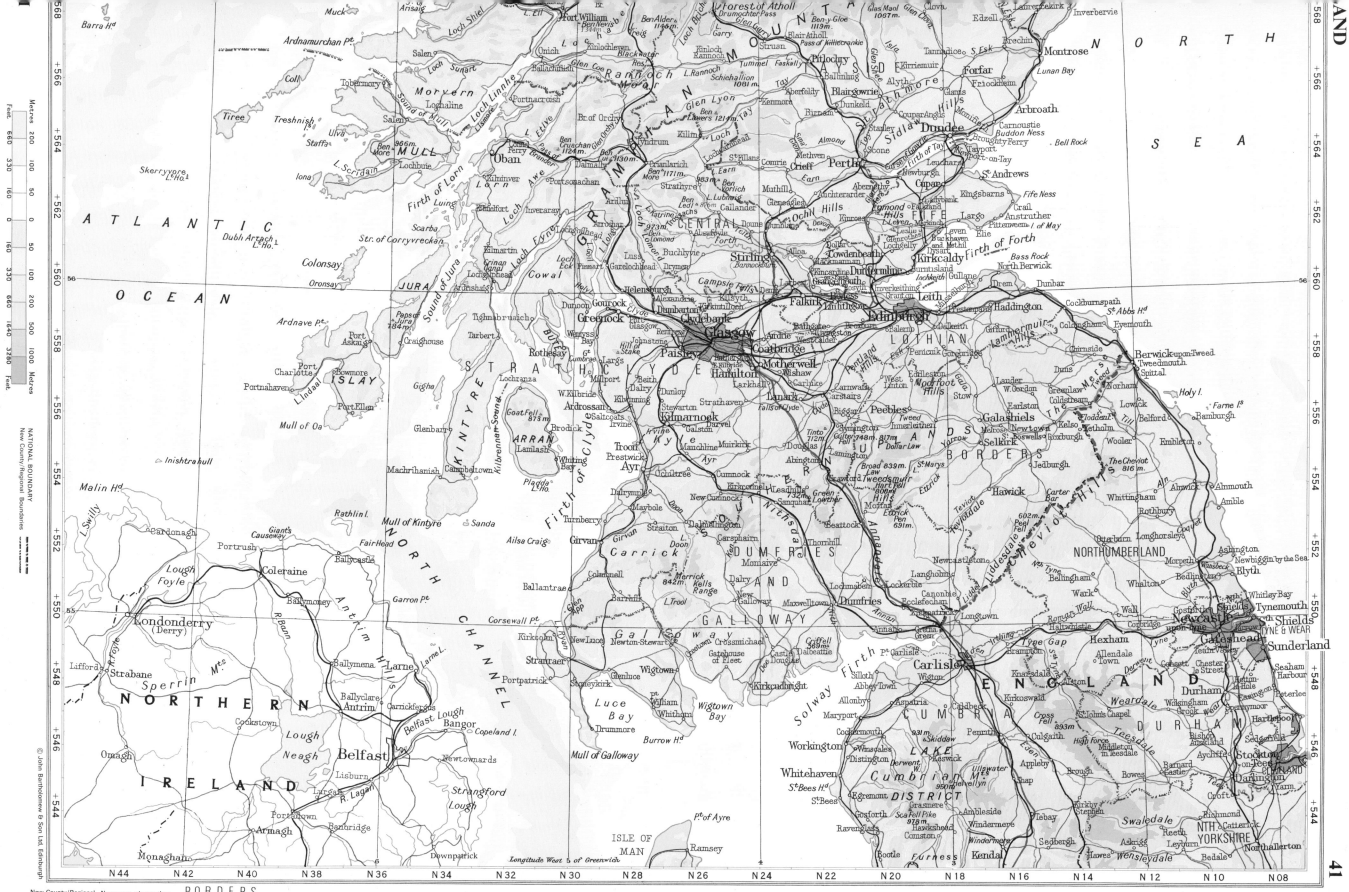

BENELUX COUNTRIES

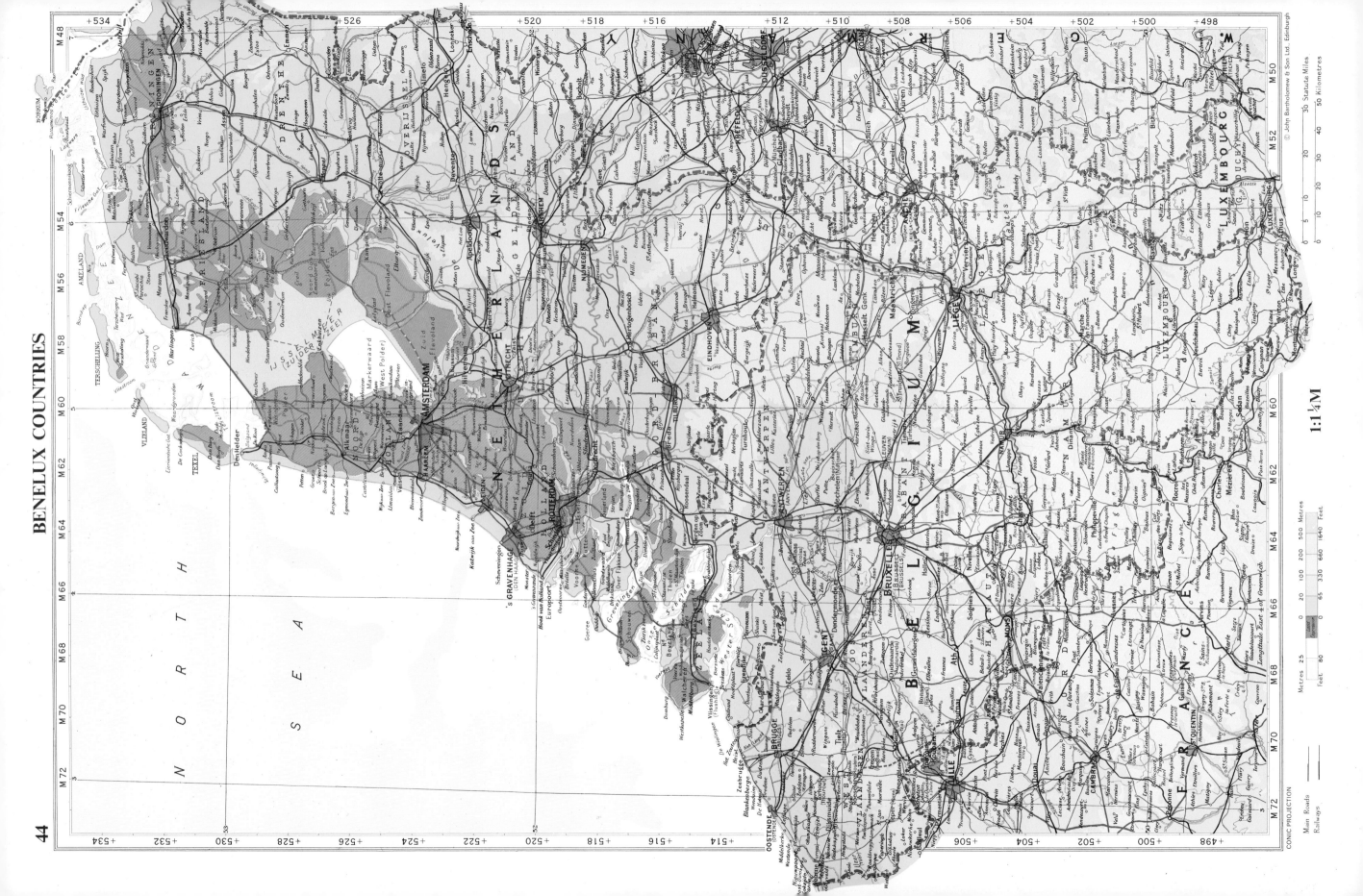

44

1:1¼M

CONIC PROJECTION

© John Bartholomew & Son Ltd. Edinburgh

Main Roads
Railways

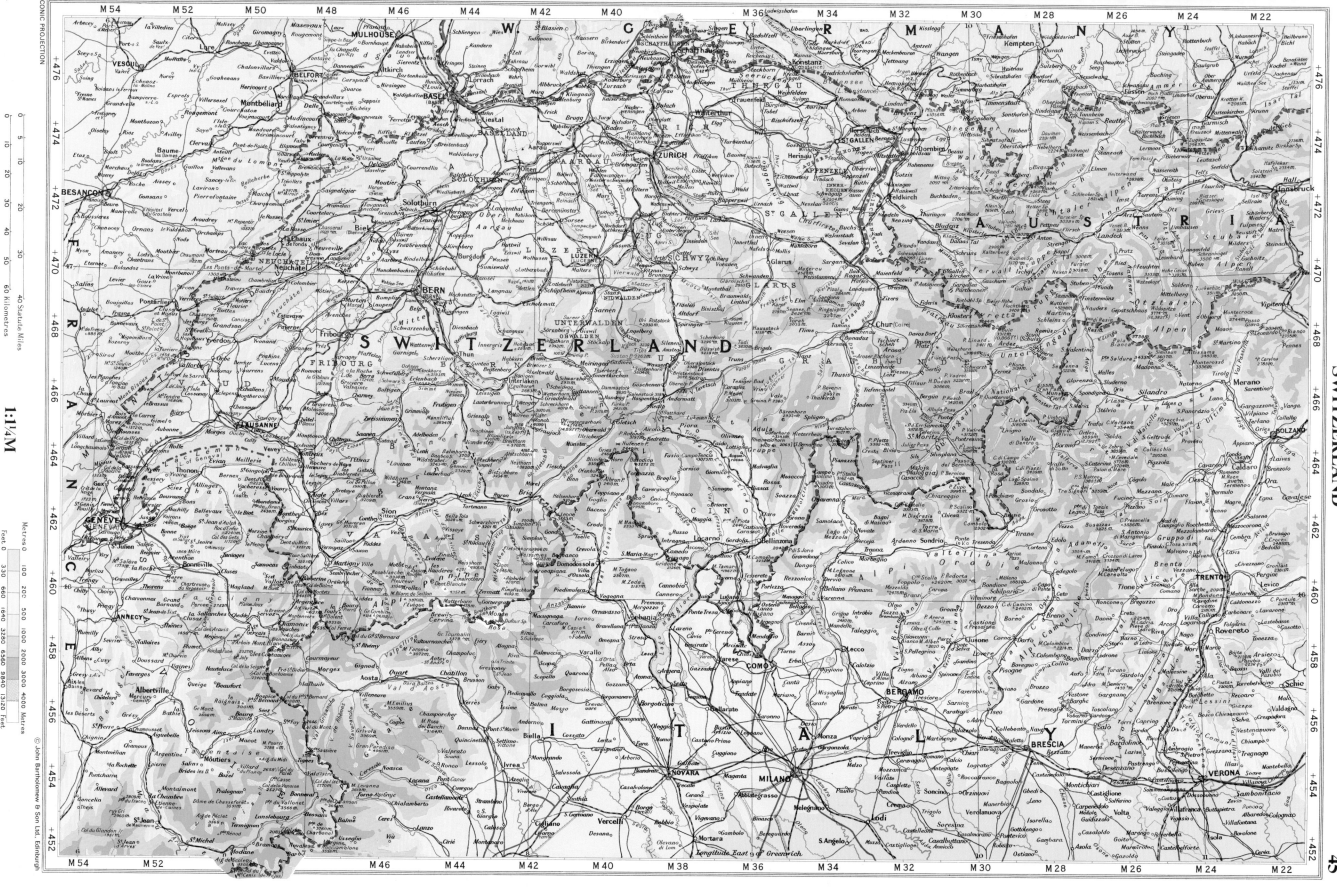

CONIC PROJECTION

1:1¼M

© John Bartholomew & Son Ltd., Edinburgh

45

46

1:4

CONIC PROJECTION

ICELAND

FÆRØERNE
(To Den.)

On the same scale

Main Roads
Railways

ATLANTIC OCEAN

180 Statute Miles
280 Kilometres

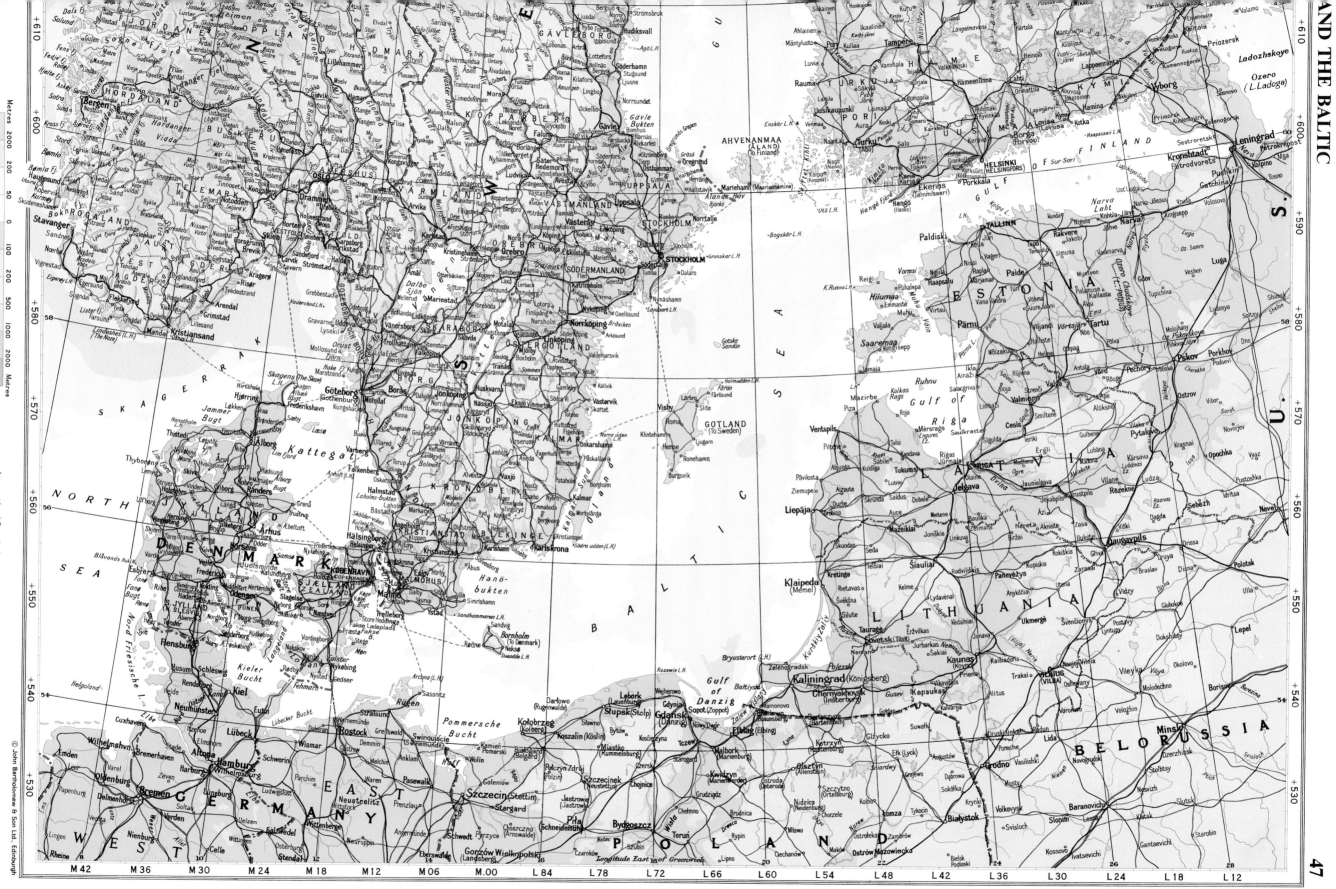

International Boundaries
State Boundaries

Metres 2000
Feet 6560

200
660

50
160

0
0

330

100
660

200
1640

500
3280

1000
6560

2000 Metres
6560 Feet

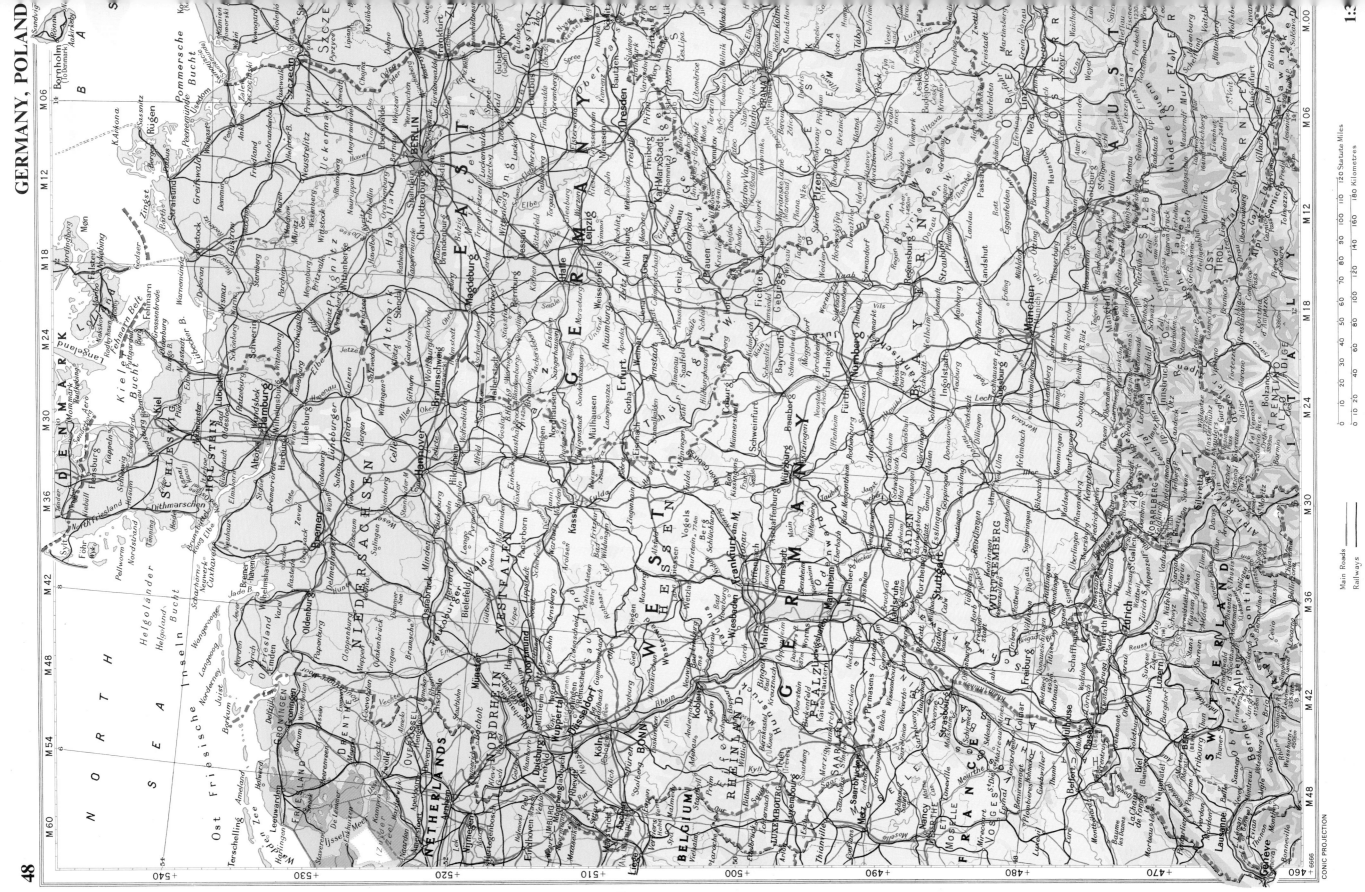

Main Roads
Railways

0 10 20 30 40 50 60 70 80 90 100 110 120 Statute Miles
0 10 20 40 60 80 100 120 140 160 180 Kilometres

CONIC PROJECTION

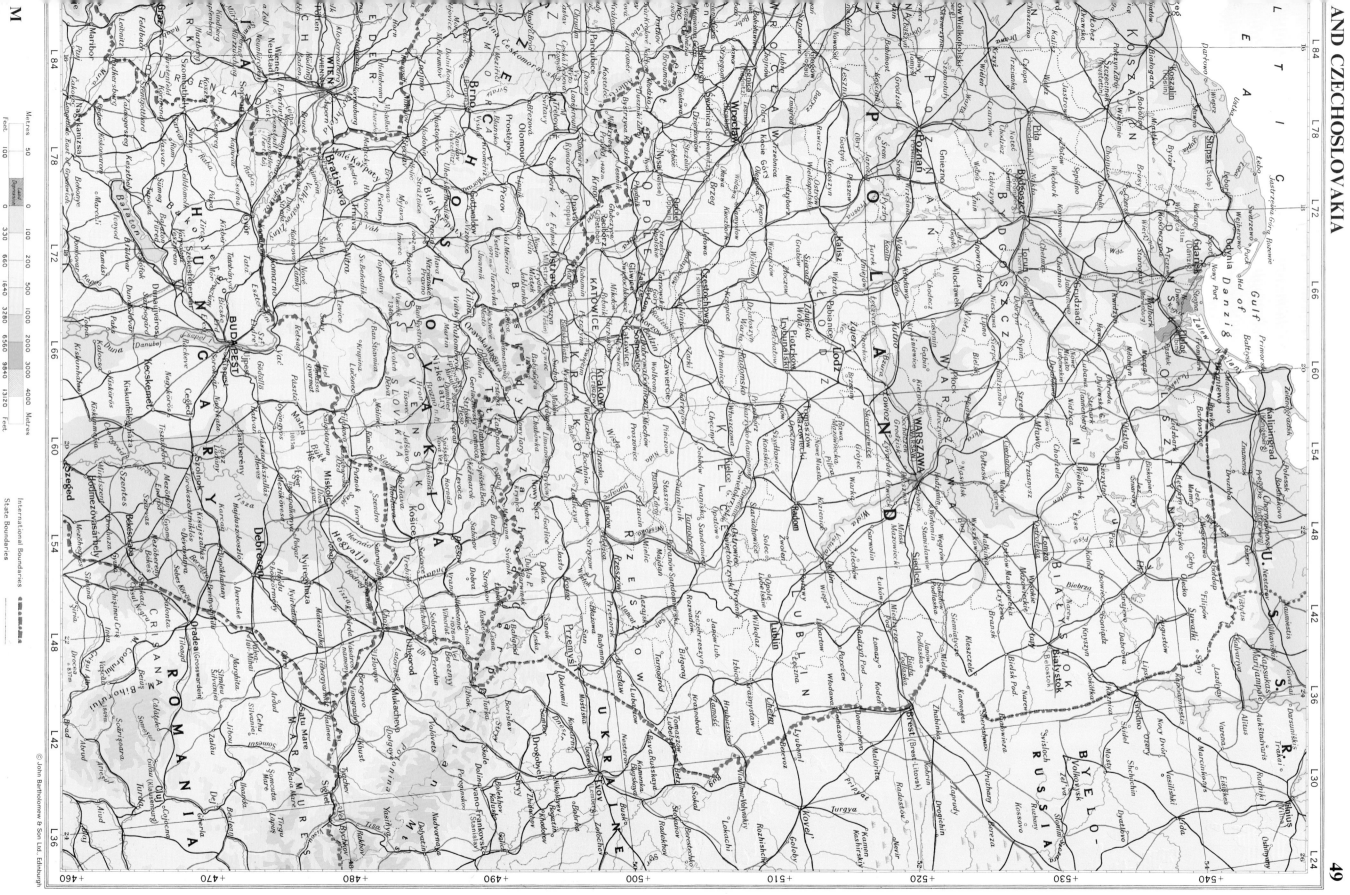

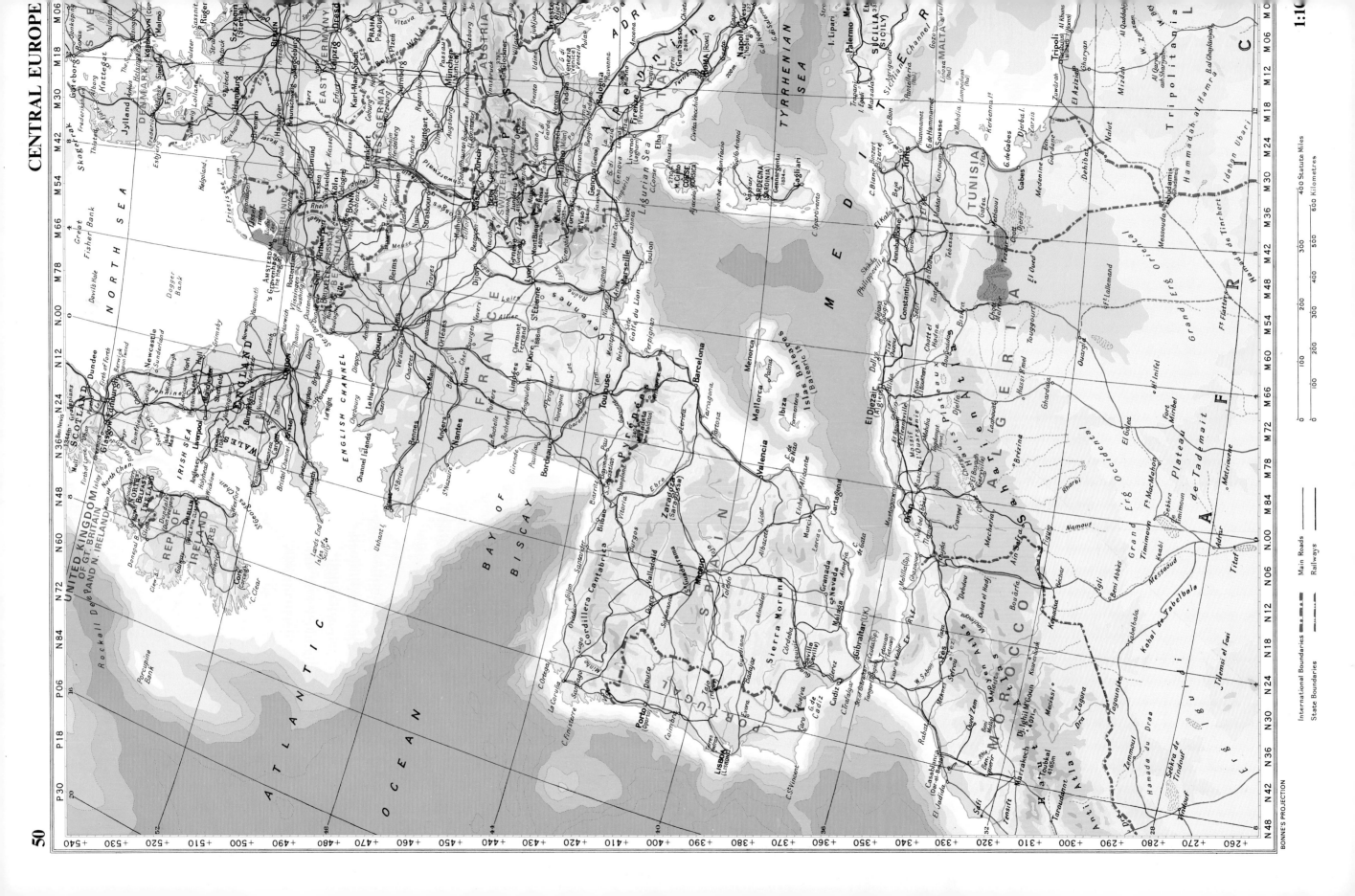

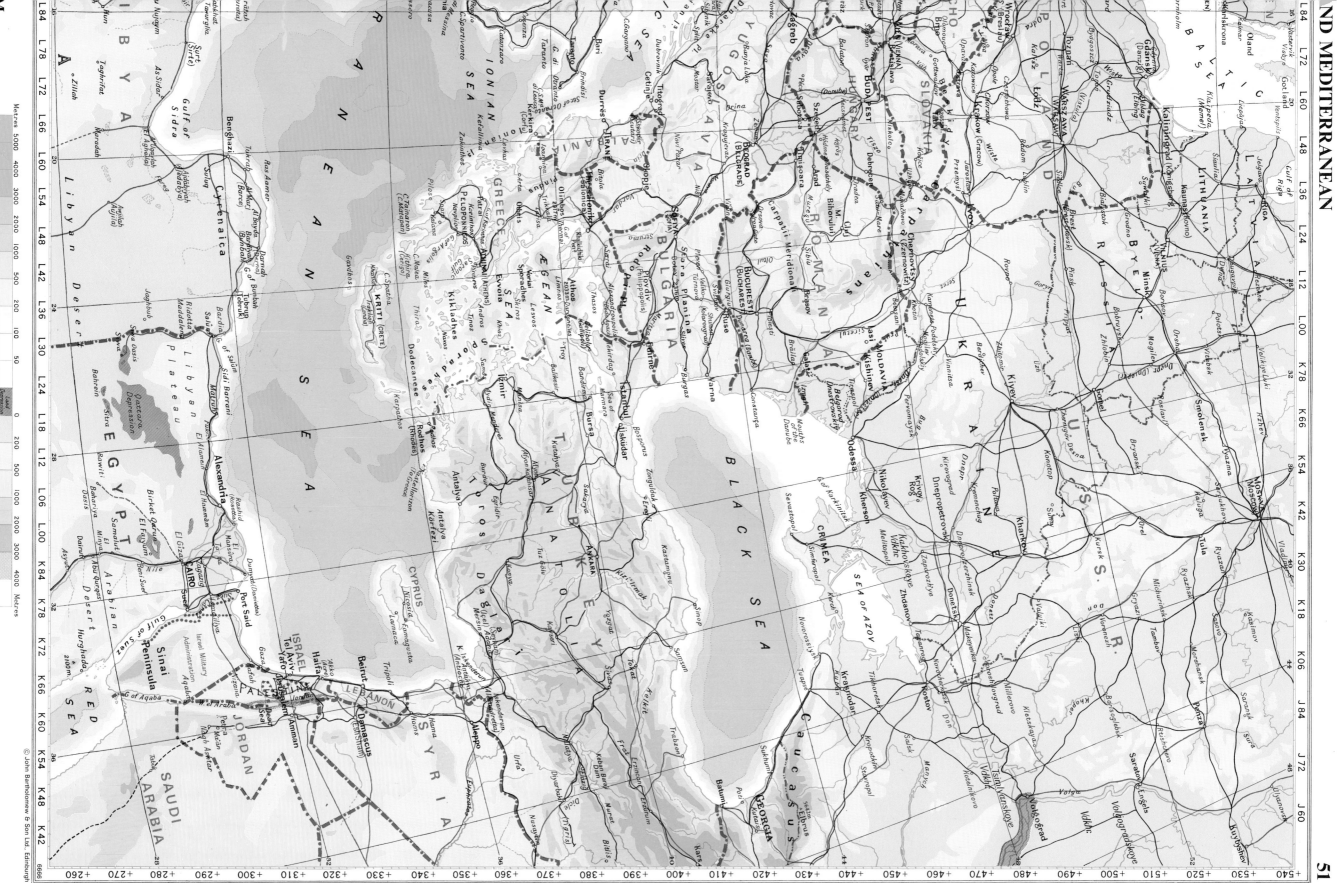

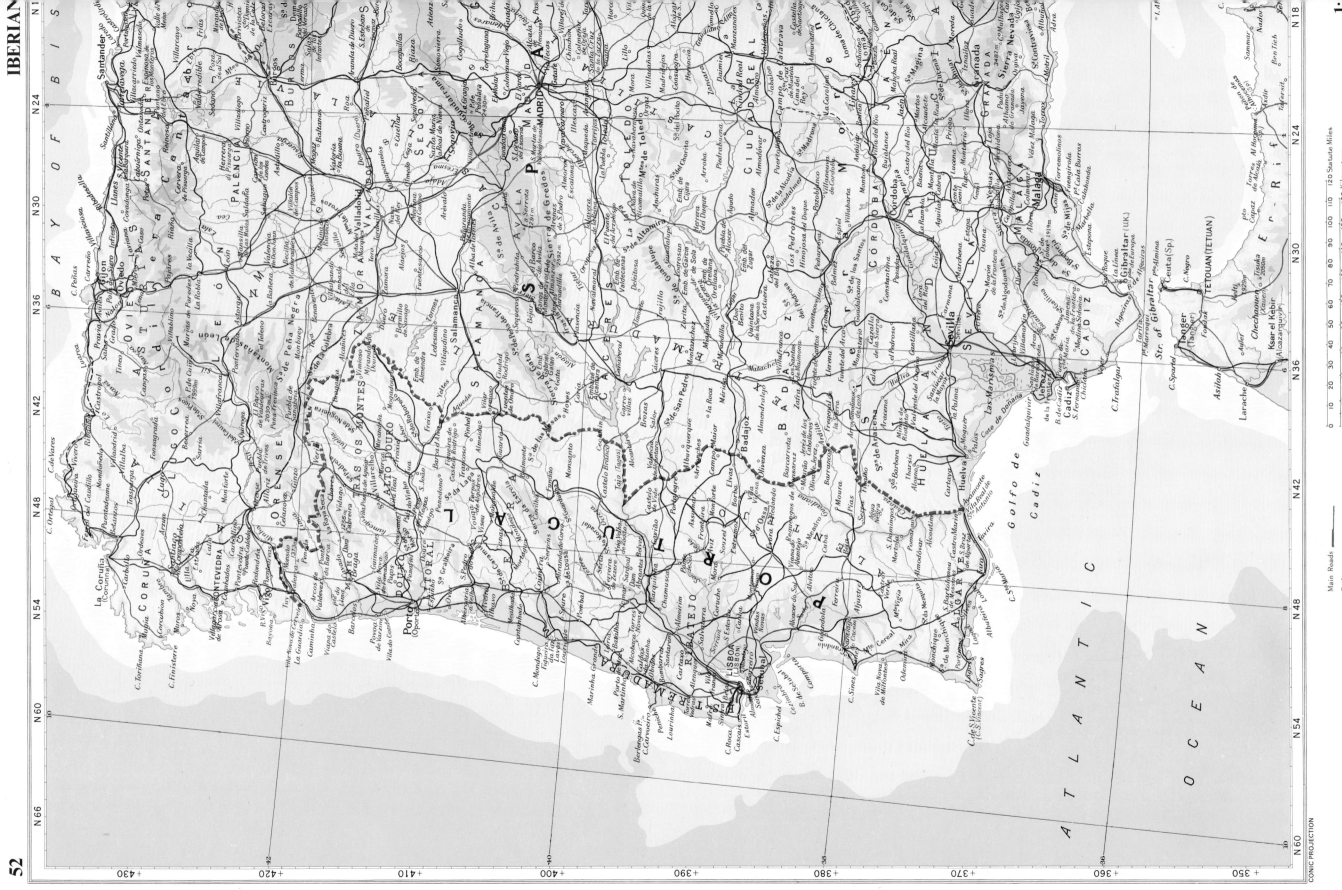

CONIC PROJECTION

1:

Main Roads
Railways

0 10 20 30 40 50 60 70 80 90 100 110 120 Statute Miles
0 10 20 40 60 80 100 120 140 160 180 Kilometres

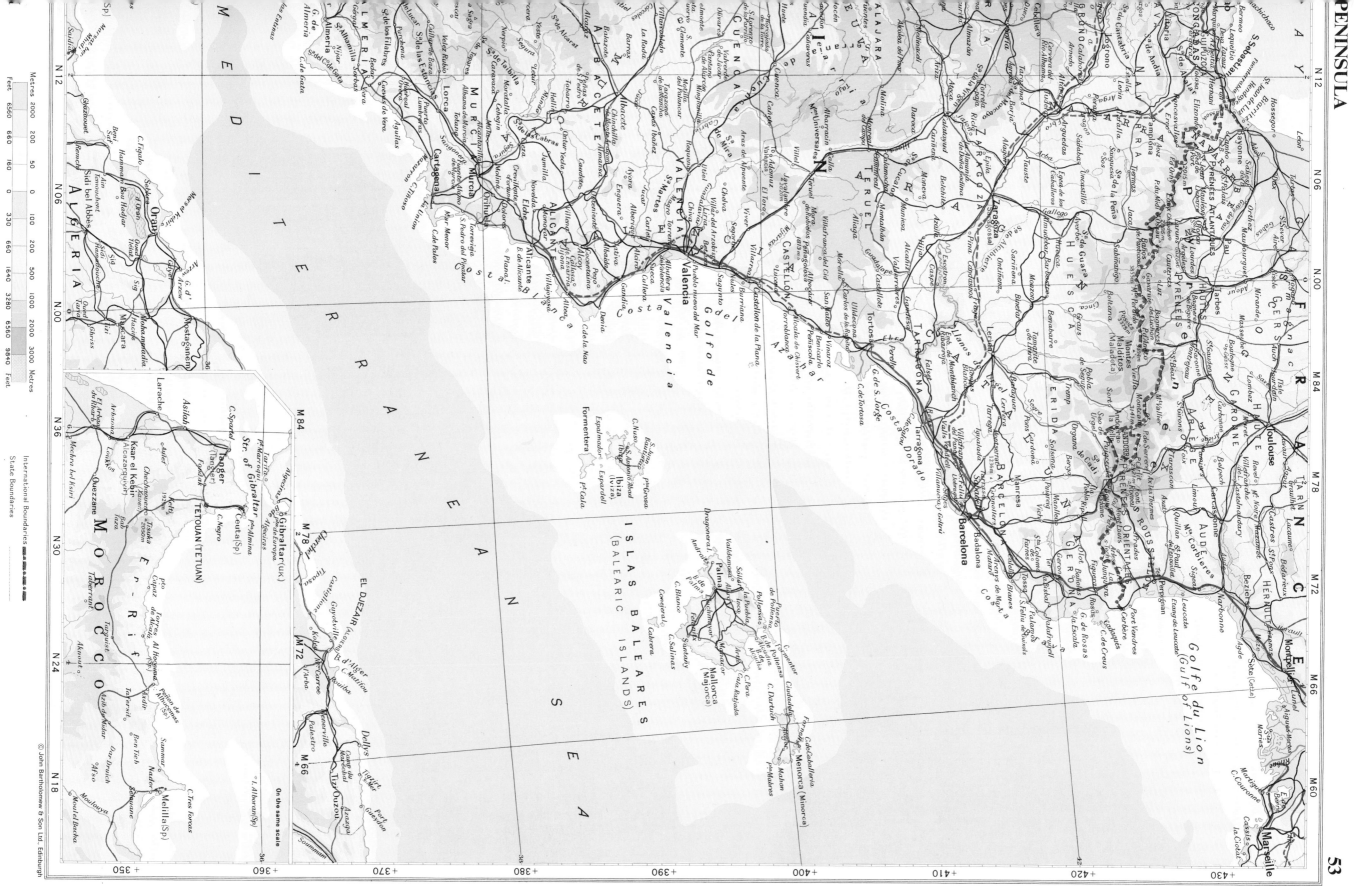

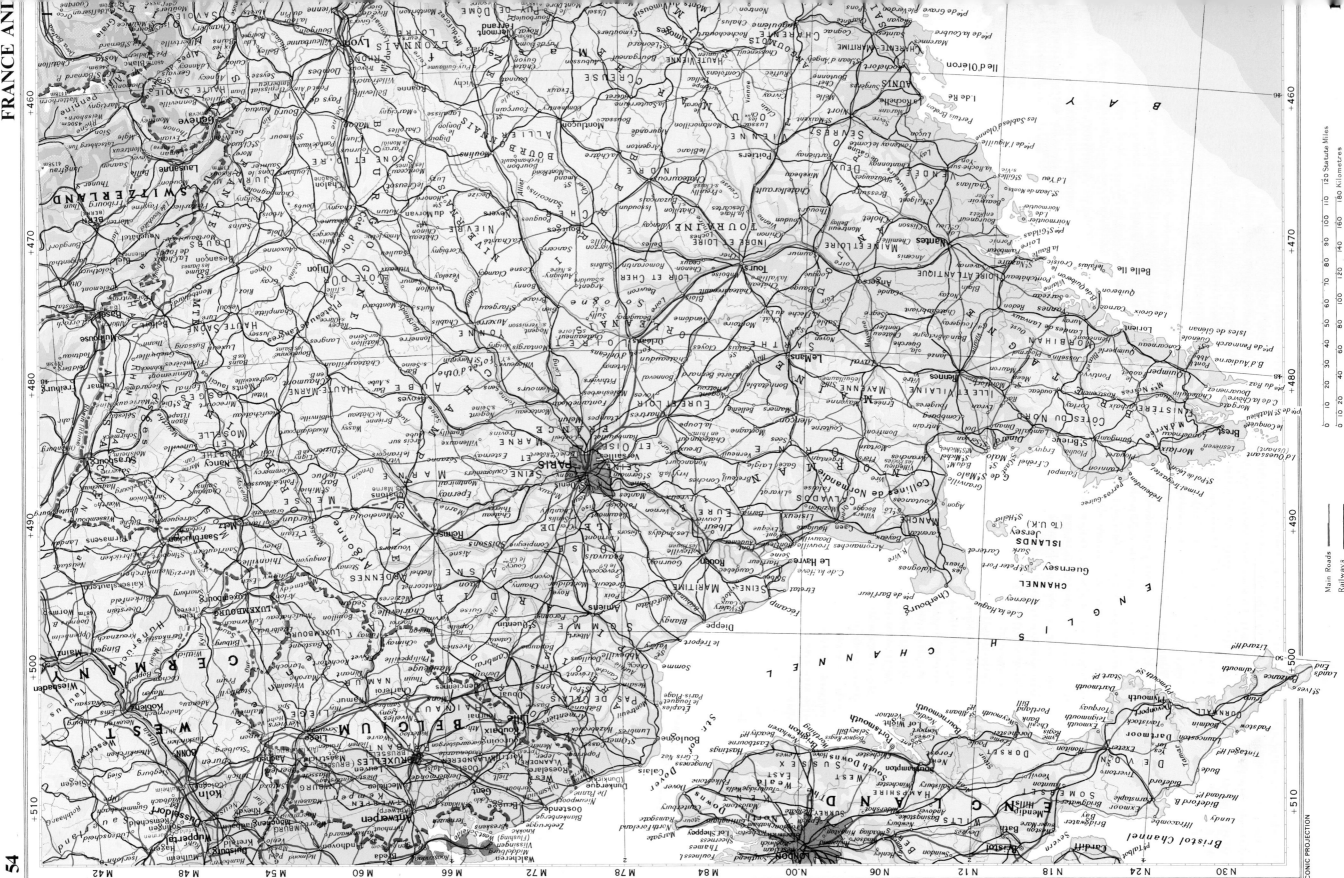

International Boundaries

State Boundaries

Metres 2000 200 50 0 330 660 1640 3280 6560 9840 13120 Feet

Feet 6560 660 160 0

Metres 200 100 200 500 1000 2000 3000 4000 Metres

ROMA (ROME)

MOLISE

S E A

Subiaco
Alatri
Castel di Sangro
Agnone
Larino
Biferno
Sanniandrea di Bari
Vieste
M. Gargano
Monte S. Angelo
S. Marco in Lamis
S. Severo
Manfredonia
G. di Manfredonia

Fiumicino
Lido di Roma
Frascati
Castel Gandolfo
Albani
M. Lepini
Frosinone
La Meta
Isernia
Campobasso
Lucera
Foggia
Cerignola

Aprilia
Nettuno
Anzio
Latina
Pontine Marshes
Pontecorvo
Liri
Cassino
Venafro
Volturno
Benevento
Bovino
Ariano Irpino
Ascoli
Cerignola
Barletta
Trani
Bisceglie
Molfetta
Bari

Terracina
Formia
Gaeta
G. di Gaeta
Capua
Caserta
Maddaloni
Avellino
Calitri
Melfi
Rionero in Vulture
Potenza
Andria
Corato
Bitonto
Minervino
Spinazzola
Altamura
Conversano
Gioia del Colle
Monopoli
Putignano
Fasano

C. Circeo
I. Ponziane
Ponza
Napoli (Naples)
Pozzuoli
Vesuvio
Portici
T. Annunziata
Nola
Nocera
M. Cervialto
Avigliano
Matera
Massafra
Ostuni
Martina Franca
Francavilla Fontana
Brindisi

Ventotene
Ischia
G. di Napoli
Salerno
Eboli
Sala Consilina
Pisticci
Metaponto
Scanzano
Mesagne
Lecce

Castellammare di Stabia
Sorrento
Amalfi
Agropoli
M. Alburno
Auletta
BASILICATA (LUCANIA)
Senise
Sinni
Noepoli
St. di Nova Siri
C. S. Vito
Taranto
Manduria
Pollino
Galatone

Capri
G. di Salerno
R. Sele
M. Cervati
Lagonegro
Morano Calabro
Golfo di Taranto
Maglie
Tricase
C. S. Maria di Leuca

TYRRHENIAN SEA

Pta. Licosa
Camerota
Sapri
M. Pollino
Scalea
Castrovillari
R. Crati
C. Trionto
Rossano
Cariati
Pta. dell' Alice

Belvedere Marittimo
Cetraro
Paola
Acri
La Sila
S. Giovanni in Fiore
Ciro
Strongoli

Amantea
Cosenza
CALABRIA
Crotone
C. Colonne

Stromboli
S. Eufemia
Nicastro
Squillace
Catanzaro
C. Rizzuto

I. Eolie o Lipari
Salina
Panarea
Tropea
C. Vaticano
Nicotera
G. di Gioia
Serra S. Bruno
G. di Squillace

Alicudi
Filicudi
Lipari
Vulcano
Palmi
Cittanova
Roccella Ionica
Siderno Marina
Monasterace Marina

Ustica
Punta del Faro
Mileto
N. S. Giovanni Montalto
Gerace
Gerace Mar.

G. di Castellammare
Castellammare
Palermo
Bagheria
Barcellona
S. Agata di Militello
C. Calavà
Messina
Reggio

C. S. Vito
Carini
Partinico
Termini Imerese
Cefalù
Tortorici
Novara di Sicilia
Str. di Messina
Melito
Melito di S. Salvo
C. Spartivento

Levanzo
Trapani
M. Nebrodi
Randazzo
Taormina

Marettimo
I. Egadi
Alcamo
Caccamo
Madonie
Bronte
Giarre

Marsala
Salemi
Corleone
Lercara Friddi
Nicosia
Troina
Etna 3323m
Adrano
Giarre
Acireale

Castelvetrano
Partanna
Prizzi
Alia
Leonforte
Agira
Paternò
Catania

Mazara del Vallo
Menfi
Castelltermini
SICILIA (SICILY)
Enna
Gulf di Catania

Sciacca
Ribera
Canicattì
Caltanissetta
Piazza Armerina
Augusta

Agrigento
Porto Empedocle
Palma
Naro
Caltagirone
Vizzini
M. Lauro
Siracusa (Syracuse)

Licata
Gela
Comiso
Palazzolo Acreide
Floridia

Vittoria
Ragusa
Avola
Noto

Modica
Scicli
Pachino
C. Passero

Pantelleria (To Italy)

MEDITERRANEAN SEA

Sicilian Channel

Malta Channel

Gozo
Victoria
Valletta
Rabat
Vittoriosa
MALTA

Linosa (To Italy)

Longitude East 12 of Greenwich

CORSE DU SUD
G. d'Ajac
Petreto Bichisano
Solenzara
Zonza
B. de Bonifacio
Bonifacio
C. Testa
La Maddalena
Caprera

Porto Vecchio
Sartène
Palau
G. de Valinco

pta. d. Scorno
Asinara
G. di Asinara
C. of Falcone

Castelsardo
Sorso
Sassari
Ozieri
M. Nieddu
Golfo Aranci
Tavolara
C. Coda Cavallo

Portos Torres
Alghero
Ittiri
Siniscola
Olbia
Tempio
Limbara

Bonorva
Bosa
Bono
Macomer
SARDEGNA (SARDINIA)
Orosei
G. di Orosei
C. Comino

Cuglieri
Suni
Nuoro
Dorgali
C. M. Santo

Oristano
Laconi
Gennargentu
Arbatax
Lanusei
Tortolì

Terralba
Villacidro
M.te Linas
Monastir
Tertenia

Iglesias
Monserrato
Quartu
Sinnai
C. Ferrato

S. Antioco
Carbonia
Cagliari
G. di Cagliari
C. Carbonara

S. Pietro
Carloforte
Calasetta
Santadi
S. Elena
Teulada

C. Altano
C. S. Marco
G. di Oristano
G. di Frasca
Guspini
Sanluri
pta. Serpeddi

G. of Palmas
C. Teulada
Botte Teulada
C. Pula
C. Spartivento

CORSE DU SUD

ALGERIA
TUNISIA

Annaba (Bône)
C. de Garde
C. Rosa
El Kala

C. Serrat
C. Blanc
Binzert (Bizerte, Bizerta)

Galite I.
Zembra
C. Bon (Ras Addar)

Tabarka
Menzel Bourguiba (Ferryville)
Ras El Djebel

La Calle
Djebel Abiod
Mateur
G. de Tunis

I. Fetzara
El Hadjar
Ain Draham
Béja
Tébourba
Djedeida
El Marsa
Carthage
TUNIS
Halq el Oued (La Goulette)
Kelibia
Menzel-Temime

Seybouse
Bouchegouf
Souk el Arba
Bou Salem
Testour
Medjerda
Medjez el Bab
Menzel bou Zelfan

Souk Ahras
Jendouba
Mechroha
Ghardimaou
Nabeul
Korba

Monts de la Medjerda
TELL
Gafour
Bou Arada
Grombalia
Hammamet
Ras Maamoura

Medjerda
Dougga
Teboursouk
Zaghouan
Dj. Zaghouan 1295m.
Maou

El Aouinet
Tadjerouine
Ebba Ksour
Nebana
Siliana
Enfida (Enfidaville)
G. de Hammamet

Maktar
Sousse (Susa)

MEDITERRANEAN SEA

57

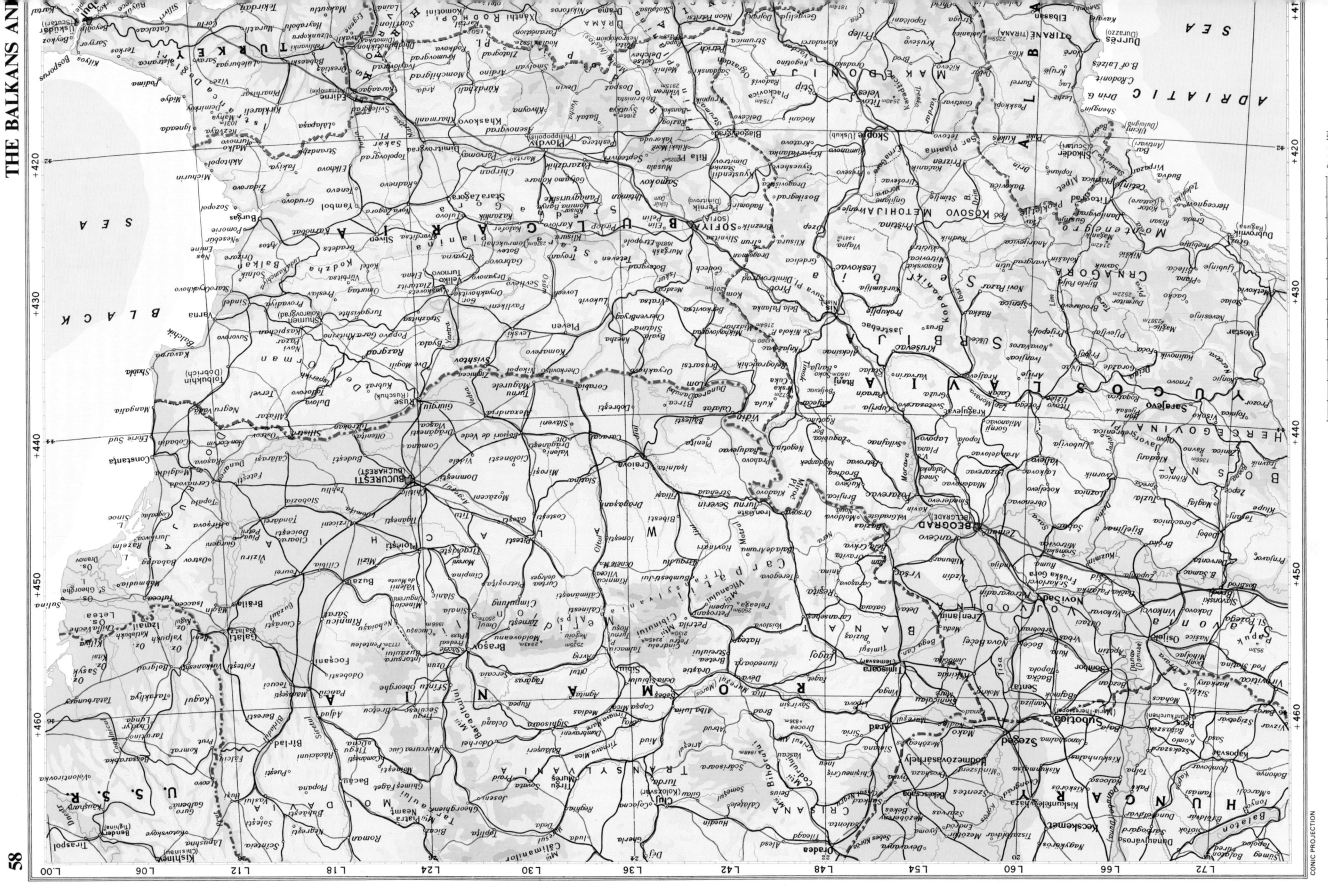

CONIC PROJECTION

Main Roads
Railways

0   10 20 30 40 50 60 70 80 90 100 110 120 Statute Miles
0   10 20   40   60   80   100 120 140 160 180 Kilometres

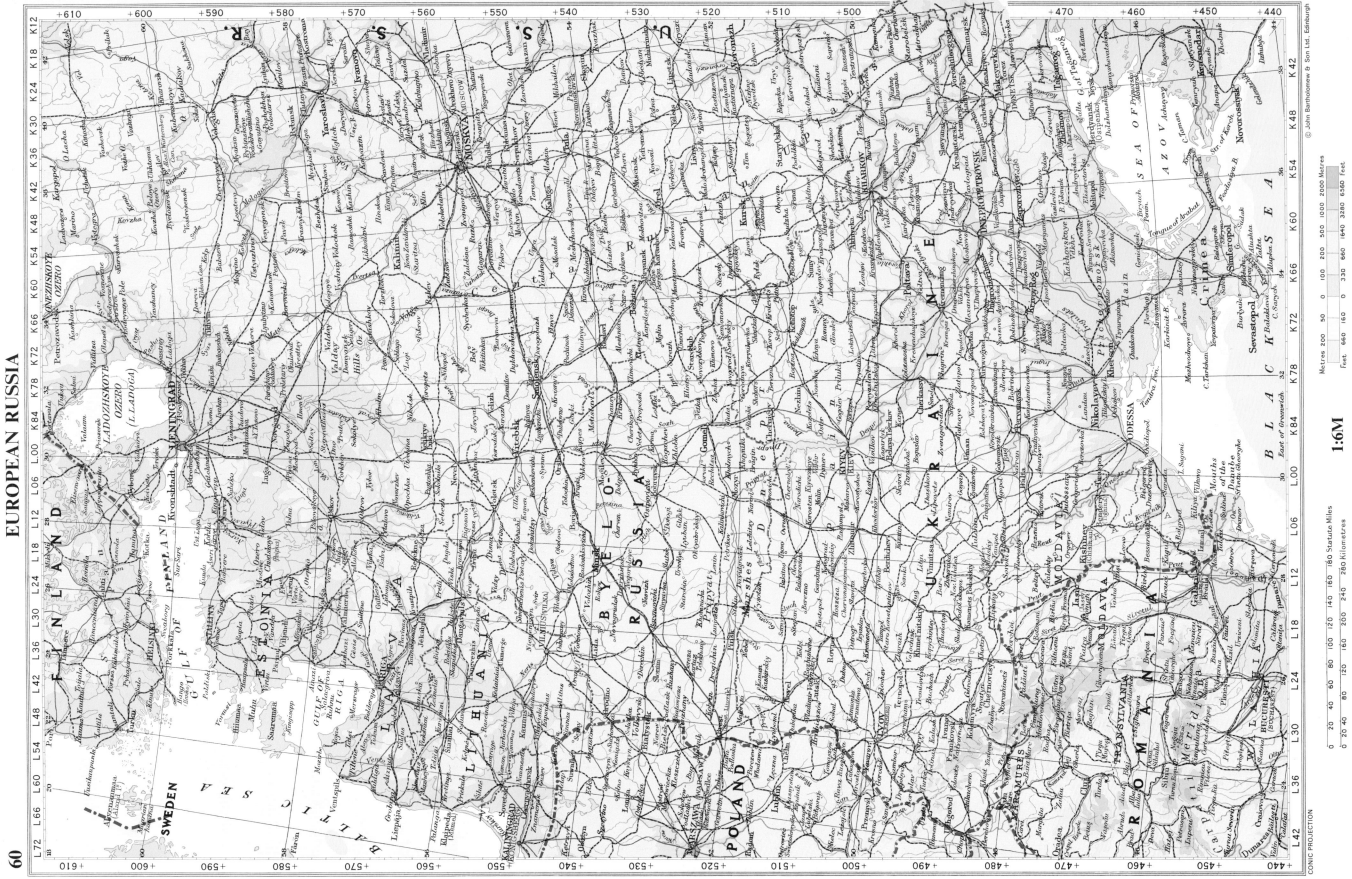

EUROPEAN RUSSIA

1:6M

CONIC PROJECTION

60

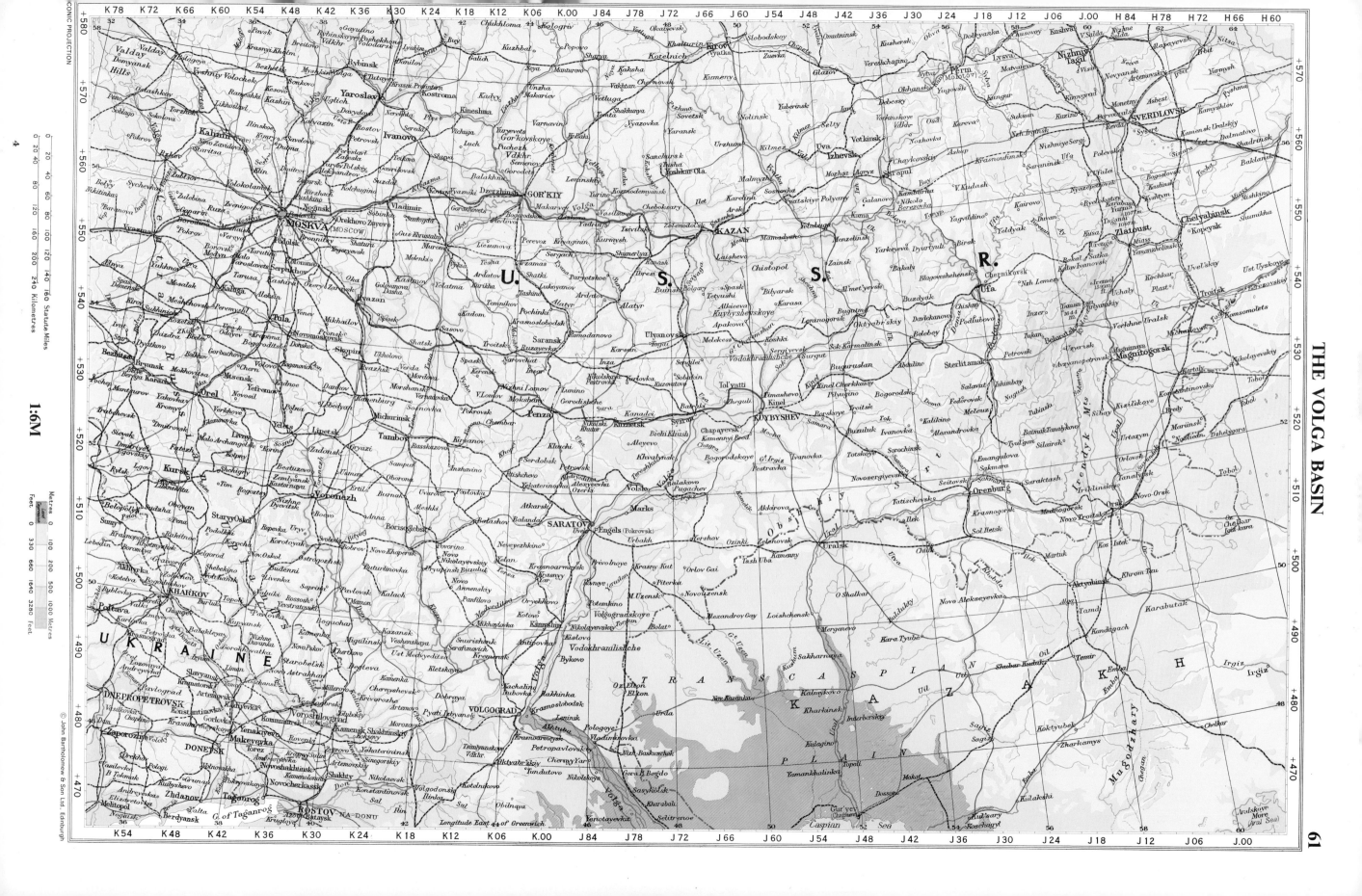

CONIC PROJECTION

© John Bartholomew & Son Ltd. Edinburgh

1:6M

U. S. S. R.

UKRAINE

KAZAKH

TRANSCASPIAN PLAIN

Caspian Sea

Longitude East 44 of Greenwich

4

61

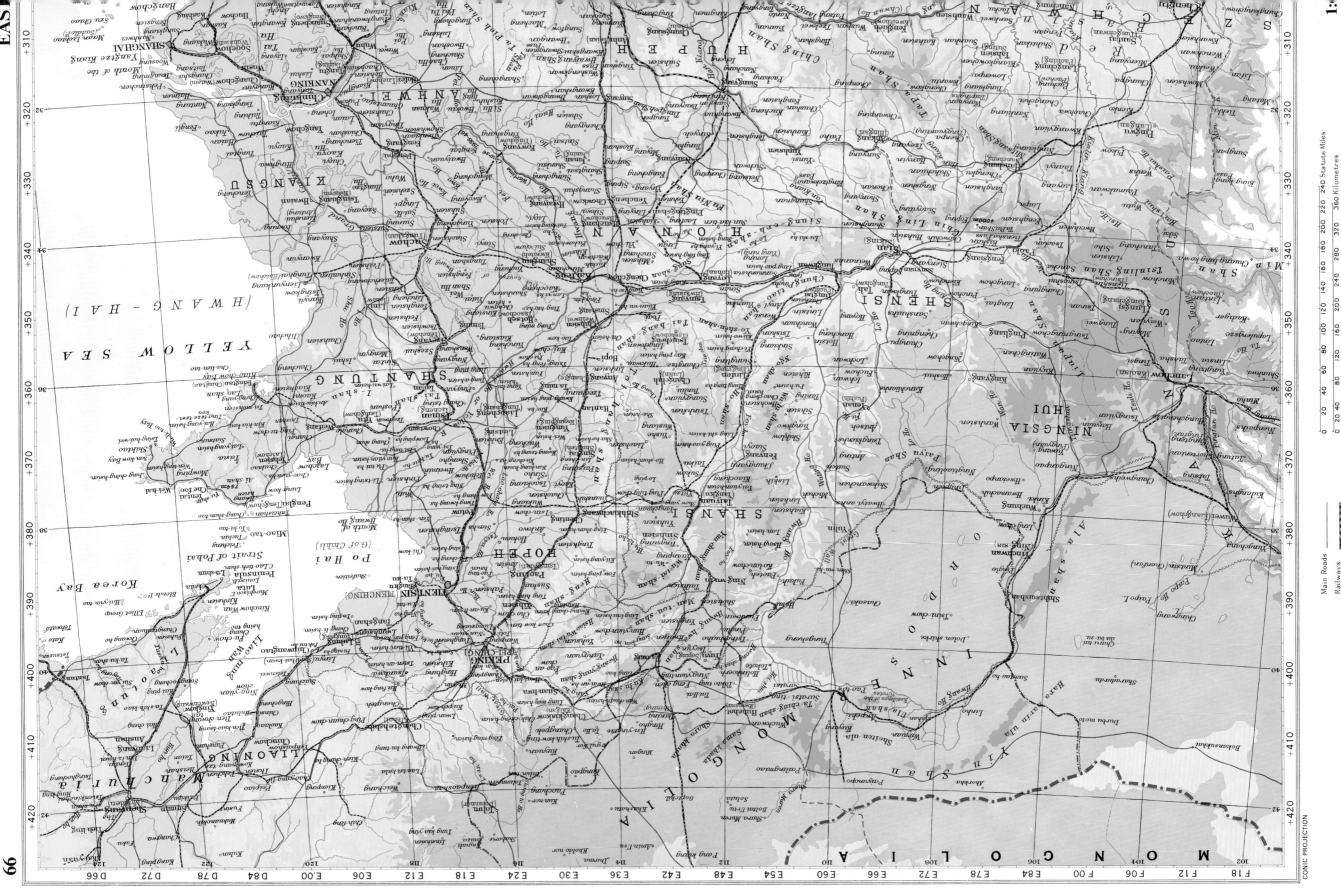

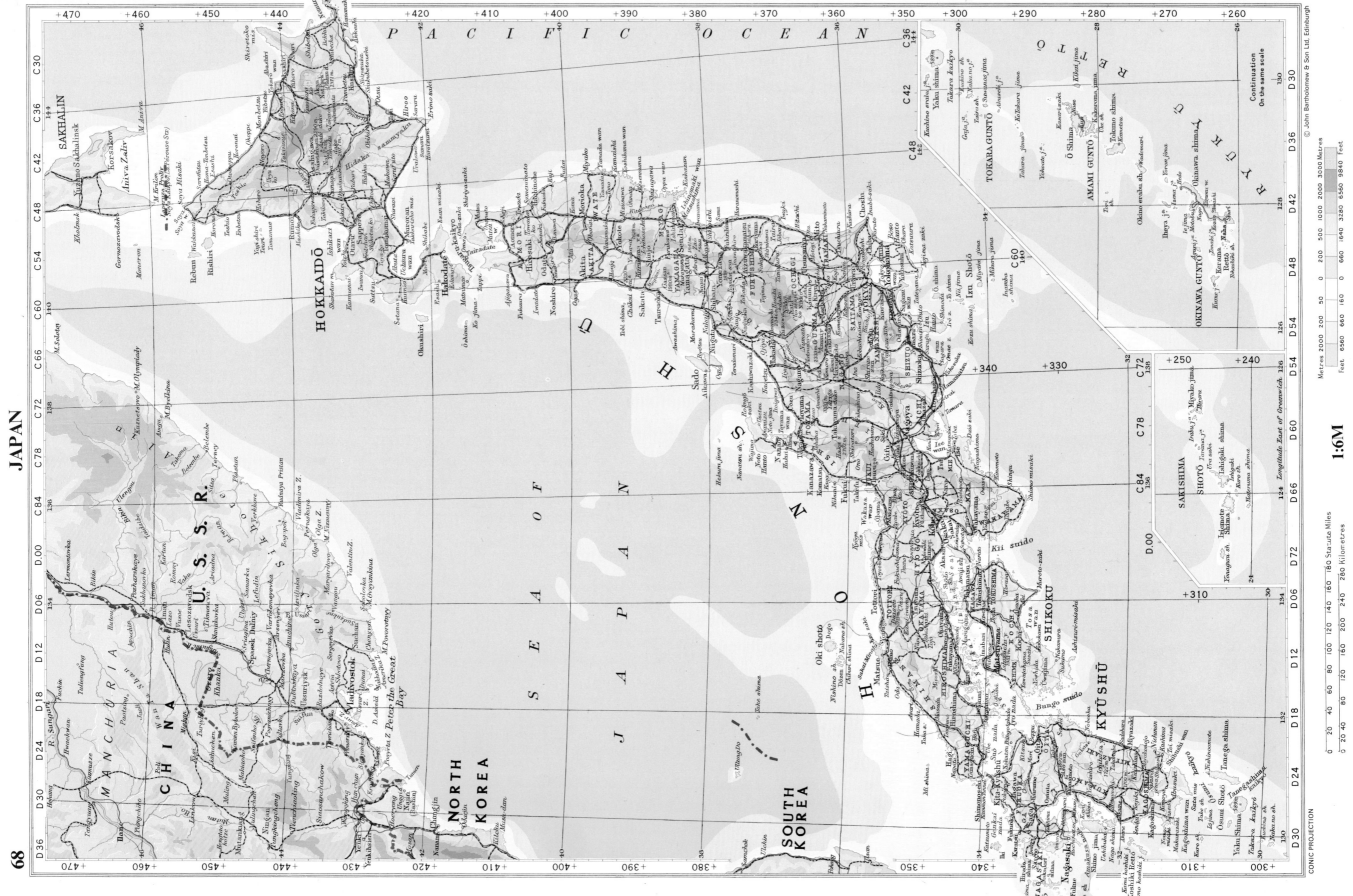

JAPAN

68

CONIC PROJECTION

1:6M

© John Bartholomew & Son Ltd. Edinburgh

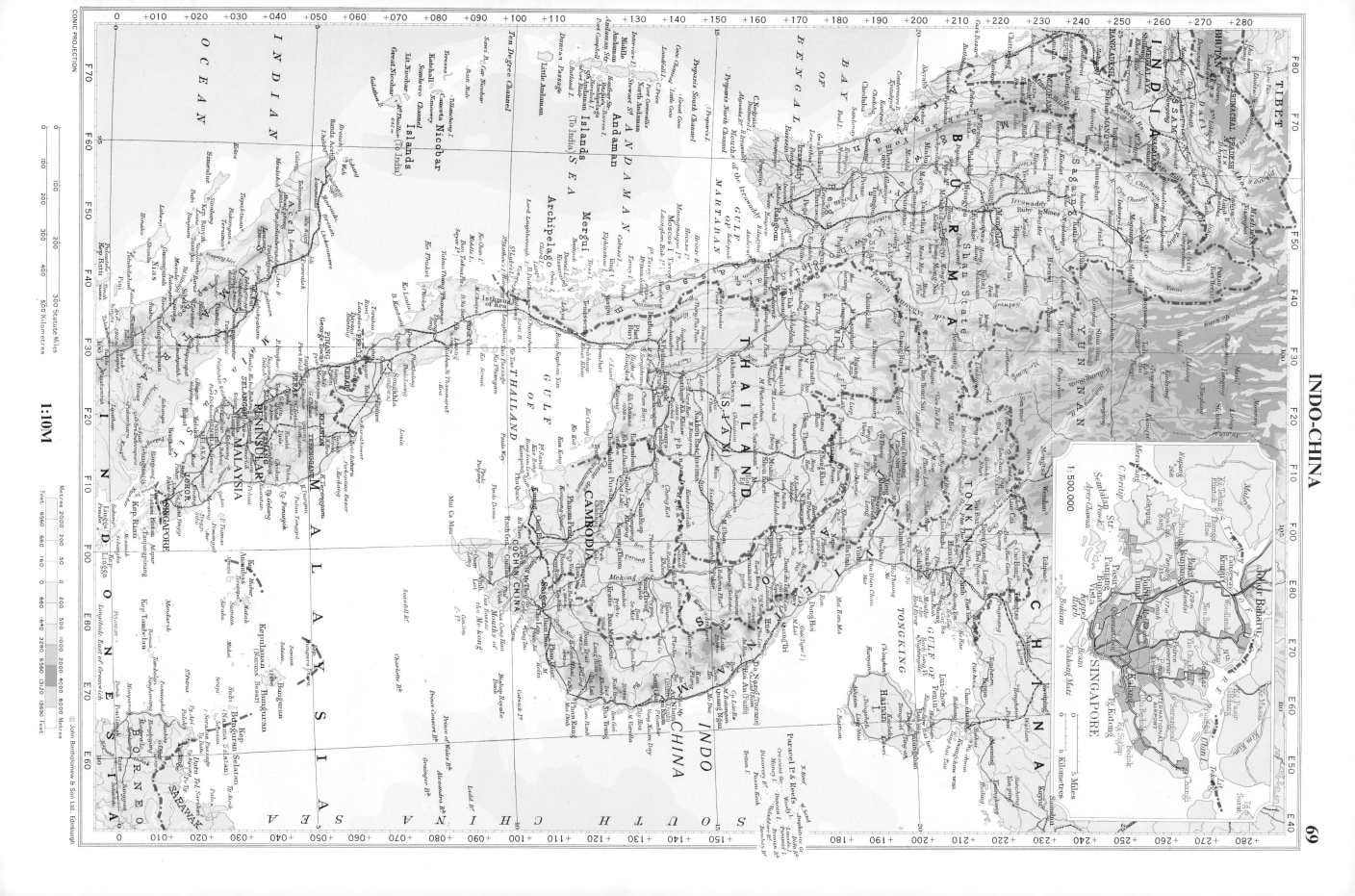

CONIC PROJECTION

1:10M

INDIAN OCEAN

BAY OF BENGAL

ANDAMAN SEA

ANDAMAN Islands (To India)

Nicobar Islands (To India)

GULF OF MARTABAN

TIBET

BURMA

YUNNAN

CHINA

THAILAND (SIAM)

GULF OF THAILAND

PENINSULAR MALAYSIA

SINGAPORE

INDONESIA

SARAWAK

BORNEO

CAMBODIA

COCHIN CHINA

INDO CHINA

TONGKING

GULF OF TONKIN

Hainan

SOUTH CHINA SEA

Mergui Archipelago

Isthmus of Kra

1:500,000

SINGAPORE

© John Bartholomew & Son Ltd. Edinburgh

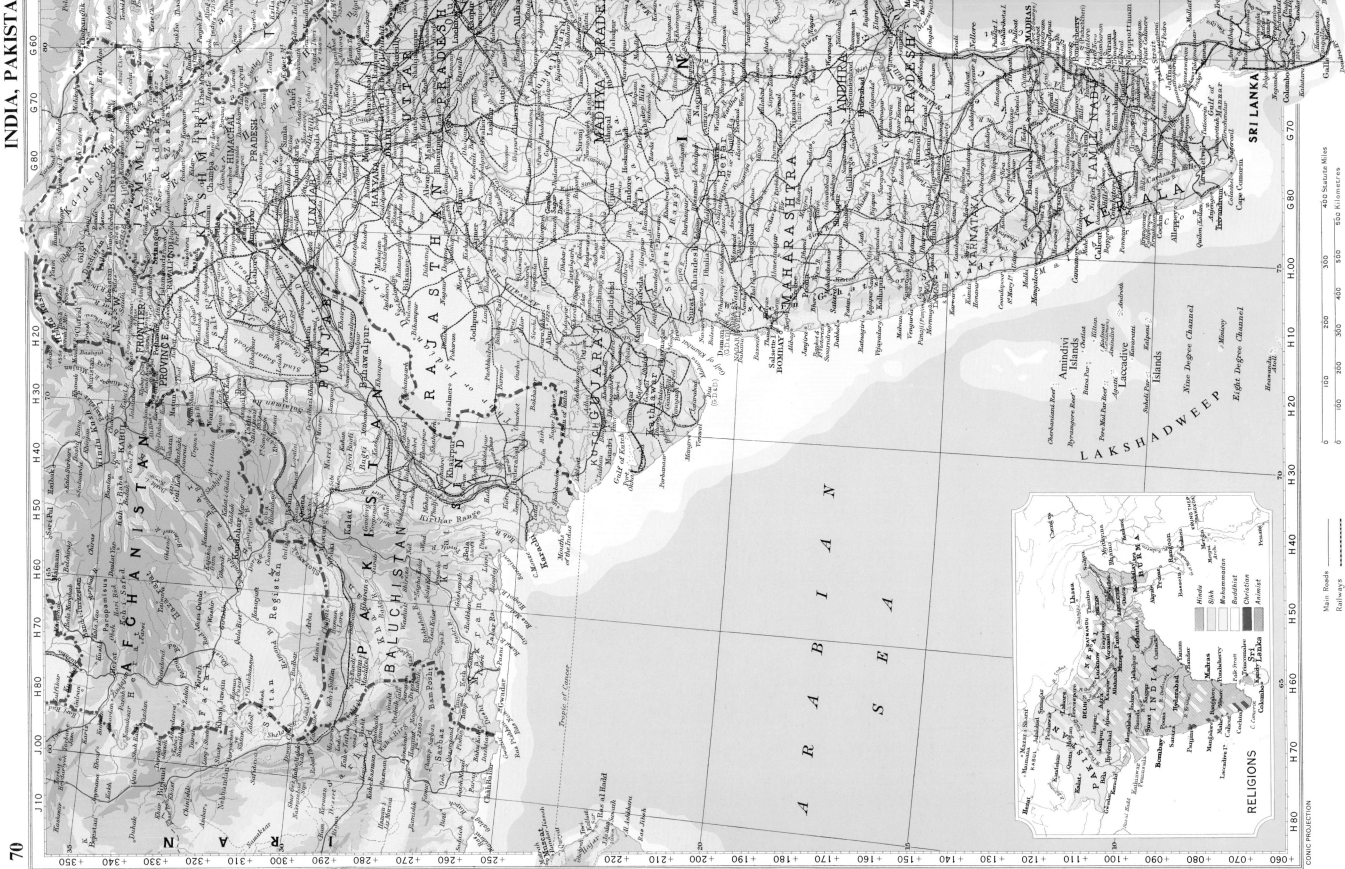

ARABIAN SEA

LAKSHADWEEP

Aminidivi Islands

Laccadive Islands

Nine Degree Channel

Eight Degree Channel

SRI LANKA

RELIGIONS

Hindu	Sikh	Muhammadan	Buddhist	Christian

Animist

Main Roads
Railways

CONIC PROJECTION

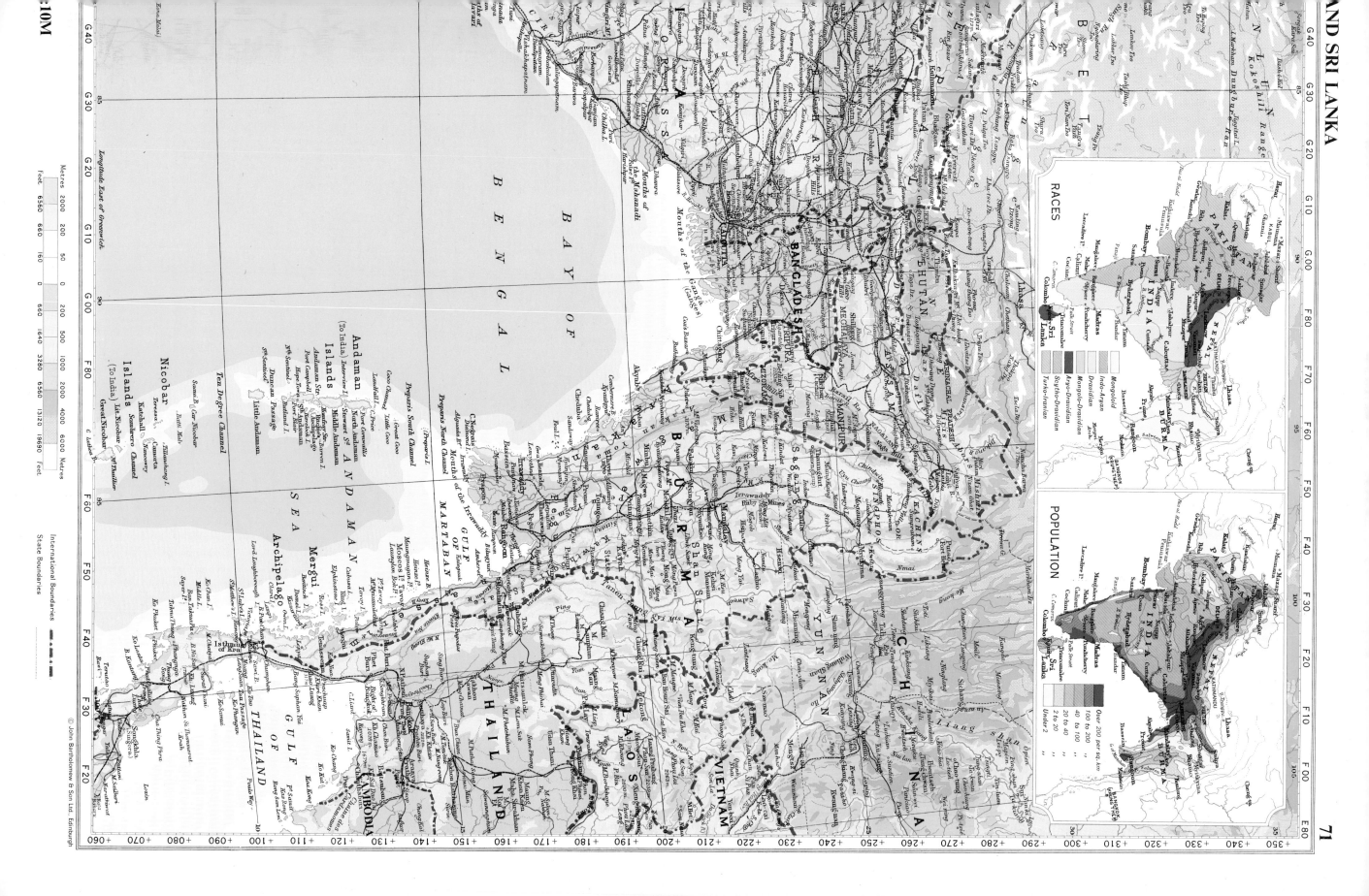

PUNJAB AND KASHMIR

1:4M

© John Bartholomew & Son Ltd. Edinburgh

CONIC PROJECTION

Main Roads
Irrigation Canals
International Boundaries
State and Division Boundaries

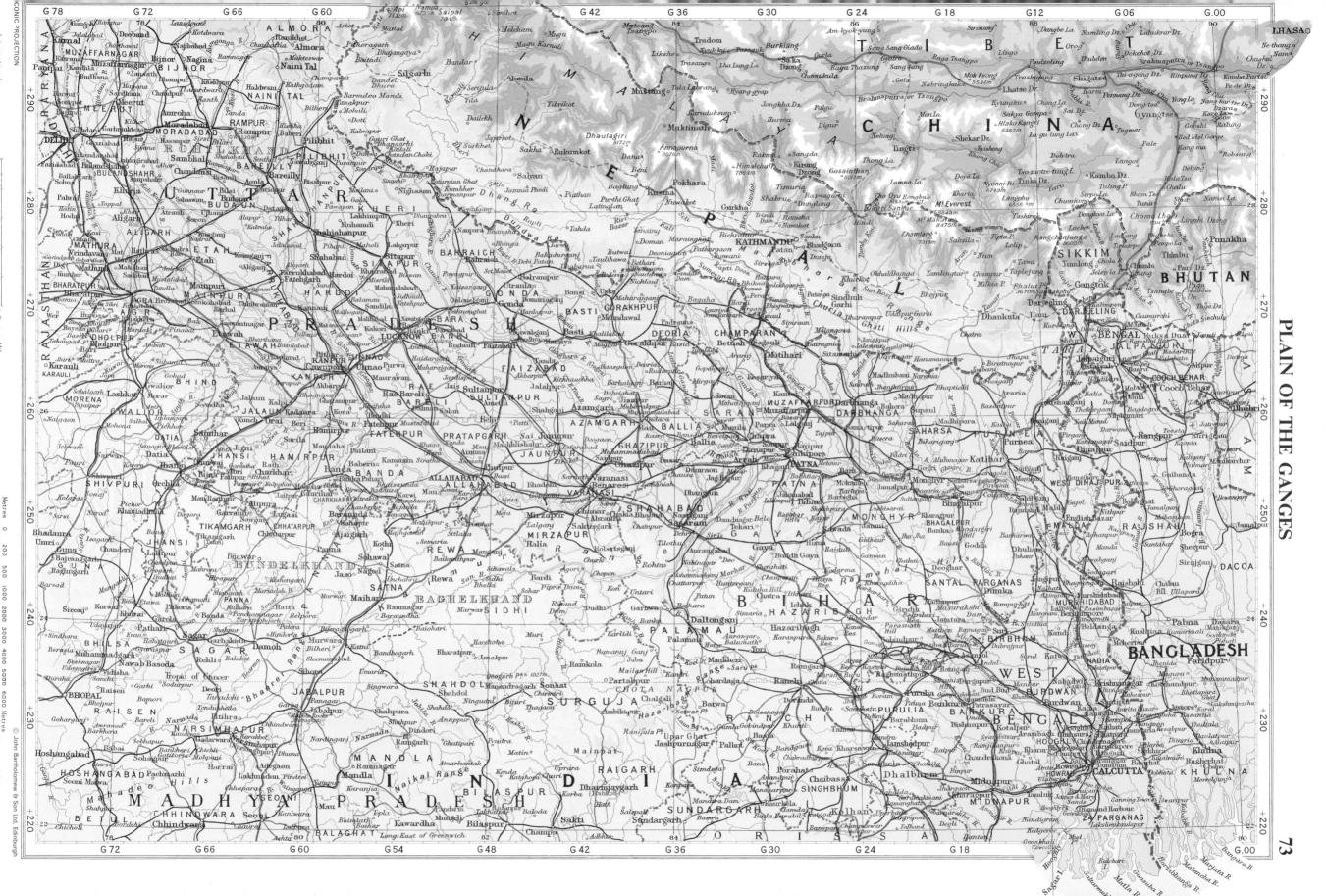

CONIC PROJECTION

1:4M

© John Bartholomew & Son Ltd, Edinburgh

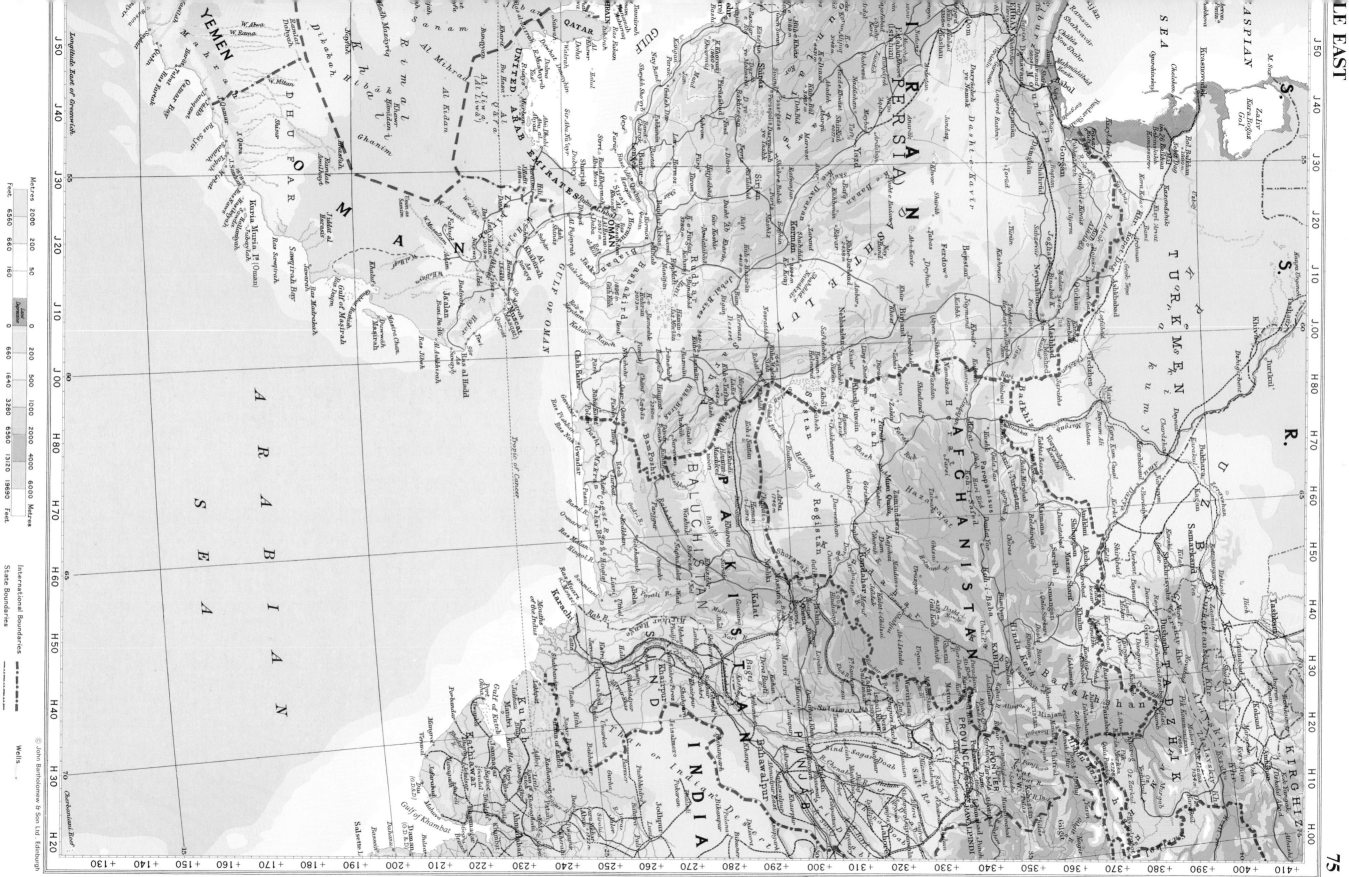

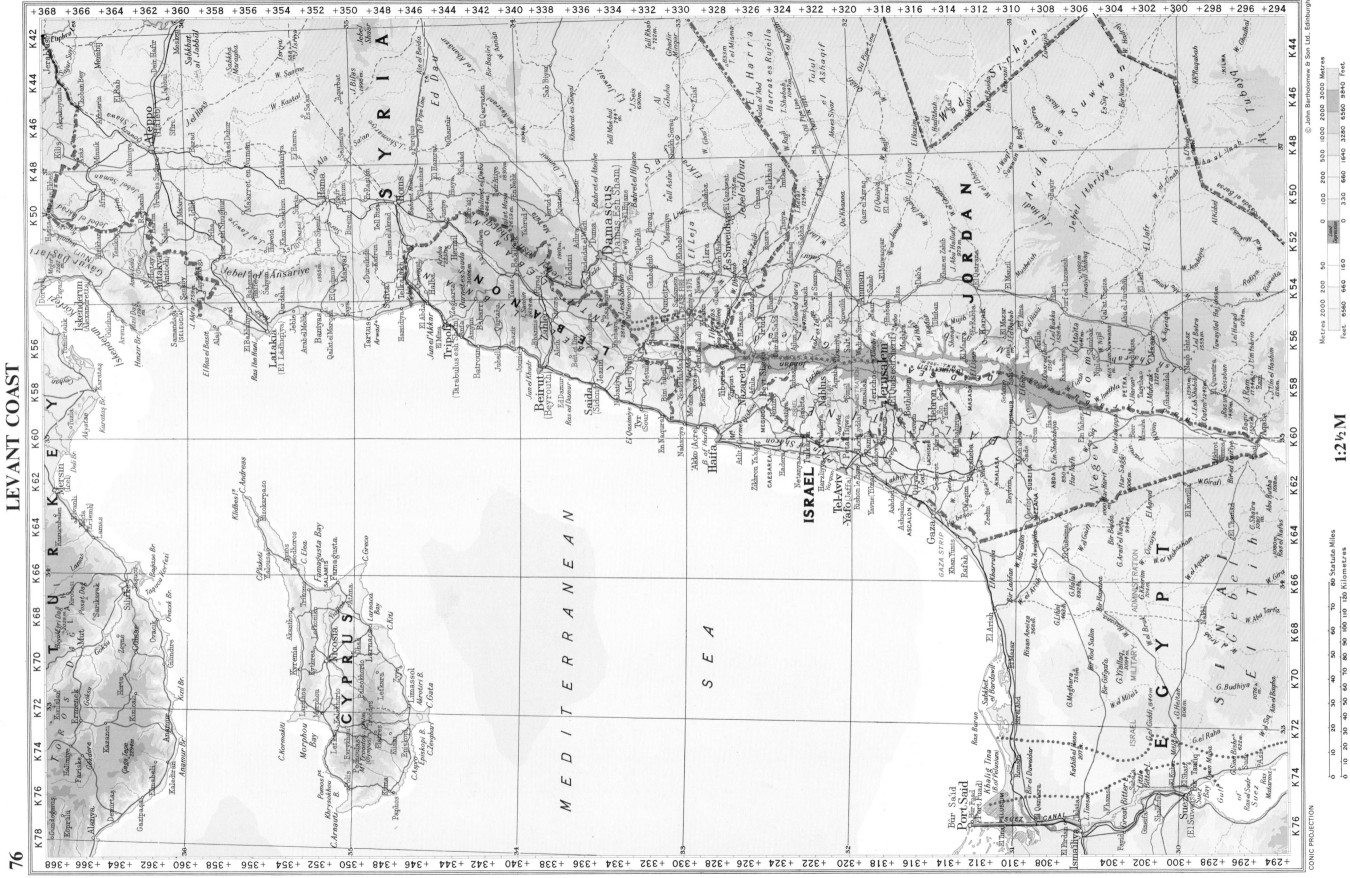

LEVANT COAST

1:2½M

CONIC PROJECTION

76

© John Bartholomew & Son Ltd. Edinburgh

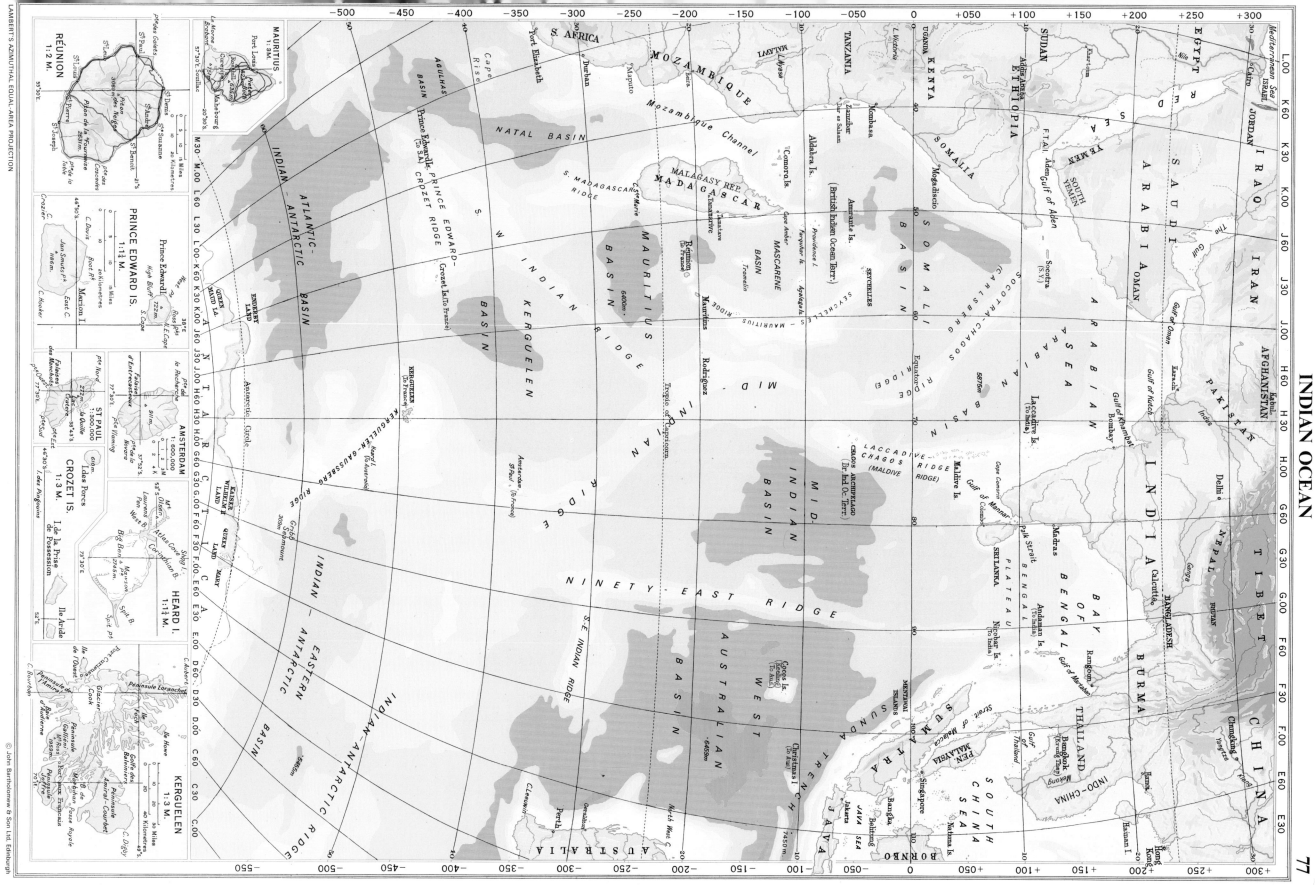

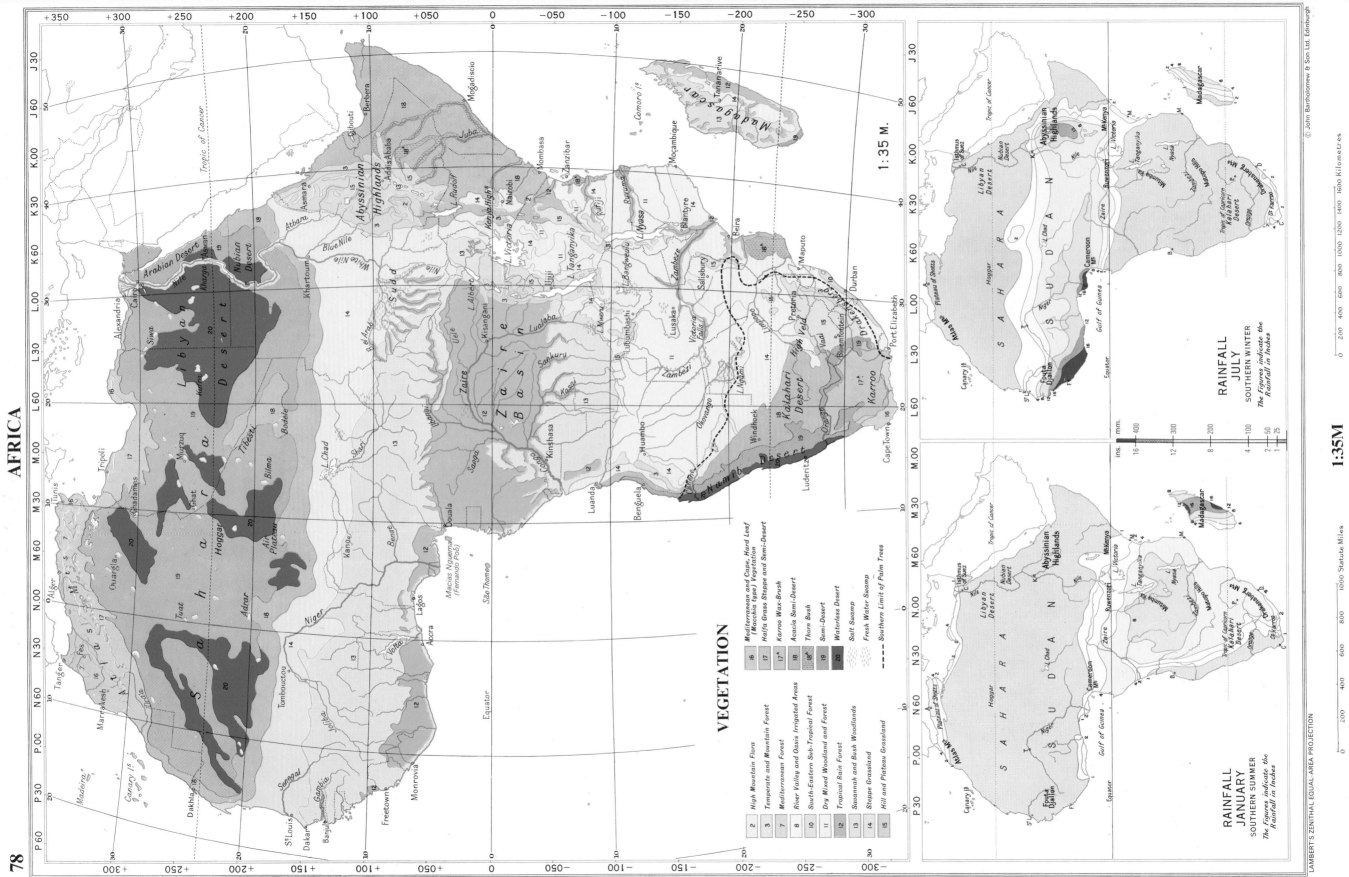

VEGETATION

2	High Mountain Flora
3	Temperate and Mountain Forest
7	Mediterranean Forest
8	River Valley and Oasis Irrigated Areas
10	South-Eastern Sub-Tropical Forest
11	Dry Mixed Woodland and Forest
12	Tropical Rain Forest
13	Savannah and Bush Woodlands
14	Steppe Grassland
15	Hill and Plateau Grassland

16	Mediterranean and Cape, Hard Leaf (Maccchia type) Vegetation
17	Halfa Grass Steppe and Semi-Desert
17*	Karroo Wax-Brush
18	Acacia Semi-Desert
18*	Thorn Bush
19	Semi-Desert
20	Waterless Desert
	Salt Swamp
	Fresh Water Swamp
---	Southern Limit of Palm Trees

1:35 M.

RAINFALL JULY
SOUTHERN WINTER
The Figures indicate the Rainfall in Inches

RAINFALL JANUARY
SOUTHERN SUMMER
The Figures indicate the Rainfall in Inches

1:35M

LAMBERT'S ZENITHAL EQUAL-AREA PROJECTION

© John Bartholomew & Son Ltd. Edinburgh

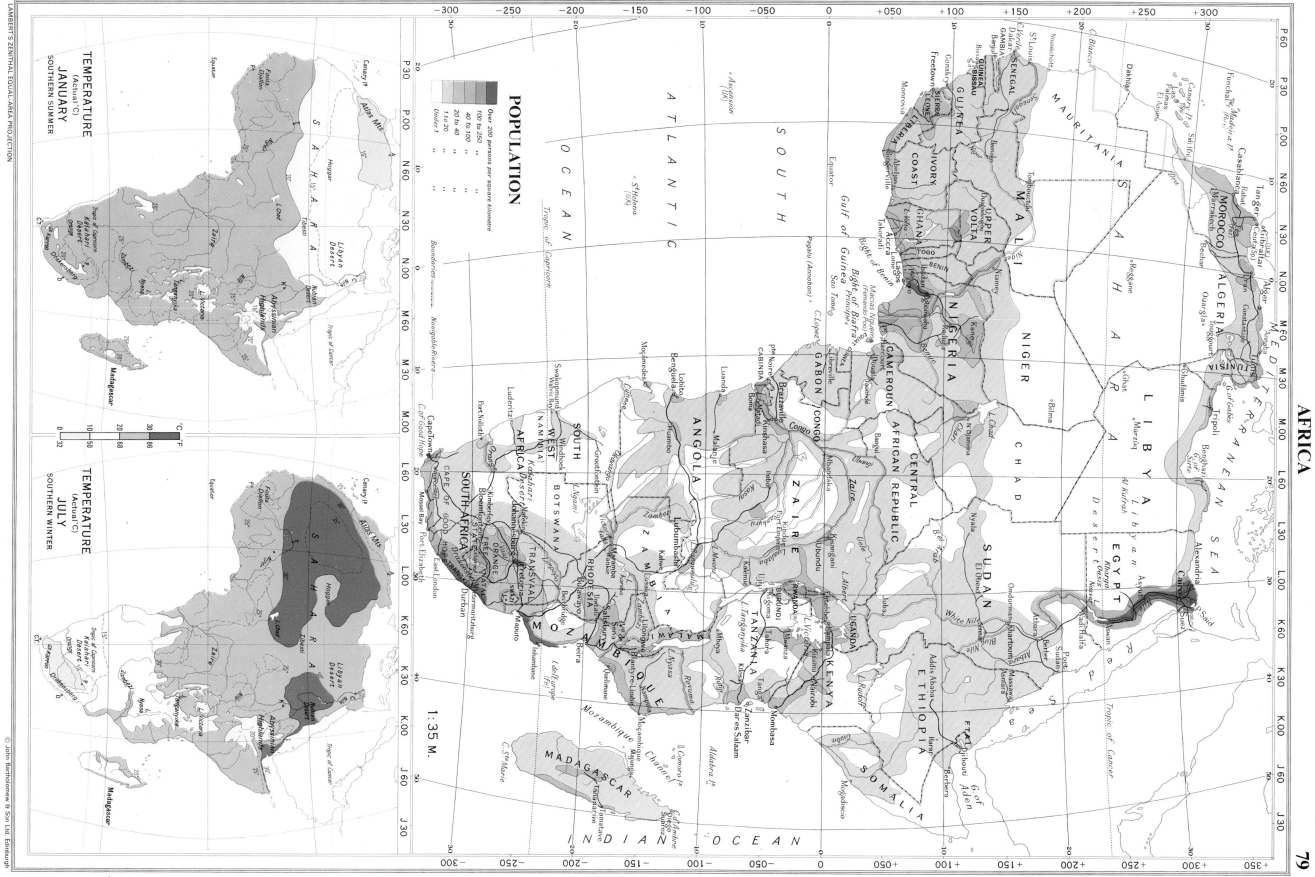

POPULATION

Over 200 persons per square kilometre
100 to 250   "   "   "
40 to 100   "   "   "
20 to 40   "   "   "
1 to 20   "   "   "
Under 1   "   "   "

TEMPERATURE (Actual °C)
JANUARY
SOUTHERN SUMMER

TEMPERATURE (Actual °C)
JULY
SOUTHERN WINTER

°C   °F
50   86
30   68
20   50
10
0   32

LAMBERT'S ZENITHAL EQUAL-AREA PROJECTION

1:35M

1:35 M.

© John Bartholomew & Son Ltd, Edinburgh

0   200   400   600   800   1000 Statute Miles

0   200   400   600   800   1000 1200 1400 1600 Kilometres

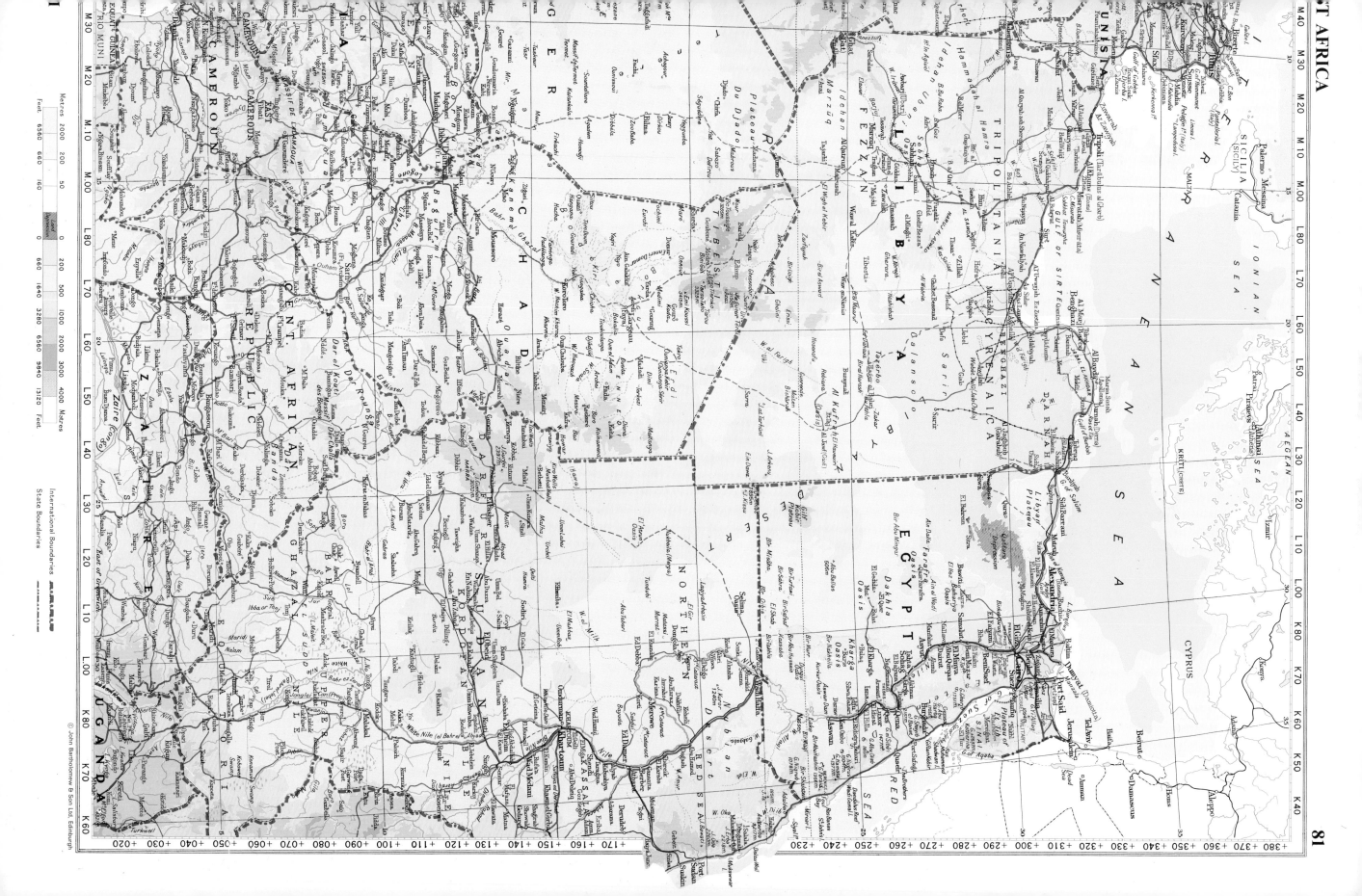

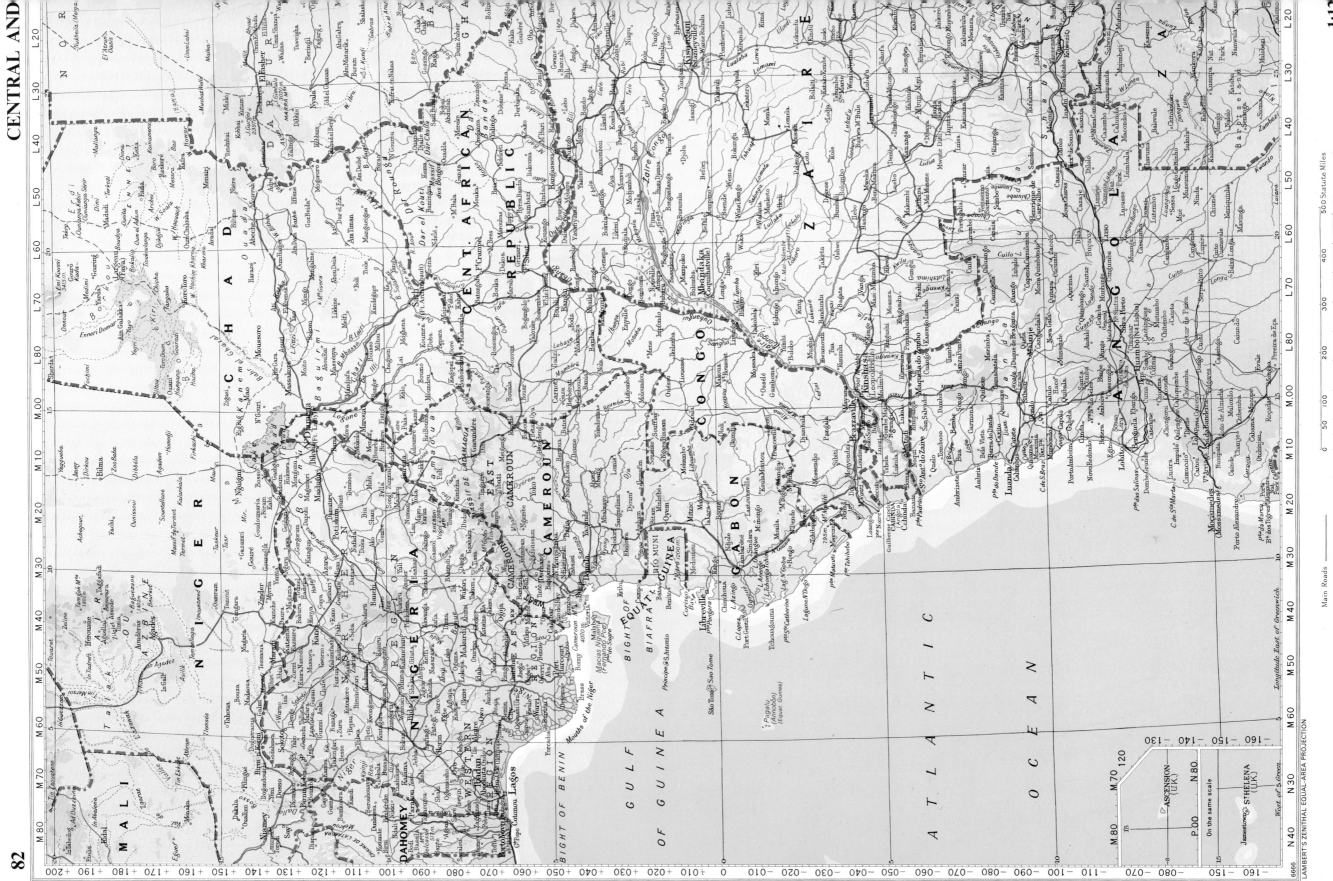

1:12

LAMBERT'S ZENITHAL EQUAL-AREA PROJECTION

Main Roads
Railways

0   50 100   200   300   400   500 Statute Miles
0   50 100   200   300   400   500   600   800 Kilometres

ASCENSION (U.K.)

St HELENA (U.K.)
Jamestown

On the same scale

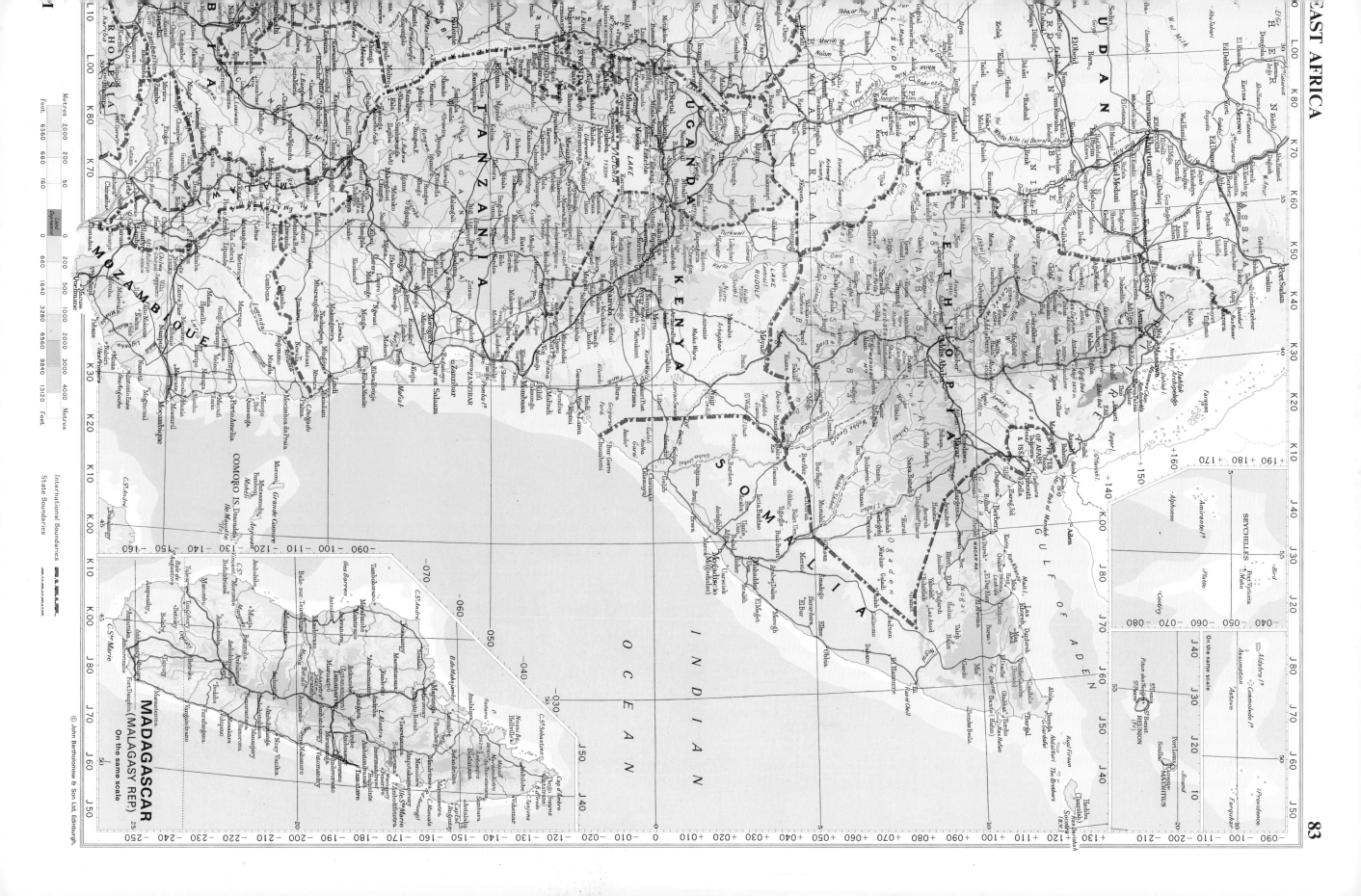

MADAGASCAR
(MALAGASY REP.)
On the same scale

International Boundaries
State Boundaries

SEYCHELLES

INDIAN

OCEAN

GULF OF ADEN

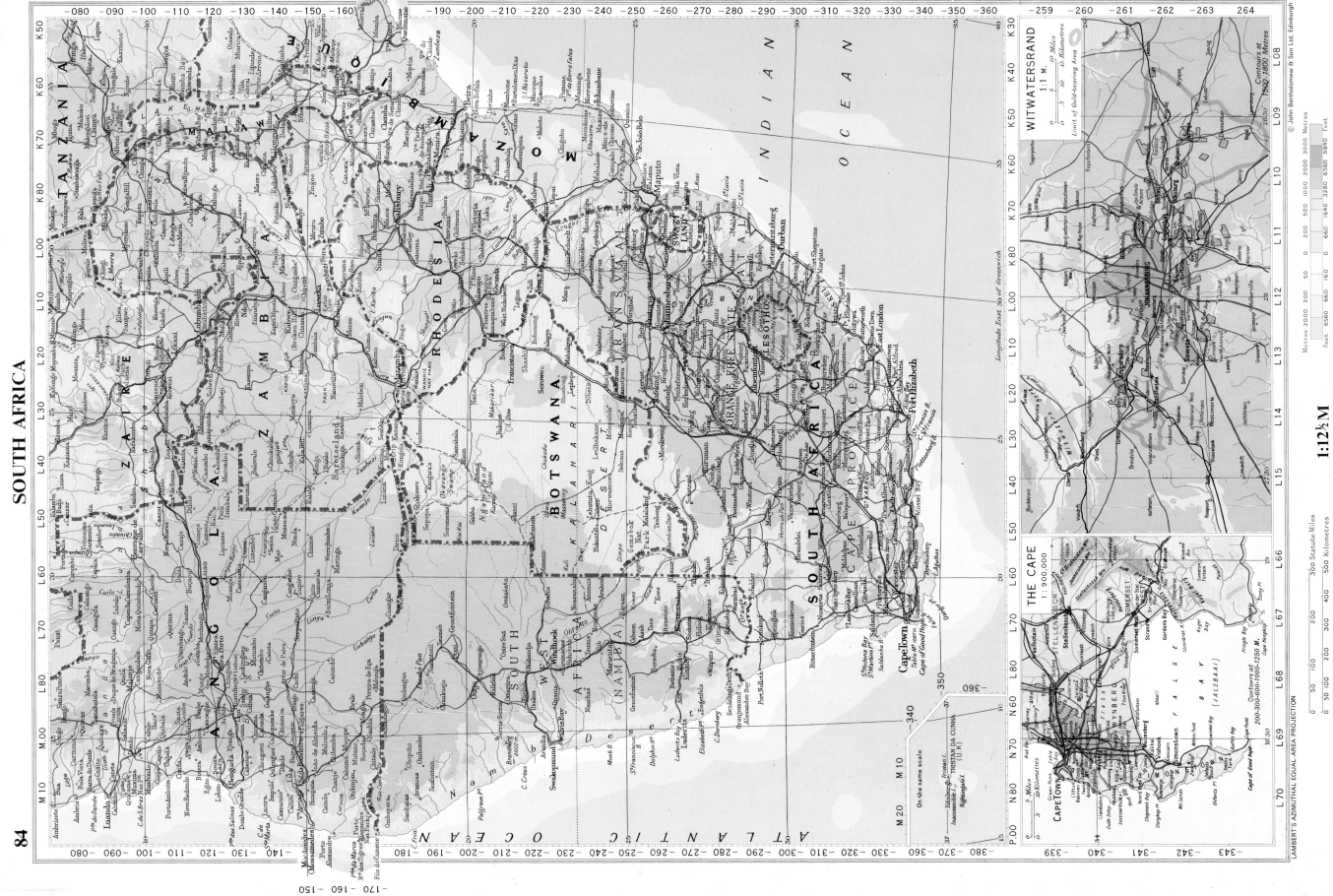

SOUTH AFRICA

84

WITWATERSRAND
1:1 M.

THE CAPE
1:900,000

1:12½M

LAMBERT'S AZIMUTHAL EQUAL-AREA PROJECTION

© John Bartholomew & Son Ltd. Edinburgh

ATLANTIC OCEAN

LAMBERT'S AZIMUTHAL EQUAL-AREA PROJECTION

1:48M

© John Bartholomew & Son Ltd, Edinburgh

PACIFIC OCEAN

NORTH AMERICA

SOUTH AMERICA

AFRICA

EUROPE

GREENLAND

ATLANTIC OCEAN

MID ATLANTIC RIDGE

MID-ATLANTIC RIDGE

North-Western Atlantic Basin

North-Eastern Atlantic Basin

Newfoundland Basin

Norwegian Basin

Cape Verde Basin

Brazilian Basin

Argentine Basin

Guinea Basin

Sierra Leone Basin

Cape Basin

South-Eastern Atlantic Basin

Agulhas Basin

Atlantic-Indian-Antarctic Basin

South Antarctic Basin

WEDDELL SEA

SCOTIA SEA

CARIBBEAN SEA

GULF OF MEXICO

WEST INDIES

Venezuela Basin

Nares Deep 6995m

Peru-Chile Trench

Cayman Trench 9219m

Puerto Rico Trench 9213m

Romanche Gap 7758m

Sandwich Trench

South Sandwich Meteor Depth 8264m

Walvis Ridge

Discovery Tablemount

Meteor Seamount 500m

Bromley Plateau 628m

Martin Vaz (Braz.)

Fernando Noronha (Braz.)

St. Paul Rocks (Braz.) 6027m

Atlantic-Antarctic Ridge

Azores-C. St Vincent Ridge

Bermuda Rise

Newfoundland Rise

Scotia Ridge

Cape Verde Islands 6104m

6407m

6603m

6075m

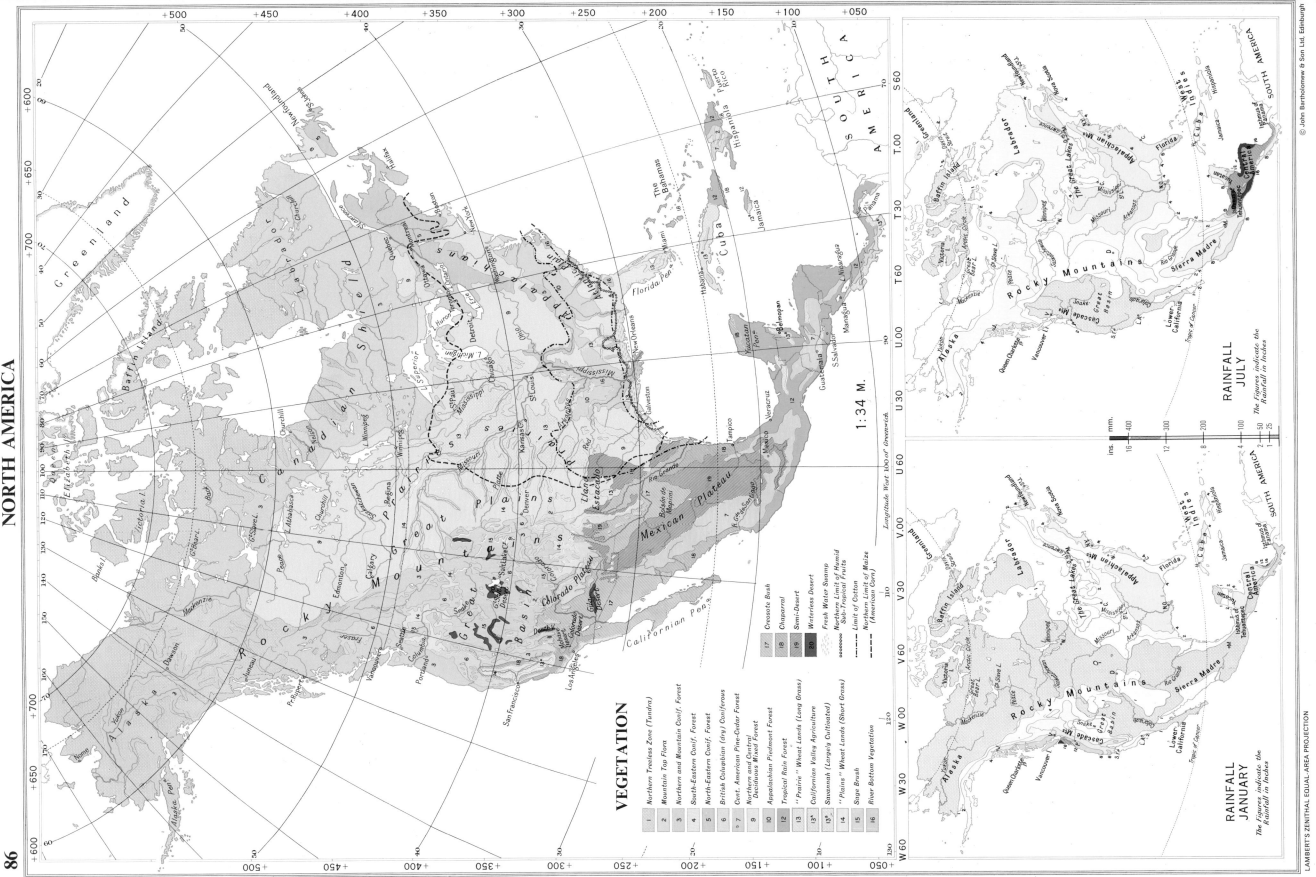

NORTH AMERICA

VEGETATION

1	Northern Treeless Zone (Tundra)
2	Mountain Top Flora
3	Northern and Mountain Conif. Forest
4	South-Eastern Conif. Forest
5	North-Eastern Conif. Forest
6	British Columbian (dry) Coniferous
7	Cent. American Pine-Cedar Forest
8	Northern and Central Deciduous Mixed Forest
9	Appalachian Piedmont Forest
10	Tropical Rain Forest
12	"Prairie" Wheat Lands (Long Grass)
13	"Plains" Wheat Lands (Short Grass)
13*	Californian Valley Agriculture
14	Savannah (Largely Cultivated)
15	Sage Brush
16	River Bottom Vegetation
17	Creosote Bush
18	Chaparral
19	Semi-Desert
20	Waterless Desert

Fresh Water Swamp
Northern Limit of Humid Sub-Tropical Fruits
Limit of Cotton
Northern Limit of Maize (American Corn)

1 : 34 M.

RAINFALL JULY

The Figures indicate the Rainfall in Inches

RAINFALL JANUARY

The Figures indicate the Rainfall in Inches

1:34M

	ins.	mm.
	16	400
	12	300
	8	200
	4	100
	2	50
	1	25

LAMBERT'S ZENITHAL EQUAL-AREA PROJECTION

© John Bartholomew & Son Ltd. Edinburgh

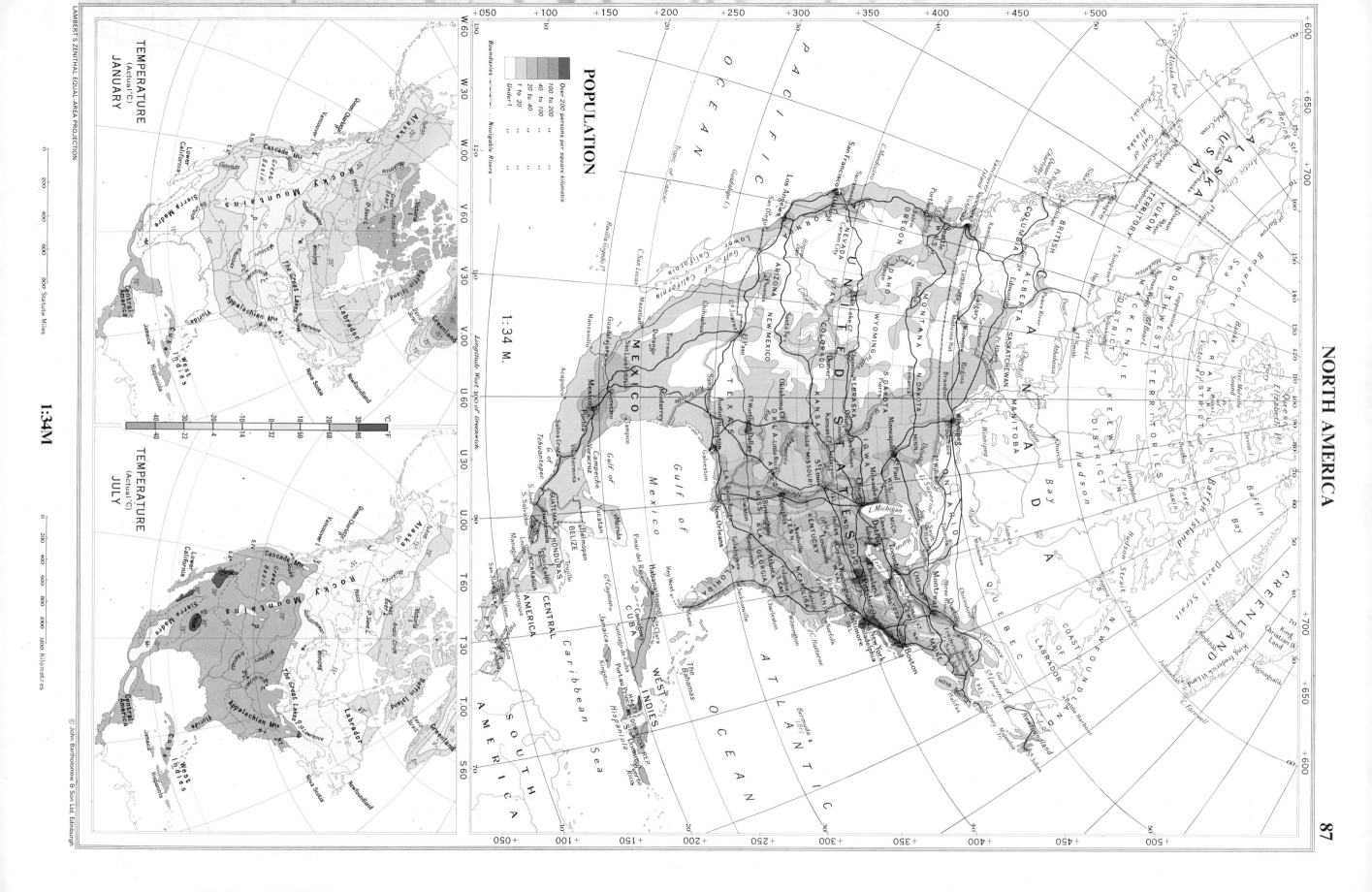

POPULATION

1:34 M.

Over 200 persons per square kilometre
100 to 200   "   "
40 to 100   "   "
20 to 40   "   "
1 to 20   "   "
Under 1   "   "

Boundaries ----------

Navigable Rivers

TEMPERATURE
(Actual°C)
JANUARY

TEMPERATURE
(Actual°C)
JULY

1:34M

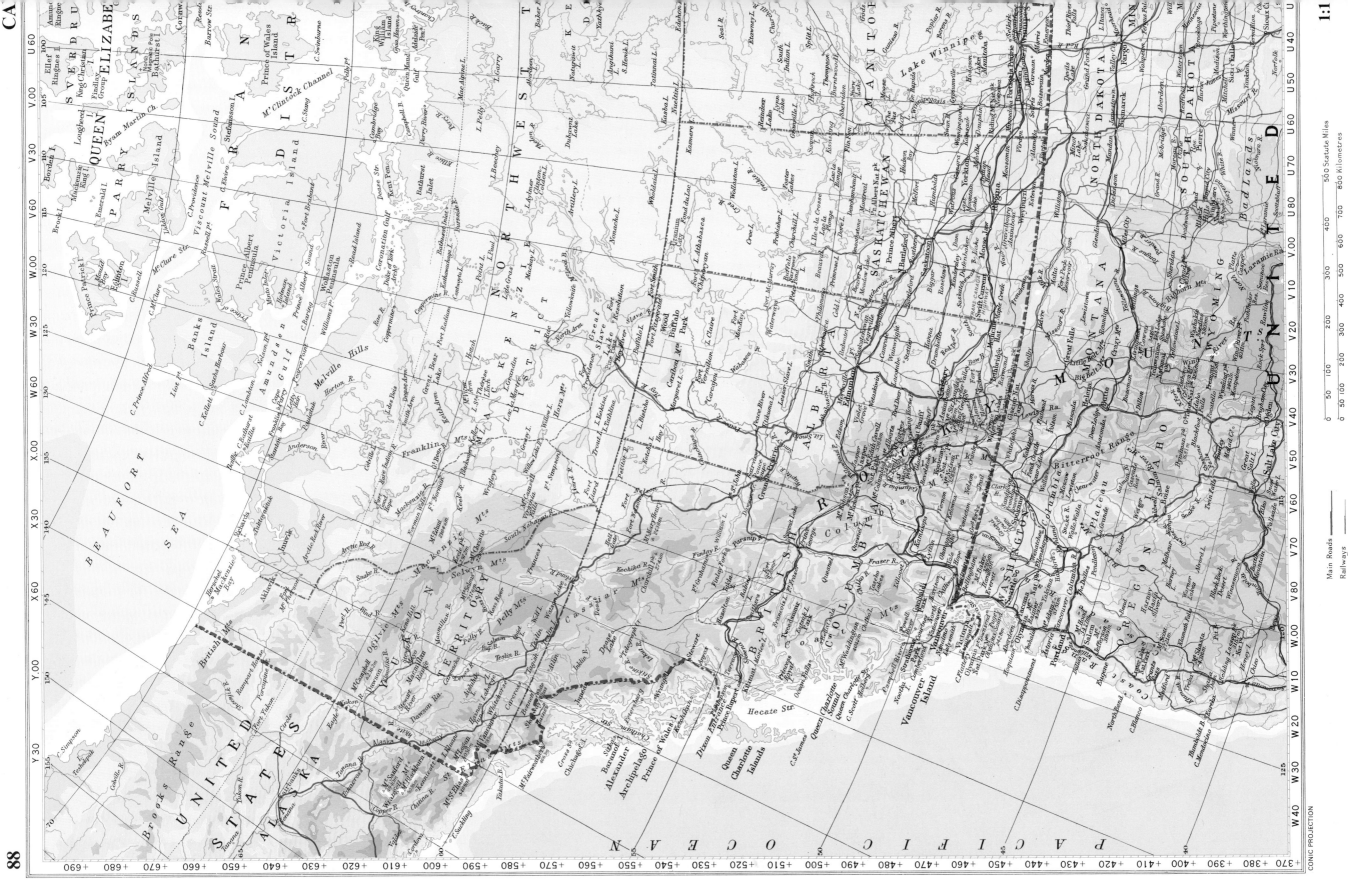

CONIC PROJECTION

Main Roads
Railways

0   50 100   200   300   400   500 Kilometres
0   100   200   300   400   500 Statute Miles
600   700   800

QUEEN ELIZABETH ISLANDS

SVERDRUP

PARRY ISLANDS

QUEEN

DISTRICT OF FRANKLIN

NORTHWEST

BEAUFORT SEA

UNITED STATES

ALASKA

Brooks Range

YUKON TERRITORY

Mackenzie Mts

DISTRICT OF MACKENZIE

Great Slave L.

Great Bear L.

BRITISH COLUMBIA

ROCKY MTS

ALBERTA

SASKATCHEWAN

MANITOBA

Lake Winnipeg

Vancouver Island

Queen Charlotte Islands

Prince of Wales I.

Alexander Archipelago

Hecate Str.

WASHINGTON

OREGON

IDAHO

MONTANA

WYOMING

NORTH DAKOTA

SOUTH DAKOTA

PACIFIC OCEAN

U N I T E D

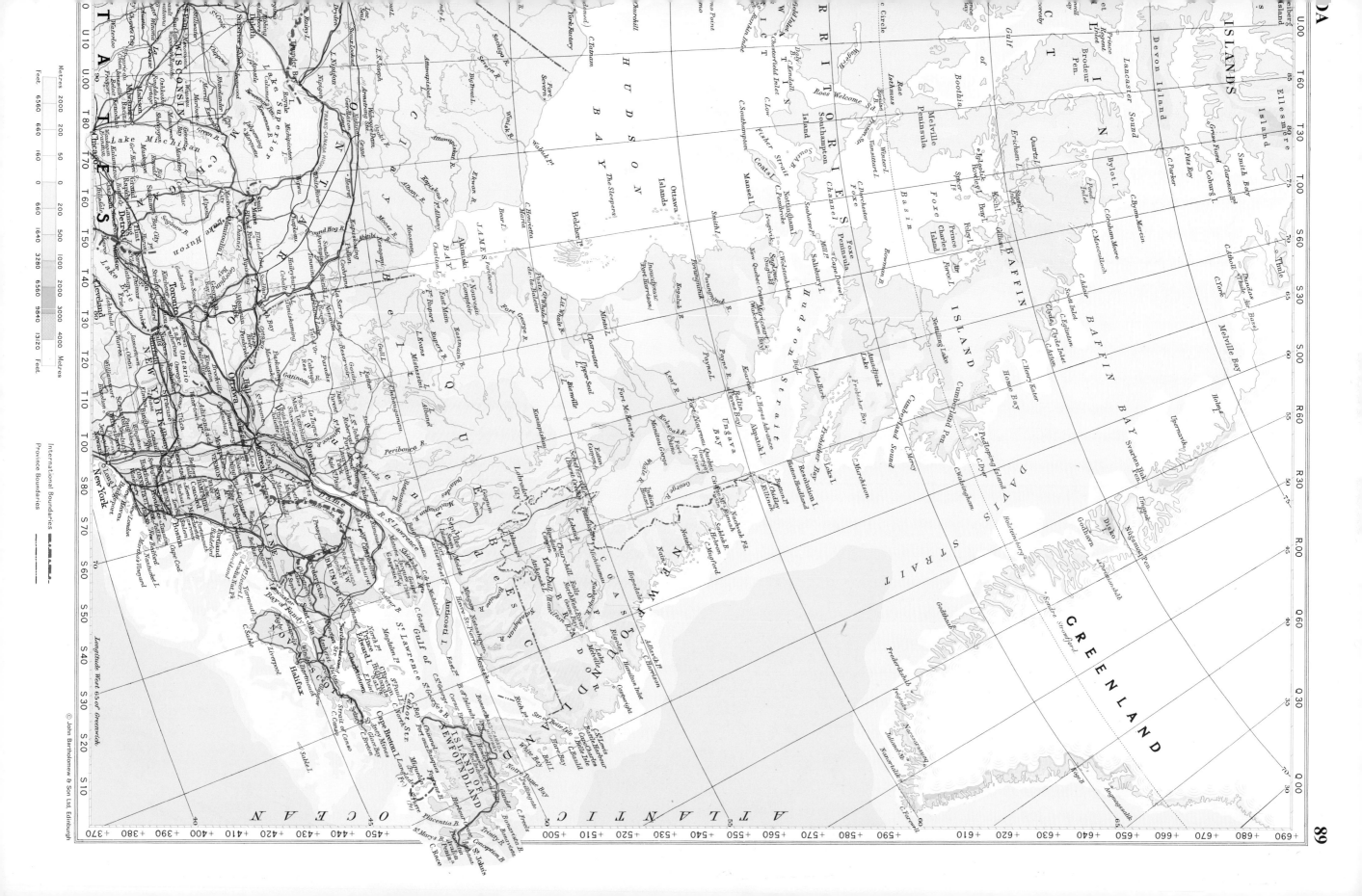

1:5M

BONNE'S PROJECTION

© John Bartholomew & Son Ltd. Edinburgh

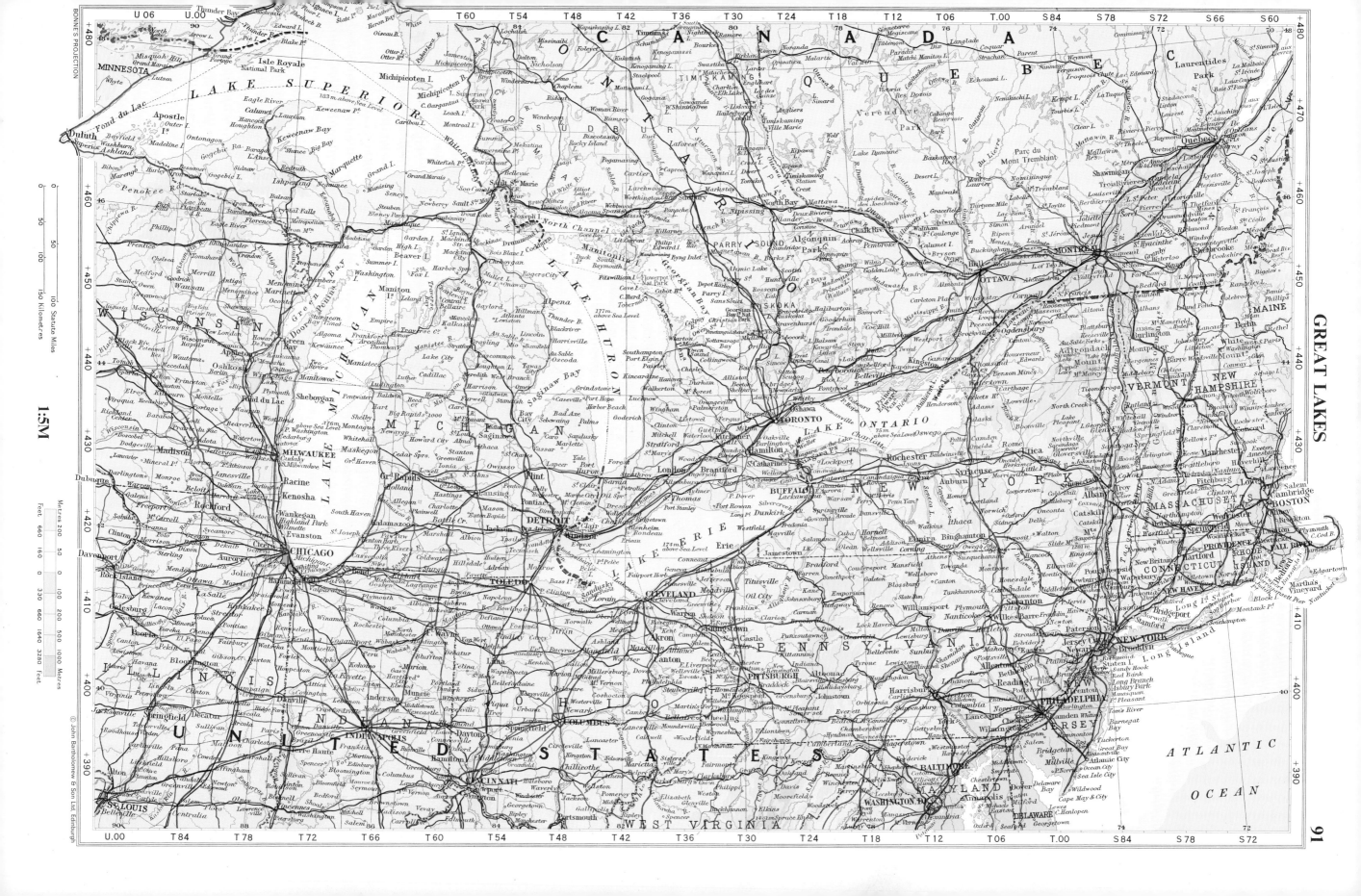

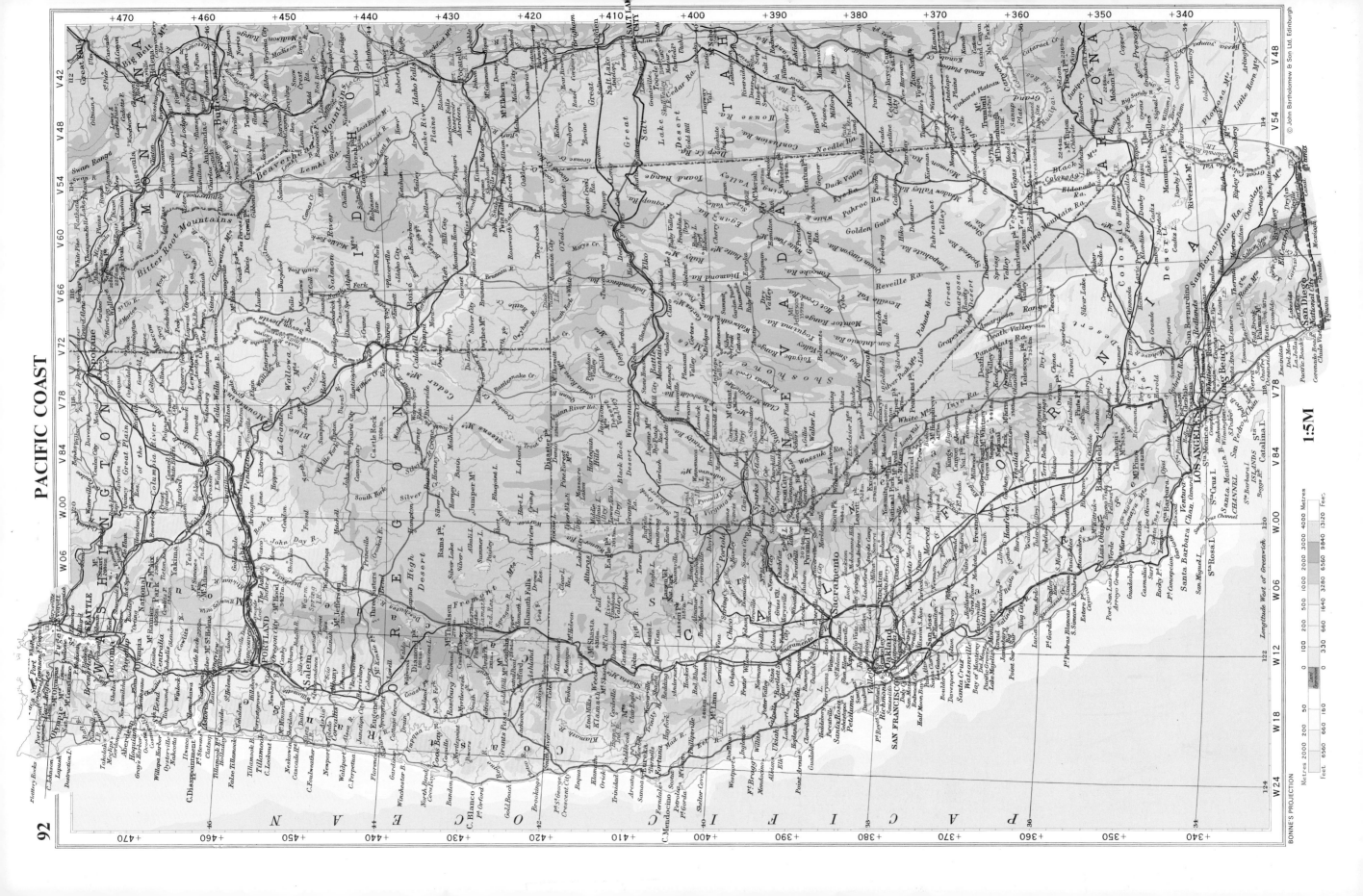

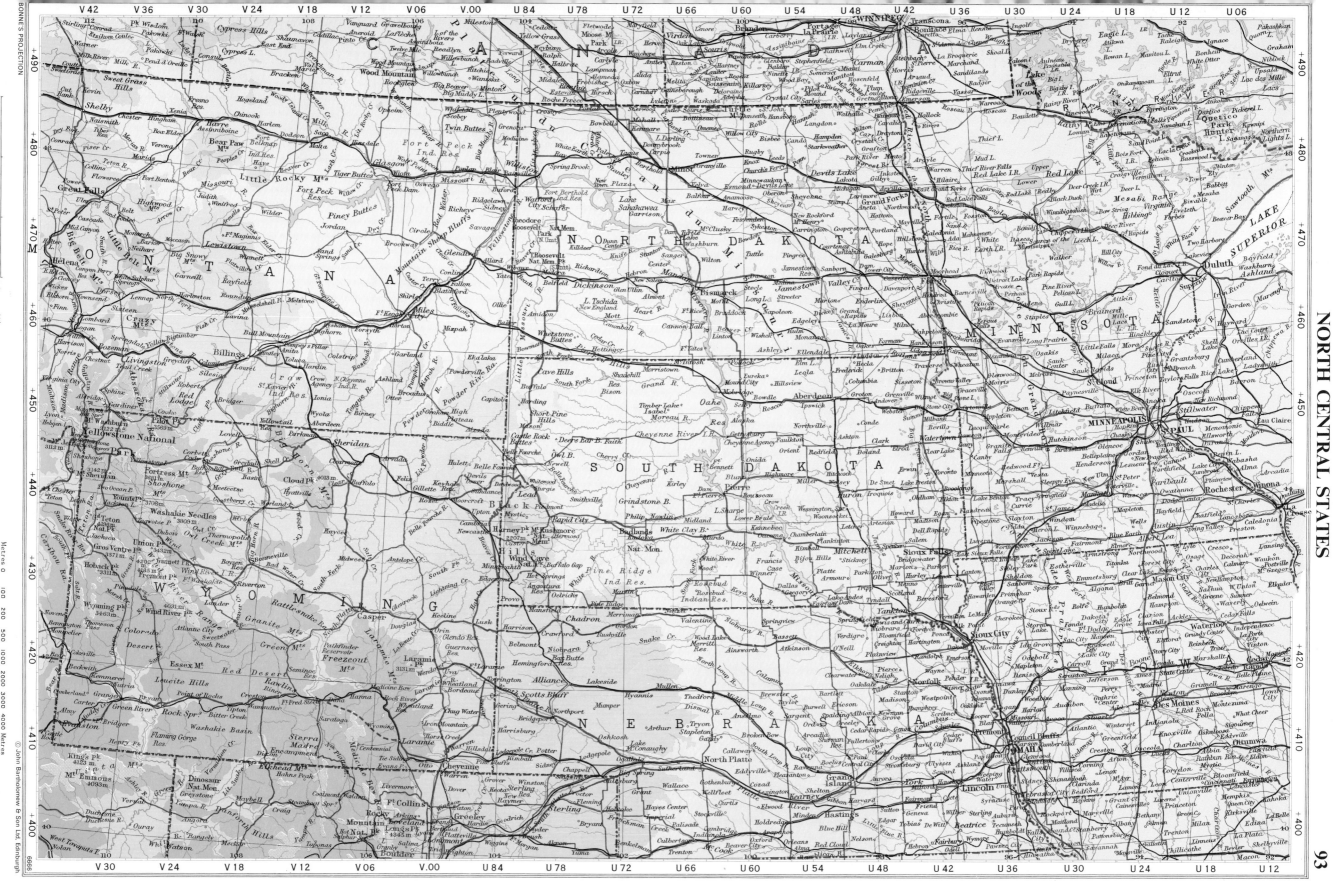

BONNE'S PROJECTION

1:5M

BONNE'S PROJECTION

Main Roads
Railways

200 Statute Miles
300 Kilometres

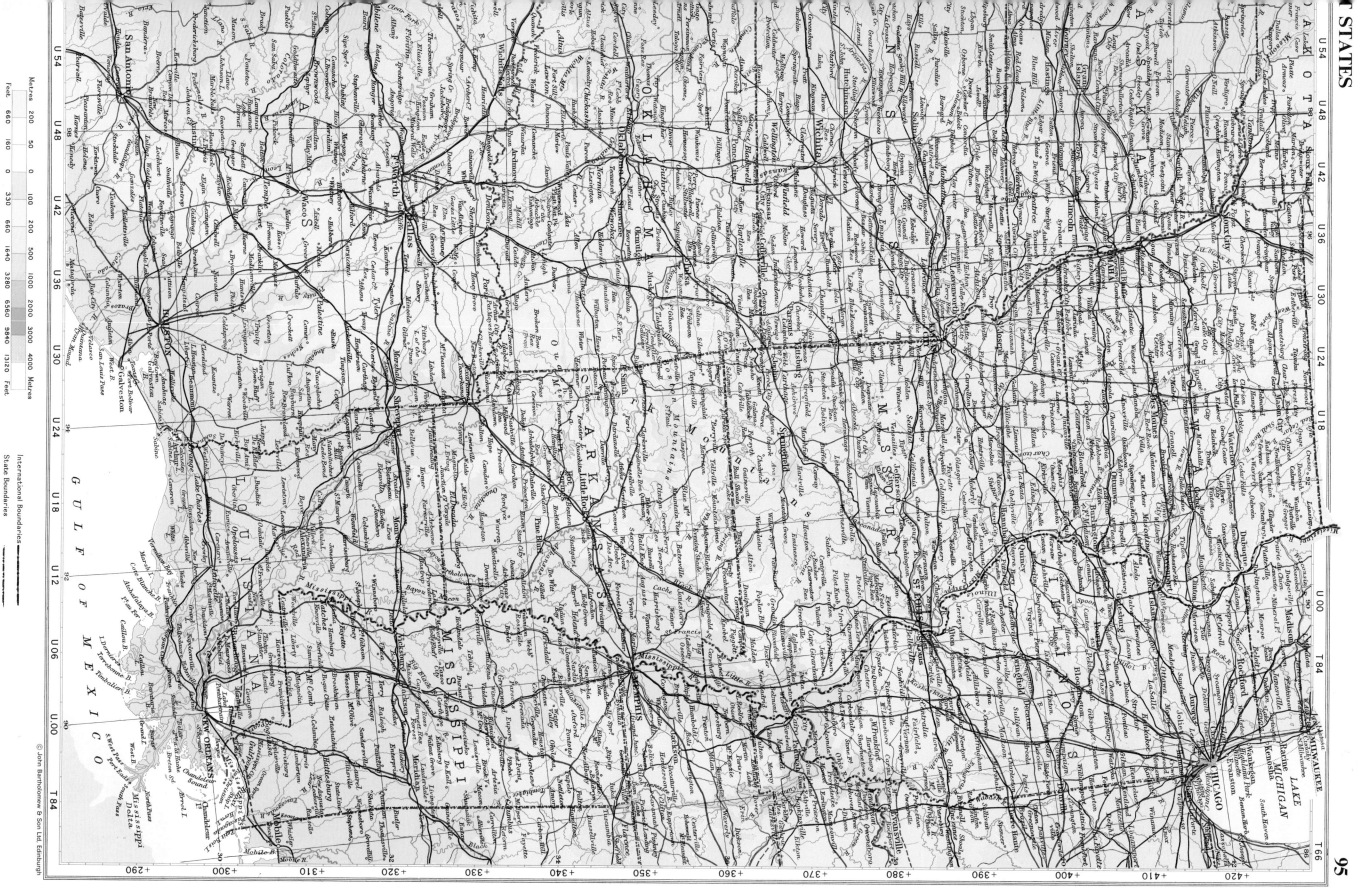

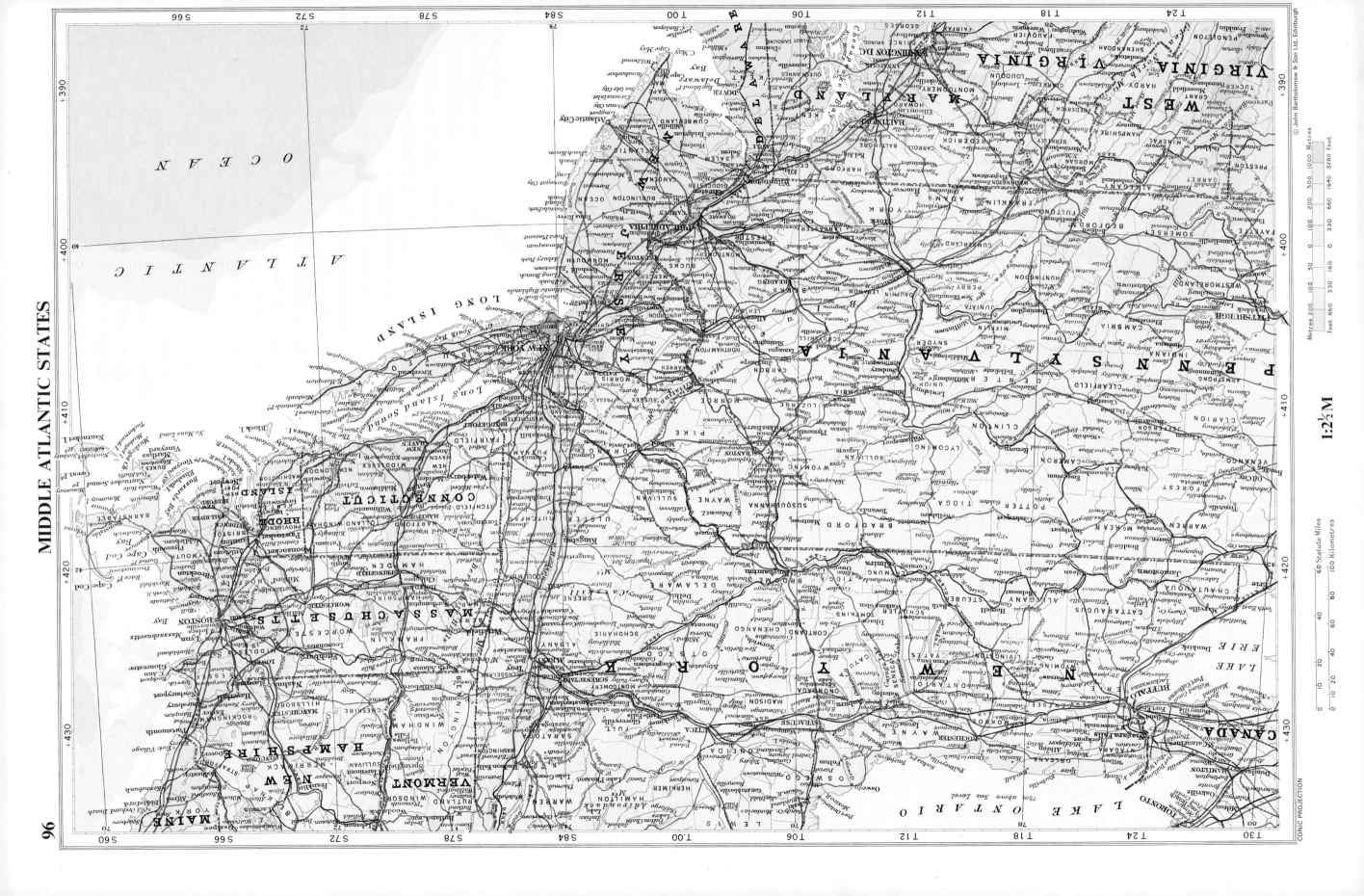

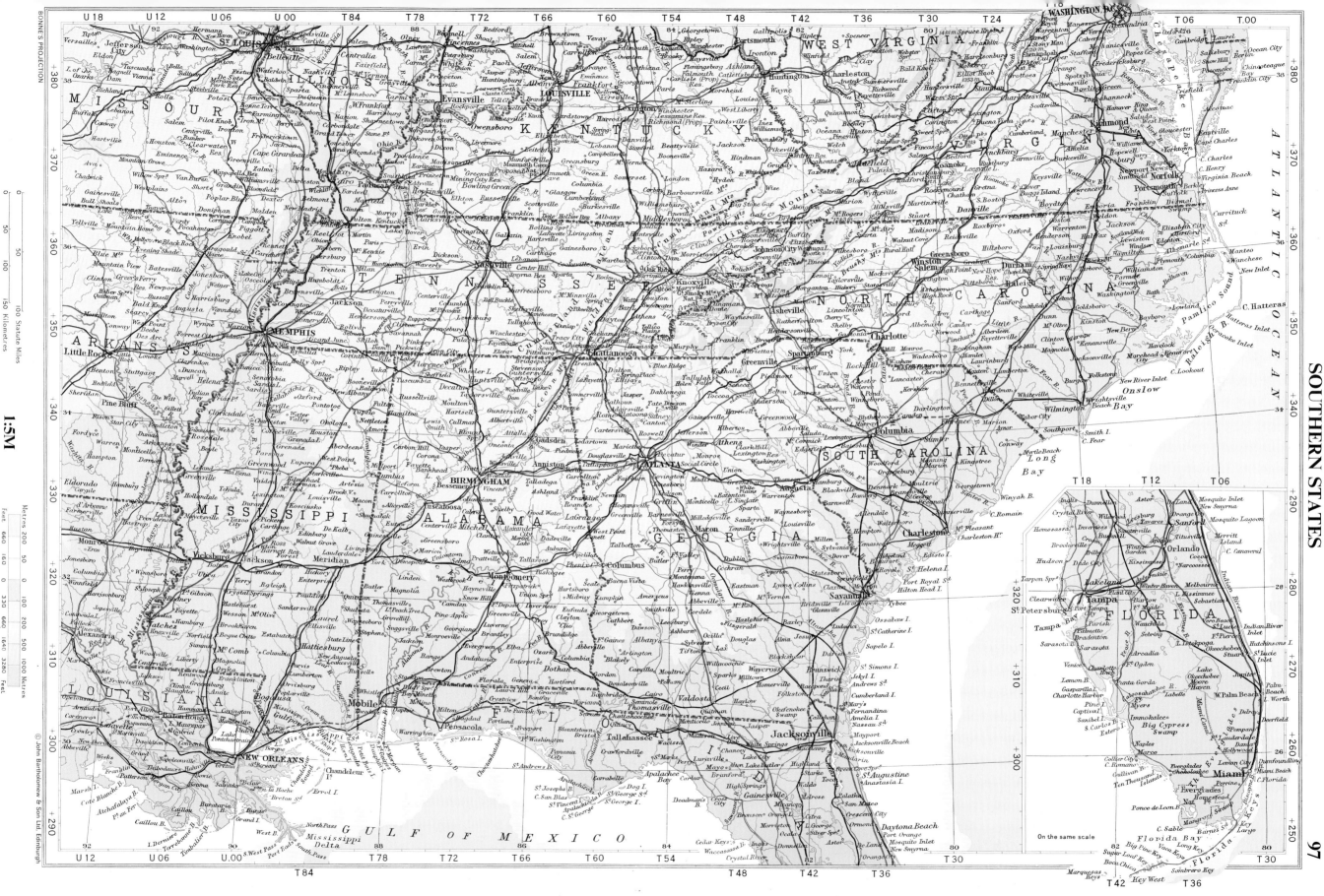

WASHINGTON, D.C.

WEST VIRGINIA

MISSOURI

ILLINOIS

KENTUCKY

VIRGINIA

ATLANTIC OCEAN

TENNESSEE

NORTH CAROLINA

ARKANSAS

SOUTH CAROLINA

MISSISSIPPI

ALABAMA

GEORGIA

LOUISIANA

FLORIDA

GULF OF MEXICO

FLORIDA

BONNE'S PROJECTION

1:5M

© John Bartholomew & Son Ltd, Edinburgh

SOUTHERN STATES

97

On the same scale

Main Roads

Railways

HAWAII
1:6¼ M.

CONIC PROJECTION

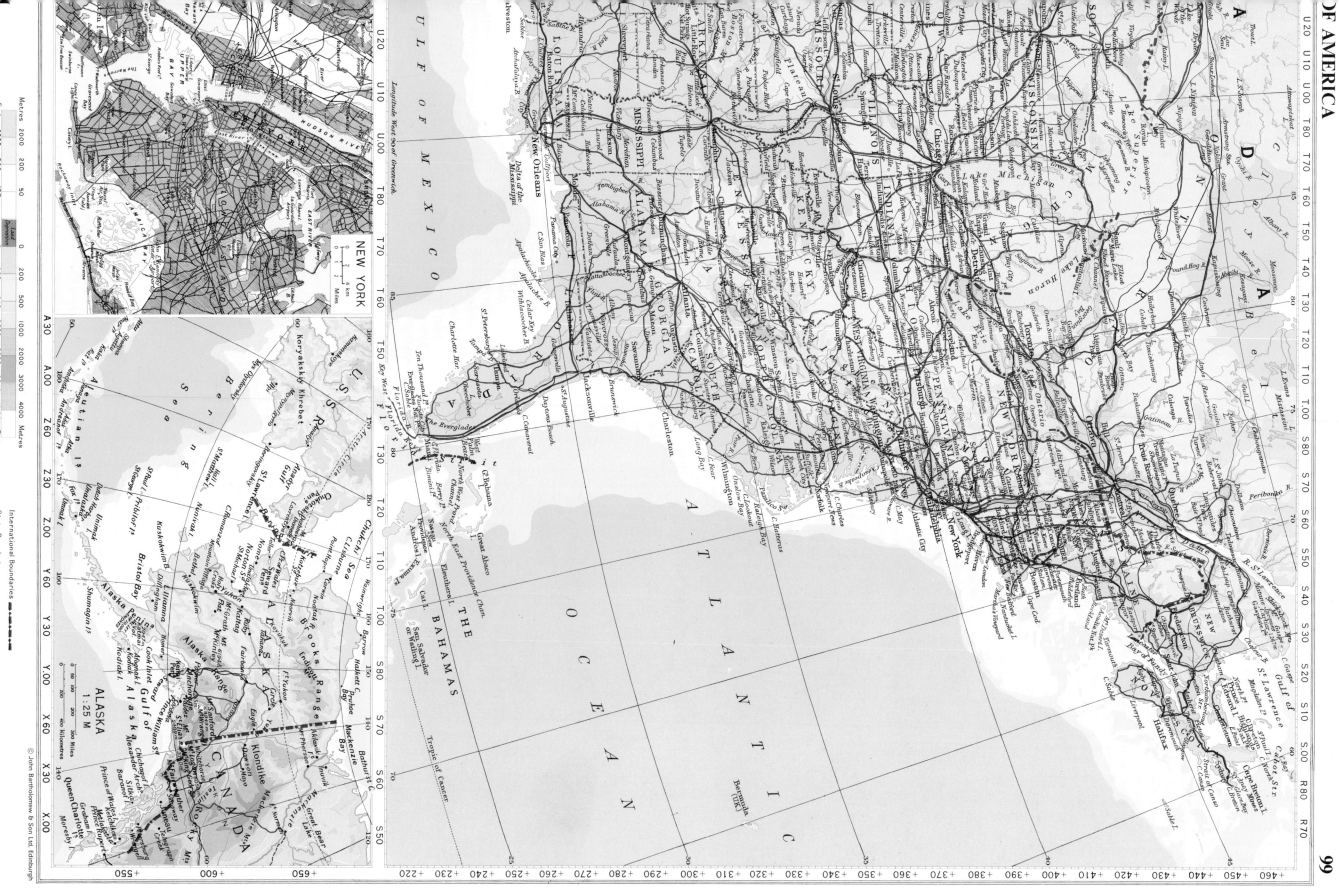

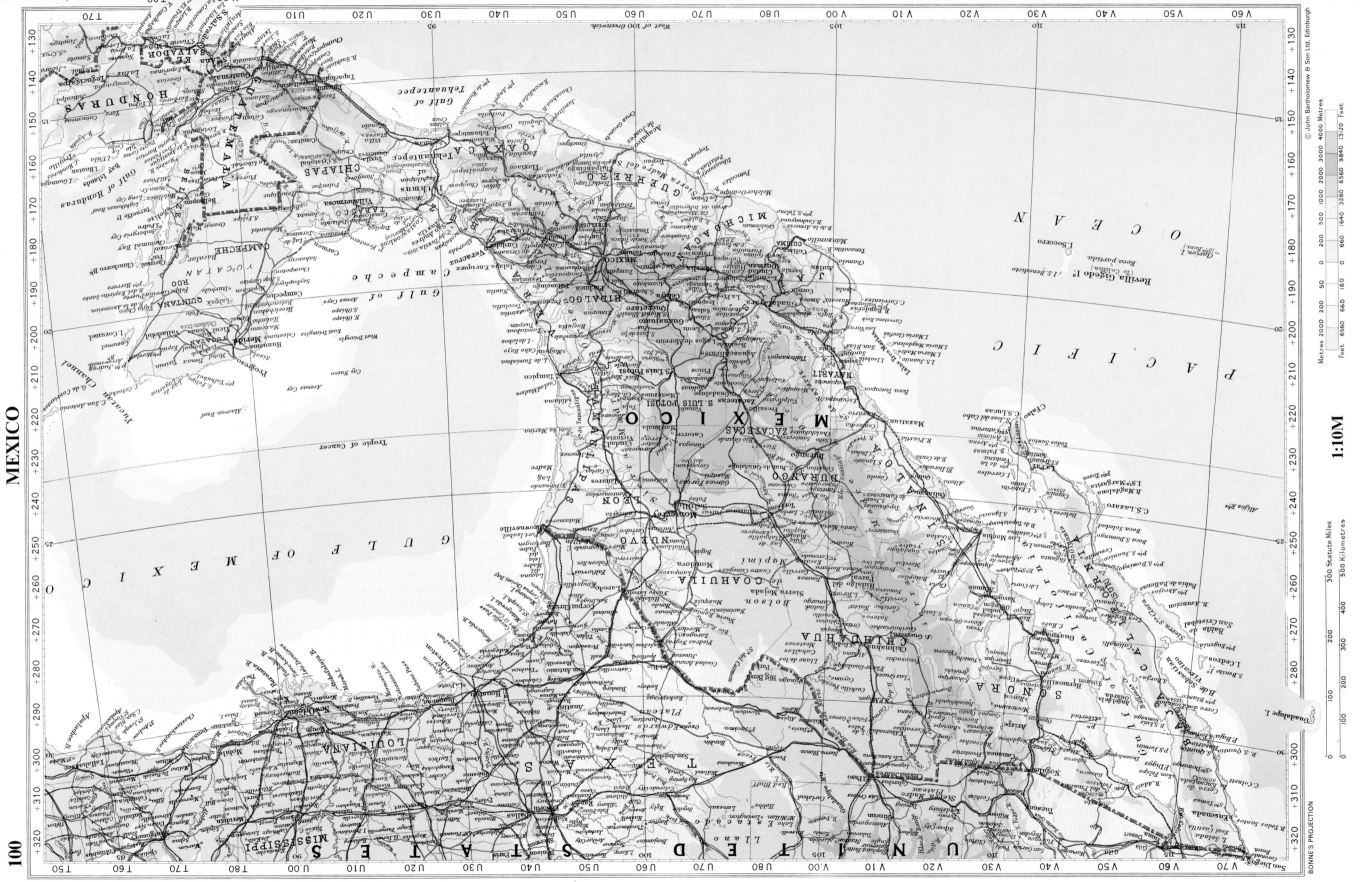

1:10M

© John Bartholomew & Son Ltd, Edinburgh

BONNE'S PROJECTION

BONNE'S PROJECTION

1:10M

© John Bartholomew & Son Ltd. Edinburgh

PANAMA CANAL
1:1,000,000

Canal ——— Railway ++++

Contours are drawn at 100 and 200 Metres

GULF OF MEXICO

ATLANTIC OCEAN

THE BAHAMAS

WEST INDIES

CUBA

GREATER ANTILLES

MEXICO

YUCATAN

QUINTANA ROO

CAMPECHE

BELIZE

GUATEMALA

HONDURAS

EL SALVADOR

NICARAGUA

CENTRAL AMERICA

COSTA RICA

PANAMA

PACIFIC OCEAN

JAMAICA

HAITI

HISPANIOLA

DOMINICAN REP.

PUERTO RICO

Virgin Is.

LEEWARD ISLANDS

LESSER ANTILLES

WINDWARD ISLANDS

CARIBBEAN SEA

COLOMBIA

VENEZUELA

GUYANA

Gulf of Darien

Mouths of the Orinoco

TRINIDAD & TOBAGO

TRINIDAD

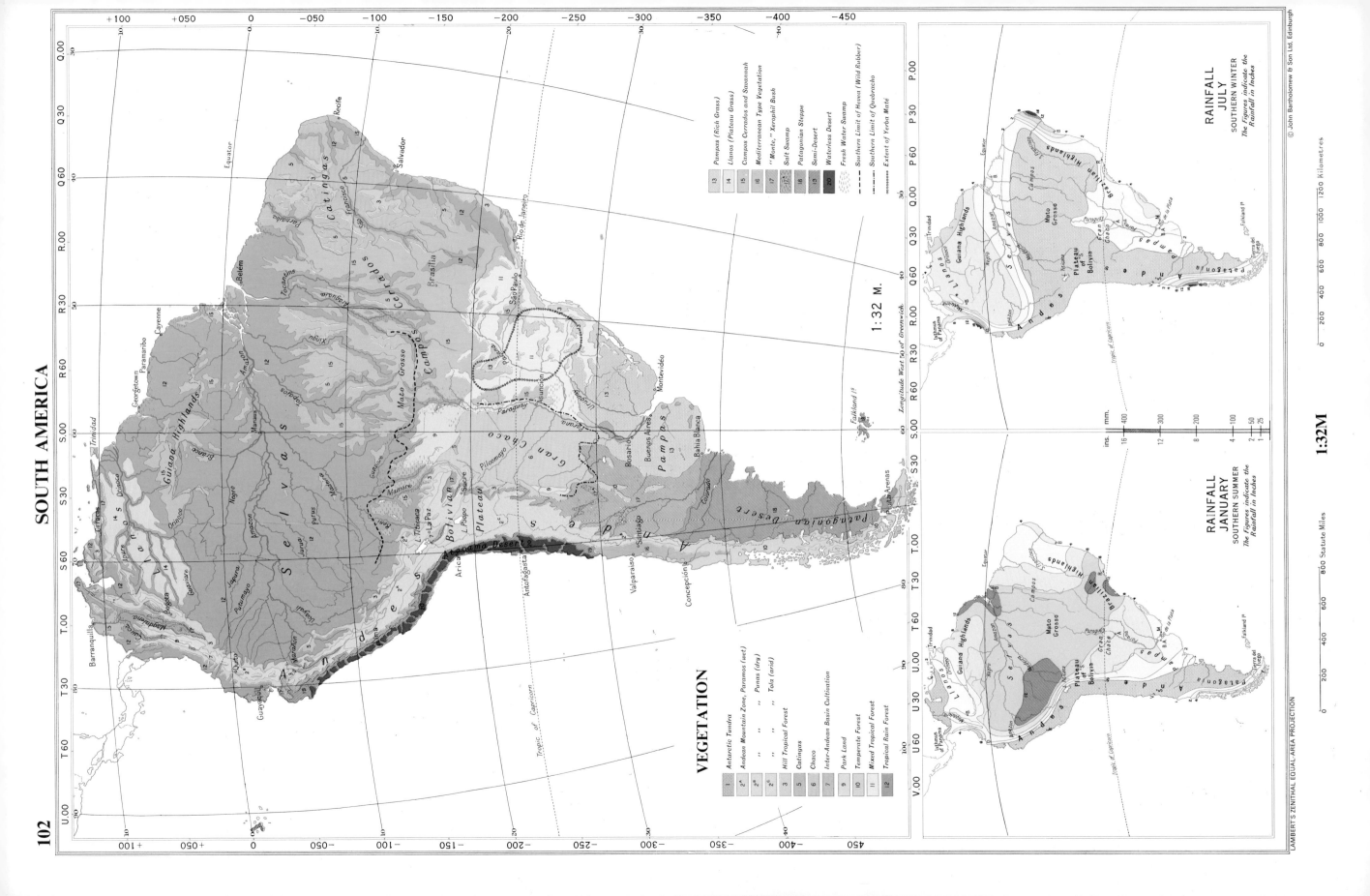

SOUTH AMERICA

102

VEGETATION

1	Antarctic Tundra
2^A	Andean Mountain Zone, Paramos (wet)
2^B	" " Punas (dry)
2^C	" " Tola (arid)
3	Hill Tropical Forest
5	Catingas
6	Chaco
7	Inter-Andean Basin Cultivation
9	Park Land
10	Temperate Forest
11	Mixed Tropical Forest
12	Tropical Rain Forest

13	Pampas (Rich Grass)
14	Llanos (Plateau Grass)
15	Campos Cerrados and Savannah
16	Mediterranean Type Vegetation
17	"Monte," Xerophil Bush
17½	Salt Swamp
18	Patagonian Steppe
19	Semi-Desert
20	Waterless Desert
	Fresh Water Swamp
— — —	Southern Limit of Hevea (Wild Rubber)
····	Southern Limit of Quebracho
–·–·–	Extent of Yerba Maté

1 : 32 M.

RAINFALL
JANUARY
SOUTHERN SUMMER
The Figures indicate the Rainfall in Inches

RAINFALL
JULY
SOUTHERN WINTER
The Figures indicate the Rainfall in Inches

ins.	mm.
16	400
12	300
8	200
4	100
2	50
1	25

© John Bartholomew & Son Ltd, Edinburgh

1:32M

LAMBERT'S ZENITHAL EQUAL-AREA PROJECTION

0   200   400   600   800 Statute Miles

0   200   400   600   800   1000   1200 Kilometres

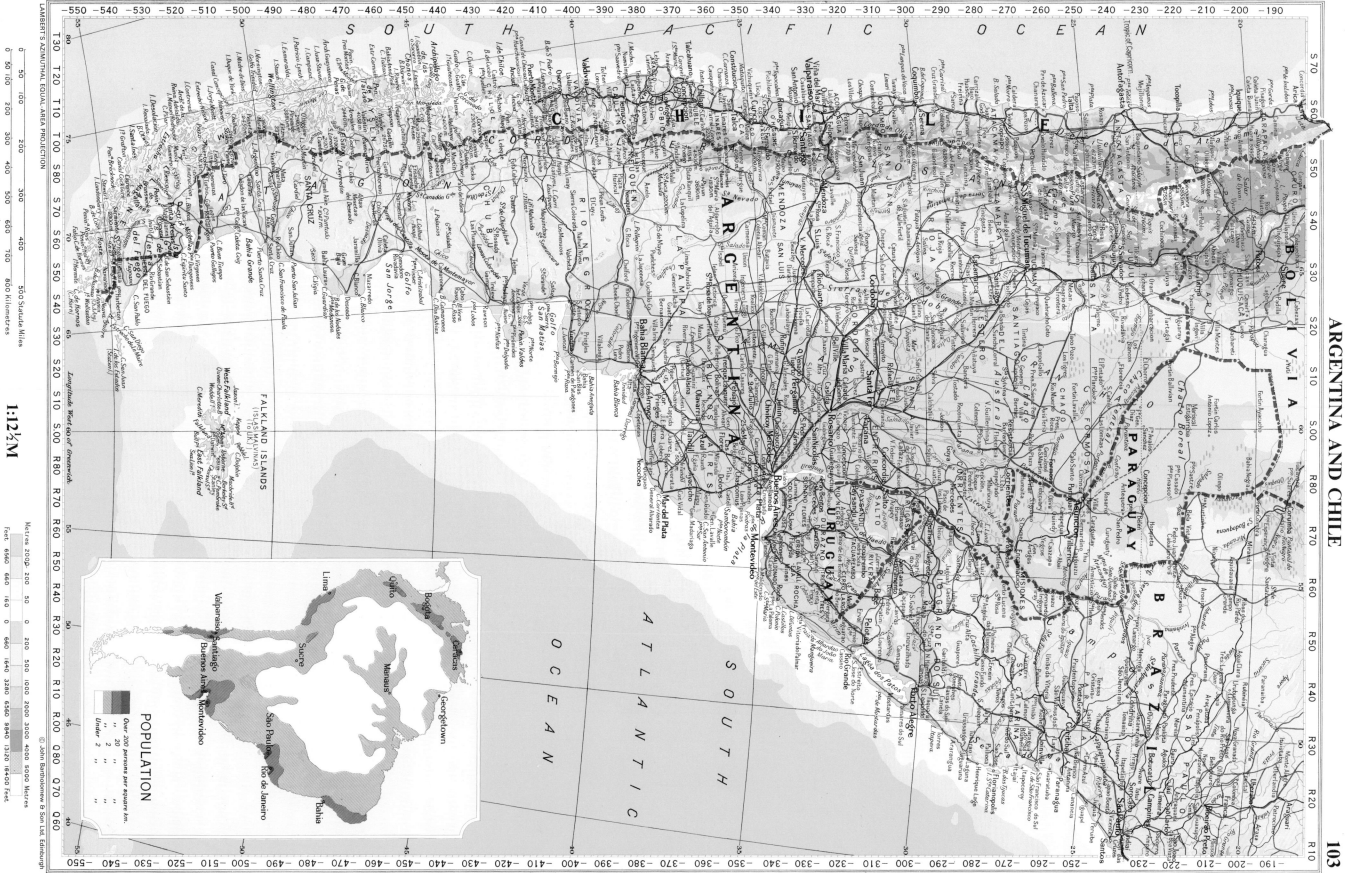

ARGENTINA AND CHILE

1:12½M

103

POPULATION

Over 200 persons per square km.
"   20   "   "   "   "
"   5   "   "   "   "
"   2   "   "   "   "
Under 2   "   "   "   "

LAMBERT'S AZIMUTHAL EQUAL-AREA PROJECTION

© John Bartholomew & Son Ltd., Edinburgh

GALAPAGOS ISLANDS
(ARCHIPIÉLAGO DE COLÓN)
(To Ecuador)

On the same scale

LAMBERT'S ZENITHAL EQUAL-AREA PROJECTION

Main Roads
Railways

500 Statute Miles
800 Kilometres

TEMPERATURE
(Actual°C)
JANUARY
SOUTHERN SUMMER

TEMPERATURE
(Actual°C)
JULY
SOUTHERN WINTER

International Boundaries
State Boundaries

© John Bartholomew & Son Ltd, Edinburgh

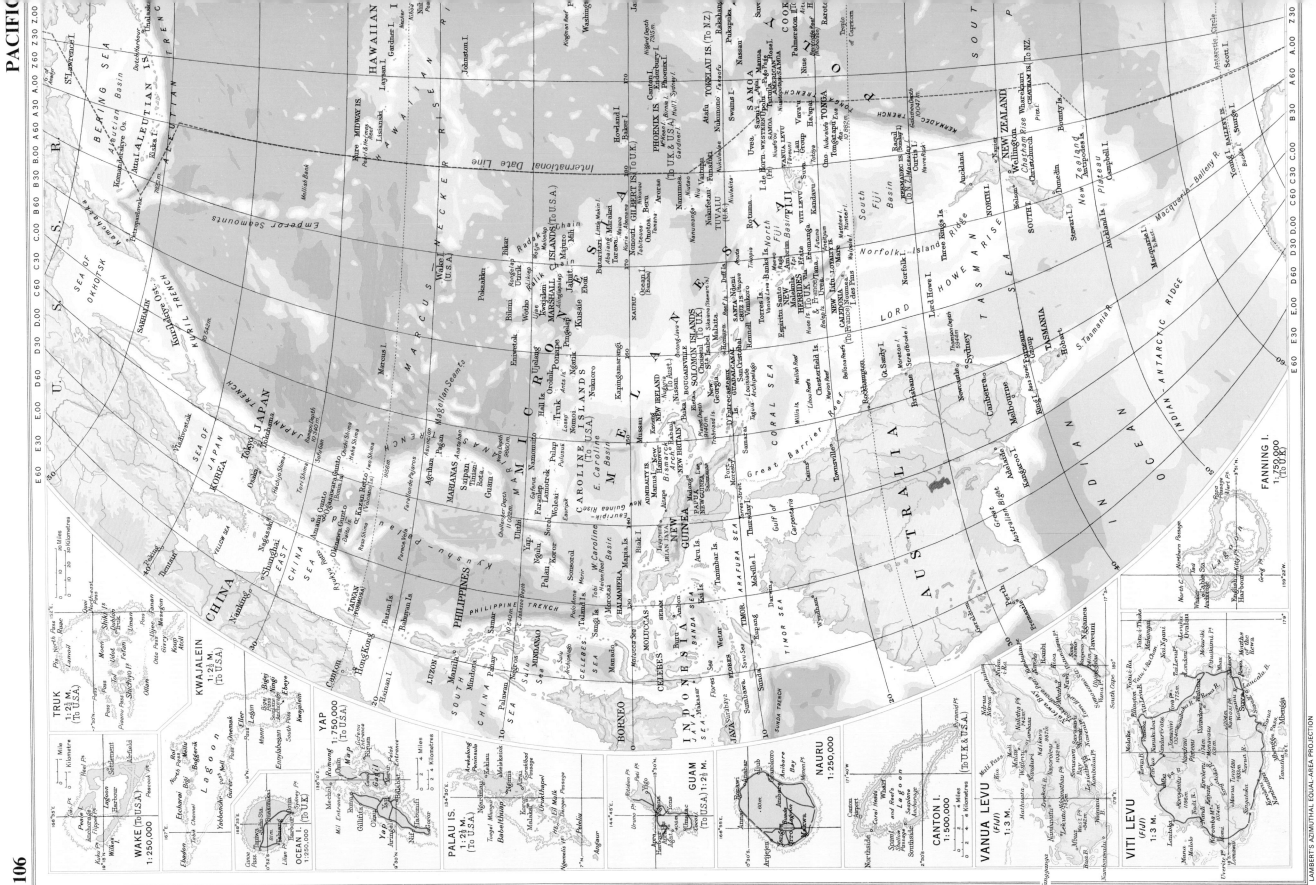

LAMBERT'S AZIMUTHAL EQUAL-AREA PROJECTION

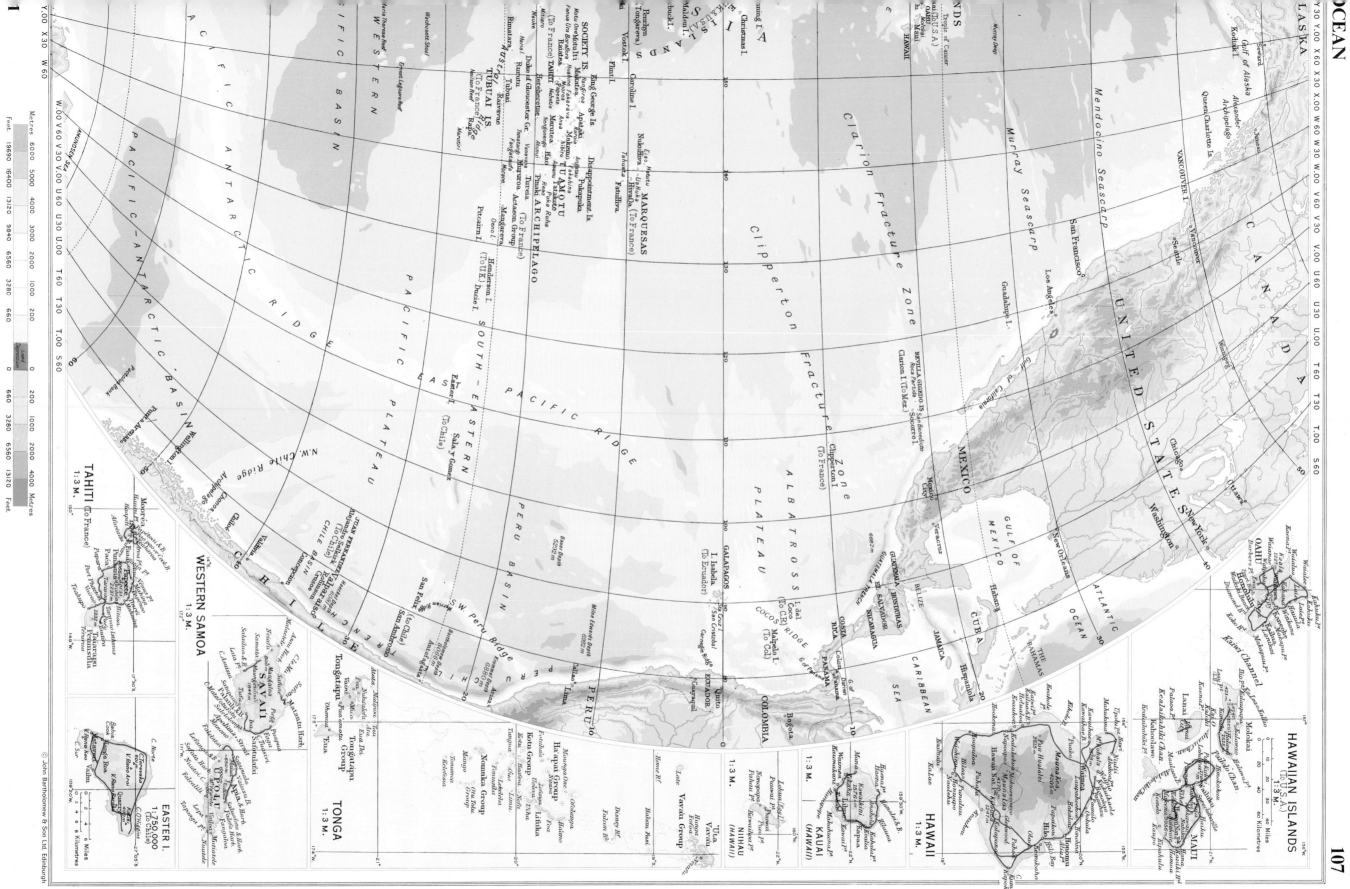

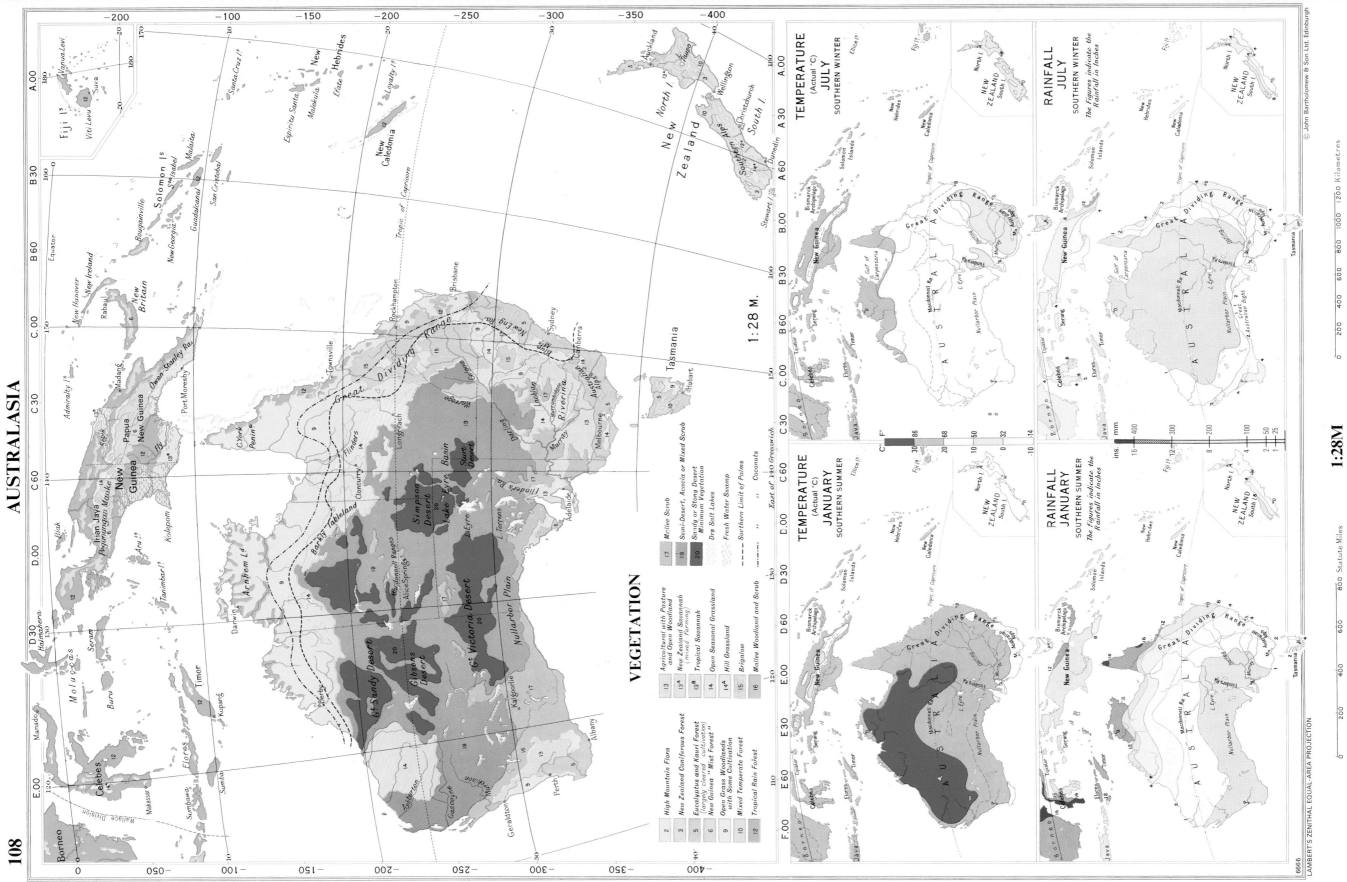

AUSTRALASIA

1:28 M.

VEGETATION

2	High Mountain Flora
3	New Zealand Coniferous Forest
5	Eucalyptus and Kauri Forest (largely cleared cultivation)
6	New Guinea "Mist Forest"
9	Open Grass Woodlands with Some Cultivation
10	Mixed Temperate Forest
12	Tropical Rain Forest
13	Agricultural with Pasture and Open Woodland
13ᴬ	New Zealand Savannah (mixed farming)
13ᴮ	Tropical Savannah
14	Open Seasonal Grassland
14ᴬ	Hill Grassland
15	Brigalow
16	Mallee Woodland and Scrub
17	Mallee Scrub
19	Semi-Desert, Acacia or Mixed Scrub
20	Sandy or Stony Desert Minimum Vegetation

Dra Salt Lakes
Fresh Water Swamp
— — — Southern Limit of Palms
· · · · · · Coconuts

TEMPERATURE (Actual °C)
JULY
SOUTHERN WINTER

RAINFALL
JULY
SOUTHERN WINTER
The figures indicate the Rainfall in Inches

TEMPERATURE (Actual °C)
JANUARY
SOUTHERN SUMMER

RAINFALL
JANUARY
SOUTHERN SUMMER
The figures indicate the Rainfall in Inches

1:28M

LAMBERT'S ZENITHAL EQUAL-AREA PROJECTION

© John Bartholomew & Son Ltd. Edinburgh

6666

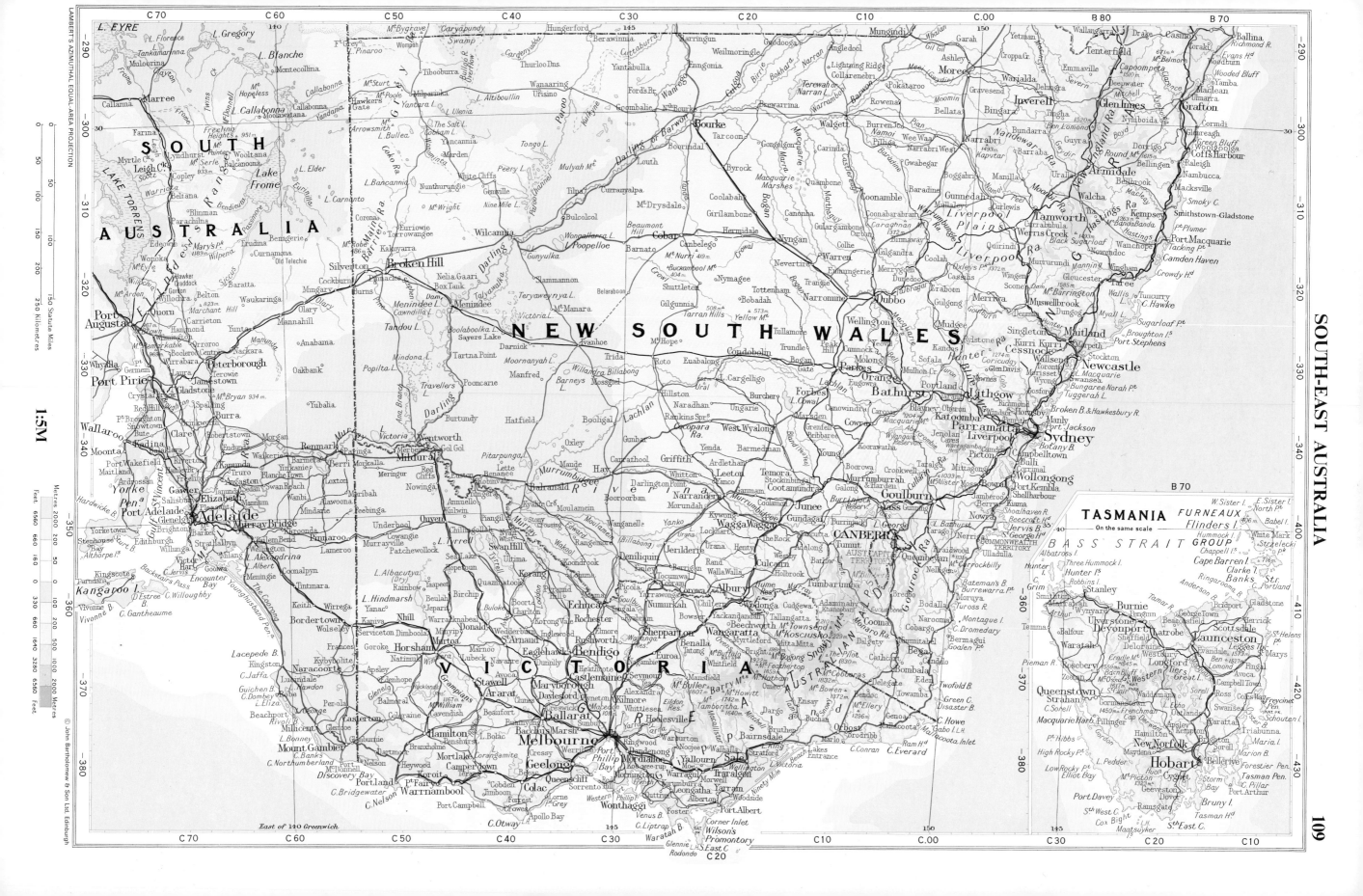

1:5M

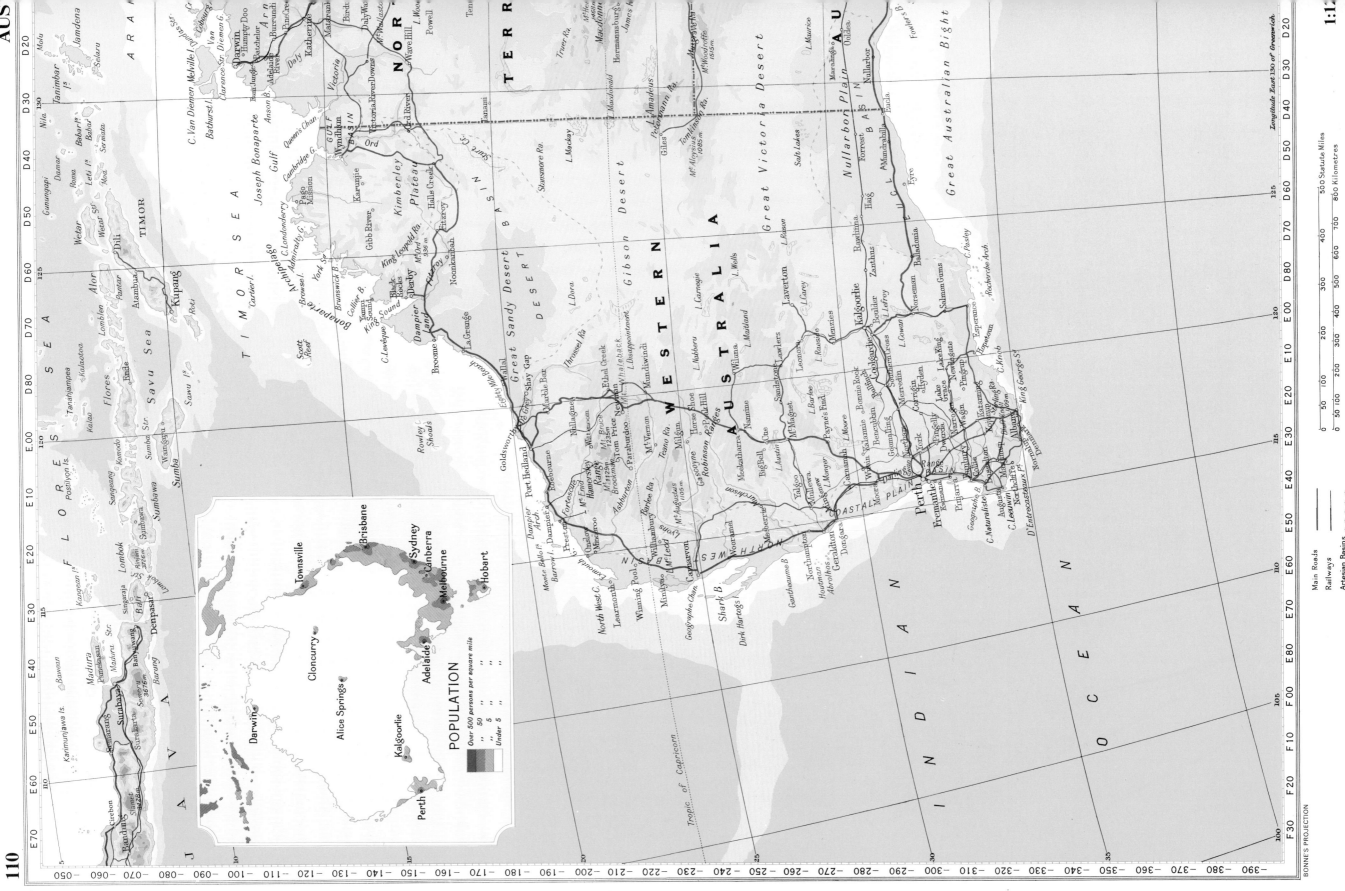

1:12

Longitude East 130° of Greenwich

D 20   D 30   D 40   D 50   D 60   D 70   D 20   D 30

NOR   TERR   AU

DARWIN

N O R T H E R N

T E R R I T O R Y

WESTERN

AUSTRALIA

Great Sandy Desert

Gibson Desert

Great Victoria Desert

Nullarbor Plain

ARTESIAN BASIN

TIMOR SEA

ARAFURA

FLORES SEA

Savu Sea

T I M O R

JAVA

Surabaya

Bandung

Semarang

Denpasar

INDIAN   OCEAN

Great Australian Bight

Perth
Fremantle

Kalgoorlie

Geraldton

Port Hedland

Broome

Derby

Carnarvon

Esperance

Albany

Tropic of Capricorn

POPULATION

Over 500 persons per square mile
50   "   "   "   "
5   "   "   "   "
Under 5 "   "   "   "

Darwin

Townsville

Cloncurry

Brisbane

Sydney
Canberra

Alice Springs

Melbourne

Adelaide

Kalgoorlie

Hobart

Perth

0   50   100   200   300   400   500 Statute Miles
0   50 100   200   300   400   500   600 Kilometres

Main Roads
Railways
Artesian Basins

BONNE'S PROJECTION

E 70 E 60 E 50 E 40 E 30 E 20 E 10 E 00 E 10 E 20 E 30 E 40 E 50 E 60 E 70 E 80 F 00 F 10 F 20 F 30

-050 -060 -070 -080 -090 -100 -110 -120 -130 -140 -150 -160 -170 -180 -190 -200 -210 -220 -230 -240 -250 -260 -270 -280 -290 -300 -310 -320 -330 -340 -350 -360 -370 -380 -390

100 105 110 115 120 125

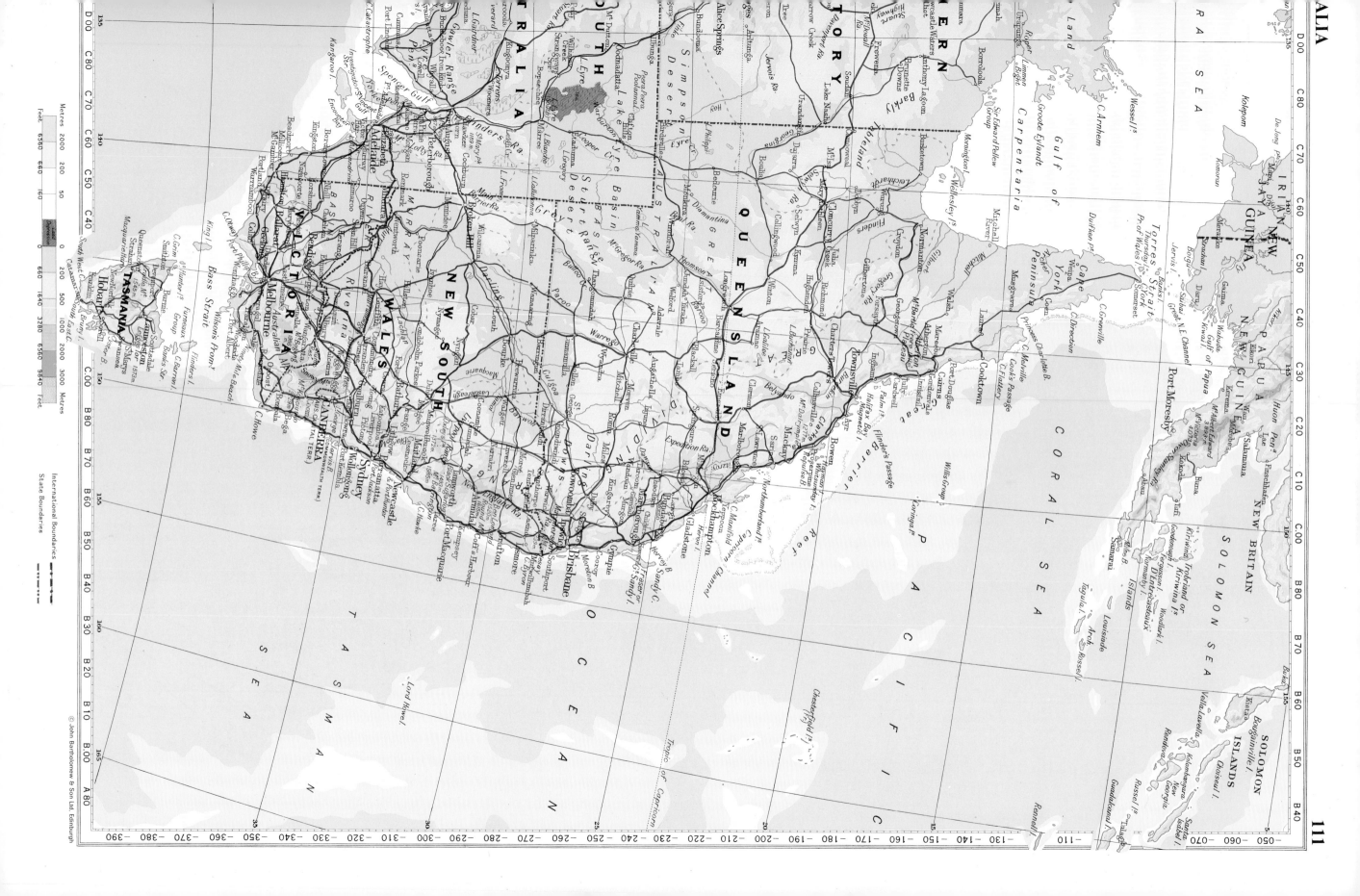

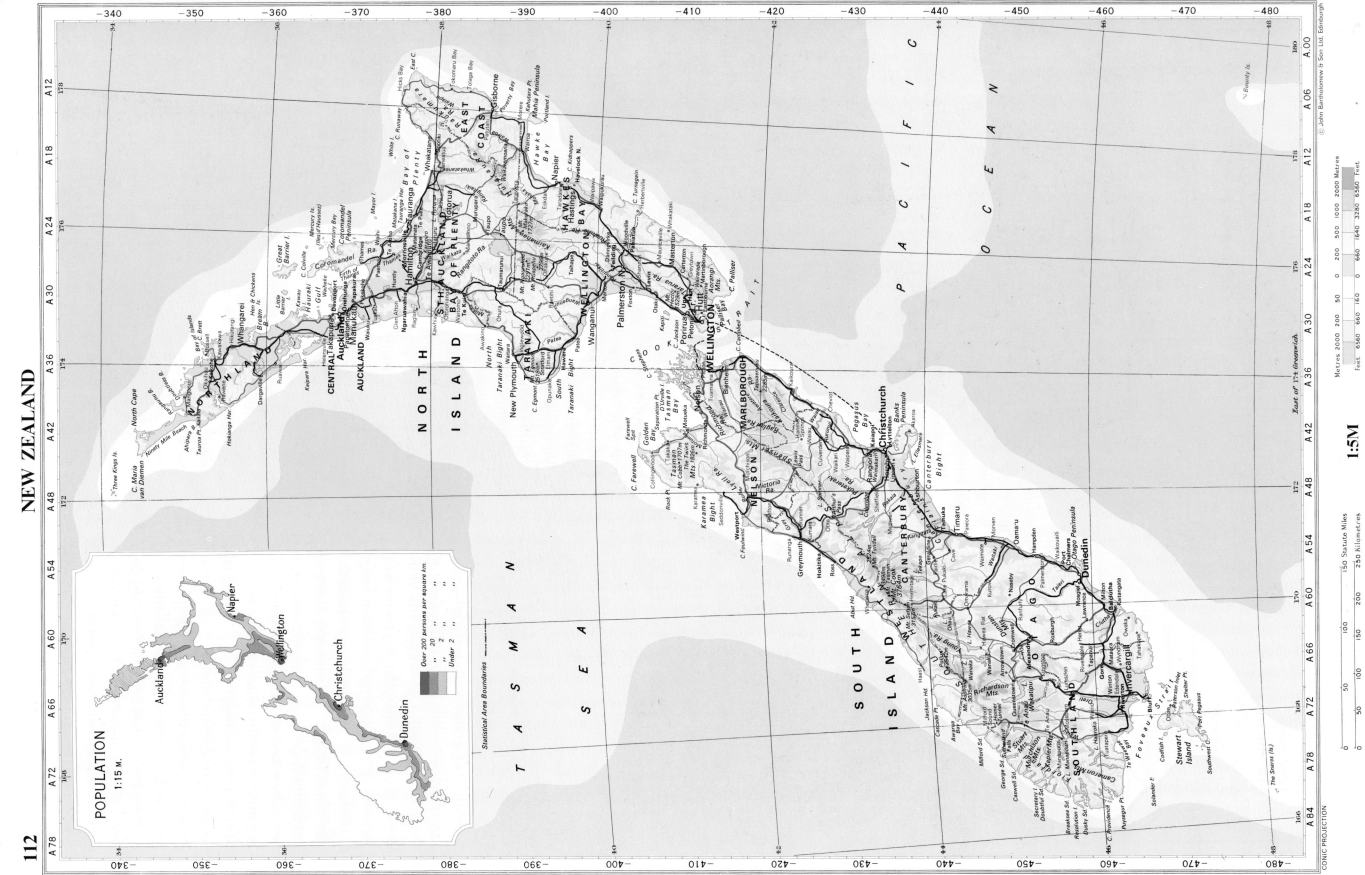

NEW ZEALAND

112

1:5M

© John Bartholomew & Son Ltd. Edinburgh

CONIC PROJECTION

POPULATION
1:15 M.

Over 200 persons per square km.
„ 20 „ „ „ „
„ 2 „ „ „ „
Under 2 „ „ „ „

Statistical Area Boundaries

Metres 2000 200 50
Feet: 6560 660 160

Metres 200 500 1000 2000 Metres
Feet: 660 1640 3280 6560 Feet

150 Statute Miles
250 Kilometres

P A C I F I C   O C E A N

T A S M A N   S E A

NORTH ISLAND

SOUTH ISLAND

GENERAL INDEX

For explanatory notes on the use of Index see page 1 of Atlas.

LIST OF ABBREVIATIONS

Afghan., Afghanistan.
Afr., Africa.
Ala., Alabama.
Alta., Alberta.
Alg., Algeria.
Antarc., Antarctica.
Arch., Archipelago.
Argen., Argentina.
Ariz., Arizona.
Ark., Arkansas.
Aust., Australia.
B., Bay, Bahia.
B.C., British Columbia.
Belg., Belgium, Belgian.
Bots., Botswana.
Bol., Bolivia.
C., Cape, Cabo.
Cal., California.
Can., Canal.
Car., Carolina.
Cel., Celebes.
Cent., Central.
Chan., Channel.
Co., County.
Col., Colony.
Colo., Colorado.
Colomb., Colombia.
Conn., Connecticut.
Cord., Cordillera.
Cr., Creek.
Czech., Czechoslovakia.
Del., Delaware.
Den., Denmark.
Dep., Department.
Des., Desert.
Dist., District.
Div., Division.

Dom., Dominican, Dominion.
E., East, Eastern.
Ecua., Ecuador.
Eiln., Eilanden.
Eng., England.
Equat., Equatorial.
Ethio., Ethiopia.
Fd., Fiord.
Fla., Florida.
Fr., French, France.
F.T.A.I., French Territory of the Afars and the Issas.
G., Gulf.
Ga., Georgia.
Geb., Gebirge.
Ger., Germany.
G.F., Goldfield.
Gt., Great.
Guat., Guatemala.
Harb., Harbour.
Hd., Head.
Hisp., Hispaniola.
Hond., Honduras.
Hung., Hungary.
I., Is., Island, Islands.
Ia., Iowa.
Ida., Idaho.
Ind., Indiana.
Ill., Illinois.
Indon., Indonesia.
It., Italian, Italy.
Iv. Cst., Ivory Coast.
Jap., Japan.
Kan., Kansas.
Ky., Kentucky.
L., Lake, Loch, Lough, Lago.
La., Louisiana.
Lab., Labrador.

Ld., Land.
Leb., Lebanon.
Lit., Little.
Lith., Lithuania.
Lr., Lower.
Madag., Madagascar.
Man., Manitoba.
Mass., Massachusetts.
Maur., Mauritania.
Md., Maryland.
Mex., Mexico.
Mich., Michigan.
Minn., Minnesota.
Miss., Mississippi.
Mo., Missouri.
Mong., Mongolia.
Mont., Montana.
Mozamb., Mozambique.
Mt., Mte., Mount, Monte.
Neb., Nebraska.
Nfd., Newfoundland.
Nev., Nevada.
N.H., New Hampshire.
N.B., New Brunswick.
Nic., Nicaragua.
N.J., New Jersey.
N. Ire., Northern Ireland.
N. Mex., New Mexico.
N.S., Nova Scotia.
N. Dak., North Dakota.
N. Car., North Carolina.
N.S.W., New South Wales.
N.-W. Terr., North-West Territories.
N.Y., New York.

N.Z., New Zealand.
O., Ohio.
Oc., Ocean.
O.F.S., Orange Free State.
S. Dak., South Dakota.
Set., Settlement.
Sol., Solomon.
Som., Somaliland.
Okla., Oklahoma.
Ont., Ontario.
Ore., Oregon.
Oz., Ozero.
Pa., Pennsylvania.
Pac., Pacific.
Pak., Pakistan.
Pan., Panama.
Para., Paraguay.
Pen., Peninsula.
P.E.I., Prince Edward Island.
Phil., Philippines.
Pk., Peak, Park.
Plat., Plateau.
Port., Portuguese, Portugal.
Prot., Protectorate.
Prov., Province.
Pt., Point.
Pto., Puerto.
Qnsld., Queensland.
Que., Quebec.
R., River, Rio.
Ra., Range.
Reg., Region.
Rep., Republic.
Res., Reservoir.
Rhod., Rhodesia.
R.I., Rhode Island.
Russ., Russia.

S.C., South Carolina.
Scot., Scotland.
Sd., Sound.
Switz., Switzerland.
Tanz., Tanzania.
Tenn., Tennessee.
Terr., Territory.
Tex., Texas.
Trans., Transvaal.
U.A.E., United Arab Emirates.
Ukr., Ukraine.
Up., Upper.
U.S.A., United State of America.
U.S.S.R., Union of Soviet Socialist Reps.
Ut., Utah.
Va., Virginia.
Val., Valley.
Venez., Venezuela.
Vict., Victoria.
Vol., Volcano.
Vt., Vermont.
W., West, Western.
Wash., Washington.
W. Indies, West Indies.
Wis., Wisconsin.
Wyo., Wyoming.
Yugosl., Yugoslavia.
Sa., Serra, Sierra.
S., South, Southern.
Sask., Saskatchewan.
Sard., Sardinia.
Sp., Spanish, Spain.
Str., Strait.
Ste., Sta., Saint, Sainte, Santa.
Swed., Sweden.

1

Aachen

Aachen, W. Germany M53+507 48
Aalen, W. Germany K45+350 76
Aalsmeer, Netherlands M30+488 44
Aalst (Alost), Belgium M62+523 44
Aalten, Netherlands M51+519 44
Aarau, Switzerland M42+474 45
Aarburg, Switzerland M46+470 45
Aardenburg, Netherlands M43+473 45
Aare, R., Switzerland M44+472 45
Aargau, canton, Switzerland M41+474 45
Aba, Zaire K88+036 83
Abacaxis, Brazil R82-040 104
Abadan, Iran J70-303 74
Abadeh, Iran J44+312 75
Abaete, Brazil R23-016 105
Abajo Mts., Utah V27+378 94
Abajo Pk., Utah V27+376 98
Abakan, U.S.S.R. F83+537 63
Abancay, Peru S78-137 104
Abashiri, Japan C34+440 68
Abashiri Bay, Japan C32+442 68
Abau, Papua New Guinea C09-102 111
Abaya, L., Ethiopia K42+062 83
Abbasabad, Iran J52+366 75
Abbeville, France T50+320 97
Abbeville, Georgia T59+320 97
Abbeville, Louisiana U12+300 95
Abbeyfeale, Ireland, Rep. N56+524 43
Abbeyleix, Ireland, Rep. N44+529 43
Abbot Ice Shelf, Antarctica 180-730 27
Abbottabad, Pakistan H11+342 72
Abdul Aziz, Jebel, Syria K30+365 74
Abdulino, U.S.S.R. J35+537 61
Abeche, Chad L56+138 81
Abeele, Belgium M74+508 44
Abelessa, Algeria M62+226 80
Abengourou, Ivory Coast N22-068 80
Abeokuta, Nigeria M70+072 80
Aberaeron, Wales N26+522 38
Aberystwyth, Wales N21+517 38
Aberdare, Wales N18+518 38
Aberdeen, Mississippi U14+450 93
Aberdeen, Montana U51+455 93
Aberdeen, S. Dakota V14+450 93
Aberdeen, Washington W23+470 92
Aberdeen L., N.-W. Terr. N12+571 40
Abernethy, Scotland N17+571 40
Abidjan, Benin N24+054 80
Abilene, Kansas U44+389 88
Abilene, Texas U58+324 95
Abingdon, Virginia 142+367 97
Abington, Massachusetts S65+421 96
Abisko, Sweden L66+683 46
Abitibi L., Ontario T28+488 89
Abitibi R., Ontario T40+500 89
Aboyne, Scotland N17+571 40
Abqaiq, Saudi Arabia J61+262 74
Abrantes, Portugal N49+395 52
Abrets, les, France M57+456 54
Abrud, Romania L42+469 58
Abruzzi, dep., Italy M07+420 56
Abtenau, Austria H14+246 70
Abu, India M10+475 48

Abu Deleig, Sudan K68+158 81
Abu Dhabi, U.A.E. J33+245 75
Abu el Jirdhan, Jordan K55+303 76
Abu Jifan, Syria J73+246 74
Abu Kemal, Syria K24+345 74
Abu Abyadh I., U.A.E. J38+243 75
Abu Mombasi, Zaire L46+034 82
Abuna, Brazil S32-098 104
Abu Qurqas, Egypt K86+278 81
Abuye Myeda, mt., Ethiopia K30-106 83
Abu Zabad, Sudan L04+122 81
Abyei, Sudan L08+096 81
Abyn, Sweden L52+650 46
Abyss, U.S.S.R. C30+685 63
Acajutla, Salvador T88+136 101
Acambaro, Mexico U64+200 100
Acaponeta, Mexico V02+225 100
Acapulco, Mexico U59+168 100
Acara & R., Brazil R20-022 105
Acarigua, Venezuela S55+095 104
Acatlan, Mexico U49+182 100
Acayucan, Mexico U41+377 100
Accomac, Virginia S42+377 97
Accra, Ghana N02+056 80
Accrington, England N14+538 37
Achaguas, Venezuela S49+075 104
Achao, Chile S81-424 103
Achil & I., Ireland, Rep. N60+539 42
Achinsk, U.S.S.R. F86+564 63
Achray, Ontario T17+459 91
Ackins I., Bahamas, The S84+225 101
Aconcagua, mt., Argentina S60-325 103
Acoyapa, Nicaragua T61+120 101
Acores, Is., Atlantic Ocean P70-390 80
Acre & B., Israel K60+329 76
Actaeon Group Tuamoru Archipelago X05-228 107
Acton Vale, Quebec S75+457 91
Ada, Minnesota U39+473 93
Ada, Oklahoma U40+348 95
Adairville, Kentucky T71+367 97
Adalia. See Antalya
Adam, Oman J15+223 75
Adama, Ethiopia K34+084 83
Adamello, mt., Italy M27+462 56
Adaminaby, New S. Wales C08-360 109
Adams, New York T06+438 91
Adam's Bridge, India/Sri Lanka G63+091 70
Adams, Mt., Washington W09+462 92
Addis Derra, Ethiopia K38+102 83
Addis Ababa, Ethiopia K38+090 83
Addison, New York T13+421 96
Addison, Pk., Sri Lanka G58+069 70
Adelaer, C., Greenland Q65+610 26
Adelaide, Cape Province L22-328 84
Adelaide, S. Australia C69-350 109
Adelaide Pen., N.-W. Terr. U45-674 88
Adelaide I., Antarctica S50-670 27
Adelboden, Switzerland M45+465 45
Adelie Ld., Antarctica C60-680 27
Adelong, New South Wales C12-354 109
Ademuz, Spain N08+401 53
Aden, Yemen South K00+130 74
Aden, G. of, Africa-Arabia J60+130 30
Adh Dhahiriya, Jordan K60+314 76
Adhoi, India H27+234 70
Adhra, Syria K51+336 76

Adi, I., New Guinea D08-042 65
Adi Kaie, Ethiopia K34+146 83
Adilabad, India G67+197 70
Adirondack Mts., New York S84+444 91
Adi Ugri, Ethiopia K38+148 83
Adi, Italy M18+451 56
Adrano, Sicily M01+376 57
Adrar, Algeria N02+276 80
Adrar, Saudi Arabia J55+201 75
Adria, Italy M18+451 56
Adrian, Michigan T55+419 91
Adriatic Sea, Italy L84+425 56
Aduwa, Ethiopia K36+140 83
Aegean Sea, Greece L39+377 59
Aelre, Belgium M69+511 44
Aerø, Denmark M27+549 47
Aershot, Belgium M61+510 44
Aesch, Switzerland M44+475 45
Afferden, Netherlands M54+516 44
Afua, Brazil R31-004 105
Afghanistan, Asia J12+239 74
Afif, Saudi Arabia K12+239 74
Afognak I., Alaska Y20+582 99
Afrin, Syria K49+365 76
Afula, Israel K58+326 76
Afyon, Turkey K87+387 74
Agab Workei, Ethiopia K48+136 83
Agadez, Niger M42+168 80
Agadir, Morocco N58+304 80
Agalta, India F82+239 71
Agartala, India F82+239 71
Agattu I., Aleutian Is. A40+518 99
Agawa, Ontario T57+476 91
Agde, France M69+433 55
Agen, France M86+442 55
Aghda, Iran J38+325 75
Agordat, Ethiopia K42+154 83
Agno, Switzerland M03+376 57
Agra, India F83+239 71
Agram. See Zagreb
Agrigento, Sicily M08+373 57
Agua, Mt., Washington W08+373 57
Aguarico, I., Mariana Is. C25+180 106
Aghnim, Greece L52+387 59
Aguaray, Argentina S22-222 103
Aguada, Puerto Rico S42+185 101
Aguadilla, Puerto Rico S42+185 101
Aguadulce, Panama T33+082 101
Aguapei, Brazil R26-042 105
Aguascalientes, Mexico U74+218 100
Agudo, Spain N29+390 52
Agudos, Brazil R24-224 105
Aguilar, Spain N28+375 52
Aguilar de Campóo, Spain N19+428 52
Aguilas, Spain N10+374 53
Aguja, Pta., Peru S35-550 103
Agulhas, C., Cape Province L60-348 84
Agusta, W. Australia E29-340 110
Ahar, Iran J77+385 74
Ahmadnagar, India H01+191 70
Ahmadpur East, Pakistan H23+291 72

Aksehir

Ahmadabad, India H14+230 70
Ahraura, India G42+250 73
Ahtopol, Bulgaria L13+421 58
Ahuachapan, Salvador T89+140 101
Ahualulco, Mexico U85+207 100
Ahus, Sweden M04+559 47
Ahvaz, Iran J67+313 74
Ahvenanmaa, Finland L60+603 47
Ahwar, Yemen, South J80+135 74
Aigle, Switzerland M48+463 45
Aijal, India F73+239 71
Aihun(ku, China D45+489 64
Aikawa, Japan C71+380 68
Ailsa Craig, I., Scotland N31+552 41
Aim, U.S.S.R. D06+588 63
Aïn Beïda, Chad M56+461 54
Ain Galaka, Chad L70+180 81
Ain Safra, Mauritania N72+194 80
Ain Sefra, Algeria N62+194 80
Ainsworth, Nebraska U60+426 95
Aintree, England N18+535 37
Aiquile, Bolivia S36+090 83
Air, France N02+437 55
Aird, R., England N07+537 37
Airdrie, Scotland N24+558 41
Aire, France N02+437 55
Aire, R., England N07+537 37
Airolo, Switzerland M38+465 45
Aiyion, Greece L48+383 59
Aiyina, I., Greece L39+377 59
Aisne, dep., France M66+495 54
Aitkin, Minnesota U22+465 93
Aiun, El, Western Sahara N80+270 80
Aix, Mt., Washington W07+469 92
Aix-la-Chapelle. See Aachen
Ajaccio & G., Corsica M38+419 57
Ajaigarh, India G58+249 73
Ajanta, India G85+205 70
Ajanta Ra. See Sahyadriparvat
Ajibba, Saudi Arabia K04+273 74
Ajmer, India H02+263 70
Ajodhya (Ayodhya), India G46+267 73
Ajoewa, Surinam R72+026 105
Akaikot, India G83+176 73
Akan Nat. Park, Japan C36+435 68
Akanthou, Cyprus K67+354 76
Akaroa, New Zealand A42+437 112
Akashi, Japan C58+408 68
Akbarpur, India G60+263 73
Akchar, Afghanistan H53+369 75
Akhisar, Turkey L13+389 74
Akhmim, Syria K46+365 76
Akhtyrka, Ukraine K61+504 60
Akimiski I., N.-W. Terr. T38+532 89
Akita, Japan C57+397 68
Akkrum, Netherlands M55+530 44
Aklavik, N.-W. Territories W86+689 88
Ako, Nigeria M26+104 82
Akola, India G77+207 70
Akpatok I., North-West Territories S49+603 89
Akra, Jebel el, Turkey K54+359 76
Akron, Colorado U80+402 94
Akron, Ohio T39+411 91
Akrotiri Pen., Crete L35+356 59
Aksaray, Turkey K66+383 74
Aksehir, Turkey K82+383 74

Aksha
Aksha, U.S.S.R. E40+503 99
Aksu, Estonia L20+585 47
Akti, Greece L35+403 59
Aktyubinsk, Kazakh. J17+504 62
Akure, Nigeria M58+072 80
Akureyri, Iceland P19+657 46
Akyab, Burma F73+202 71
Alabama, state, U.S.A. I70+326 99
Alabama R., Alabama I74+313 99
Alaejos, Spain N31+413 52
Alagoas, Brazil Q35-096 105
Alagoa de Baixo, Brazil Q44-082 105
Alagoinhas, Brazil Q35-096 105
Alagon, Spain N07+417 52
Alaja, Syria K55+358 76
Alajuela, Costa Rica T55+100 101
Aakurti, U.S.S.R. K85+672 62
Alakpa, Nigeria M64+086 81
Al' Ala, Saudi Arabia K41+267 74
Alameda, California W14+377 92
Alameda, Saskatchewan W14+496 88
Alamogordo, New Mexico V06+330 94
Alamogorda Res., New Mex. U87+346 94
Alamos, Mexico V24+271 100
Alamosa, Colorado V06+374 94
Åland, See Alvenanmeri
Ålands Hav, Sweden-
  Finland L64+600 47
Alapaevsk, U.S.S.R. H80+578 61
Alashir, Turkey L09+384 74
Ala Shan, China F10+394 64
Alaska, state, U.S.A. Y00+630 99
Alaska, G. of, Alaska X60+586 99
Alaska Pen., Alaska Y60+560 99
Alaska Highway, Alaska-Can. X38+632
Alatyr, U.S.S.R. J80+548 61
Alavus, Finland L38+626 46
Alawoona, S. Australia C57-348 109
Al'Ayn, Oman J31+196 75
Alaysky Khrebet, Kirgiz H20+400 62
Alazeyskoye Plat., U.S.S.R. C10+680 63
Abérique, Spain N11+390 53
Abbacete, Spain N11+390 53
Abbada, Spain N03+389 53
Alba Iulia, Romania L39+461 58
Albanel, L., Quebec S78+511 90
Albania, S. Europe L60+410 51
Albany, Alabama I70+342 99
Albion, Michigan I59+423 91
Albany, Georgia I61+367 97
Albany, Kentucky I61+367 97
Albany, Missouri U26+403 95
Albany, New York S83+426 91
Albany, Oregon W19+446 92
Albany, W. Australia E13-350 110
Albany R., Ontario T52+514 89
Al Bayda', Libya L49+326 81
Albarracin, Spain N09+405 53
Alberton, Victoria C20-386 109
Albertville, Prince Edward I. S24+468 90
Albi, France M77+439 55
Albina, Surinam R56+054 105
Albion, Michigan I59+423 91
Albion, New York T19+432 91
Albufeira, Portugal N49+371 52
Albuñol, Spain N19+368 52
Albuquerque, New Mexico V10+350 94
Albury, New South Wales N42+392 52
Alcácer do Sal, Portugal N51+384 52
Alcalá de Chisvert, Spain M99+403 53
Alcalá de Henares, Spain N20+405 52
Alcázar de San Juan, Spain N19+394 52
Alcira, Spain N03+391 53
Alcoláca, Portugal N54+395 52
Alcoléa del Pinar, Spain N15+410 53
Alcoutim, Portugal N45+375 52
Alcoy, Spain N03+387 53
Adabra Is., Indian Ocean J76-093 77
Adama, Chihuahua, Mexico V06+288 100
Adama, Tamaulipas, Mexico U49+229 100
Aldan & R., U.S.S.R. D58+588 63
Aldan R., U.S.S.R. K19+516 61
Alessandria, Italy M38+448 56
Ålesund, Norway M53+625 46
Aletschhorn, mt., Switzerland M42+465 45

Aleutian Is., Bering Sea A00+512 99
Aleutian Ra., Alaska Y40+580 26
Alexander Arch., Alaska X05+575 99
Alexander I., Antarctica S60-700 27
Alexandra, New Zealand A63-452 112
Alexandra, Victoria C26-372 109
Alexandretta. See Iskencerun
Alexandria, Egypt L00+310 81
Alexandria, Louisiana U14+312 95
Alexandria, Minnesota U32+459 93
Alexandria, Ontario S88+453 91
Alexandria, Virginia T13+388 96
Alexandria, L. S. Aust. C65-355 109
Alexandroupolis, Greece L25+408 59
Altamachi, Bolivia S38-167 104
Altamaha R., Georgia T43+318 99
Altamira, Brazil R44-032 105
Altamura, Italy L80+408 57
Altan Bulag, Mongolia E81+503 63
Altar, Mexico V40+307 100
Altata, Mexico V18+246 100
Aitdorf, Switzerland M38+469 45
Aitea, Spain N00+386 53
Altenburg, E. Germany M16+510 48
Altin Kopru, Iraq K05+358 74
Altmark, E. Germany M20+527 48
Alto Molocue, Mozambique K44-156 83
Alton, Illinois U01+390 95
Alton, Missouri U09+367 97
Altona, Germany M30+535 48
Altoona, Pennsylvania T21+405 96
Altrincham, England N14+534 37
Alstätten, Switzerland M33+474 45
Alturas, California W03+415 92
Altus, Oklahoma U56+346 95
Altyn Tagh, China G30+380 30
Al Ugla, Saudi Arabia K43+258 74
Al Uj, Saudi Arabia J66+228 74
Aloksne, Latvia L18+574 47
Alula, Somalia J56+118 83
Alumine, Argentina S66-392 103
Alupka, U.S.S.R. K65+444 60
Alushta, U.S.S.R. K63+446 60
Alvho, Sweden M01+615 47
Alva, Oklahoma U52+368 95
Alvarado, Mexico U35+188 100
Alvear, Argentina S22-352 103
Alvesta, Sweden M03+569 47
Alvin, Texas U32+294 95
Alvito, Portugal N48+383 52
Alvord, L., Oregon V82+424 92
Alwar, India G81+275 72
Alward, New Brunswick S33+462 90
Alyab, Sudan K68+172 81
Alyth, Scotland N19+566 41
Alytus, Lithuania L36+544 47
Amadi, Sudan L44+059 81
Amadjuak, N.-W. Territories S75+641 89
Amadjuak L., N.-W. Terr. S65+648 89
Amakusa Nada, Japan D32+325 68
Amalfi, Italy M03+407 57
Amaliás, Greece L52+378 59
Amami Gunto, Japan D34+283 68
Amanalco, Mexico U60+192 100
Amantea, Italy L84+392 57
Amapá, Brazil R34+020 105
Amarante, Italy J77+320 74
Amarante, Burma F53+218 71
Amaravti, India G73+210 70
Amargosa, Brazil Q59-130 105
Amarillo, Texas U68+352 94
Amasra, Turkey K74+418 74
Amasya, Turkey K55+406 74
Amatignak, U.S.A. A05+508 99
Amatitlán, Guatemala U04+145 100
Amazon, Mths. of the, Brazil R30+006 105
Amazonas, R., Brazil R33-020 105
Amb, Pakistan H12+343 72
Ambala, India G79+304 72
Ambam, Cameroun M22+024 82
Ambar, Iran J06+318 75
Ambarchik, U.S.S.R. B15+697 63
Ambato, Ecuador T22-013 104
Ambatolampy, Madagascar J66-132 83
Ambelau, England N18+544 37
Amberg, Germany M18+494 48
Ambergris Cay, Bahamas, The S70+212 101
Ambergris Cay, Belize T78+180 101
Ambérieu, France M58+460 54
Ambert, France M68+455 54
Ambikapur, India G41+231 73
Ambilobe, Madagascar J66-132 83
Ambleside, England N18+544 37
Amblève, Belgium M53+504 44
Ambohimahasoa, Madagascar J78-212 83
Amboni Boeni, Madagascar J80-164 83
Ambositra, Madagascar J76-206 83
Ambriz, New Hebrides A67+169 106
Ambriz, Angola M10-080 82
Ambrizete, Angola M12-074 82
Amd, Yemen, South J72+154 74
Ameca, Mexico U85+205 100
Ameland, I., Netherlands M55+534 44
Amelia, Italy M16+426 56
American Falls, Idaho V47+428 92
American Fork, Utah V41+404 94
Americus, Georgia T56+320 99
Amersfoort, Netherlands M57+520 44
Amersham, England N04+517 39
Amethi, India G49+262 73
Amfilokía, Greece L43+392 59
Amga & R., U.S.S.R. D18+610 63
Amgu, U.S.S.R. C74+457 63
Amherst, Massachusetts S75+424 96
Amherst, Nova Scotia S25+458 90
Amherst I., Ontario M62+521 44
Amherstburg, Ontario M76+499 54

Angra
Amik Lake, Ontario T28+456 91
Amirdivi I., Indian Oc. H14+110 70
Amingaon, India F79+263 71
Aminuis, S.-W. Africa L64-236 84
Amirante Is., Indian Ocean J40-060 77
Amla, Saudi Arabia K11+206 74
Amlah, Saudi Arabia J89+173 74
Amlwch, Wales N26+534 38
Amm Adam, Sudan K54+164 81
Amman, Jordan K54+319 76
Ammanford, Wales N24+518 38
Amol, Iran J46+364 75
Amorgós, I., Greece L24+372 59
Amos, Quebec T18+488 89
Amoy, See Hsiamen.
Amparo, Brazil R10-225 105
Amqui, Quebec S44+485 90
Amraho, Sudan K78+186 81
Amran, Yemen K06+157 74
Amreli, India H23+214 70
Amriswil, Switzerland M34+475 45
Amritsar, India H01+316 72
Amroha, India G69+289 73
An, Burma F66+198 71
Anabama, S. Australia C59-328 109
Anabta, Jordan K59+323 76
Anandpur, India G81+312 72
Anantapur, India G74+146 70
Anar, Iran J28+309 75
Anarak, Iran J38+333 75
Anardara, Afghanistan H80+328 75
Anatolia, Turkey K80+390 74
Anatuya, Argentina S17-284 103
Anchorage, Alaska A15+645 63
Anchuras, Spain N29+395 52
Anchuma, mt., Bolivia S51-160 104
Ancón, Peru T14-118 104
Ancona, Italy M09+435 56
Ancud, Chile S82-418 103
And Fd., Norway L83+692 46
Andacollo, Argentina S64-371 103
Andalgalá, Argentina S38-275 103
Andalsnes, Norway M44+626 46
Andaman Is. and Sea,
  Bay of Bengal F65+124 71
Andeer, Switzerland M33+466 45
Andelingen, Switzerland M38+476 45
Andenne, Belgium M59+505 44
Andermatt, Switzerland M38+466 45
Anderson, Indiana I64+401 91
Anderson, S. Carolina T46+345 97
Anderson R., N.-W. Terr. W40+684 88
South America S70-429 103
Andevoranto, Madagascar J66-189 83
Andhra Pradesh, India G70+167 70
Andikithira, I., Greece L40+358 59
Andimilos, I., Greece L35+368 59
Andiparos, I., Greece L30+370 59
Andizhan, Uzbek H15+409 62
Andkhui, Afghanistan H59+369 75
Andoas Nuevo, Ecuador T11-023 104
Andorra & rep., Pyrenees M81+425 53
Andover, England N09+512 39
Andover, Massachusetts S67+427 96
Andover, S. Dakota U47+454 93
Åndoya, Norway L86+691 46
Andrada, Mozambique K60-186 84
Andreanof Is., Aleutian Is. Z73+513 99
Andreas, C., Cyprus K62+357 76
Andreyevka, Ukraine K57+488 60
Andria, Italy L83+412 57
Andro, N. Dakota U48+477 93
Andros I., N.-W. Terr. U60+628 88
Angkor, Khmer F06+134 69
Angledool, New S. Wales C12-291 109
Anglesey, I., Wales N27+533 38
Angliers, Quebec T25+475 91
Angmagssalik, Greenland Q55+660 26
Angola, Chile S76-379 103
Angola, New York T24+426 96
Angola, W. Africa L76-100 82
Angora. See Ankara
Angoulême, France M89+456 54
Angoumois, prov., France M89+459 54
Angra, Brazil Q86-229 105

2

Augusta, Georgia T42+334 97
Augusta, Kansas U42+377 95
Augusta, Kentucky T54+387 97
Augusta, Maine S59+444 90
Augusta, Sicily L89+372 52
Augusta, Wisconsin U07+447 91
Augustów, Poland L43+538 49
Augustus, Mt., W. Australia E12-246 110
Auletta, Italy L37+406 57
Aumale, Algeria M68+360 80
Aunis, prov., France N08+461 54
Aura, Finland L44+606 47
Aurangabad, India G33+247 73
Auray, France N18+477 54
Aurillac, France M76+449 55
Aurora, Illinois T80+418 91
Aurora, Ontario T27+440 91
Aus, S.-W. Africa L82-266 84
Au Sable, Michigan T50+445 91
Au Sable Forks, New York S82+445 91
Austin, Minnesota U07+447 91
Austin, Nevada V73+395 92
Austin, Texas U46+303 95
Austin, L., W. Australia E12-276 110
Austral Is., Pacific Oc. Y00-250 107
Australia, Australasia 110-111
Australian Alps, Vic.-N.S.W. C10-368 109
Australian Capital Terr.
  Australia C06-355 109
Austria, Central Europe M06+474 50
Autlan, Mexico U87+197 100
Autun, France M64+470 54
Auvergne, prov., France M72+454 55
Auxerre, France M69+478 54
Aux Sources, Mt.-
  Lesotho L06-288 84
Ava, Burma F54+218 71
Avallon, France M66+475 54
Avalon Pen., Newfoundland R52+473 90
Avaré, Brazil R24-231 105
Avanos, S.-W. Africa M12-184 84
Aveiro, Portugal N52+406 52
Avellaneda, Argentina R80-347 103
Avelino, Italy M01+409 57
Avenir, French Guiana R53+048 105
Aversa, Italy M05+410 57
Avesnes, France M66+501 54
Avesta, Sweden L83+601 47
Aveyron, dep., France N37+441 55
Aviemore, Scotland N23+572 40
Avigliano, Italy L86+408 55
Avignon, France M61+440 55
Aviz, Portugal N47+391 52
Avoca, Iowa U32+414 95
Avoca, Tasmania C14-418 109
Avola, Sicily L89+369 57
Avon, co., England N15+515 38
Avon R., England N10+523 37
Avon R., Scotland N20+574 40
Avranches, France N08+487 54
Awaji Shima, Japan D00+344 68
Awe L., Scotland N32+563 41
Awjilah, Libya L52+292 81
Awusa L., Ethiopia K40+070 83
Axat, France M77+428 55
Axel, Greece L43+397 59
Axel Heiberg, North-West
  Territories U15+790 89
Axminster, England N18+508 38
Ayabaca, Peru T28-046 104
Ayacucho, Argentina R82-371 103
Ayacucho, Peru S85-132 104
Ayaguz, U.S.S.R. G59+480 62
Ayakkum, U.S.S.R. F66+593 63
Ayamonte, Spain N44+372 52
Ayancik, Turkey K61+419 74
Ayaviri, Peru S64-147 104
Aydin, Turkey L13-379 74
Ayerbe, Spain N04+423 53
Ayion Oros, Greece L35+403 59
Aylesbury, England N05+518 38
Aylmer, Ontario T36+428 91
Aylmer, L., N.-W. Territories V20+643 88
Aylsham, England N03+528 39
Aylwin, Quebec T06+460 91
Aymores, Brazil Q67-196 105
Ayora, Spain N06+390 53
Ayr, Queensland C15-195 111
Ayr & R. Scotland N28+555 41
Ayun, Saudi Arabia K08+265 74
Ayutla, Mexico U55+169 100
Ayuthaya, Thailand F27+144 69
Aywalik, Turkey L20-394 74
Azaila, Belgium N03+413 53
Azamgarh, India G41+261 73
Azare, Nigeria M58+116 81
Azaz, Syria K48+366 76
Azerbaydzhanskaya, rep.-
  U.S.S.R. J80+410 62
Azi, Latvia L27+563 47
Azogues, Ecuador T23+026 104
Azov, Sea of, U.S.S.R. K48+460 60
Azpeitia, Spain N14+432 53
Aztec, New Mexico V15+367 98
Azua, Dominican Rep. S64+184 101
Azuaga, Spain N34+382 52
Azul, Argentina R89-367 103
Azzan, Yemen D.R. J74+144 74
Az Zubayr, Iraq J74+304 74
Azzaila, Spain N03+413 73

Babahoya, Ecuador T26-018 104
Babai, I., Indonesia D32-080 65
Babati, Tanzania K56-042 83
Babel I., Tasmania C11-399 109
Babenna, Syria K54-356 76
Babine L., Brit. Columbia W38+550 88
Babispe, Mexico V23+305 100
Babol, Iran J44+366 75
Baboua, Nigeria M40+126 82
Babuyan Is., Philippines D80+192 64
Babylon, Iraq K03+326 74
Bacabal, Brazil R69-053 105
Bacadehuachi, Mexico V24+298 100
Bacalar, Mexico U24+090 100
Bacan, I., Indonesia D45+006 65
Bacău, Romania L18+465 58
Bacerac, Mexico V23+303 100
Bach long Vi, I., N. Vietnam E74+202 69
Back R., N.-W. Territories U40+660 88
Backbone Mts., W. Va.-Md. T27+393 96
Bäckefors, Sweden M17+588 47
Backergunge, Bangladesh F88+224 71
Backstairs Pass., S. Aust. C72-357 109
Bac-Ninh, N. Vietnam E83+212 69
Bacoachi, Mexico V24+309 100
Bacolod, Philippines D72+106 65
Bacup, England N13+537 37
Bada, Saudi Arabia K48+269 74
Badajoz, Brazil R17-026 105
Badajoz, Spain N41+389 52
Badalona, Spain M17+415 53
Badarma, U.S.S.R. F15+578 63
Badas, Brunei E33+046 65
Bad Axe, Michigan T48+438 91
Bad Ems, W. Germany M44+503 48
Baden, Germany M43+480 48
Baden, Switzerland M40+475 45
Baden-Baden, Germany M40+487 48
Badin, Pakistan H36+246 70
Bad Kissingen, W. Germany M29+502 48
Bad Lands, Nebraska, etc. U80+426 98
Badnera, India G72+218 70
Badrinath, India G63+308 70
Baduen, Somalia J74+070 83
Badulla, Sri Lanka G53+070 70
Baena, Spain N26+376 52
Baerle-Duc, Belgium M60+514 44
Baeza, India G35+257 73
Baeza, Turkey K28+316 75
Baffin B., N.-W. Territories S30+714 89
Baffin I., N.-W. Territories S60+680 89
Bafia, Cameroon M24+046 81
Batoulabé, Mali N64+136 80
Baf'q, Iran J21+291 75
Bafra, Turkey K54+415 74
Bagata, Zaire L72-038 82
Bage, Brazil R54-312 103
Bagenalstown. See Muine Bheag
Baghdad, Iraq K04+334 74
Bagherhat, Bangladesh G01+227 73
Baghin, Iran J19+302 75
Baghpat, India G76+290 72
Bagnulun Hd. Ireland, Rep. N41+522 43
Bagley, Minnesota U32+475 93
Bagnell, Missouri U16+382 97
Bagnols-sur-Ceze, France M62+442 55
Bagotville, Quebec S65+484 90
Baguio, Philippines D86+165 65
Bahadurgarh, India G76+283 72
Bahamas, The, West Indies T10+250 101
Bahama, I., Grand, Bahamas, The T20+266 101
Bahawalpur, Pakistan H19+294 72
Baheri, India G63+287 73
Bahia. See Salvador
Bahia Blanca, Argentina S13-386 103
Bahia de Caráquez, Ecuador T33-007 104
Bahia Laura, Argentina S39-483 103
Bahia Negra, Paraguay R79-202 103
Bahia Solano, Colombia T14+063 104
Bahraich, India G50+276 73
Bahrain, The Gulf J37+261 75
Bahret el Ateibe, Syria K50+335 76
Bahret el Hijane, Syria K50+333 76
Bahu Kalat, Iran H81+257 75
Bahus, Brazil R48-184 105
Baiao, Brazil R26-028 105
Baibokoum, Chad L28+078 81
Baidaratskaya B., U.S.S.R. J14+526 61
Baie St Paul, Quebec S63+474 91
Baie Verte, New Brunswick S25+460 90
Baiji, Iraq K09+350 74
Baikal, L., U.S.S.R. F51+617 63
Bailén, Spain N26+381 52
Baile-Atha-Cliath. See Dublin
Baillie, N.-W. Territories W50+706 88
Baimak Tanalykovo, U.S.S.R. J14+526 61
Bainbridge, Georgia T57+309 97
Bairnsdale, Victoria C14-378 109
Baital Faqih, Yemen K10+146 74
Baitk Bogdo, China F80+450 64
Baixo Longa, Angola L66-164 84
Baja California, state, Mexico V60+300 100
Bajan, Mexico U68+265 100
Bakel, U.S.S.R. J37+552 61
Bakel, Senegal N74+148 80
Baker, Montana U86+463 93
Baker, Oregon V77+448 92
Baker, I., Pacific Ocean Z70+004 106
Baker, L., N.-W. Territories U40+644 88
Baker, Mt., Washington W10+483 98
Baker, Mt., Arizona V38+344 94
Bakersfield, California V38+354 92
Bakhasar, India H23+247 70
Bakhtiari. See Machilipatnam
Baklol, India H24+247 70
Bakonyerdo, Hungary L72+473 49
Baku, Azerbaydzhan J50+405 62

Balabac Str., Philippines E20-076 65
Balaghat, India G58+220 70
Balakava, U.S.S.R. F79+552 63
Balakava, U.S.S.R. K68+445 60
Bala Murghab, Afghanistan H70+356 75
Balancan, Mexico U10+178 100
Balaquer, Spain M83+418 53
Balashov, U.S.S.R. K11+515 61
Balasore, India G18+215 71
Balat, Egypt L04+256 81
Balaton, L., Hungary L74+469 49
Balazote, Spain N13+389 53
Balboa, Panama T27+090 101
Balbriggan, Ireland. Rep. N37+536 42
Balcarce, Argentina R80-379 103
Balchik, Bulgaria L11+434 58
Balclutha, New Zealand U10+353 95
Bald Knob, Arkansas U63+479 93
Bald Knob, W. Virginia C30-413 109
Bali, L., Indonesia E30-084 65
Balikesir, Turkey L13+397 74
Balikpapan, Borneo E19-012 65
Balkh, Afghanistan H49+368 75
Balkhash & Oz., Kazakh H00+469 62
Ballabgarh, India G76+283 72
Ballaghaderreen, Ireland, Rep. N31+567 42
Ballantrae, Scotland N31+567 41
Ballarat, Victoria C60-210 111
Ballater, Scotland N18+570 40
Balli, Mali N52+154 80
Ballina, Ireland, Rep. N49+533 42
Ballina, N.S. Wales B69-289 109
Ballinasloe, Ireland, Rep. N49+533 43
Ballindine, Ireland. Rep. N54+537 42
Ballingarry, Ireland. Rep. N53+525 43
Ballinluig, Scotland N22+566 41
Ballinrobe, Ireland. Rep. N55+536 42
Ballinskelligs B., Ireland. Rep. N62+518 43
Ballston Spa, New York S83+430 96
Ballybay, Ireland, Rep. N41+541 42
Ballybofey, Ireland, Rep. N47+548 42
Ballybunion, Ireland, Rep. N56+525 43
Ballycastle, Ireland, Rep. N37+552 42
Ballyclare, N. Ireland N36+547 42
Ballyconnell B. Ireland, Rep. N45+541 42
Ballycotton B. Ireland, Rep. N48+521 43
Ballyduff, Ireland, Rep. N50+535 43
Ballygawley, N. Ireland N44+540 42
Ballyhaise, Ireland, Rep. N53+538 42
Ballyhaunis, Ireland, Rep. N53+543 42
Ballyjamesduff, Ireland, Rep. N47+534 43
Ballymahon, Ireland, Rep. N37+549 42
Ballymena, N. Ireland N39+551 42
Ballymoney, N. Ireland N35+544 42
Ballymote, Ireland, Rep. N51+541 42
Ballynahinch, N. Ireland N33+543 42
Ballyquintin Pt., N. Ireland N44+528 42
Ballyragget, Ireland, Rep. N49+545 43
Ballyshannon, Ireland, Rep. N53+53i 42
Ballyvaghan, Ireland, Rep. N55+531 43
Balmoral, Victoria C49-372 109
Balomeo, Angola M00-124 82
Balotra, India H16+258 70
Balrampur, India G47+274 73
Balramald, New S. Wales C39-346 109
Balsam, L., Ontario T23+446 91
Balta, Ukraine L02+479 60
Baltanas, Spain N26+419 52
Baltic Sea, N.-W. Europe 47
Baltimore, Ireland, Rep. N56+515 43
Baltimore, Maryland T10+393 96
Baltinglass, Ireland, Rep. N40+529 43
Baltistan, Kashmir H60+275 70
Baltiysk, U.S.S.R. L60+547 47
Baluchistan, Pakistan H60+275 70
Balurghat, India G07+252 73
Balya, Nigeria M08+116 81
Bama, Nigeria M08+126 80
Bamako, Mali N48+126 80
Bamba, Cent. Afr. Rep. L56+056 88
Bamberg, W. Germany M25+499 48
Bamenda, Cameroon M30+058 81
Bamfield, Michigan T53+446 91
Bamian, Afghanistan H43+348 75
Bampton, England N21+510 38
Bampur, Iran H87+272 75
Banas, R., India H24+247 70
Banat, Romania, state L50+455 58
Banayan, Saudi Arabia J53+232 75
Banbridge, N. Ireland N38+544 42
Banbury, England N08+521 38
Ban Chamai, Thailand F32+082 69
Banda, India G58+255 73
Banda, Atjeh, Sumatra F59+056 65
Banda Sea, Indonesia D50-055 65
Bandar. See Machilipatnam
Bandar Abbas, Iran J22+272 75

Bandar Jissah, Oman J08+235 75
Bandar Shah, Iran J36+370 75
Bandera, Argentina S13-289 103
Banderas, B., Mexico V03+206 100
Bandiagara, Mali N22+140 80
Bandikui, India G81+269 70
Bandin Tologo, China F07+412 64
Band-i-Qir, Iran J66+316 74
Bandirma, Turkey L12+404 74
Bandol, France M56+431 55
Bandol & R., Ireland, Rep. N52+517 43
Bandundu, Zaire L76-034 82
Bandung, Java E75-068 65
Baned, Cuba T05+210 101
Bañeza, la, Spain N35+422 52
Banff, Scotland N15+577 40
Banff & Park, Alberta V63+510 88
Bangalore, Congo L12+040 83
Bangalore, India G74+131 70
Bangassou, Cent. Afr. Rep. L42+048 81
Bangka, I., Indonesia E84-022 65
Bangkok. (Krung Thep),
  Thailand G27+138 69
Bangladesh, S. Asia G05+246 71
Bang Mun Nak, Thailand F28+160 65
Bangor, Maine S53+448 90
Bangor, N. Ireland N34+546 42
Bangor, Pennsylvania T02+408 96
Bangor, Wales N25+532 38
Bang Saphan Yai, Thailand F33+113 69
Bangui, Cent. Afr. Rep. L68+044 81
Bangweulu L., Zambia L02-112 83
Ban Houei Sai, Laos F27+203 69
Bania, Cent. Afr. Rep. L84+040 82
Banica, Dominican Rep. S69+190 101
Baniyas, Syria K54+352 76
Baniyas, Syria K56+332 76
Banja Luka, Yugoslavia L77+448 56
Banjarmasin, Indonesia E32-034 65
Ban Jaruga, Yugoslavia L79+454 56
Banjul, Gambia P10+134 80
Banka, India G18+249 73
Banki, India G26+203 71
Bankipore, India G29+256 73
Banks I., N.-W. Territories W00+730 88
Banks I., Queensland C46-102 111
Banks Is., Pacific Ocean A40-437 112
Banks Pen., New Zealand A40-437 112
Banks Str., Tasmania C12-406 109
Bann R., India G17+232 73
Bann R., N. Ireland N37+544 42
Bannu, Pakistan H26+330 72
Bañolas, Spain M73+421 53
Baños de Montemayor, Spain N35+403 52
Ban-pot, Thailand F31+160 69
Banzare Coast, Antarctica D65-660 27
Bansda, India G43+272 73
Bansi, India H09+208 70
Banswara, India H03+236 70
Bantalor, New Brunswick S38+463 90
Ban Thakham, Thailand F34+089 69
Bantry & B., Ireland, Rep. N57+517 43
Banu, Afghanistan H34+356 75
Banyak Kep., Indonesia F46+022 65
Banyo, Cameroon M20+068 81
Banyuwang, Java E34+082 65
Banzville, See Bandundu
Bapaume, France M73+501 54
Baquedano, Chile S58-230 103
Baquba, Iraq K02+337 74
Bar, Yugoslavia L65+421 58
Bara, Sudan K88+138 81
Barabanki, India G53+270 73
Baraboo, Wisconsin T89+435 91
Baracoa, Cuba S87+203 101
Barada, Syria K47+359 76
Barahona, Dominican Rep. S66+182 101
Barail Ra., India F70+252 71
Baraimi, U.A.E. J26+243 75
Barak R., India J31+266 75
Baramula, Kashmir H04+342 72
Baranagar, India G09+227 73
Baranof I., Alaska X00+570 99
Baranovichi, U.S.S.R. L23+532 60
Baranów, Poland L51+505 49
Barão de Melgaço, Brazil S10+177 105
Barataria, B., Louisiana U00+292 95
Barbacena, Brazil Q83-212 105
Barbados, I., Windward Is. R88+132 101

Barbosa, Colombia T19+016 104
Barcelona, Venezuela S27+101 104
Barcelonnette, France N74+144 80
Barcelos, Portugal N74+148 80
Barco de Avila, el, Spain N33+404 52
Barcoo, R., Queensland C34-242 111
Bardera, Somalia K45+245 73
Bardi, India G45+245 73
Bardsey I., Wales L30+318 81
Bardstown, Kentucky T63+378 97
Bareilly, India G63+284 73
Barents Sea, Arctic Ocean K30+750 62
Barentsova, I., Arctic Ocean L50+785 62
Barfrush. See Babol
Bargal, Somalia J54+112 83
Barh, India J64+304 74

Index

Index

Curico, Chile S67-350 103
Curiplaya, Colombia S89-003 104
Curitiba, Brazil R25-256 103
Curitibanos, Brazil R34-273 103
Curlewis, New South Wales B88-311 109
Curnamona, S. Australia C63-316 109
Curora, Mozambique K42-116 83
Currabubula, New S. Wales B86-312 109
Curraes Novos, Brazil Q39-062 105
Curralinho, Brazil R28-017 105
Currane, L. Ireland, Rep. N61+518 43
Currann Pen., (Corraun),
  Ireland, Rep. N59+539 42
Currituck Sd., N. Carolina T04-364 97
Curtis, I., Pacific Ocean Z80-305 106
Curuay, Gde. do, L., Brazil R62-022 105
Curuca, Brazil R17-006 105
Curupachi, Brazil R76-076 105
Curuzú Cuatia, Argentina R78-298 103
Curwensville, Pennsylvania T21+410 96
Cury, Brazil R63-039 105
Cushendall, N. Ireland N36+551 42
Cushendun, N. Ireland N36+551 42
Cushing, Oklahoma U40+359 95
Custer, S. Dakota U82+437 93
Cut Bank, Montana V44+486 93
Cuthbert, Georgia T59+318 97
Cuttack, India G24+204 71
Cutra L., India G24-204 71
Cuxhaven, W. Germany M38+539 48
Cuzco, Peru S72-135 104
Cyclades, See Kikladhes, Is.
Cygnet, Tasmania C18-432 109
Cynthiana, Kentucky T56+385 97
Cyrenaica, Libya L50-292 81
  terranean Sea K72-350 76
Cyrene. See Shahhat
Czechoslovakia, rep.
  Central Europe 50-51
Czersk, Poland L72+538 49
Czestochowa, Poland L65+508 49
Dabakala, Ivory Coast N26+084 80
Dabaro, Colombia J68+064 83
Dabeiba, Colombia T07+070 104
Dabie, Poland M02+534 48
Dabola, Guinea N66+108 80
Dabrowa Górnicza, Poland L65+504 49
Dacca, Bangladesh F87+237 71
Dadanawa, Guyana R88+028 104
Dade City, Florida T56+281 97
Dadni, India G82+286 72
Dagana, Senegal P04+164 80
Dagaria, Somalia K06+106 83
Dagash, Sudan K70+190 81
Dagda, Latvia L15+561 47
Dagenham, England M89+515 39
Dagupan, Philippines D88+160 65
Dahlak Arch., Ethiopia K28+156 83
Dahomey, rep. See Benin
Daimiel, Spain N22+391 52
Dairen, See Luta
Dairut, Egypt K86+276 81
Daisetsuzan Nat. Park, Japan C44+435 68
Dajarra, Queensland C63-218 111
Dakar, Senegal P14+146 80
Dakhla, Mauritania P06+236 80
Dakovica, Yugoslavia L58+424 58
Dal, Norway M22+603 47
Dal Alv, Sweden L80+602 47
Dalandzadgad, Mongolia F02+437 64
Dala, Angola L58-112 82
Dalbandin, Pakistan G30+290 70
Dalbeattie, Scotland N23+549 41
Dalbo Sjön, Sweden M12+589 47
Dalby, Queensland B83-270 111
Dalen, Netherlands M49+527 44
Dalen, Norway M42+595 47
Dalgety, New S. Wales C07-364 109
Dalhart, Texas U75+360 98
Dalhousie, New Brunswick S38+481 90
Dalhousie, India G84+325 72
Dalkeith, Scotland N18+559 41
Dalkey, Ireland, Rep. N36+533 43
Dallas, Texas U41+328 95
Dallas, The, Oregon W07+456 92
Dalmacio Velez, Argentina S22-327 103
Dalmatia, Yugoslavia L82+437 56
Dalmatovo, U.S.S.R. H73+562 61
Dalmellington, Scotland N25+554 41
Daloa, Ivory Coast N38+070 80
Dalry, Scotland N28+557 41
Dalrymple, Mt., Queensland B84+325 72
Dalton, England N19+542 37
Dalton, Ontario T54+481 91
Datongani, India G35+240 73
Dalwhinnie, Scotland N25+569 40
Daly, N. Terr., Australia D22-126 110
Daly Waters, N. Terr., Aust. D10-162 110
Dam, Surinam R60+046 105
Damanhur, Egypt K88+310 81
Daman, l., Indonesia D38-072 65
Damar, l., Indonesia D38-072 65
Damascus (Damas), Syria K52+335 75
Damavand, mt. Iran J48+360 75
Damghan, Iran L38-068 82
Damietta, Egypt K89+314 81
Damiya, Jordan K57+321 76
Damman Ad. Saudi Arabia J57+265 75
Damoh, India G63+238 73
Dampier, Arch., W. Aust. E22-204 110
Dampier Land, W. Australia D73-174 110
Dampier Str., Indonesia D26-007 65
Dana, Mt., California V85+379 92
Danbury, Connecticut S81+414 96
Danby, California V62+347 92
Dandenong, Victoria C29-380 109
Danforth, Maine S47+457 90
Danger Pt., Cape Province L64-348 84

Dangra Yum L., Tibet G20+310 71
Danilov, U.S.S.R. K29+582 60
Dankaz, Ethiopia K44+124 83
Danmark Fd., Greenland P85+810 26
Dannemora, Sweden L74+603 34
Dannevirke, New Zealand A23-400 112
Danville, New York T16+426 96
Danube (Dunarea, Donau) R.,
  Cent. Europe L70+450 51
Danville, Illinois T76+401 95
Danville, Kentucky T59+376 97
Danville, Pennsylvania T10+410 96
Danville, Virginia T26+366 97
Danzig, See Gdansk
Danzig, G. of, Poland L66+546 49
Daolatabad, Afghanistan H60+364 75
Daqq-e-Patargan,
  Iran-Afghanistan H88+341 75
Daraban Kalan, Pakistan H28+317 72
Daraw, Egypt K72+240 81
Darb, Saudi Arabia K16+175 74
Darbhanga, India G24+262 73
Dardanelles, Turkey L23+400 74
Darende, Turkey K45+386 74
Dar-es-Salaam, Tanzania K34-070 83
Dargai, Pakistan H19+345 72
Dargan, India G33+217 71
Dargaville, New Zealand A59+348 112
Dargo, Victoria C16-375 109
Darien, Georgia T39+314 97
Darien, G. of, Colombia T10+082 104
Darjeeling, India G10+270 73
Darling Ra., W. Australia E22-314 110
Darling, R., N. S. Wales C44-336 109
Darling Downs, Queensland C00-276 111
Darlington, Nova Scotia S21+447 90
Darlington, S. Carolina T29+343 97
Darlington, Wisconsin U01+426 95
Darlington Point, N.S.W. C24-346 109
Darkowo, Poland L82+544 49
Darmstadt, W. Germany M38+499 48
Daroca, Spain N08+411 53
Dart, C. Antarctica W10-720 27
Dart R., England N22+505 38
Dartmoor, England N23+506 38
Dartmouth, Victoria C53-380 109
Dartmouth, Nova Scotia S21+447 90
Darton, India G24+400 74
Daru, I., Papua New Guinea C41-091 111
Darun, Iran J58+330 75
Daruvar, Yugoslavia L77+456 56
Darwen, England N15+537 37
Darwin, N. Terr., Australia D24-124 110
Darwin, mt., Chile S56-548 103
Darwin Mt., Rhodesia K80-168 84
Daryabad, India G51+269 73
Daryácheh e Bakteigan L.,
  Iran J36+295 75
Daryácheh-ye-Namak, Iran J50+348 75
Daryácheh-ye-Rezá'iyeh, Iran J88+378 74
Dasara, Bangladesh G00+239 73
Dashibalbar, Mongolia E34+495 64
Dashk R., Pakistan H78+256 70
Dasht Ab, Iran J21+289 75
Dashti, Iran H82+255 75
Daska, Pakistan H04+323 72
Daspalla, India G23+203 71
Daspur, India G21+220 73
Datia, India G69+256 73
Datu, India G86+318 72
Datagani, India G63+280 73
Daudnagar, India G33+250 73
Daugavgriva, Latvia L36+570 47
Daugavpils, Latvia L21+559 47
Daulatabad, India G88+200 70
Daule, Ecuador T30-018 104
Dauleteabad, Iran J35+361 75
Dauphin, Manitoba U04+509 88
Dauphin, prov., France M56+449 55
Davao & G., Philippines D57+070 65
Davenport Ra., N.T., Aust. D00-209 111
Davenport, Iowa U04+415 95
Daventry, England N07+523 37
David, Panama T44+085 101
David City, Nebraska U43+412 95
Davignab, S.-W. Africa L62-276 84
Davis Mts., Texas U84+308 94
Davis Sea, Antarctica F60-650 27
Davos Dorf, Switzerland M31+468 45
Davos Platz, Switzerland M31+468 45
Davy Sd., Greenland W60+580 26
Dawlish, England F41+170 71
Dawna Ra., Burma F41+170 71
Dawson, Georgia T57+318 97
Dawson, Minnesota U36+449 93
Dawson, New Mexico V00-366 94
Dawson, N. Dakota U59+469 93
Dawson, Yukon X25+643 88
Dawson Ra., Yukon X22+629 88
Dawson Creek, B.C. W02+558 88
Dawsonville, Georgia T55+344 97
Dax, France N06+437 55
Daylesford, Victoria C35-374 109
Dayton, Tennessee T60+355 97
Dayton, Ohio T55+398 91
Daytona Beach, Florida T36+292 97
De Aar, Cape Province L36-308 84
Dead Sea, Jordan-Israel K56+314 76
Deakin, S. Dakota U82+446 98
Deal, England M82+512 39
Dean, Forest of, England S27-304 103
Dean Funes, Argentina S27-304 103
Dease L., Brit. Columbia W55+592 88
Dease Lake, Brit. Columbia W55+592 88
Dease Str., N.-W. Terr. V20+682 88
Death Valley, California V72+366 92
Deauville, France N00+494 54
Debar, Yugoslavia L57+416 58
Debec, New Brunswick S46+461 90
Debess, U.S.S.R. J36+576 61
Deblin, Poland L49+506 49
Debno, Poland L92+527 48
Debra Markos, Ethiopia K42+104 83
Debrecen, Hungary L51+475 49
Derecske, Hungary L47+546 49

Decaturville, Tennessee T79+355 97
Deccan, India G80+130 70
Deception, I., South Shetlands S04-630 27
Déčin, Czechoslovakia M05+508 48
Decize, France M69+468 54
Decorah, Iowa U11+412 95
Dedeagach. See Alexandroupolis
Dedham, Massachusetts S67+423 96
Dédougou, Upper Volta N20+122 80
Dedza, Malawi K64-142 83
Dee R., Scotland N12+571 40
Dee R., Scotland N12+548 37
Dee R., Wales N18+530 38
Deel R., Ireland, Rep. N54+526 43
Deep Creek L., Maryland T26+395 96
Deepwater, New S. Wales B79-294 109
Deer I., Maine S52+442 90
Deer Lake, Newfoundland R74+492 90
Deer Lodge, Montana V46+464 92
Deer River, Minnesota U23+473 93
Defferrari, Argentina R87-384 103
De Funiak Springs, Florida T67+307 97
Degana, India H02+270 70
Degerfors, Sweden L62+642 46
De Gerlache Str., Antarctica S20-650 27
Degrad, Brazil R39+021 105
De Grey, R., W. Australia E02-204 110
Deh Bid, Iran J41+306 75
Dehdez, Iran J58+318 75
Dehra (Dehra Dun), India G71+303 72
Dehrud, Iran J50+290 75
Deim Zubeir, Sudan L22+078 81
Deinze, Belgium M69+510 44
Deir 'Ali, Syria K52+332 76
Deir Atiye, Syria K49+341 76
Deir ez Zor, Syria K29+354 74
Deir Hafir, Syria K44+361 76
Deir Shemil, Syria K52+352 76
Dej, Romania L37+471 49
De Kalb, Mississippi T82+328 97
De Kalb, Illinois T82+419 95
De Kastri, U.S.S.R. C55+515 63
Dekoven, Kentucky T79+376 97
Delano, California V45+385 98
Delano Pk., Utah V44+384 94
Delavan, Wisconsin T82+427 91
Delaware, state, U.S.A. T03+391 99
Delaware B., Del.-New Jersey T01+391 96
Delaware City, Delaware T03+396 96
Delaware R., New York, etc. T01+405 96
Delden, Netherlands M50+523 44
Delegate, New S. Wales C06-370 109
Deleitosa, Spain N33+396 52
Delft, Netherlands M63+519 44
Delfzijl, Netherlands M48+533 44
Delgado C., Mozambique K26-108 83
Delger, Mongolia E56+457 64
Delgo, Sudan K86+200 81
Delhi, India G77+286 72
Delhi, New York T00+423 96
Dellenbaugh, Mt., Arizona V51+363 92
Dellys, Algeria M66+366 80
Delmenhorst, W. Germany M39+530 48
Del Norte, Colorado V08+376 94
Deloraine, Tasmania C20-415 109
Del Rio, Texas U66+294 94
Delta, Colorado V18+387 94
Delta, Louisiana U06+324 97
Delta, Missouri T89+372 97
Delta, Pennsylvania T08+397 96
Delta, Utah V46+396 94
Delungra, New S. Wales B85-296 109
Demanda, Sa. de la, Spain N18+422 52
Demchok, Tibet G63+326 70
Deming, New Mexico V18+323 94
Demini Dagh, Turkey L10+391 74
Demmin, E. Germany M12+539 48
Demopolis, Alabama T77+325 97
Denbigh, Wales N20+532 38
Denbigh, co., England N20+532 38
Denderleeuw, Belgium M66+509 44
Dendermonde, Belgium M65+511 44
Denekamp, Netherlands M48+533 44
Den Haag. See 's Gravenhage
Denham Ra., Queensland C08-260 111
Denia, Spain M89+388 53
Deniliquin, New S. Wales C30-356 109
Denison, Texas U32+420 95
Denison, Iowa U39+338 95
Denizli, Turkey L05+377 74
Denmark, New S. Wales B86-324 109
Denmark, S. Carolina T37+333 97
Denmark, kingdom, W. Eur.
Denmark Str., Greenland, etc. Q00+670
Den Oever, Netherlands M60+529 44
Den Blanche, mt., Switz. M44+460 45
De Panne, Belgium M74+511 44
Denton, Maryland T05+389 91
Denton, Texas U42+332 95
D'Entrecasteaux Is.,
  Papua New Guinea B80-100 111
D'Entrecasteaux Pt.,
  W. Australia E24-348 110
Denver, Colorado V00+397 94
Deoband, India G74+297 72
Deobhog, India G44+200 71
Deogarh, India G32+214 71
Deoghar, India G89+320 72
Deoli, India G88+257 70
Deoria, India G37+265 73
De Pere, Wisconsin T78+445 91
Deposit, New York T03+421 91
Depot Harbor, Ontario T31+453 91
Dera, Syria K53+326 76
Dera Bugti, Pakistan H35+291 70
Dera Ghazi Khan, Pakistan H26+301 72
Dera Ismail Khan, Pakistan H25+318 72
Dera Nanak, India G89+320 72
Derbent, U.S.S.R. J89+422 62
Derby, W. Australia D68-172 110
Derby & co. England N09+529 37
Derby, co., England N09+529 37
Derg, L., Ireland, Rep. N47+546 42
Derg L. Ireland, Rep. N50+530 43
Derg R. N. Ireland N46+547 42

De Ridder, Louisiana U20+308 95
De Rijp, Netherlands M61+525 44
Dermott, Arkansas U07+336 95
Derna, (Dernah), Libya L44+326 81
Dernberg C., S.-W. Africa L86-278 84
Derravaragh L., Ireland. Rep. N44+537 42
Derryveagh Mts.,
  Ireland, Rep. N49+550 42
Derudeb, Sudan K54+174 81
De Ruyter, New York T05+428 96
Derventa, Yugoslavia L73+450 56
Derwent R., England N12+548 37
Derwent R., England N05+538 37
Derwent R., Tasmania C22-424 109
Derwent Water, England N19+546 37
Des Arc, Arkansas U09+350 97
Deschaillons, Quebec S72+466 91
Descalvados, R. Argentina S50-468 44
Deshambault L., Sask. V00+546 88
Des Moines & R., Iowa U22+416 95
Desna, R. Ukraine K84+512 60
Desolacion, I., Chile S84-532 103
Desolation R., Greenland R25+610 26
De Soto, Missouri U04+382 95
Dessau, E. Germany M16+518 48
Deta, Romania L53+454 58
Detroit, Michigan T48+424 91
Detroit Lakes, Minnesota U35+468 93
Dett, Rhodesia L18-186 84
Deurne, Netherlands M55+515 44
Deux-Sèvres, dep., France N03+466 54
Déva, Romania L43+459 58
Dévavanya, Hungary L54+471 49
Deventer, Netherlands M53+523 44
Deveron R., Scotland N15+577 40
Devil's Elbow, Scotland N21+569 41
Devils Lake, N. Dakota U53+481 93
Devizes, England L34+417 58
Devin, Bulgaria L37+471 49
Devon, co., England N22+508 38
Devon I., N.-W. Territories T60+750 89
Devonport, England N25+504 38
Devonport, New Zealand A31-368 112
Devonport, Tasmania C22-412 109
De Witt, Arkansas U08+343 97
Dewsbury, England N10+537 37
Dexter, Maine S56+450 90
Dexter, Missouri U04+368 95
Dezful, Iran J70+324 74
Dhaba, Saudi Arabia K56+274 74
Dhahran, Saudi Arabia J58+263 75
Dhak, Pakistan H15+325 72
Dhamar, Yemen K04+147 74
Dhampur, India K69+293 73
Dhamra, India G18+208 71
Dhamtari, India G50+208 70
Dhang Ra., Nepal G48+282 73
Dhangain, India G34+252 73
Dhank, Oman J23+236 75
Dhankuta, Nepal G16+270 73
Dhariya, Saudi Arabia K13+247 74
Dhariyagath, India G41+224 73
Dharmkot, India G88+309 72
Dharmsala, India G82+322 72
Dharwar, India K55+315 76
Dhaulagiri, mt., Nepal G40+287 73
Dhiban, Jordan K55+315 76
Dhidhimotikhon, Greece L21+413 58
Dhionisiadhes. See Yianisahes Is.
Dholera, India H27+222 70
Dholpur, India G50+208 70
Dhond, India H01+184 70
Dhubri, India G00+260 73
Dhula, Yemen, South J71+150 74
Dhulia, India H01+209 70
Dhurma, Saudi Arabia J84+246 74
Dharwa, Saudi Arabia A31-368 112
Dia I., Crete L29+354 59
Diamantina, Argentina S04-320 103
Diamantina, Brazil R69-144 105
Diamantina, Brazil Q81-182 105
Diamantina, l., Queensland C53-242 111
Diamond Harbour, India G10+222 73
Diamond, I., Burma F64+159 71
Dibah, U.A.E. J28+257 75
Dibai, U.A.E. J28+253 75
Dibbah, Jebel, Saudi Arabia K56+278 74
Dibbela, Niger G10+184 81
Dibit, Somalia J72+060 83
Dibrugarh, India F60+274 71
Dickinson, N. Dakota U77+469 93
Dickson, Tennessee T75+362 95
De, France M60+448 55
Diefenbaker L., Saskatchewan V10+510 88
Diego Garcia, I., Indian Oc. H35-100 25
Diego Suarez, Madagascar J64-124 83
Dien Bien Phu, N. Vietnam F12+212 69
Dieppe, France M84+499 54
Diest, Belgium M60+510 44
Dieterbrug, Netherlands M52+529 44
Dig, India G76+274 72
Digby, Nova Scotia S35+446 90
Digby Neck, Nova Scotia S37+444 90
Dighal, Yemen, South J70+146 74
Digne, France M53+441 55
Digoin, France M66+465 54
Dijon, France K53+326 91
Dikwa, Nigeria M06+120 81
Dili, Timor I. Indonesia D56-086 65
Dillon, Montana V46+452 92
Dilolo, Angola L48-118 82
Dimbokro, Ivory Coast N28+068 80
Dimitrovo (Pernik), Bulgaria L42+426 58
Dimla, Bangladesh G06+261 73
Dimotika. See Dhidhimotikhon
Dinagat, I., Philippines D56+100 65
Dinajpur, Bangladesh G08+256 73
Dinan, France N12+485 54
Dinanagar, India G87+322 72
Dinant, Belgium M60+503 44
Dinapur, India G29+256 73
Dinar, Turkey K89+381 74
Dinard, France N13+486 54

Index

Index

14

Index

Index

Groot Natuna, I. Indonesia E70+039 65
Grossevichi, U.S.S.R. C63+479 63
Gross Glockner, Austria M15+471 48
Grosswardein. See Oradea
Groton, New York T09+426 96
Groton, S. Dakota U49+455 93
Grozny, U.S.S.R. J87+435 62
Grudziadz, Poland L67+535 49
Grues, l. aux, Quebec S63+471 91
Grundarfjörd, Scotland N33+579 40
Grüsch, Switzerland M32+470 45
Gruyère, Lac de, Switz. M47+467 45
Gruz, Yugoslavia (Georgia). rep., U.S.S.R. K10+422 62
Gryböw, Poland L55+496 49
Gsteig, Switzerland M46+464 45
Guabito, Panama T46+096 101
Guacanayabo, G. de, Cuba T14+206 101
Guachipas, Argentina S33-256 103
Guadalajara, Spain N19+406 52
Guadalajara, Mexico U80+206 100
Guadalcanal, Spain N35+381 52
Guadalcanal, I., Solomon Is. B30-095 106
Guadalcazar, Mexico U62+226 100
Guadalquivir, R., Spain N30+376 52
Guadalupe I., Mexico U75+227 100
Guadalupe Mts., New Mexico, Texas V00+320 94
Guadalupe R., Texas U47+296 98
Guadalupe-y-Calvo, Mexico V11+262 100
Guadarrama, Spain N25+407 52
Guadarrama, Sa. de, Spain N24+410 52
Guadeloupe, I., Leeward Is. S10+162 101
Guadiana, R., Spain N45+383 52
Guadix, Spain N19+373 52
Gualo & G. de, Chile S88-436 103
Guaitecas, Is., Chile S82-439 103
Guajara-Mirim, Brazil S32-108 104
Gualeguatuba, Brazil S17-050 104
Gualeguaychu, Argentina R81-330 103
Guam, I., Pacific Ocean C30+140 106
Guamini, Argentina S15-370 103
Guamo, Colombia T00+040 104
Guanabacoa, Cuba T43+232 101
Guanabara, Brazil Q82-228 104
Guanaceví, Mexico V06+259 100
Guanahani. See San Salvador
Guanajuato, Mexico U67+212 100
Guanare, Venezuela S58+090 104
Guanarito, Venezuela S54+087 104
Guandacol, Argentina S52-295 103
Guanipati, Venezuela S11+074 104
Guane, Cuba T54+223 101
Guanica, Puerto Rico S41+180 101
Guanta, Venezuela S27+102 104
Guantanamo, Cuba T02+202 101
Guapi, Colombia T17+026 104
Guaples, Costa Rica T53+102 101
Guapore (Rondonia), Brazil S31-118 104
Guapore, R., Brazil-Bolivia S16-128 104
Guaqui, Bolivia S54-166 104
Guarapuava, Brazil R40-255 103
Guarda, Portugal N43+406 52
Guasaves, Mexico V25+298 100
Guasdualito, Venezuela S64+072 104
Guatache, Argentina S22-378 103
Guatire, R., Colombia S56+036 104
Guaxupe, Brazil R10-212 105
Guayabal, Venezuela S43+080 104
Guayaquil, Ecuador T29-022 104
Guaymas, Mexico V35+279 100
Guazapares, Mexico V15+273 100
Gubin. See Guben
Gubio, Angola L64-076 82
Gudivatam, India M46+361 80
Guelma, Algeria M70+363 80
Guelph, Ontario T32+436 91
Guéret, France M79+462 54
Guernsey, I., Channel Is. N15+495 54
Guernsey Res., Wyoming U89+424 93
Guerrero, Mexico V13+284 100
Guerrero, state, Mexico U56+267 100
Gugera, Pakistan H10+309 72
Guiana Highlands, S. Amer. R80+028 104
Guija, Mozambique K74-244 84
Guildford, England N03+512 39
Guildford, Maine S56+452 90
Guillaumes, France M49+441 55
Guimaraes, Brazil Q88-020 105
Guimarães, Portugal N50+414 52
Guinea-Bissau, N.W. Afr. P00+120 80
Guinea, West Africa N60+110 80
Guinea, G. of, N.-W. Africa M70+030 82
Guines, Cuba T42+231 101
Guingamp, France N19+485 54
Guiria, Venezuela S13+106 104
Guise, France M68+499 54
Gusisil, Vol., Nicaragua T67+127 101
Gujarat, state, India H07+218 70
Gujar Khan, Pakistan H11+333 72
Gujranwala, Pakistan H05+321 72
Gujrat, Pakistan H05+326 72
Gulargambone, N.S.W. C09-314 109
Gulbarga, India G78+173 70
Gulbene, Latvia L20+571 47
Gulfport, Mississippi T84+304 95
Gulgong, New South Wales C03-326 109
Gulistan, Pakistan H50+306 70
Gul Koh, Afghanistan H42+334 75
Gul L., Quebec T11+498 89
Gullane, Scotland N17+560 41
Gulpaigan, Iran J59+334 75
Gulpen, Netherlands M55+508 44
Gulran, Afghanistan H80+351 75
Gulu, Uganda K76+026 83
Gum, Ethiopia K20+116 83
Gummersbach, W. Germany M45+510 48
Gümüljina. See Komotini
Gümüsane, Turkey K33+404 74
Guna, India G76+246 73
Gunbad-i-Qabuz, Iran J28+373 75

Gunbar, New South Wales C28-341 109
Gunchu, Japan D14+338 68
Gundagai, N.S. Wales C12-351 109
Gunisao R., Manitoba U40+540 88
Gunnedah, New S. Wales B88-310 109
Gunning, New South Wales C05-348 109
Gunnislake, England N25+505 38
Gunnison, Colorado V12+386 94
Gunnison, Utah V42+392 94
Guntakal, India G75+152 70
Guntersville & L., Alabama T68+344 97
Guntur, India G57+164 70
Gunza, Kashmir H01+346 72
Gurdaspur, India G87+320 72
Gurdon, Arkansas U19+338 95
Gurgaon, India G78+285 72
Gurgl, Austria M24+469 48
Gurha, Nepal G32+280 73
Gurla Mandhata, mt., Tibet G51+304 70
Gurnigel, Switzerland M45+468 45
Gursköy, Norway M56+623 46
Gurupa, Brazil R39-015 105
Gurupa, l., Brazil R39-010 105
Guru Sikhar, India H13+247 70
Gur'yev, Kazakh J50+470 62
Gusev, U.S.S.R. L47+546 47
Gushi, Iran H78+277 75
Guspini, Sardinia M38+396 57
Gustav Holm, Kap, Greenland Q05+670 26
Güstrow, E. Germany M17+538 48
Guthrie, Iowa U27+416 95
Guthrie, Kentucky T73+367 97
Guthrie, Oklahoma U44+358 95
Guyana, S. America R84+050 104
Guyenne, prov., France M82+446 54
Guymon, Oklahoma U68+368 94
Guyra, New South Wales B80-302 109
Guzman, Mexico U82+196 100
Gwa, Burma F62-176 71
Gwabegar, New S. Wales C06-306 109
Gwadar, Pakistan H76+251 70
Gwalior, India G71+262 73
Gwanda, Rhodesia L06-210 84
Gwatar, Iran H81+251 75
Gweebarra B., Ireland, Rep. N51+549 42
Gwelo, Rhodesia L02-194 84
Gwent, co., Wales N18+517 38
Gwydir, R., New S. Wales B83-304 109
Gwynedd, co., Wales N24+529 38
Gyangtse, Tibet G03-289 71
Gydanski Pol., U.S.S.R. G80+700 62
Gympie, Queensland B74-261 111
Gyömpe, Hungary L74-477 49
Gyöngyös, Hungary L52+465 49
Gypsumville, Manitoba U51+516 88
Gyula, Hungary L53-380 74
Gzhatsk, U.S.S.R. K60+555 60

Haacht, Belgium M62+510 44
Haag, Switzerland M33+472 45
Haaksbergen, Netherlands M33+472 45
Haarlem, Netherlands M49+522 44
Habana, Cuba T44+232 101
Habay, Yemen, South J77+146 74
Habbaniyah, Iraq K07+334 74
Habiganj, Bangladesh F81+244 71
Habikino, Japan C51+405 68
Hachinohe, Japan C51+405 68
Haddington, Scotland N16+560 41
Hadera, Israel K60+324 76
Haderslev, Denmark M33+552 47
Hadhramaut, Yemen, South J76+155 74
Hadin, Turkey K53-380 74
Haeju, Korea D58-380 64
Haerhpin, China D45+455 64
Hafar al Ats, Saudi Arabia J84+284 74
Haffe. See Babenna
Hafnarfjördhur, Iceland P41+641 46
Hagen, Germany M45+514 48
Hageri, Estonia L32+591 47
Hagerstown, Maryland T16+397 96
Hagi, Japan D21+344 68
Hague, C. de la, France N12+497 54
Hahnville, Louisiana U03+299 97
Haibak, Afghanistan H42+362 75
Haicheng. See Tunghai
Haichow. See Tunghai
Hai cheng. See Tunghai
Haidar Pasha, Turkey L05+410 74
Haifa, Israel K60+328 76
Haig, W. Australia D54-309 110
Haikou, China E58+200 67
Haiphong, N. Vietnam E80+208 69
Haiti, rep., West Indies S74+190 101
Haiuoto, Finland L52+650 46
Hainan I., China E60+190 67
Hainan Str., China E60+200 67
Hainaut, prov., Belgium M66+505 44
Haines, Alaska X02+594 88
Hajduszoboszlo, Hungary L52+477 49
Hajipur, India G28+257 73
Hajjar, China F72+369 64
Hakkari, Turkey K07+376 74
Hakodate, Japan C55+418 68
Hala, Pakistan H40+258 70
Halacho, Mexico U01+204 100
Halberstadt, E. Germany M21+591 47
Halden, Norway M21+591 47
Haleb, Lebanon. See Aleppo
Halebiye, Syria K31+357 74
Halen, Belgium M59+509 44
Halesworth, England M81+524 39
Halia, India G45+268 73
Halib, Saudi Arabia J31+227 75
Haliburton, Ontario T21+450 91
Halifax, N. Carolina T08+366 97
Halifax, Queensland B74-184 111
Halifax & Harb., N.S. S22+446 90
Halkett C., Alaska Y10+708 99
Hall, W. Germany M32+491 48

Hall Is., Caroline Is. B76+080 106
Hall Ld. Greenland R30+810 26
Halle, E. Germany M18+515 48
Halle, Belgium M65+507 44
Halmahera I., Indonesia D42+006 65
Halmstad, Sweden M13+567 47
Hälsingborg, Sweden M14+561 47
Halstead, Kansas U46+360 95
Halys, C., Turkey K54+417 74
Hama, Syria K50+351 76
Hamada, Japan D17+349 68
Hamadan, Iran J70+348 74
Hamamatsu, Japan C74+347 68
Haman, Iraq K05+312 74
Hamar, Saudi Arabia J83+224 74
Hamar, Norway M23+608 47
Hambantota, Sri Lanka G53+061 70
Hamburg, New York T23+427 96
Hamburg, Pennsylvania T06+405 96
Hamburg, S. Carolina T41+335 97
Hamburg, W. Germany M34+521 48
Hämeenlinna, Finland L33+610 47
Hamelin, W. Germany M34+521 48
Hami, Yemen, South J61+148 74
Hamidiya, Syria K54+347 76
Hamilton, Alabama T78+342 97
Hamilton, New Zealand A28-378 112
Hamilton, N. Carolina T14+359 97
Hamilton, Ohio T57+394 91
Hamilton, Scotland N24+558 41
Hamilton, Tasmania C19-426 109
Hamilton, Victoria C48-378 109
Hamilton, Washington W08+480 88
Hamilton Inl., Labrador R75+543 89
Hamilton L., Arkansas U18+344 95
Hamilton L., Texas U51+308 98
Hamilton R. (Churchill), Lab. S10+530 89
Hamina, Finland L16+605 47
Hamirpur, India G59+259 73
Hamlet, N. Carolina T28+349 97
Hamley Bridge, S. Australia C68-344 109
Hamm, W. Germany M43+517 48
Hamme, Belgium M65+511 44
Hammerfest, Norway L38+706 46
Hammersley Ra., W. Aust. E15-220 110
Hammond, Indiana T75+416 91
Hammond, Louisiana U02+305 95
Hammond, S. Australia C70-325 109
Hammonton, New Jersey S85+396 96
Hamont, Belgium M57+512 44
Hampden, N. Dakota U52+486 93
Hampshire, co., England N08+510 39
Hampton, Arkansas U15+335 97
Hampton, Iowa U18+427 95
Hampton, New Brunswick S34+455 90
Hampton, New Hampshire S65+430 90
Hampton, S. Carolina T37+329 97
Hamun-i-Helmand,
Hamun-i-Puzak, Afghanistan H80+314 75
Hanakiya, Saudi Arabia K24+253 74
Hanau, W. Germany M36+501 48
Hanchung, China E78+331 66
Hancock, Michigan T81+473 90
Hancock, New York T02+419 96
Handeni, Tanzania K42-054 83
Hanford, California V87+466 92
Hangchow, China D89+303 67
Hangchow B., China D80+306 66
Hangu, Pakistan H24+335 72
Han Kiang, China E60+328 64
Hankinson, N. Dakota U41+461 93
Hanko (Hango), Finland L42+599 47
Hankong, China E04+254 64
Hankow (Wuhan), China E34+306 66
Hanle, Kashmir G66+328 70
Hanmer, New Zealand A43-425 112
Hanna, Alberta V41+514 88
Hanna, Wyoming V06+414 93
Hannibal, Missouri U06+414 93
Hannover, Germany M32+524 48
Hano-bukten, Sweden M02+558 47
Hanover, N. Vietnam E85+210 69
Hanover, Pennsylvania T12+398 96
Hanover, Virginia T14+377 97
Hanover, l., Chile S88-510 103
Hanstholm, Denmark M66+515 44
Hanyang, China E34+305 67
Hanyin, China E68+329 66
Hao, I., Tuamotu Arch. X20-190 107
Hapara, Japan C50+444 68
Hapur, India G73+287 72
Haraiya, India G45+268 73
Harak, Saudi Arabia K48+256 74
Harardera, Somalia K56+334 83
Harardera, Somalia J79+236 74
Hara Usu Nur, Mongolia F76+480 64
Harbin. See Haerhpin
Harbor Beach, Michigan T46+438 91
Harbor Spring, Michigan T60+455 91
Harburg Wilhelmsburg, Ger. M30+534 48
Harda, India G77+223 70

Hardanger Fjell, Norway M42+609 47
Hardanger Fd., Norway M54+601 47
Hardenberg, Netherlands M50+526 44
Harderwijk, Netherlands M56+523 44
Hardin, Montana V16+457 93
Harding, Natal L00-306 84
Hardoi, India G59+274 73
Hardwar, India G71+299 72
Hardwicke B., S. Australia C76-348 109
Hardy, Pen., Chile S52-555 103
Hare l., Newfoundland R64+512 90
Hare I., Quebec S58+479 91
Hareidland, Norway M54+624 46
Harelbeke, Belgium M70+509 44
Hargeisa, Somalia K06+094 83
Hari, R., Sumatra, Indon F10-016 65
Harib, Saudi Arabia J85+152 74
Harihar, India G85+146 70
Harim, Syria K51+362 76
Haripur, Pakistan H12+340 72
Hariq, Saudi Arabia J81+237 74
Harishpur, India G21+201 71
Harlan, Iowa U32+416 95
Harlan, Kentucky T47+368 97
Harlech, Wales N25+529 38
Harlem, Montana V22+485 93
Harlequin Hills, Nevada V84+415 92
Harlingen, Netherlands M57+532 44
Harlingen, Texas U46+262 94
Harlowton, Montana V29+464 93
Harmanli. See Kharmanli
Harnai, Pakistan H42+302 70
Harney L., Oregon V85+432 92
Harney Pk., S. Dakota U81+438 93
Harney Basin, Oregon W00+436 98
Harnosand, Sweden L73+626 46
Harper, Liberia N46+044 80
Harper, l., Okney, Scot. N19+590 40
Harrington Harbour, Quebec R87+505 89
Harris, & Sd., of Scotland N41+578 40
Harrisburg, Illinois T82+378 95
Harrisburg, Pennsylvania T12+403 96
Harrison, Arkansas U18+362 95
Harrison, Michigan T59+440 91
Harrison, C., Labrador R67+548 89
Harrison, C., Brit. Columbia W10+498 88
Harrisonburg, Virginia U10+318 97
Harrisonville, Virginia F73+480 63
Harrisonville, Missouri U26+386 95
Harrodsburg, Kentucky T59+378 97
Harrogate, England N09+540 37
Harrow, England N02+516 39
Harsova, Romania L12+447 58
Harspranget, Sweden L61+668 46
Harstad, Norway L81+689 46
Hart, Michigan T68+437 91
Hartford, Connecticut S76+418 96
Hartland, New Brunswick S45+464 90
Hartlepool, England N07+547 37
Hartsville, Tennessee T67+364 97
Hartsville, S. Carolina T42+343 97
Harvard, Illinois T82+425 91
Harvard, Mt., Colorado V08+385 94
Harvey, New Brunswick S42+457 90
Harvey, N. Dakota U60+478 93
Harwell, England N08+516 39
Harwich, England M82+519 39
Haryana, state, India G84+291 72
Harz, mts., Germany M27+516 48
Hasan Dagh, Turkey K66+382 74
Hasan Kuli, Turkmen J37+378 62
Hasanpur, India G70+293 73
Hasbeya, Lebanon H82+314 75
Hassan, India G80+130 70
Hassayampa, Arizona V46+334 98
Hasselt, Netherlands M58+509 44
Hastiere, Belgium M61+502 44
Hastings, England M86+509 39
Hastings, Michigan T62+427 91
Hastings, Minnesota U16+448 93
Hastings, Nebraska U50+406 95
Hastings, New Zealand A19-396 112
Hastings's Ra., New S. Wales B80-312 109
Hateg, Romania L42+456 58
Hatfield, England N06+536 37
Hatfield, New South Wales C37-339 109
Hatha, Saudi Arabia K27+228 74
Hathras, India G71+276 73
Hat-tinh, N. Vietnam E85+184 69
Hatteras, C., N. Carolina T03+352 97
Hattiesburg, Mississippi T86+312 95
Hatton Headline, N.-W. Terr. S30+611 89
Hatvan, Hungary L62+477 49
Hat Yai, Thailand F27+071 65
Haudères, les, Switzerland M45+461 45
Haugesund, Norway M58+594 47
Haukipudas, Finland L28+652 46
Haukivesi, Finland L10+622 46
Haura, Yemen, South J74+139 74
Haut Volta. See Upper Volta
Haut Rhin, dep., France
Hauraki Gulf, New Zealand A30-367 112
Hauranui Mts.,
New Zealand A28-414 112
Hauroko L., New Zealand A76-460 112
Hausa, Jordan K43+299 76
Haut Atlas, mts., Morocco N50+320 80
Hauta, Yemen, South J80+135 74
Havana. See Habana
Havana L., Cal.-Ariz. V56+346 92
Havelange, Belgium M59+504 44
Haveland, E. Germany M14+527 48
Havelock, New Brunswick S32+460 90
Havelock I., Andaman Is. F72+119 71

Jaguari, *Brazil* R58–295 **103**
Jaguariaira, *Brazil* R28–242 **105**
Jaguaruna, *Brazil* R24–286 **103**
Jahanabad, *India* G30+252 **73**
Jahangirabad, *India* G71+284 **72**
Jahra, *Kuwait* J74+294 **74**
Jahrum, *Iran* J38+284 **75**
Jaicos, *Brazil* Q66–074 **105**
Jaipur, *India* G84+268 **70**
Jaipur, *India* G21+208 **71**
Jais, *India* G51+263 **73**
Jaisalmer, *India* H24+268 **70**
Jajarm, *Iran* J22+370 **75**
Jakarta, *Java, Indonesia* E79+062 **65**
Jäkkvik, *Sweden* L78+663 **46**
Jakobi, *Estonia* L21+592 **47**
Jakobstad. *See* Pietarsaari
Jalalabad, *Afghanistan* H28+345 **72**
Jalalpur, *India* G44+263 **73**
Jalalpur, *Pakistan* H22+295 **72**
Jalalpur, *Pakistan* H04+327 **72**
Jalapa, *Nicaragua* T65+139 **101**
Jalapa Enriquez, *Mexico* U42+195 **100**
Jalasjärvi, *Finland* L43+625 **46**
Jalaun, *India* G64+260 **73**
Jaldak, *Afghanistan* H50+319 **75**
Jalgaon, *India* G86+210 **70**
Jalisco, state, *Mexico* U80+200 **100**
Jalk, *Iran* H74+276 **75**
Jalor, *India* H14+252 **70**
Jalpaiguri, *India* G07+265 **73**
Jaluit, I., *Marshall Is.* A64+060 **106**
Jamaica, I., *West Indies* T14+181 **101**
Jamaja, *Estonia* L48+580 **47**
Jamalabad, *Iran* J73+373 **74**
Jamalpur, *Bangladesh* G00+249 **73**
Jamalpur, *India* G21+253 **73**
Jamberoo, *New S. Wales* B86–346 **109**
Jambi, *Sumatra, Indonesia* F08-016 **65**
Jamdena, I., *See* Yamdena
James B., *Canada* T30+530 **89**
James Ras., *N. Terr., Aust.* D15–241 **110**
James R., *S. Dakota* U50+442 **98**
James R., *Virginia* T20+377 **97**
Jamesburg, *California* W10+364 **92**
James Ross, I., *Antarctica* R75–640 **27**
Jamestown, *New York* T25+421 **91**
Jamestown & Res., *N. Dakota* U52+469 **93**
Jamestown, *S. Australia* C68–332 **109**
James W. Ellsworth Ld.
Antarctica U40–770 **27**
Jamiltepec, *Mexico* U47+162 **100**
Jammer Bugt, *Denmark* M36+573 **47**
Jammu & Kashmir H01+327 **72**
Jammu & Kashmir, *India-Pakistan* H00+350 **70**
Jamnagar, *India* H30+224 **70**
Jampur, *Pakistan* H26+296 **72**
Jamrad, *Afghanistan* H42+331 **75**
Jamrao, *Pakistan* H35+255 **70**
Jämsä *Finland* L29+619 **47**
Jamshedpur, *India* G22+228 **73**
Jamui, *India* G22+249 **73**
Jamuna R., *Bangladesh* G02+250 **73**
Jandaq, *Iran* J34+341 **75**
Jandiala, *India* G89+315 **72**
Janesville, *Wisconsin* T84+427 **95**
Jangipur, *India* G11+245 **73**
Jani Khel, *Pakistan* H27+328 **72**
Janjira, *India* H12+184 **70**
Jan Mayen, I., *Arctic Ocean* N55+710 **62**
Janos, *Mexico* V18+310 **100**
Jansath, *India* G73+293 **72**
Jansenville, *Cape Province* L30–330 **84**
Januaria, *Brazil* Q86–154 **105**
Janze, *France* N09+480 **54**
Jaoho, *China* D06+472 **64**
Jaora, *India* G89+236 **70**
Japan & Sea of, *E. Asia* C60+400 **64**
Japen, I., *See* Yapen I.
Japur R., *Brazil* S45+019 **104**
Japvo Mt., *India* F65+256 **71**
Jaragua, *Brazil* R25–265 **103**
Jaragua, *Brazil* R26–157 **105**
Jarales, *New Mexico* V12+346 **94**
Jaramillo, *Argentina* S43–472 **103**
Jarandilla, *Spain* N34+402 **52**
Jardim, *Brazil* Q40–065 **105**
Jardines de la Reina, *Cuba* T24+211 **101**
Jarji, *Nigeria* M46+108 **80**
Jarocin, *Poland* L75+520 **49**
Jaromer, *Czechoslovakia* L85+504 **49**
Jarosław, *Poland* L44+500 **49**
Järpen, *Sweden* M09+634 **46**
Jarrow, *England* N09+550 **37**
Jarvis I., *Pacific Ocean* Y60–002 **106**
Järvsö, *Sweden* L83+617 **47**
Jashpurnagar, *India* G35+229 **73**
Jask, *Iran* J13+257 **75**
Jason I., *Falkland Is.* S07–510 **103**
Jasper, *Florida* T48+305 **97**
Jasper, *Georgia* T57+345 **97**
Jasper, *Texas* U24+310 **95**
Jasper & Park, *Alberta* V80+533 **88**
Jassy. *See* Iasi.
Jastrowie, *Poland* L79+534 **49**
Jaswantnagar, *India* G66+269 **73**
Jaszberény, *Hungary* L60+475 **49**
Jath, *India* G88+170 **70**
Jativa, *Spain* N03+390 **53**
Jatoba, *Brazil* Q50–092 **105**
Jaú, *Brazil* R21–222 **105**
Jauche, *Belgium* M60+507 **44**
Jauf, *Saudi Arabia* K31+299 **74**
Jauhari, *Saudi Arabia* J46+165 **75**
Jauja, *Peru* T02–117 **104**
Jaumave, *Mexico* U57+234 **100**
Jaunjelgava, *Latvia* L29+566 **47**
Jaunpur, *India* G44+258 **73**
Java, I., *Indonesia* E60–073 **65**
Javari, R., *Peru-Brazil* S78–065 **104**
Javier, I., *Chile* S86–471 **103**
Jawa, *Nigeria* M24+128 **81**
Jawalamukhi, *India* G82+318 **72**
Jayapura, *Indonesia* C57+026 **65**
Jazir, *Oman* J20+186 **75**
Jebba, *Nigeria* M62+090 **80**
Jeble, *Syria* K54+354 **76**
Jech Doab, *Pakistan* H14+321 **72**
Jedabya, *Libya* L58+306 **81**
Jedburgh, *Scotland* N15+555 **41**
Jedede, *Saudi Arabia* K29+218 **74**
Jefferson, *Georgia* T51+341 **97**
Jefferson, *Wisconsin* T82+430 **95**
Jefferson, Mt., *Oregon* W11+446 **92**
Jefferson City, *Missouri* U13+386 **95**
Jeffersonville, *Indiana* T64+383 **97**
Jehol. *See* Chêng-têhshih.
Jekabpils, *Latvia* L25+565 **47**
Jelgava, *Latvia* L37+566 **47**
Jelsava, *Czechoslovakia* L59+486 **49**
Jemeppe, *Belgium* M62+505 **44**
Jena, *E. Germany* M21+509 **48**
Jenin, *Jordan* K58+325 **76**
Jenipapo, *Brazil* R84–064 **104**
Jennings, *Louisiana* U16+302 **95**
Jenolan Caves, *New S. Wales* C00–339 **109**
Jeparit, *Victoria* C48–362 **109**
Jeppo, *Finland* L44+634 **46**
Jerablus, *Syria* K42+368 **76**
Jerash, *Jordan* K55+323 **76**
Jeremie, *Haiti* S84+187 **101**
Jerez, *Mexico* U78+228 **100**
Jerez de la Frontera, *Spain* N37+367 **52**
Jeriban, *Somalia* J66+072 **83**
Jericho, *Jordan* K57+319 **76**
Jericho, *Queensland* C24–234 **111**
Jerilderie, *New S. Wales* C26–354 **109**
Jerome, *Arizona* V43+348 **94**
Jerruck, *Pakistan* H40+250 **70**
Jersey, I., *Channel Is.* N13+492 **54**
Jersey City, *New Jersey* S84+407 **96**
Jerseyshore, *Pennsylvania* T14+412 **96**
Jerusalem, *Israel-Jordan* K59+318 **76**
Jervis B., *New South Wales* B86–351 **109**
Jervois Ra., *N. Terr., Aust.* C83–225 **111**
Jesenik, *Czechoslovakia* L77+503 **49**
Jesselton, *N. Borneo* E24+060 **65**
Jessore, *Bangladesh* G04+231 **73**
Jesup, *Georgia* T41+316 **97**
Jesus I., *Quebec* S81+457 **91**
Jesus Maria, *Argentina* S25–310 **103**
Jesus Maria, *Mexico* V16+282 **100**
Jetalsar, *India* H26+217 **70**
Jeypore, *India* G44+189 **71**
Jezzin, *Lebanon* K57+335 **76**
Jhal, *Pakistan* H45+282 **70**
Jhalrapatan, *India* G82+246 **70**
Jhang Maghiana, *Pakistan* H16+313 **72**
Jhansi, *India* G68+254 **73**
Jhau, *Pakistan* H56+262 **70**
Jhelum, *Pakistan* H08+330 **72**
Jhelum R., *Pakistan* H14+325 **72**
Jhunjhunu, *India* G87+281 **72**
Jiachan, *Tibet* G53+316 **70**
Jianpur, *India* G40+262 **73**
Jibhalanta, *Mongolia* F49+480 **63**
Jicaro, *Nicaragua* T65+138 **101**
Jičin, *Czechoslovakia* L88+505 **49**
Jidd, *Iraq* K32+328 **74**
Jidda, *Saudi Arabia* K35+215 **74**
Jiggitai L., *Tibet* G19+350 **71**
Jihlava, *Czechoslovakia* L87+494 **49**
Jildiah, Jebel, *Saudi Arabia* K15+277 **74**
Jimena de la Frontera, *Spain* N32+365 **52**
Jimenez, *Mexico* U64+290 **100**
Jimenez, *Mexico* V00+270 **100**
Jimma, *Ethiopia* K48+076 **83**
Jim Thorpe, *Pennsylvania* T05+408 **96**
Jind, *India* G82+293 **72**
Jinotega, *Nicaragua* T66+131 **101**
Jipijapa, *Ecuador* T33–012 **104**
Jirgalanta, *Mongolia* F80+480 **63**
Jirm, *Afghanistan* H25+368 **75**
Jisha, *Saudi Arabia* J61+253 **74**
Jisresh Shughur, *Syria* K52+358 **76**
Jiul R., *Romania* L37+441 **58**
Jiza, *Jordan* K54+317 **76**
João Pessoa, *Brazil* Q28–071 **105**
Jodhpur, *India* H12+263 **70**
Joensuu, *Finland* L01+626 **46**
Jofane, *Mozambique* K64–214 **84**
Jogjakarta, *See* Yogyakarta
Johannesburg, *Transvaal* L12–262 **84**
John o' Groats, *Scotland* N18+586 **40**
Johnsonburg, *Pennsylvania* T22+415 **96**
Johnson City, *Tennessee* T44+363 **97**
Johnston I., *Pacific Ocean* Z28+170 **106**
Johnstown, *Ireland, Rep.* N41+534 **43**
Johnstown, *New York* S85+430 **96**
Johnstown, *Pennsylvania* T24+403 **96**
Johore Baharu, *Malaya* F08+015 **69**
Joinville, *Brazil* R23–263 **103**
Joinville, *France* M59+484 **54**
Joinville I., *Antarctica* R60–630 **27**
Jokkmökk, *Sweden* L61+666 **46**
Jol Plat., *Saudi Arabia* J65+154 **74**
Joliet, *Illinois* T78+415 **95**
Joliette, *Quebec* S81+460 **91**
Jolo, I., *Philippines* D82+059 **65**
Jonava, *Lithuania* L34+551 **47**
Jonesboro, *Arkansas* U04+358 **95**
Jonesboro, *Georgia* T56+335 **97**
Jonesboro, *Illinois* T86+374 **97**
Jonesboro, *Louisiana* U16+322 **97**
Jonesport, *Maine* S46+445 **90**
Joniškis, *Lithuania* L39+562 **47**
Jönköping, *Sweden* M05+578 **47**
Jonquière, *Quebec* S67+484 **90**
Jonuta, *Mexico* U13+180 **100**
Joplin, *Missouri* U27+372 **95**
Jordan, *Minnesota* U22+447 **93**
Jordan, *Montana* V12+473 **93**
Jordan, *S.-W. Asia* K53+310 **74**
Jordan, R., *Israel* K57+323 **76**
Jordan R., *Utah* V42+407 **94**
Jorhat, *India* F65+267 **71**
Jorje Montt, I., *Chile* S88–513 **103**
Jorna da Del Muerto,
New Mexico V11+330 **94**
Joseph Bonaparte Gulf,
W. Australia D40–130 **110**
Jostedalsbre Glacier, *Norway* M47+616 **47**
Jotunheimen, *Norway* M42+615 **34**
Joux, L. de, *Switzerland* M52+466 **45**
Jowai, *India* F76+254 **71**
Juan de Fuca Str.,
U.S.A.-Canada W20+479 **98**
Juan Fernandez I.,
Pacific Ocean T25–345 **107**
Juan Stuven, I., *Chile* T00–479 **103**
Juárez, *Argentina* R89–376 **103**
Juarez, *Mexico* U01+188 **100**
Juba, *Sudan* K80+050 **81**
Jubba, *Saudi Arabia* K23+280 **74**
Jubbulpore. *See* Jabalpur
Jubeil, *Lebanon* K56+341 **76**
Jubi, C., *Morocco* N78+280 **80**
Jucaro, *Cuba* T23+216 **101**
Juchitan, *Mexico* U31+164 **100**
Judenburg, *Austria* M02+471 **48**
Judique, *Nova Scotia* S09+459 **90**
Judith, *Montana* V28+477 **93**
Judith Pt., *Rhode Island* S67+414 **91**
Juian, *China* D85+278 **67**
Juichow. *See* Kaoan
Juist, I., *Germany* M48+537 **48**
Juiz de Fora, *Brazil* Q80–217 **105**
Jujuy, *Argentina* S32–242 **103**
Jukao, *China* D86+324 **66**
Jukkasjarvi, *Sweden* L52+679 **34**
Julaco, *Bolivia* S46–209 **104**
Julesburg, *Colorado* U74+410 **94**
Juli, *Peru* S57–162 **104**
Juliaca, *Peru* S61–156 **104**
Julianstown, *Ireland, Rep.* N38+537 **42**
Julio de Castilhos, *Brazil* R52–293 **103**
Jullundur, *India* G86+313 **72**
Jumaima, *Iraq* K08+298 **74**
Jumet, *Belgium* M63+504 **44**
Jumilla, *Spain* N08+385 **53**
Jumin, *Iran* J08+345 **75**
Jumla, *Nepal* G47+293 **73**
Jumna (Yamuna), R., *India* G58+260 **73**
Junagarh, *India* H27+216 **70**
Junan, *China* E33+330 **66**
Junction City, *Kansas* U41+390 **95**
Jundiai, *Brazil* R11–232 **105**
Juneau, *Alaska* W86+585 **99**
Junee, *New South Wales* C14–349 **109**
Jungfrau, mt., *Switzerland* M42+465 **45**
Jungfraujoch, *Switzerland* M42+465 **45**
Jungkiang, *China* E68+259 **67**
Junin, *Argentina* S67–400 **103**
Junin, *Argentina* S06–345 **103**
Junin, *Chile* S61–198 **103**
Junin, *Peru* T06–112 **104**
Juning. *See* Junan
Juniper, *New Brunswick* S43+466 **90**
Juniye, (Jounie) *Lebanon* K56+340 **76**
Junsele, *Sweden* L78+637 **46**
Juojarvi, *Finland* L08+628 **46**
Jupia, *Brazil* R39–208 **105**
Juquila, *Mexico* U45+163 **100**
Jura, dep., *France* M54+467 **54**
Jura, mts., *France-Switz.* M54+463 **54**
Jura I. & Sd. of, *Scotland* N35+560 **41**
Jurado, *Colombia* T17+072 **104**
Jurbarkas, *Lithuania* L43+551 **47**
Jurf ed Darawish, *Jordan* K55+307 **76**
Jüri, *Estonia* L30+594 **47**
Juruá, R., *Brazil* S40–045 **104**
Juruena & R., *Brazil* R83–128 **104**
Juruty, *Brazil* R67–020 **105**
Jusiye, *Syria* K50+344 **76**
Jussy, *Switzerland* M52+462 **45**
Justlahuaco, *Mexico* U48+174 **100**
Justo Daract, *Argentina* S31–338 **103**
Jutahy, *Brazil* S42–027 **104**
Juticalpa, *Honduras* T64+146 **101**
Jutland. *See Jylland*
Juuka, *Finland* L05+632 **46**
Juwain, *Afghanistan* H80+316 **75**
Juwara, *Oman* J16+190 **75**
Jylland, *Denmark* M36+562 **47**
Jylland, South, *Denmark* M36+552 **47**
Jyväskylä, *Finland* L26+623 **46**
K2, Mt, *Kashmir* G81+359 **72**
Kabaena, I., *Indonesia* D79–054 **65**
Kabala, *Sierra Leone* N70+096 **80**
Kabale, *Uganda* L00–014 **83**
Kabalega Falls, *Uganda* K80+020 **83**
Kabba, *Nigeria* M54+078 **80**
Kabia, I., *Indonesia* D87–061 **65**
Kabinda, *Zaire* L32–062 **82**
Kabongo, *Zaire* L26–074 **82**
Kabul & R., *Afghanistan* H34+346 **75**
Kabunda, *Zaire* L04–126 **83**
Kabwe, *Zambia* L10–144 **83**
Kačanik, *Yugoslavia* L53+424 **58**
Kachiry, *Kazakh* G84+530 **62**
Kachkar, *U.S.S.R.* H84+544 **61**
Kachuga, *U.S.S.R.* E84+540 **63**
Kadaura, *India* G61+260 **73**
Kadina, *S. Australia* C74–340 **109**
Kadiri, *India* G70+141 **70**
Kadiyevka, *Ukraine* K39+486 **60**
Kadoka, *S. Dakota* U69+438 **93**
Kadom, *U.S.S.R.* K15+546 **61**
Kadugli, *Sudan* L02+110 **81**
Kaduna, *Nigeria* M46+106 **80**
Kadur, *India* G84+136 **70**
Kadyy, *U.S.S.R.* K11+577 **61**
Kadzand, *Netherlands* M70+514 **44**
Kaesong, *Korea* D52+380 **64**
Kaf, *Saudi Arabia* K46+315 **74**
Kafakumba, *Congo* L38–096 **82**
Kafanchan, *Nigeria* M40+096 **80**
Kafia Kingi, *Sudan* L34+092 **81**
Kafra, *Chad* L44+162 **81**
Kafr Behum, *Syria* K50+351 **76**
Kafrun, *Syria* K52+348 **76**
Kagan, *Uzbek* H63+396 **62**
Kagi. *See* Chiai
Kagmar, *Sudan* K88+144 **81**
Kagoshima, *Japan* D27+316 **68**
Kagoshima B., *Japan* D28+311 **68**
Kagul, *Moldavia* L11+459 **60**
Kahafa, *Saudi Arabia* K10+270 **74**
Kahama, *Tanzania* K74–038 **83**
Kahoka, *Missouri* U10+404 **95**
Kahra, *Yemen* J89+141 **74**
Kahror, *Pakistan* H18+296 **72**
Kahta, *Turkey* K38+381 **74**
Kahuta, *Pakistan* H09+336 **72**
Kai-Kep, *Indonesia* D14–058 **65**
Kaiama, *Nigeria* M66+096 **80**
Kaiapoi, *New Zealand* A44–434 **112**
Kai-chow, *China* E30+357 **66**
Kaieteur Fall, *Guyana* R87+052 **104**
Kai fêng, *China* E33+348 **66**
Kaigo, *Sudan* K80+060 **81**
Kaihwa. *See* Wenshan
Kaikoura, *New Zealand* A38–424 **112**
Kaikoura Ra., *New Zealand* A40–421 **112**
Kailas Ra., *India-Tibet* G78+352 **70**
Kaimanawa Mts., *N.Z.* A24–390 **112**
Kaimganj, *India* G64+275 **73**
Kaimur Ra., *India* G48+245 **73**
Kaipara Harb., *New Zealand* A35–364 **112**
Kaira, *India* H13+226 **70**
Kairana, *India* G77+294 **72**
Kairouan, *Tunisia* M30+358 **81**
Kairovo, *U.S.S.R.* J16+558 **61**
Kaisarie. *See* Kayseri
Kaišedorys, *Lithuania* L33+549 **47**
Kaiserslautern, *W. Germany* M43+494 **48**
Kaiser Wilhelm II Ld.,
Antarctica G00–670 **27**
Kaitangata, *New Zealand* A61–463 **112**
Kaithal, *India* G81+297 **72**
Kai-yuan, *China* D66+427 **66**
Kajaani, *Finland* L13+642 **46**
Kajiado, *Kenya* K50–018 **83**
Kajiki, *Japan* D26+317 **68**
Kajuri Kach, *Pakistan* H31+321 **72**
Kakamari, *Uganda* K64+034 **83**
Kakamega, *Kenya* K60+002 **83**
Kakh, *Iran* J08+342 **75**
Kakhovskoye Vdkhr., *Ukr.* K62+471 **60**
Kakia, *Botswana* L40–248 **84**
Kakisa, L., *N.-W. Terr.* V76+607 **88**
Kakori, *India* G55+269 **73**
Kakoyarra, *New S. Wales* C51–317 **109**
Kaksha, *U.S.S.R.* J80+582 **61**
Kalabagh, *Pakistan* H21+330 **72**
Kalabaka, *Greece* L50+397 **59**
Kalabo, *Zambia* L44–150 **84**
Kalabsha, *Egypt* K74+234 **81**
Kalach, *U.S.S.R.* K24+504 **61**
Kaladan, *Burma* F72+211 **71**
Kalahari Des., *Botswana* L40–238 **84**
Kalajoki, *Finland* L36+643 **46**
Kalakan, *U.S.S.R.* E19+552 **63**
Kalakepen, *Sumatra* F43+028 **65**
Kalámai, *Greece* L47+370 **59**
Kalamáta. *See* Kalámai.
Kalamazoo, *Michigan* T63+424 **91**
Kalamboa, *Sudan* L30+126 **81**
Kalamos I., *Greece* L55+386 **59**
Kala Nao, *Afghanistan* H71+350 **75**
Kalanaur, *India* G82+289 **72**
Kalangali, *Tanzania* K66–062 **83**
Kalannie, *W. Australia* E18–302 **110**
Kala Sarkari, *Afghanistan* H46+358 **75**
Kalat, *Pakistan* H50+270 **70**
Kalat-i-Ghilzai, *Afghanistan* H49+320 **75**
Kalat-i-Nadiri, *Iran* J01+371 **75**
Kalaw, *Burma* F50+207 **71**
Kale, *Burma* F65+232 **71**
Kalediran, *Turkey* K74+362 **74**
Kalémié *Zaire* L04–060 **83**
Kalewa, *Burma* F64+232 **71**
Kalgan. *See* Changkiakow
Kalgoorlie, *W. Australia* D82–307 **110**
Kalikino, *U.S.S.R.* J35+528 **61**
Kalimnos, I., *Greece* L19+370 **59**
Kalingapatnam, *India* G35+184 **70**
Kalinin, *U.S.S.R.* K56+568 **60**
Kaliningrad, *U.S.S.R.* L57+547 **47**
Kalinino, *U.S.S.R.* E70+599 **63**
Kalispell, *Montana* V56+479 **98**
Kalisz, *Poland* L71+518 **49**
Kaliua, *Tanzania* K80–050 **83**
Kalix Älv, *Sweden* L56+676 **46**
Kalixfors, *Sweden* L59+677 **46**
Kalka, *India* G78+308 **72**
Kalkaska, *Michigan* T61+448 **91**
Kalkfeld, *S.-W. Africa* L84–208 **84**
Kalkfontein, *Botswana* L54–222 **84**
Kalkwerk, *S.-W. Africa* L76–268 **84**
Kallavesi, *Finland* L14+628 **46**
Kallim, *Chad* L54+128 **81**
Kalloni, *Greece* L23+392 **59**
Kall Sjön, *Sweden* M12+637 **46**
Kalmar, *Sweden* L82+567 **47**
Kalmar Sund, *Sweden* L82+565 **47**
Kalmykovo, *Kazakh* J50+490 **62**
Kalna, *India* G10+232 **73**
Kalocsa, *Hungary* L66+465 **49**
Kalokhorio, *Cyprus* K72+351 **76**
Kalol, *India* H14+234 **70**
Kalpi, *India* G62+261 **73**
Kaltag, *Alaska* Y50+640 **99**
Kaluga, *U.S.S.R.* K52+545 **60**
Kalule, *Zaire* L24–096 **82**
Kalundborg, *Denmark* M23+557 **47**
Kalundu, *Zambia* L02–104 **83**
Kalutara, *Sri Lanka* G61+065 **70**
Kalvariya, *Lithuania* L41+544 **47**
Kalyan, *India* H11+192 **70**
Kalyazin, *U.S.S.R.* K44+572 **60**
Kama, R., *U.S.S.R.* J22+608 **62**
Kamah, *Labrador* S22+590 **89**
Kamaishi, *Japan* C48+393 **68**
Kamalampaka, *Tanzania* K86–056 **83**
Kamalia, *Pakistan* H08+307 **72**
Kaman, *India* G77+276 **72**
Kamaran, I., *Red Sea* K14+154 **74**
Kamasin, *India* G54+255 **73**
Kamassa, *Cameroun* M10+078 **81**
Kamchatka, *U.S.S.R.* B40+560 **63**
Kamen, *U.S.S.R.* G52+538 **62**
Kamenets Podolskiy, *Ukraine* L21+488 **60**
Kamenskoye, *U.S.S.R.* B00+625 **63**
Kamensk Shakhtinski,
U.S.S.R. K28+483 **61**
Kamensk Ural'skiy, *U.S.S.R.* H79+564 **61**
Kamet, Mt., *India* G64+309 **70**
Kami Iwani, *Japan* D10+351 **68**
Kamina, *Zaire* L30–088 **82**
Kamloops, *Brit. Columbia* W02+507 **88**
Kamnik, *Yugoslavia* M02+462 **56**
Kamouraska, *Quebec* S59+476 **90**
Kampa Dzong, *Tibet* G09+283 **71**
Kampala, *Uganda* K74+002 **83**
Kampen, *Netherlands* M54+526 **44**
Kampot, *Khmer* F05+106 **69**
Kamptee, *India* G64+212 **70**
Kamsack, *Saskatchewan* U71+513 **88**
Kamyshin, *U.S.S.R.* J88+501 **61**
Kamyshlov, *U.S.S.R.* H74+568 **61**
Kanab, *Utah* V45+370 **94**
Kannauj, *India* G61+270 **73**

Index

23

Krakow, Poland L60+501 49
Kramatorsk, Ukraine K45+487 106
Krammer, Netherlands M65+517 44
Kranj, Yugoslavia M04+463 56
Kranystaw, Poland L41+510 49
Kranz, U.S.S.R. L57+549 47
Krapina, Yugoslavia L85+462 56
Krasino, Novaya Zemlya J35+708 62
Krasnobrod, Poland L44+505 49
Krasnodar, U.S.S.R. K37+451 62
Krasnograd, Ukraine K58+494 60
Krasnoufimsk, U.S.S.R. J14+566 61
Krasnovisher, U.S.S.R. J17+602 62
Krasnovodsk, Turkmen J44+401 62
Krasnoyarsk, U.S.S.R. F71+562 63
Krasnyi Kholm, U.S.S.R. K48+581 60
Krasnyi Kut, U.S.S.R. J78+509 61
Krasny Yar, U.S.S.R. K02+507 61
Krefeld, W. Germany M51+513 48
Kremenchug, Ukraine K69+491 60
Kremensk, U.S.S.R. K10+497 61
Krems, Austria L87+484 49
Kretinga, Lith. L53+559 47
Kreuzlingen, Switzerland M35+476 45
Kribi, Cameroun M30+030 81
Krimml, Austria M17+472 48
Krishna, R., India G63+166 70
Krishnanagar, India G09+234 73
Krishnangar Res., India G81+126 70
Krivoy Rog, Ukraine K70+478 60
Krizevci, Yugoslavia L81+460 56
Kik. I., Yugoslavia M02+451 56
Kroken, Norway M43+631 46
Krokom, Norway M04+653 46
Kroměříž, Czechoslovakia L76+493 49
Kronoby, Finland L42+637 46
Kronshtadt, U.S.S.R. L02+600 60
Kroonstad, Orange Free State L16+276 84
Kropotkin, U.S.S.R. K28+454 62
Krotoszyn, Poland L76+517 49
Krško, Yugoslavia L87+459 56
Krugersdorp, Transvaal L14+262 84
Kruishoutem, Belgium M69+509 44
Krujë, Albania L62+415 58
Krumbach, W. Germany M28+482 48
Krung Kao, Kenya K22+018 83
Krung Thep, Thailand F27+138 69
Krupnik, Bulgaria L40+418 58
Krusevac, Yugoslavia L52+436 58
Kruspils, Latvia L24+565 47
Kryvz, Poland L84+529 49
Ksar el Boukhari, Algeria M74+358 80
Kuala Kangsar, Malaya F25+049 69
Kuala Kerai, Malaya F16+054 69
Kuala Klawang, Malaya F18+030 69
Kuala Lipis, Malaya F20+032 69
Kuala Lumpur, Malaya F20+032 69
Kuandang, Celebes D72+008 65
Kuantan, Malaya F10+037 65
Kuba, S.-W. Africa L74-242 84
Kubis, S.-W. Africa L80-268 84
Kuching, Sarawak E58+016 65
Kuchow. See Jungkiang
Kudat, Sabah E20+069 65
Kudymkar, U.S.S.R. J33+593 62
Kuhak, Iran H71+271 75
Kuh Banan, Iran J22+315 75
Kuh-e-Bul, Iran J55+305 75
Kuh Furgan, Iran J22+279 75
Kuh-i-Bul, Iran J43+308 75
Kuh-i-Dinar, Iran J51+310 75
Kuh-i-Kashgah, Iran J28+284 75
Kuhpayeh, Iran J45+327 75
Kuhrud, Iran J53+337 75
Kuhsan, Afghanistan H82+347 75
Kukatush, Ontario T43+481 91
Kukawa, Nigeria M08+128 81
Kukes, Albania L58+421 58
Kukong (Shiukwan), China E38+248 67
Kulachi, Pakistan H27+320 72
Kulakh, Saudi Arabia K25+212 74
Kuldiga, Latvia L48+570 47
Kuldja, Sinkiang, China G51+440 62
Kulhakangri Mt., Tibet F87+280 71
Kulu, India H04+144 70
Kulunda, U.S.S.R. E52+559 63
Kulwin, Victoria C44-350 109
Kumara, New Zealand A52-426 112
Kumari, Ghana N10+068 80
Kumasi, Ghana N74+114 80
Kumbakonam, India G76+273 73
Kumta, India G98+143 70
Kunduz, Afghanistan H36+367 75
Kungchang. See Lungsi

Kure, Japan D15+342 68
Kure, I., Hawaiian Is. Z80+288 106
Kureika, U.S.S.R. G05+670 62
Kuressare, Estonia L45+582 47
Kurgan, U.S.S.R. H57+556 62
Kuria Muria Is., Arabian Sea J22+175 75
Kurigram, Bangladesh G02+258 73
Kurikka, Ostrova, U.S.S.R. C00+458 63
Kurnool, India G72+159 70
Kurow, New Zealand A57-446 112
Kurram, Pakistan H29+339 72
Kurri Kurri, N.S. Wales B82-328 109
Kursk, U.S.S.R. K53+517 60
Kurski Zaliv, U.S.S.R. L55+550 47
Kurtalan, Turkey K18+384 74
Kuru, Finland L37+619 47
Kuruman, Cape Province L40-276 84
Kurume, Japan D27+332 68
Kurunegala, Sri Lanka G58+076 70
Kusa, U.S.S.R. J04+553 61
Kusaie, I., Caroline Is. B10+053 106
Kushersk, U.S.S.R. J30+584 61
Kushiro, Japan C33+430 68
Kushk, Afghanistan H75+348 75
Kushka, Turkmen H77+352 62
Kushtia, Bangladesh G05+239 73
Kushva, U.S.S.R. J02+584 61
Kuskokwim R., Alaska Y80+590 99
Kusma, Nepal G38+282 73
Kutahya, Turkey L01+393 74
Kutai, R., Borneo, Indon. E26+004 65
Kut-al-Hai, Iraq J84+322 74
Kutatjane, Sumatra, Indon. F44+034 65
Kutch, & Gulf of, India H23+232 70
Kutch, Rann of, India H30+240 70
Kutchan, Japan C56+429 68
Kutin, Yugoslavia L80+455 56
Kutno, Poland L64+522 49
Kutsing, China F07+255 67
Kutu, Ethiopia K64+090 83
Kutum, Sudan L32+140 81
Kuusjärvi, Finland L05+659 46
Kuusamo, Finland L07+627 46
Kuwait & state, The Gulf J72+294 74
Kuyang, China E60+414 66
Kuybyshev, U.S.S.R. J58+531 61
Kuybyshev, U.S.S.R. G68+559 62
Kuybyshevskoye Vdkhr., U.S.S.R. J60+548 61
Kuyan, U.S.S.R. F22+544 63
Kuzhbal, U.S.S.R. K05+585 61
Kuzino, U.S.S.R. J04+571 61
Kuznetsk, U.S.S.R. J81+530 61
Kuzomen, Surinam R62+051 105
Kuzovatovo, U.S.S.R. J75+536 61
Kvaloy I., Norway L65+702 46
Kvaløy, Norway L68+697 46
Kvarken, Ostra, Sweden L56+634 46
Kvarner, G. of, Yugoslavia M05+448 56
Kvesmenes, Norway L52+218 84
Kwajalein Is., Marshall Is. A80+088 106
Kwakhanai, Botswana L52-218 84
Kwakoegron, Surinam R62+051 105
Kwangchow, China E23+267 67
Kwangchow Wan, China E40+232 67
Kwangnam, China E40+232 67
Kwangning, China F00+241 67
Kwangshun, China F00+241 67
Kwangping, China E82+261 67
Kwangsuan prov., China E72+238 67
Kwangtung, prov., China E36+235 67
Kwangyuan. See Shangkiao
Kwania, L., Uganda K74+016 83
Kwan-tung (Luta) Pen., China D86+388 66
Kweichin, China E15+307 66
Kweichow. See Fengkieh
Kweihwa. See Huhehot
Kweiping, China E59+254 67
Kweisui. See Huhehot
Kweitei, China E59+233 67
Kweiteh. See Shangkiu
Kweiyang, China E80+266 67
Kwei-yang, China E45+258 67
Kwidzyn, Poland L66+538 49
Kwitao, Burma F44+257 71
Kwoka, mt., New Guinea D15-006 65
Kyabram, Victoria C50-363 109
Kyakhta, U.S.S.R. E81+504 63
Kyalite Crossing, N.S.W. C40-349 109
Kyangin, Burma F58+182 71
Kyaring Nor, China F46+348 64
Kyaukpadaung, Burma F72+208 71
Kyaukpyu, Burma F69+195 71
Kyaukse, Burma F53+215 71
Kybybolite, S. Australia C54-369 109
Kyelang, India G78+326 72
Kyi R., Tibet F80+298 71
Kymi, Finland L19+605 47
Kyneton, Victoria C33-373 109
Kyoga L., Uganda K74+014 83
Kyoto, Japan C85+350 68
Kyrenia, Cyprus K70+353 76
Kyshtym, U.S.S.R. H86+557 61
Kythera, Cyprus K69+352 76
Kyūshū, I., Japan D24+330 68
Kyustendil, Bulgaria L44+423 58
Kyusyur, U.S.S.R. D45+708 63
Kywong, New South Wales C20-350 109
Kyzyl, U.S.S.R. F63+517 63
Kyzyl Kum, Uzbek, etc. H70+423 62
Kyzylsk, U.S.S.R. J06+526 61
Kyzyl Orda, Kazakh H57+450 62
Laania, Finland L19+684 46
La Argentina, Argentina S70-503 103
La Ascuncion, Venezuela S23+110 104
Laban, Jordan K56+309 76
La Banda, Argentina S25-277 103
Labe, Guinea N74+114 80

Labrador, Canada 89
Labrea, Brazil S28-072 104
La Brea, Honduras T76+134 101
La Brea, Trinidad S08+102 104
Labuan, N. Sabah E29+054 65
Labuk B., Sabah E14+061 65
La Canoa, Venezuela S23+086 104
La Carlota, Argentina S20-334 103
La Carolina, Spain N22+383 52
La Ceiba, Venezuela S66+094 104
Lacepede B., S. Australia C62-367 109
Lac Frontiere, Quebec S60+467 90
Lachine, Quebec S82+455 91
Lachlan R., New S. Wales C30-338 109
Lachmangarh, India G89+278 72
Lachute, Quebec S87+457 91
Lackawanna, New York T23+428 96
Lackawaxen, Pennsylvania T00+415 96
Lacken Res., Ireland, Rep. N39+532 43
La Cocha, Argentina S33-278 103
Lacombe, Alberta V53+522 88
La Concordia, Salvador T85+134 101
La Copelina, Argentina S46-372 103
La Coruña, Spain N51+433 52
La Crosse, Wisconsin U07+438 93
La Cruz, Mexico V01+279 100
Ladakh Ra., Tibet G60+322 70
Ladis, Iran H82+289 75
Ladoga, L. See Ladozhskoye Ozero
Ladozhskoye Oz., Russia K84+606 60
Ladwa, India G77+300 72
Lady Neunes B., Antarctica A70-730 27
Ladysmith, British Columbia W23+490 88
Ladysmith, Natal L02-288 84
Ladysmith, Wisconsin U07+455 93
Lae, Papua New Guinea C18-068 111
Laesö, I., Denmark M24+573 47
La Esperanza, Honduras T62+384 97
La Estrada, Spain N51+427 52
Lafayette, Georgia T62+347 97
La Fayette, Indiana T71+404 91
Lafayette, Louisiana U12+302 95
La Florencia, Argentina S13-241 103
Lahijan, Iran J60+372 75
Laholm, Sweden M12+565 47
Lahore, Pakistan H04+316 72
Lahti, Finland L26+610 47
Lai, C. N. Vietnam E77+171 69
Laibach. See Ljubljana
Lai-chau, N. Vietnam F11+222 69
Laichow. See Yehsien
Laigle, France M86+488 54
Laila, Saudi Arabia J79+223 74
Laingsburg, Cape Province L56-330 84
Lairg, Scotland N26+580 40
Laishev, U.S.S.R. J63+554 61
Laives, Italy M22+465 45
Laja, L., Chile S68-374 103
Lajao, Brazil Q69-192 105
La Japonesa, Argentina S39-386 103
Lajes, Brazil R32-278 103
La Junquera, Spain M73+424 53
La Junta, Colorado U53+380 94
Lakatraisk, Sweden L53+663 46
Lake Andes, S. Dakota U52+432 93
Lake Charles, Louisiana U19+302 95
Lake City, Florida T45+300 97
Lake City, Michigan T61+444 91
Lake District, England N19+546 37
Lake Edward, Quebec S73+477 91
Lake Pleasant, New York S86+434 96
Lake Providence, Louisiana U07+328 95
Lakes Entrance, Victoria C12-378 109
Lakeview, Minnesota U12+469 93
Lakewood, New Jersey S85+400 96
Lakewood, New York T26+422 96
Lakewood, Ohio T40+415 91
Lakhimpur, India F65+272 71
Lakhpat, India H24+325 72
Lakkor I.so., Tibet G36+320 71
Lakonia, Greece L45+369 59
Lakota, Ivory Coast N34+060 80
Laksa, N. Dakota U30+481 93
Lakse Fd., Norway L20+705 46
Lakshadweep, Indian Ocean H13+115 70
Laktsang, Tibet G42+303 71
Lala Musa, Pakistan H06+327 72
Lalbagh, India G10+242 73
Lalgani, India G29+259 73
La Libertad, Ecuador I35-022 104

La Libertad, Guatemala U01+167 100
La Libertad, Nicaragua 161+123 101
La Ligua, Chile S67-324 103
Lalin, Spain N49+426 52
Lalitpur, India G69+247 73
La Maddalena, I., Sardinia M34+413 57
La Malbaie, Quebec S03+476 91
Lamar, Colorado U76+381 94
Lamar, Missouri U26+374 95
Lamastre, France M63+450 55
Lambach, Austria M07+481 48
Lamballe, France N15+485 54
Lambayeque, Peru 130-066 104
Lambert I., Ireland, Rep. N36+535 43
Lambert's Ld., Greenland P30+790 26
Lambertville, New Jersey 100+403 96
Lambia, Greece L49+379 59
Lame, Chad M02+092 81
Lamego, Portugal N47+411 52
Lameroo, S. Australia C57-354 109
Lamesa, Texas L45+389 59
Lamia, Greece L45+389 59
Lamlash, Scotland N31+555 41
Lammermuir Hills, Scotland N16+559 41
Lamotrek Is., Caroline Is. C30+075 106
La Moure, N. Dakota U50+464 93
Lampa, Peru S80-153 104
Lampazos, Mexico U62+270 100
Lampedusa, I., Medit. Sea M12+355 81
Lampeter, Wales N25+521 38
Lamphun, Thailand F35+186 69
Lampton, C., N.-W. Terr. W20+710 88
Lampton, I., Burma F41+108 71
Lamu, Kenya K24-024 83
Lanak, Peru 117-063 104
Lanark, Scotland N23+557 41
Lancashire, co., England N16+537 37
Lancaster, England N17+540 37
Lancaster, New Hampshire S69+445 91
Lancaster, New York 122+429 96
Lancaster, Pennsylvania 108+401 96
Lancaster, S. Carolina 134+347 97
Lancaster, Wisconsin U04+429 91
Lancaster Sd., N.-W. Terr. 160+734 89
Lanchow, China F07+360 66
Landeck, Austria M27+471 48
Landen, Belgium M60+508 44
Lander, Wyoming V22+429 93
Landernau, France N26+484 54
Landes, dep., France N04+440 55
Landi Khana, Pakistan H23+342 72
Landi Kotal, Pakistan H23+342 72
Landon, Sweden M04+636 46
Landovery, Wales N13+519 38
Landsberg, W. Germany M25+481 48
Landsberg. See Gorzow Wielkopolski
Land's End, England N34+500 38
Landshut, W. Germany M17+490 48
Landskrona, Sweden M13+559 47
Langå, Denmark M31+563 47
Langadhas, Greece L41+408 59
Langchung, China E84+315 66
Langeland, I., Denmark M26+549 47
Langenthal, Switzerland M43+472 45
Langeland, I., Denmark L34+615 47
Lang Jökull, Iceland P30+646 46
Langkawi I., Malaya F31+063 69
Langlade, I., Atlantic Oc. R68+468 90
Langogne, France M67+447 55
Langøy, Norway M00+687 46
Langport, England N17+511 38
Langres, France M58+478 54
Langsa, Sumatra I-42+045 65
Långsele, Sweden L78+632 46
Lang-Son, N. Vietnam E79+218 69
Långträsk, Sweden L58+654 46
Languedoc, France M26+549 47
Länkäaret, Belgium M56+510 44
Lankor I.so, Tibet G42+325 71
Lannion, France N21+488 54
Lansdale, Pennsylvania 102+402 96
Lansing, Michigan 157+428 91
Lansingburg, New York S82+428 91
Lan Tao, China E36+223 67
Lanzarote, I., Canary Is. N82+290 80
Laoag, Philippines D87+182 65
Lao Bao, S. Vietnam E80+165 69
Lao-chang-Ho R., China E23-378 66
Lao-Cai, N. Vietnam F07+225 69
Laon, France M69+496 54
La Oroya, Peru 106-115 104
Laos, S.-E. Asia F10+192 69
Lao shan, China D86+363 66
Lapalisse, France M68+462 54
Lapeer, Michigan 150+431 91
La Pedada, Argentina S06-309 103
La Palma, I., Canary Is. P30+286 80
La Paragua, Venezuela S21+070 104
La Paz, Argentina R88-307 103
La Paz, Argentina S45-334 103
La Paz, Bolivia S49-165 104
La Paz, Honduras 176+143 101
La Paz, Mexico V32+241 100
Lapeenranta, Finland L11+610 47
Lapland, N. Europe L57+680 46
Lappträsk, Sweden L39+660 46
Laprida, Argentina S06-378 103
Lappajärvi, Finland L38+631 46
La Porte, Indiana T70+416 96
La Porte City, Iowa U13+424 95
Laptevykh Sea, U.S.S.R. D70+750 63
Lapsul Românesc, Romania L36+475 49
Lapy, Poland L43+530 49
Laqit, Kuwait J71+290 74
La Quiaca, Argentina S34-222 103
Lar, Iran J33+276 75
Larache, Morocco N38+350 80
Laragne, France M55+443 55

Litoměřice, Czechoslovakia M05+505 48
Little R., Missouri T88+363 97
Little Belt Mts., Montana V34+468 93
Little Current, Ontario T42+460 91
Little Falls, Minnesota U26+464 93
Little Falls, New York S89+430 96
Little Horn Mts., Arizona V52+334 92
Little River, Newfoundland A43+437 112
Little Rock, Arkansas U14+348 95
Little Smoky R., Alberta V74+546 88
Littleton, Colorado V00+396 94
Littleton, New Hampshire S70+443 91
Little Valley, New York T23+423 96
Luan, China E22+318 64
Liuchow, China E64+243 67
Lupan Shan, China E84+356 66
Liusvaara, Karelia K77+626 46
Live Oak, Florida T48+303 97
Liverpool, New South Wales B85+339 109
Liverpool, Nova Scotia S28+440 90
Liverpool & B., England N18+534 37
Liverpool Coast, Greenland P35+710 26
Liverpool Plains, N.S.W. C00+312 109
Livingston, Alabama T79+326 97
Livingston, Guatemala T82+158 100
Livingston, Montana V33+457 93
Livingston, Tennessee T62+364 97
Livingstone, Zambia U30+307 95
Livingstone, See Maramba
Livingstonia, Malawi K66+108 83
Livny, U.S.S.R. K45+524 60
Livo Joki, Finland L18+655 46
Livorno, Italy M28+435 56
Livramento, Brazil R63+308 103
Liwale, Tanzania K42+098 83
Liwa, Oman J21+246 75
Lizard & Pt., England N31+500 38
Ljubljana, Yugoslavia M03+461 56
Ljubuški, Yugoslavia L75+432 56
Llanguihue, L., Chile S76+411 103
Llanelly, Wales N19+530 38
Ljungdalen, Sweden M13+628 46
Ljusdal, Sweden L83+618 47
Llandaff, Wales N24+519 38
Llandeilo, Wales N24+519 38
Llandrindod Wells, Wales N20+522 38
Llandudno, Wales N23+533 38
Llanelli, Wales N25+517 38
Llanerchymedd, Wales N26+533 38
Llangollen, Wales N29+434 52
Llanidloes, Wales N26+528 38
Llano Estacado, New Mex. U78+340 94
Llanrhaeadr, Wales N20+528 38
Llanrwst, Wales N23+531 38
Lerena, Spain N36+383 52
Lleyn Pen., Wales N27+529 38
Lliamna, L., Alaska Y30+595 99
Llico, Chile S72-347 103
Lloydminster, Saskatchewan V30+534 88
Lluchmayor, Balearic Is. M72+395 53
Loango, Congo M20+046 82
Lobbes, Belgium M64+504 44
Loberia, Argentina R83-382 103
Lobito, Angola M08+124 82
Lobos, Argentina R86-352 103
Lobstick L., Labrador S30+540 89
Locarno, Switzerland M37+462 45
Lochalsh, Ontario T56+484 91
Lochalsh, Kyle of, Scotland N35+564 41
Lochbuie, Scotland N35+564 41
Locharron, Scotland N33+574 40
Lochearnhead, Scotland N26+564 41
Lochgelly, Scotland N21+551 41
Lochgilphead, Scotland N33+560 41
Lochinver, Scotland N31+582 40
Lochmaben, Scotland N21+551 41
Lochmaddy, Scotland N43+576 40
Lochnagar, Scotland N20+570 40
Lochy, L., Scotland N29+570 40
Lockerbie, Scotland N20+551 41
Lockhart, New South Wales C21-353 109
Lock Haven, Pennsylvania T15+411 96
Lockport, New York T22+431 96
Loc Ninh, S. Vietnam E81+118 65
Lochristi, Belgium M49+471 45
Lodenoye Pole, U.S.S.R. K69+608 60
Lodhran, Pakistan H20+295 72
Lodi, Wisconsin T87+434 91
Lödingen, Norway L84+684 46
Lodwar, Kenya K56+030 83
Lodz, Poland L63+518 49
Loenen, Netherlands M54+521 44
Loewoek, Celebes, D73+010 65
Lofer, Austria M14+476 48
Lofoten Is., Norway M16+680 46
Logan, Montana V39+459 93
Logan, Utah V42+418 94
Logan, Mt., Quebec S40+489 90
Logan, Mt., Yukon X30+606 88
Logansport, Indiana T68+408 95
Logone R., Cameroun-Chad. M00+104 81
Logroño, Spain N15+424 53
Lohardaga, India G32+234 73
Lohari, India G85+285 72
Loikaw, Burma F46+197 71
Loir, R., France N02+476 54
Loire Atlantique, dep., Fr. N11+474 54
Loiret-et-Cher, dep., France M82+475 54
Loja, Ecuador T25+040 104
Loja, Spain N25+372 52
Lokeren, Belgium M66+511 44
Lokka, Finland L14+678 46
Lökken, Denmark M32+574 47
Lökken, Norway M32+631 46
Loko, Sudan K84+044 81
Lokoja, Nigeria M50+078 80
Loks I., N-W. Territories S26+620 89
Lola, Angola M08+144 82
Lolland, Denmark M20+546 47

Lom, Bulgaria L41+438 58
Loman, Minnesota U23+485 93
Lomas, Argentina R80-348 103
Loma Tina, mt., Dom. Rep. S64+186 101
Lombardia, dep., Italy M30+457 56
Lombardia, Montana V39+461 93
Lombien, I. & Str., Indonesia D70-085 65
Lombok, I. & Str., Indonesia E24-088 65
Lome, Togo M84+062 80
Lomela, Zaire L40-022 82
Lomie, Cameroun M08+032 81
Lommel, Belgium M58+512 44
Lomond L., Scotland N28+562 41
Lomond Hills, Scotland N20+562 41
Lomza, Poland L48+532 49
Loncoche, Chile S77-394 103
Londiani, Kenya K54-002 83
Londinium, England N01+515 39
London, Ontario T37+430 91
Londonderry, & co.,
Northern Ireland, N44+550 42
Londonderry, C., W. Aust. D49-138 110
Londonderry, I., Chile S64-550 103
Long Beach, S. Carolina T03+338 99
Long I., Bahamas, The T01+234 101
Long I., New York S78+408 96
Long I., Nova Scotia S38+443 90
Long I., Maine S56+466 90
Long I., Ontario T70+496 89
Long I., Scotland N29+562 41
Long Ra., Newfoundland R74+500 90
Longa, Brazil Q73-054 105
Long Beach, California V79+338 92
Long Beach, New Jersey S85+396 96
Long Branch, New Jersey S84+403 96
Longchamps, Belgium M56+500 44
Longford, Tasmania C18-416 109
Longford & co., Ireland, Rep. N47+537 42
Long Island Sd. N.Y., etc. S77+411 96
Long Island City, New York S84+407 96
Long Melford, England M86+521 39
Longmont, Colorado V01+402 94
Long Point I., Ontario T32+426 91
Long Prairie, Minnesota U29+460 93
Longreach, Queensland C35-232 111
Longs Pk., Colorado V04+402 94
Longtown, England N01+474 38
Longueuil, Quebec S81+456 91
Longueil, France M57+494 54
Longuyon, France N28+324 95
Longview, Washington W18+461 92
Longwy, France N45+495 54
Long-Xuyen, S. Vietnam E87+104 69
Lonneker, Netherlands M48+522 44
Lons Saunier, France M57+467 54
Looc, Philippines D78+123 65
Looe, England N27+504 38
Lookout, C., N. Carolina T07+347 99
Loolmalasin, mt., Tanzania K56-030 83
Loop Hd., Ireland, Rep. N60+526 43
Lopei, China D24+476 64
Lopez C., Gabon M38-006 82
Lopik, Netherlands M60+520 44
Lop Nor, Sinkiang, China F88+404 64
Lopphavet, Norway L54+704 46
Lora Hamun, Pakistan H61+292 70
Lorain, Ohio T43+414 91
Loralai, Pakistan H38+304 70
Lorca, Spain N10+377 53
Lord Howe I., Pacific Ocean B35-314 106
Lordsburg, New Mexico V22-324 94
Loreto, Brazil R00-226 105
Loreto, Brazil R02-073 105
Lorica, Colombia T04+092 104
Lorient, France N20+478 54
Lorne, Victoria C36-386 109
Lorn, Firth of, Scotland N34+563 41
Lorrach, W. Germany M44+476 48
Lorraine, prov., France M53+487 54
Los Andes, Chile S64-328 103
Los Angeles, California V79+341 92
Los Angeles, Chile S74-375 103
Los Blancos, Argentina S16-235 103
Loshan, China F08+296 67
Lošinj I., Yugoslavia M04+445 56
Los Lamentos, Mexico V04+305 100
Los Menucos, Argentina S49-408 103
Los Pozos, Argentina S89-408 103
Los Santos, Panama T32+080 101
Los Santos de Maimona, Spain N38+385 52
Lossiemouth, Scotland N20+577 40
Los Teques, Venezuela S42+103 104
Los Tigres, Argentina S16-258 103
Lostwithiel, England N28+504 38
Los Vilos, Chile S69-319 103
Lot, dep., France M80+446 55
Lot, R., France M85+445 55
Lota, Chile S79-371 103
Lotbinière, Quebec S72+466 91
Lot-et-Garonne, dep., France M87+443 55
Lothian, reg., Scotland N18+559 41
Lottigna, Switzerland M36+465 45
Loubet Coast, Antarctica S25-680 27
Loudeac, France N16+482 54
Loudima, Congo M12-042 82
Loudon, Tennessee T56+357 97
Loudun, France N00+470 54
Louga, Senegal P08+154 80
Loughborough, England N07+528 37
Loughor, Wales N24+517 38
Loughrea, Ireland, Rep. N51+532 43
Louhans, France M59+466 54
Louisa, Kentucky T46+381 97
Louisburg, N. Carolina T20+362 97
Louisburg, Quebec S78+463 91
Louisiade Arch.,
Papua New Guinea B70-110 111
Louisiana, U.S.A. U20+306 99
Louis Trichardt, Transvaal L00-232 84
Louisville, Colorado V02+400 94
Louisville, Kentucky T65+383 97
Louisville, Mississippi T84+331 97
Louvain, See Leuven
Louveigne, Belgium M62+509 44
Louviers, France M83+492 54
Lovech, Bulgaria L52+643 46
Loveland, Colorado V00+404 94
Lovell, Wyoming V21+448 93
Loviisa (Lovisa), Finland L23+605 47
Lovington, New Mexico U80+329 94
Low, C., N-W. Territories T64+634 91
Lowa, Zaire L24-014 82
Lowell, Massachusets S68+427 91
Lowell, Michigan T62+429 91
Lower Brule, S. Dakota U57+441 93
Lowestoft, England M80+525 39
Lowicz, Poland L60+521 49
Lowland, N. Carolina T09+353 97
Lowriet, Belize T81+182 101
Lowville, New York T03+438 91
Loxton, S. Australia C57-345 109
Loyang, China E45+348 66
Loyang, China E63+244 67
Loyalty Is., Pacific Ocean A80-210 106
Lozère, dep., France M68+444 55
Loznica, Yugoslavia L65+445 58
Luampa, Zambia L34-152 84
Luan, See Changchih
Luanda, Angola M10-090 82
Luang Prabang, Laos F17+198 69
Luarca, Spain N40+435 52
Luashi, Zaire L38-110 82
Lubaczow, Poland L42+501 49
Lubana, Latvia L20+569 47
Lubartow, Poland L45+515 49
Lubben, E. Germany M07+520 48
Lubbock, Texas U70+336 94
Lubeck, W. Germany M26+539 48
Lübeck, Victoria C45-368 109
Lübecker B.,
E. & W. Germany M24+541 48
Lubefu, Zaire L32-046 82
Lublin, Poland L45+512 49
Lublin, Poland L45+512 49
Lubliniec, Poland L68+507 49
Lubnaig, L. Scotland N26+563 41
Lubumbashi, Zaire L14-118 83
Luc, le, France M52+434 55
Lucala, Angola L88-094 82
Lucan, Ireland, Rep. N39+534 43
Lucania, See Basilicata.
Lucca, Italy M27+439 56
Luce, Jamaica T19+185 101
Luce B., Scotland N29+548 41
Lucena, India G85+309 72
Lucena, Spain N27+374 52
Lucena, Philippines D78+139 65
Lucera, Italy L88+415 57
Lucerne, See Luzern.
Luch, U.S.S.R. K17+570 61
Luchow, China E88+288 67
Luchow (Hotei), China E17+319 66
Lucinda, Pennsylvania T27+413 96
Lucindale, S. Australia C58-370 109
Luckenwalde, E. Germany M08+519 48
Luckenwalde, E. Germany M11+521 48
Lucknow, India G54+268 73
Lucknow, Ontario T39+440 91
Lucon, France N07+465 54
Luderitz, S-W. Africa L88-266 84
Ludhiana, India G85+309 72
Ludington, Michigan T69+440 91
Ludlow, England N16+524 38
Ludvigshafen, W. Germany M40+495 48
Ludwigslust, E. Germany M21+533 48
Ludza, Latvia L14+565 47
Luebo, Zaire L52-054 82
Luga, U.S.S.R. L01+587 60
Lugano & L. di, Switz. M36+460 45
Lugansk, Ukraine K34+486 60
Lugh Ferrandi, Somalia K14+036 83
Lugo, Spain N45+430 52
Lugoj, Romania L48+457 58
Lugovaia, Kazakh. H13+430 62
Lugovoia, Yemen J14+157 74
Luhaiya, Yemen J14+157 74
Luhit R., India F54+276 71
Luhsien, See Luchow.
Luhwang Shan I., China D77+297 67
Luichow Pen., China E66+208 64
Luime, Angola L84-108 82
Luitpold Cst., Antarctica Q20-770 27
Lujan, Argentina R83-345 103
Lujan, Argentina R83-330 103
Lujan, Paraguay R75-252 103
Lukala, Zaire M04-056 82
Lukovit, Bulgaria L35+432 58
Lukoyanov, U.S.S.R. K03+550 61
Lukula, Zaire M12-054 82
Lule Alv, Sweden L47+656 46
Lulea, Sweden L18+656 46
Luluabourg, Zaire L46-058 82
Lulung, China E07+398 66
Lumberton, N. Carolina T24+346 97
Lumbres, France M78+507 54
Lumsden, New Zealand A69-457 112
Luna, Arkansas U06+334 97
Lunan B., Scotland N15+566 41
Lund, Sweden M11+557 47
Lundu, I., England N28+512 38
Lune, R., England N16+542 37
Lüneburg, W. Germany M28+533 48
Lunel, France M66+437 55
Luneville, France M51+486 54
Lungan, See Pingwu.
Lungki, China E13+246 67
Lungnan, China F03+349 66
Lungsi, China E18+252 67
Lungyen, China F03+349 66
Luni, India H11+260 70
Lunino, U.S.S.R. J89+536 61
Lunz, Austria L90+478 48
Luoperi, China D83+446 64
Lupeh, China D83+446 64
Lupiro, Tanzania K50-084 83
Lupkow, Poland L48+493 49

Luputa, Zaire L38-072 82
Luray, Virginia T21+387 91
Lurgan, N. Ireland N38+544 42
Luribay, Bolivia S46-170 104
Lure, Norway M13+664 46
Lusaka, Zambia L10-154 84
Lusambo, Zaire L40-050 82
Lusambo, Zaire L44-084 82
Lushnji, Albania L62+409 59
Lushun, China D82+388 66
Lusk, Wyoming U86+427 93
Luss, Scotland N28+561 41
Lüta, China ·D80+389 66
Luther, Michigan T65+441 91
Luton, England E13+409 66
Lutsen, Minnesota U04+476 91
Lutsk, Ukraine L28+508 60
Lütvia, Belgium M64+505 44
Luvia, Finland L50+613 47
Luxembourg, and Grand-duchy of,
N-W. Europe M54+497 44
Luxembourg, prov., Belg. M57+500 44
Luxeuil, France M52+478 54
Luxor, Egypt K74+256 81
Luzern, & canton, Switz. M40+471 45
Luzern, Philippines D85+150 65
Luzon, I., Philippines D75+200 64
Luzon Str. Philippines D75+200 64
Luzy, France M66+468 54
Lvov, Ukraine L36+498 60
Lwanhsien, China E07+397 66
Lwan-ping, China E13+409 66
Lyallpur, Pakistan H15+314 72
Lybster, Scotland N20+583 40
Lycksele, Sweden L68+646 46
Lydavenai, Lithuania L41+556 47
Lydda, Israel K61+320 76
Lydenburg, Transvaal L88-252 84
Lydney, England N16+517 38
Lyell, Mt., California V85+378 92
Lyell, Mt., Brit. Columbia V72+17 88
Lyell Ra., New Zealand A46-416 112
Lykens, Pennsylvania T11+405 96
Lyme B., England N18+506 38
Lyme Regis, England N18+507 38
Lymington, England N09+508 39
Lynchburg, Virginia T25+374 97
Lyndhurst, S. Australia C70-303 109
Lynn, Massachusets S65+425 96
Lynton, England N23+512 38
Lyon, Montana V39+448 93
Lyonnais, prov., France M65+458 54
Lyons, Georgia T44+322 97
Lyons, Kansas U49+384 95
Lyons, New York T12+430 96
Lyons, R., W. Australia E27-243 110
Lys, R., Belgium, etc. M69+509 44
Lysamis, Kenya K42-016 83
Lyse, Poland L51+534 44
Lysekil, Sweden M21+583 47
Lyss, Switz. M46+471 45
Lyster, Quebec S69+464 91
Lysva, U.S.S.R. J14+581 61
Lytham St Annes, England N18+537 37
Lyttelton, New Zealand A43-436 112
Lytton, British Columbia W09+502 88
Ma'an, Jordan K56+302 76
Maarheeze, Netherlands M57+513 44
Maarianhamina. See Mariehamn.
Ma'arret en Numan, Syria K50-357 76
Maas, R., Netherlands M55+518 44
Maasbree, Netherlands M54+514 44
Maaseik, Belgium M55+511 44
Maasssluis, Netherlands M65+519 44
Maastricht, Belgium M56+508 44
Maatsuyker Is., Tasmania C22-436 109
Mabote, Mozambique K66-222 84
Mabrouk, Mali N0S+194 80
Mabuki, Tanzania K70-030 83
Macadam, New Brunswick S44+456 90
Macae, Brazil Q32-059 105
Macaé, Brazil Q32-059 105
McConnellsburg, Pa. T18+399 96
McCook, Nebraska U66+402 94
Macalister, mt., New S. Wales C02-345 109
Macaloje, Mozambique K52-120 83
Macao (Port.), China E38+223 67
Macapa, Brazil R36+001 105
Macas, Ecuador T19-024 104
Macau, Brazil Q40-051 105
McCammon, Idaho V43+426 94
Macclesfield, England N13+533 37
McClintock Chan., N-W. Ter. U70+714 88
McClure, C., N-W. Ter. W08+746 88
McClure Str., N-W. Ter. V70+738 88
McConnellsburg, Pa. T18+399 96
Macdonald, L., W. Australia D37-234 110
Macdonnel Ranges, N. Terr., Aust. D15-232 110
Macdougall Ra., N. Terr. Aust. D00-196 111
Macedonia, rep., (Bandar), India G52+162 70
Macerata, Italy M09+433 56
Macerata, Italy M09+433 56
McGill, Nevada V59+395 92
Macgillycuddy's Reeks,
Ireland, Rep. N59+520 43
McGregor, Texas U44+314 95
McGregor Ra. Queensland C43-268 111
Mach, Pakistan H48+298 70
Machala, Ecuador T29-032 104
Machareti, Bolivia S19-208 104
Machias B., Maine S44+446 90
Machias, Maine S45+448 90
Machilipatnam (Bandar), India G52+162 70
Machiques, Venezuela S75+100 104
Machiwara, India G83+309 72
Machu Picchu, Peru S37-128 104
Machynlleth, Wales N23+526 38
Macias Nguema, Equat.-Guinea M38+036 80
Macin, Romania L11+452 58
McIntosh, S. Dakota U68+459 93
Mackay, Alberta V40+570 88
Mackay, Queensland H48+298 70
Mackay, L., N-W. Australia D37-226 110
Mackay, L., W. Australia G52+162 70
McKeesport, Pennsylvania T29+404 96

Monterey, Virginia T27+384 97
Monterey, B. of, California W14+367 92
Monteria, Colombia S34-272 103
Monteros, Argentina S34-272 100
Monterrey, Mexico U27-221 101
Monte San Angelo, Italy L84+417 57
Montes Claros, Brazil Q82-167 105
Montevideo, Minnesota U35+449 103
Montevideo, Uruguay R67-349 104
Monte Vista, Colorado V08+376 94
Montezuma, Georgia T54+324 97
Montfort-sur-Meu, France N12+481 54
Montgomery, Alabama T68+324 97
Montgomery, Missouri U09+390 95
Montgomery, Wales N19+526 38
Monthey, Switzerland M48+463 45
Monticello, Arkansas U10+336 95
Monticello, Georgia T54+333 97
Monticello, Maine S47+465 99
Monticello, New York S88+416 91
Monticello, Utah V26+380 94
Montijo, B. de, Panama T36+076 101
Montilla, Spain N28+375 52
Mont Joli, Quebec S49+486 90
Montlucon, France M74+464 54
Montmagny, Quebec S63+470 90
Montmedy, France M58+495 54
Montmirail, France M69+489 54
Montmorency, Quebec S67+469 91
Montoursville, Pennsylvania T12+412 96
Montpelier, Idaho V38+423 94
Montpelier, Vermont S76+443 91
Montpellier, France M67+436 55
Montreal, Quebec S44+493 90
Mont-St Jean, Belgium M64+507 44
Mont-St-Michel & B., Fr. N09+487 54
Montserrat, I., Leeward Is. S13+168 101
Montreuil Bellay, France M79+505 54
Montreuil, France M87+431 55
Montrose, Colorado V17+384 94
Montrose, Pennsylvania T06+418 96
Montrose, Scotland N15+567 41
Moorhead, Minnesota U41+469 93
Moorsel, Belgium M65+509 44
Moorslede, Belgium M72+509 44
Moose L., Manitoba U62+540 88
Moose R., Ontario T42+505 89
Moose Jaw, Saskatchewan V04+504 88
Moosehead L., Maine S58+456 90
Moosic L., Mts., Pennsylvania T03+417 96
Moosomin, Saskatchewan U70+501 88
Moosonee, Ontario T34+511 89
Mopti, Mali N24+142 80
Moquegua, Peru S66-172 104
Mora, Ethiopia K54+104 83
Mora, Cameroun M06+110 81
Mora, Minnesota U20+459 93
Mora, Portugal N49+389 52
Mora, Spain N23+397 52
Mora, Italy M35+456 56
Mora, Sweden M03+610 47
Moradabad, India G67+288 73
Mora de Rubielos, Spain N05+403 53
Moramanga, Malagasy Rep. J70-190 83
Morano Calabro, Italy L83+399 57
Morar, India G70+262 73
Morar L., Scotland N34+569 40
Morat. See Murten
Moratalla, Spain N11+382 53
Morava R., Yugoslavia L53+444 58
Moravia, Czechoslovakia L75+493 49
Moravska Trebova, Czech. L79+498 49
Morawhanna, Guyana R88+083 104
Moray Firth, Scotland N22+577 40
Morbihan, dep., France N18+479 54
Mordialloc, Victoria C59-380 88
Morden, Manitoba U50+493 61
Morea. See Pelop.
Morea, Greece L46+376 59
Moreau R., S. Dakota U72+452 98
Morecambe & B., England N17+451 37
Moreda, Spain N20+374 52
Moree, New South Wales C01-295 109
Moreira, Brazil S21-006 104
Moreton B., Queensland A13-390 112
Moreton, New Zealand M42+464 45
Morella, Mexico U67+196 100
Morella, Spain N01+406 53
Morelia, Mexico U65+284 100
Morelos, Mexico V13+267 100
Morelos, state, Mexico U54+186 100
Morena, India G76+261 73
Morena, Sa., Spain N24+383 52
Morenci, Arizona V26+332 94
Moreton R., Queensland B68-267 111
Morez, France M54+465 54
Morgan City, Louisiana U07+297 95
Morgan, N. Carolina T40+357 97

Morobe, Papua New Guinea C15-078 111
Morocco, N.-W. Africa N30+326 80
Morogoro, Tanzania K44-068 83
Morokwen, Cape Province L36-262 84
Moron, Cuba T22+221 101
Moron, Venezuela S49+110 104
Morona, Ecuador T15-028 104
Morondava, Malagasy Rep. K04-204 83
Moron de la Frontera, Spain N33+371 52
Mors, Denmark M38+568 47
Morshansk, U.S.S.R. K19+534 61
Mortagne, France M87+485 54
Mortagua, Portugal N49+404 52
Mortain, France N06+486 54
Mortlake, Victoria C43-381 109
Morundah, New S. Wales C22-349 109
Moruya, New S. Wales B89-360 109
Morven, Queensland A53-448 112
Morvi, India H24+228 70
Morwell, Victoria C22-382 109
Moscow, Idaho V72+467 92
Moscow. See Moskva
Moselle, dep, France M48+489 54
Moselle, R., France M53+489 54
Mosera I. See Masira I.
Mosgiel, New Zealand A58-458 112
Moshupa, Botswana L28-248 84
Mosjoen, Norway M11+658 46
Moskenesoya, Norway M11+680 46
Moskva, U.S.S.R. K45+558 60
Mosquera, Brazil R21-012 104
Mosquera, Colombia S63+094 104
Mosquito Bank, Nicaragua T46+132 101
Moss, Norway M26+595 47
Mossamedes, Angola M16-152 84
Mossburn, New Zealand A70-457 112
Mossel B., Cape Province L46-342 84
Mossgiel, New South Wales C33-333 109
Mossoro, Brazil Q44-052 105
Mossurize, Mozambique K72+206 84
Moss Vale, New S. Wales B88-346 109
Most, Czechoslovakia M08+505 48
Mostaganem, Algeria N00+358 80
Mostardas, Brazil R35-310 103
Mostar, Yugoslavia L73+433 58
Mosul, Iraq K12+365 74
Mota del Marques, Spain N31+416 52
Motala, Sweden M45+461 47
Motatan, Venezuela S63+094 104
Motherwell, Scotland N24+558 41
Motier, Switzerland M48+469 45
Motiers, Switzerland M50+469 45
Motihari, India G30+266 73
Motril, Spain N22+367 52
Mott, N. Dakota U84+211 100
Motueka, New Zealand A42-411 112
Motul, Mexico T84+211 100
Moturoa, New Zealand A36-390 112
Moudon, Switzerland M48+469 45
Moudros, Greece L29+399 59
Moudjeria, Chad L68+088 81
Moukden. See Shenyang
Moula, Gabon M24-020 82
Moulamein & R., N.S.W. C36-351 109
Moulins, France M70+466 54
Moulmein, Burma F44+164 71
Moulouya R., Morocco N22+330 80
Moulton, Alabama T74+344 97
Mound City, Illinois T85+370 97
Mound Grove, Missouri U14+371 97
Mountain Home, Arkansas U15+363 97
Mountain Sheep Bluffs, Montana V03+473 93
Mountain Ayr, Iowa U26+407 95
Mount Barker, S. Australia C67-351 109
Mount Bellew, Ireland, Rep.

Mount Stewart, P.E.I. S17+464 90
Mount Union, Pennsylvania T18+404 96
Mount Vernon, Illinois T84+384 95
Mount Vernon, Indiana T77+380 95
Mount Vernon, Kentucky T57+374 97
Mount Vernon, New York T13+387 91
Moura, Brazil S10-016 104
Moura, Portugal N45+381 52
Mourão, Portugal N44+384 52
Mourne R., N. Ireland N36+542 42
Mourne Mts., N. Ireland N45+548 42
Moussoro, Chad L80+136 81
Moutier, Switzerland M46+473 45
Moutohora, New Zealand A14-383 112
Mowlaik, Burma F64+236 71
Mowming, China E54+217 67
Mowping, China D80+374 66
Moy R., Ireland, Rep. N55+541 42
Moyale, Kenya K36+034 83
Moyobamba, Peru T12-062 104
Mozambique, rep., E. Africa K70-200 84
Moziga, U.S.S.R Q55+840 26
Mozyr, Belorussia L05+520 60
Mpanda, Tanzania K84-064 83
Mporokoso, Zambia K88-094 83
Mstislavl, Belorussia K80+541 60
Mtakuja, Tanzania K86-072 83
Mtarica, Mozambique K48-128 83
Mito Andei, Kenya K40-028 83
Mtoko, Rhodesia K76-174 84
Mtsensk, U.S.S.R. K51+533 60
Mu, R., Burma F57+228 71
Muaddhidham, el, Saudi Arabia K43+278 74
Muang Chaiya, Thailand F35+093 69
Muang Chana, Thailand F26+070 69
Muang Nan, Thailand F26+188 69
Muang Langsuan, Thailand F35+100 69
Muang Palien, Thailand F32+073 69
Mubarraz, Saudi Arabia K62+256 74
Mubende, Uganda K82+004 83
Muchinga Mts., Zambia K80-116 83
Muckish, Ireland, Rep. N48+551 42
Muckros Hd., Ireland, Rep. N52+546 42
Mudanya, Turkey L07+404 74
Mudawwara, Jordan K54+294 76
Muddusjarvi, Finland L19+691 46
Mudgee, New S. Wales C02-327 109
Mudhnib, Saudi Arabia K04+259 74
Muford C. Labrador S13+582 89
Mugia, Spain N55+431 52
Mugla, Turkey L10+372 74
Muglad, Sudan L14+110 81
Muhamdi, India G58+279 73
Muhammadgarh, India J05+375 75
Muharraq, The Gulf J56+264 75
Mühldorf, W. Germany M15+482 48
Mühlehorn, Switzerland M35+471 45
Mühlhausen, W. Germany M27+512 48
Muhu, Estonia L41+586 47
Muhu Vain, Estonia L40+588 47
Munak, Uzbek. J06+438 62
Muine Bheag, Ireland, Rep. N42+527 43
Mukalla, Yemen, South J65+146 74
Mukdahan, Thailand F01+164 69
Mukden. See Shenyang
Mukhtuul, U.S.S.R. E30+607 63
Mukinath, Nepal G37+291 73
Muktsar, India H03+305 72
Mula, Spain N08+380 53
Mulanje, Mt., Malawi K56-156 83
Mulchen, Chile S73-377 103
Mulgrave, Nova Scotia S08+456 90
Mulhacen, Mexico V42+268 100
Mülheim, W. Germany M48+510 48
Mülheim, W. Germany M49+515 48
Mulhouse, France M46+477 54
Mulki, India H01+131 70
Mull Hd., Orkney, Scot. N18+594 40
Mull, I. Scotland N36+564 41
Mull, Sd. of, Scotland N35+565 41
Mullaittivu, Sri Lanka G55+093 70
Mullaley, New South Wales C01-311 109
Muller Peg., Borneo E27-284 110
Mullet L., Michigan T57+455 91
Mullewa, W. Australia D75+050 65
Mullingar, Ireland, Rep. N44+535 43
Mullion Creek, N.S.W. C05-332 109
Muloorwurtina, S. Australia C60-301 109
Mulroy B. Ireland, Rep. N46+552 42
Multan, Pakistan H21+302 72
Multia, Finland L31+624 46
Mumbondo, Angola M04-104 82
Mumbwa, Zambia L18-150 82
Muna, Indonesia D75+050 65
Muncie, Indiana U00+421 91
Mundo Novo, Brazil Q63-118 105
Mungari, Mozambique K68-174 84
Mungindi, N.S.W.-Qnsld. C06-289 109
Munich. See Munchen
Muniesa, Spain N05+410 53
Munkfors, Sweden M09+599 47
Munro, Louisiana U12+324 95
Münster, Switzerland M27+466 45
Münster, Switzerland M41+465 45
Münster, W. Germany M41+472 45
Münster. See Munchen

Murbat, Oman J31+171 75
Murca, Portugal N45+414 52
Murcheh Khur, Iran J52+331 75
Murchison, C., N.-W. Terr. S24+636 89
Murchison Falls, see Kabalega Falls
Murchison Mts., N.Z. A76+452 112
Murchison, R., W. Aust. E22-266 110
Murcia, Spain N07+380 53
Murdo, S. Dakota U65+438 93
Muresul (Maros), R.,—
Romania L54+462 58
Murfreesboro, Tennessee T68+358 93
Muri, Switzerland M40+473 45
Murias de Paredes, Spain N37+429 52
Müritz See, E. Germany M14+534 48
Murjo, mt., Java E55-066 65
Murmansk, U.S.S.R. K70+690 62
Muroran, U.S.S.R. C54+423 68
Muros, Spain N54+428 52
Murphy, N. Carolina T54+351 97
Murphysboro, Illinois T86+378 95
Murray, Kentucky T80+366 95
Murray, Utah V42+406 98
Murray R., N.S.W., etc. C39-352 109
Murray Bridge, S. Australia C65-352 109
Murray Harbour, P.E.I. S15+460 90
Murray River, P.E.I. S16+460 90
Murrayville, Victoria C53-353 109
Murree, Pakistan H10+339 72
Murren, Switzerland M43+466 45
Murrumbidgee, R., N.S.W. C35-346 109
Murrumburrah & Harden,
New South Wales C10-346 109
Murrurundi, N.S.W. B85-318 109
Mursan, India G72+275 72
Murshidabad, India G10+243 73
Mursur, Oman J22+249 75
Murten & See, Switzerland M47+469 45
Murtoa, Victoria C45-357 109
Mururoa I., Tuamotu Arch. X10-215 107
Murwara, India H06+258 81
Murzuq, Libya M06+258 81
Mus, Turkey K21+388 74
Musa Kala, Afghanistan H61+323 75
Musalamya, Saudi Arabia J65+275 74
Muscat (Masqat), Oman J09+236 75
Muscat & Oman. See Oman
Muscatine, Iowa U06+414 95
Musemir, Yemen, South K02+134 74
Musgrave Harb., Nfd. R52+495 90
Musgrave Ra., New Guinea C40-063 111
Musgrave Ra., S. Australia D20-260 110
Musheramore, Ireland, Rep. N54+520 43
Mushie, Zaire L78-030 82
Muskeget Chan., Mass. S62+413 96
Muskegon, Michigan T68+432 91
Muskegon R., Michigan T62+440 91
Muskogee, Oklahoma U33+359 95
Muskwaro, L., Quebec S06+506 90
Musmar, Sudan K56+180 81
Musoma, Tanzania K68-064 83
Musselburgh, Scotland N18+559 41
Mussidan, France M88+450 55
Mussuma, Angola L48-142 82
Mustahil, Ethiopia K02+052 83
Mustajidda, Saudi Arabia K19+266 74
Mustang, Nepal G37+291 73
Mustang L., Texas U43+276 94
Musters, L., Argentina S56-455 103
Muswellbrook, N.S.W. B85-323 109
Mut, Egypt L06+254 81
Mut, Turkey K70+366 74
Mutano, Zambia L22-124 82
Mutano, Angola M01-166 84
Mutorai, U.S.S.R. F27+615 63
Mutshatsha, Zaire L34-056 82
Mutsu B, Japan C53+411 68
Mutton I., Ireland, Rep. N57+528 43
Mutumbo, Angola L76-134 82
Mutupet, India G66+104 70
Muwale, Tanzania K68-064 83
Muy, le, France M50+435 55
Muya, Japan D02+342 68
Muya, U.S.S.R. E24+563 63
Muy Muy, Nicaragua T63+127 101
Muzaffarabad, Kashmir H09+344 72
Muzaffargarh, Pakistan H23+301 72
Muzaffarnagar, India G74+294 72
Muzaffarpur, India G27+261 73
Muzhi, U.S.S.R. H63+655 62
Muzquiz, Mexico U69+278 100
Muztagh Ata, Sinkiang, China G89+383 72
Mwanza, Tanzania K72-026 83
Mweelrea, Ireland, Rep. N59+536 42
Mweru L., Zaire L08-090 83
Mwinilunga, Zambia L34-120 82
Myall, L., New S. Wales B77-325 109
Myanaung, Burma F58+82 71
Myaungmya, Burma F52+238 71
Myebon, Burma F69+201 71
Myemolektikat, Mt., Burma F37+134 71
Myingyan, Burma F57+214 71
Myitkyina, Burma F45+254 71
Myjava, Czechoslovakia L74+488 49
Mymensingh, Bangladesh F87+248 71
Myohaung, Burma F71+206 71
Myrdal, Norway M47+607 47
Myrtle Creek, S. Australia C71-304 109
Myrtleford, Victoria C19-366 109
Myslowice, Poland L67+502 49
Mysore. See Karnataka
Mystic, S. Dakota U82+441 93
Mziha, Tanzania K44-058 83
Mzimba, Malawi K68-120 83

Naaf, Bangladesh F75+210 71
Naarden, Netherlands M59+523 44
Naas, Ireland, Rep. N40+532 43
Nabadwip, India G10+234 73
Nabadwip, Iran J43+274 75
Nabatiye, Lebanon K57+334 76
Nabberu, L., W. Australia D87-257 110
Nabha, India G83+304 72
Nacaome, Honduras T75+136 101
Nachvak B., Labrador S21+592 89
Nacimiento, Mexico U71+292 100
Nackara, S. Australia C65-328 109

Index

Ngulu, I., Pacific Ocean C78+075 106
Ngwasi, Tanzania K46-086 83
Nha-Trang, S. Vietnam E65+123 69
Nhill, Victoria C50-363 109
Niafounke, Mali N24+160 80
Niagara, Ontario T25+433 91
Niagara Falls, New York T24+431 91
Niagara Falls, Ontario T24+431 91
Niah, Sarawak E38+037 65
Niamey, Niger M78+134 80
Nia Nia, Zaire L14+014 83
Niapa, mt., Borneo F44+011 65
Nias, I., Indonesia F44+011 65
Nicaragua, rep., Cent. Amer. T62+130 101
Nicaragua L., Nicaragua T63+116 101
Nicastro, Italy L82+390 57
Nice, France M47+437 55
Nicobar Is., Indian Ocean
Nicolet, Quebec S76+462 91
Nicoque, Mozambique K36-128 83
Nicosia, Cyprus K70+352 76
Nicoya & Pen., Costa Rica T62+100 101
Nidau, Switzerland M47+471 45
Nidd R., England N10+540 37
Nidzica, Poland L57+533 49
Niedere Tauern, Austria M06+473 48
Niedersachsen, W. Germany M42+528 48
Nielle, Ivory Coast N34+102 80
Nièvre, Chad L50+142 81
Nièvre, dep., France M68+471 54
Nigde, Turkey K62+380 74
Niger, rep., W. Africa M30+156 81
Niger R., W. Africa N10+150 80
Nigeria, W. Africa M40+100 80
Nighasan, India G55+282 73
Nigula, Estonia L20+595 47
Niigata, Japan C66+379 68
Niihau, I., Hawaiian Is., Y60+220 106
Nitaka Chain, Taiwan D84+240 67
Nijil, Jordan K57+305 76
Nile, R., N. Africa K72+250 81
Niles, Michigan T68+418 91
Nikitros, Greece L34+412 58
Nikki, Benin M72+098 80
Nikko Nat. Park, Japan C64+368 68
Nikolayevsky, U.S.S.R. J87+501 61
Nikolayev, Ukraine K78+470 60
Nikolayevsk-na-Amure,
  U.S.S.R. C56+533 63
Nikolo Kozelsk. Ukraine K71+476 60
Nikolskaya Pestrovka, U.S.S.R. J84+538 61
Nikolsk Berezovka, U.S.S.R. J35+561 61
Nikopol, Ukraine K63+476 60
Niksar, Turkey K48+407 74
Niksic, Yugoslavia L66+428 58
Nila, I., Indonesia D33+068 65
Nimach, (Neemuch), India H00+245 70
Nimes, France M64+439 55
Nimgiri, India G59+196 71
Nimmitabel, New S. Wales C05-365 109
Nine de Julio, Argentina S05-354 99
Ninety Mile Beach, Victoria C16-382 109
Nineveh, Iraq K11+366 74
Ningan, China D33+444 64
Ningerh, China E86+373 66
Ninghai, China D81+293 67
Ninghsien, China E37+267 67
Ningpo, China D80+298 67
Ning-sia. See Yingchwan
Ningteh, China E03+267 67
Ning-wu-fu, China E46+390 66
Ning-yüan-ting, China E44+403 66
Ninh-binh, N. Vietnam E84+203 69
Ninh Hoa, S. Vietnam E66+140 65
Ninove, Belgium M66+508 44
Niobrara R., Nebraska U71+424 98
Nioet, mt., Borneo F60+010 65
Nioro, Mali N58+152 80
Niort, France N03+463 54
Nipani, India G69+191 70
Nipawin, Saskatchewan
Nipe, B. de, Cuba T04+208 101
Nipigon, Ontario T80+492 89
Nipigon, L., Ontario T80+500 89
Nipissing, L., Ontario T29+462 91
Nirmal, India G69+191 70
Nis, Yugoslavia L49+433 58
Nisab, Saudi Arabia J81+149 74
Nishapur. See Neyshabur.
Nishino, Japan C77+348 68
Nishio, Japan C71+366 59
Nisiros, I., Greece L17+366 59
Nissan, Solomon Islands B60-053 106
Nissi, Estonia L34+591 47
Niterói, Brazil Q79-228 105
Nith, R., Scotland N22+550 41
Nitra, Czechoslovakia L71+483 49
Niue, I. Cook Islands Z30+190 106
Nivelles, Belgium M64+506 44
Nivernais, prov. France M68+471 54
Nizamabad, India G71+187 70
Nizampatnam, India G55+159 70
Nizana, Israel K63+309 76
Nizhne Chirskaya, U.S.S.R. K12+484 61
Nizhne Udinsk, U.S.S.R. F35+549 63
Nizhni Pesha, U.S.S.R. J73+668 62
Nizhniy Serogoyz, Ukraine K64+469 60
Nizhniy Kresty, U.S.S.R. B25+687 63
Nizhiy Lomov, U.S.S.R. K02+536 61

Nizhniy Tagil, U.S.S.R. J01+579 61
Nizke Tatry, Czechoslovakia L63+490
Njombe, Tanzania K60-094 83
Nkhota-Kota, Malawi K64-130 84
Nkongsamba, Cameroun M30+050 81
Nmai R., Burma F41+264 71
Noagarh, India G47+204 71
Noakhali. See Sudharam
Noanama, Colombia T13+047 104
Noatak R., Alaska Y60+675 99
Nobber, Ireland, Rep. N40+538 42
Nochistlan, Mexico U44+174 100
Noerbo, Norway M56+587 47
Nogales, Arizona V36+313 94
Nogaro, France N00+438 55
Nogent-le-Rotrou, France M85+483 54
Nogent-sur-Seine, France M69+485 54
Noginsk, U.S.S.R. K40+558 60
Nohar, India H02+292 72
Noirmoutier, I. de, France N14+470 54
Nokhtuysk, U.S.S.R. E11+600 63
Nola, Cent. Afr. Rep. L84+034 82
Nola, Italy M03+409 57
Nome, Alaska Z00+642 99
Nomeny, Is., Quebec T00+465 91
Nomoi, Is., Caroline Islands B65+060 106
Nonacho L., N.-W. Terr. V30+614 88
Nonancourt, France M83+488 54
Nong-han, Thailand F11+174 69
Nong Khai, Thailand F13+179 69
Nongoma, Natal K80-280 84
Nong-son, S. Vietnam E72+156 69
Nonni, R. (Nun), China D64+488 64
Nonno, Ethiopia K46+084 83
Nonoava, Mexico V10+274 100
Nonouti, I. Gilbert Islands A35-005 106
Nöo, Estonia L21+583 47
Noojee, Victoria C24-379 109
Noonthorungee, N.S.W. C46-310 109
Noordeloos, Netherlands M60+519 44
Noordwolde, Netherlands M53+529 44
Nootka I., Brit. Columbia W41+498 88
Nootongoro, Tanzania K62-032 83
Nora, Sweden M00+595 47
Noranda, Quebec T25+482 91
Nord, dep. France M71+505 54
Nord Cap (Horn), Iceland P44+665 46
Nordenshelda, Arkh., U.S.S.R. F55-762
Nordhausen, E. Germany M25+515 48
Nordkapp, Norway L25+711 46
Nordkyn Halvoy, Norway L12+709 46
Nördlingen, W. Germany M27+489 48
Nordost Rundingen, Greenland N60+810
Nordreisa, Norway L44+698 46
Nordrhein-Westfalen, W. Ger. M48+518 48
Nord Slesvig. See Jylland, South
Nordvik, U.S.S.R. E53+739 63
Nore, Norway M36+601 47
Nore R., Ireland, Rep. N42+523 43
Norfolk, Virginia T08+369 97
Norfolk, co., England M84+527 39
Norfolk Broads, England M81+527 39
Norfolk I. Pacific Ocean A72-290 106
Norfolk Res., Arkansas U14+364 95
Norgama, Pakistan H50+286 70
Noril'mesund, Norway M53+603 47
Norily, U.S.S.R. G06-694 62
Norman, N.-W. Territories W32+649 88
Norman, Oklahoma U44+352 95
Normanby I., Papua New Guinea
  B84-100 111
Normanton, Queensland C53-176 111
Norman Wells, N.-W. Terr. W40+652 88
Norquin, Argentina S64-377 103
Norquinco, Argentina S66-418 103
Norris, L., Tennessee T54+364 97
Norris Arm, Newfoundland R61+491 90
Norristown, Pennsylvania T02+402 96
Norrköping, Sweden L83+586 47
Norrsundet, Sweden L78+610 47
Norrtalie, Sweden L68+598 47
Norseman, W. Australia D80-321 110
Norsholm, Sweden L84+585 47
North C., Antarctica A80-700 27
North C., New Zealand A42-344 112
North C., Nova Scotia S02+461 91
North Chan., Ontario T50+461 91
North Chan., Scot.-N. Ire. N33+550 42
North Downs, England M87+513 39
North I., New Zealand 112
North Sea, W. Europe 34
North Adams, Massachusetts S78+427 96
Northallerton, England N08+543 37
North Bay, Ontario T27+463 91
North Bend, Oregon W25+434 96
North Berwick, Scotland N16+560 41
North Borneo (Sabah),
  Borneo E21+054 65
North Bourke, N.S.W. C24-300 109
North Carolina, state, U.S.A. T40+358 91
North Creek, New York S84+437 91
North Dakota, state, U.S.A. U78+472 98
Northern Circars, India G50+165 70
Northern Ireland, Brit. Isles N40+544 34
Northern Territory, Aust. 110-111
Northfield, Minnesota U19+445 93
North Land. See Severnaya Zemlya
North Lisbon, Wisconsin U01+439 91
North Little Rock, Arkansas U13+348 95
North Platte, Nebraska U64+411 94
North Pole, Arctic Ocean 26
North Riding, see North Yorkshire
North Ronaldsay, I. & Firth,
  Orkney, Scotland N14+594 40
North Shields, England N09+550 37
North Sydney, Nova Scotia S02+462 90
North Tonawanda, N.Y. T23+430 96
North Truchas Pk., n. Mex. V04+360 94
Northumberland, co., Eng. N13+553 37
Northumberland, Pa. T11+409 96

Northumberland Str..
  New Brunswick, etc. S27+465 90
North Vancouver, B.C. W19+494 88
Northville, New York S86+433 91
North West C., W. Aust. E35+218 110
North-West River, Labrador S01+537 89
North-West Territories, Can. 88-89
Northwood, Iowa U19+434 95
Northwood, Iowa N15+532 37
Norton, Kansas U60+398 95
Norton, New Brunswick S34+456 90
Norton Sd., Alaska Z00+636 99
Norwalk, Connecticut S81+411 96
Norwalk, Ohio T46+413 91
Norway, Michigan T77+458 91
Norway, king.,-N.-W. Europe 46-47
Norwich, Connecticut S72+415 96
Norwich, England M82+526 39
Norwich, New York T03+425 96
Norwood, New York T00+447 91
Noshiro, Japan C60+402 68
Nossegem, Belgium M63+509 44
Nosy Be, I., Madagascar J70-134 83
Noto, Sicily L89+368 57
Noto Pen, Japan C80+372 68
Notodden, Norway M38+595 47
Notre Dame B., Nfd. R60+497 90
Notre Dame Mts., Quebec S53+476 90
Notre-Dame-du-Lac, Quebec T32+446 91
Nottingham & co., England N07+530 37
Nottingham I., N.-W. Terr. T17+636 89
Nouakchott, Mauritania P06+180 80
Nova Chaves, Angola L52-108 82
Nova Cruz, Brazil Q32-064 105
Nova Gaïa, Angola L74-102 82
Nova Goa (Panjim),
  Goa, Daman & Diu H07+156 70
Nova Lisboa, See Huambo
Novara, Italy M38+454 56
Nova Scotia, prov. Canada S20+450 105
Nova Venecia, Brazil Q63-188 105
Novaya Sibir, Ostrov, U.S.S.R.
  C10+750 63
Novaya Zemlya, U.S.S.R. J20+730 62
Nova York, Brazil Q84-068 105
Nové Zamky, Czech. L71+480 49
Novgorod, U.S.S.R. K82+586 60
Novi, Yugoslavia M01+451 56
Novi Pazar, Bulgaria L17+434 58
Novi Pazar, Yugoslavia L57+431 58
Novi Sad, Yugoslavia L61+453 58
Novo Alekseyevka, Kasakh. H66+453 62
Novocherkassk, U.S.S.R. K29+474 61
Novokuznetsk, U.S.S.R. G17+538 62
Novo Mesto, Yugoslavia M01+458 56
Novomoskovsk, U.S.S.R. K43+479 60
Novo Nikolayevsky, U.S.S.R. K58+487 61
Novorossiysk, U.S.S.R. K44+448 62
Novoshakhtinsk, U.S.S.R. K31+477 61
Novosibirsk, U.S.S.R. G42+550 62
Novosibirskiye Ostrova, U.S.S.R.
  C60+755 63
Novo Troitsk, U.S.S.R. J21+545 61
Novourgench, Uzbek H86+415 61
Nozay, France N10+476 54
Nsanje, Uganda K86-008 83
Nuanetsi, Rhodesia K8-214 84
Nueces R., Texas U48+283 94
Nueltin L., N.-W. Terr. U56+602 88
Nuevo, G. Argentina S28-426 103
Nuevo Laredo, Mexico U57+274 100
Nuevo Leon, state, Mexico U60+262 100
Nügssuaq, Pen., Greenland R35+700 26
Nuits St Georges, France M60+471 54
Nukumrkah, Victoria C27-361 109
Nukus, Uzbek J02+424 61
Nules, Spain N01+398 53
Nullagine, W. Australia E00-218 110
Nullarbor Plain, W. Aust. D40-306 110
Numazu, Japan C67+351 68
Numfoor I., New Guinea D01-010 65
Nunchia, Colombia S74+056 104
Nuneaton, England N09+525 37
Nunivak I., Alaska Z15+600 99
Nunkiang, China D59+490 64
Nuoro, Sardinia M34+403 57
Nuqui, Colombia T14+057 104
Nurmes, Finland L05+636 46
Nürnberg, Germany M24+494 48
Nurpur, India G84+323 72
Nurri, Sardinia M35+397 57
Nusaybin, Turkey K23+371 74
Nushki, Pakistan H54+296 70
Nutrias, Venezuela S56+079 104
Nuwara Eliya, Sri Lanka G56+070 70
Nyada, Sweden L72+629 46
Nyah, Victoria C40-352 109
Nyaker, Sweden L64+638 46
Nyala, Sudan L30+120 81
Nyalikungu, Tanzania K70-026 83
Nyamlell, Sudan L18+092 81
Nyandoma, U.S.S.R. K29+617 62
Nyantza, Tanzania K82-030 83
Nyanza, Rwanda L00-024 83
Nyasa, L., Malawi K64-118 83
Nyasaland, (Malawi) K4-Afr. K66-120 83
Nyazepetrovsk, U.S.S.R. J03+561 61
Nyda, U.S.S.R. H11+667 62
Nyeri, Kenya K48-004 83
Nyhammar, Sweden M00+603 47

Nyiregyháza, Hungary L50+479 49
Nykobing, Denmark M19+547 47
Nykobing, Denmark M37+568 47
Nyköping, Sweden L78+587 47
Nylstroom, Transvaal L10-246 84
Nyamagee, New South Wales
  C22-321 109
Nymboida & R., N.S.W. B75-299 109
Nyngan, New South Wales C17-316 109
Nyon, Switzerland M53+464 45
Nyonga, Tanzania K78-068 83
Nyons, France M59+444 55
Nysa, Poland L76+505 49
Nysted, Denmark M19+546 47
Nyurba, U.S.S.R. E10+634 63
Nyuya, U.S.S.R. E22+606 63
Nzega, Tanzania K70-042 83

Oababatiya, Israel K58+324 76
Oacoma, S. Dakota U56+438 93
Oahe Res., S. Dakota U62+450 93
Oahu, I., Hawaiian Islands Y45+212 107
Oakan, Japan C34+434 68
Oakbank, S. Australia C57-331 109
Oakes, N. Dakota U48+462 93
Oakham, England N04+527 37
Oakland, California W14+378 92
Oakland, Maryland T26+394 91
Oakley, Kansas U66+390 94
Oakville, Ontario T28+435 91
Oamaru, New Zealand A34-451 112
Oates Ld., Antarctica B50-700 27
Oatlands, Tasmania C16-423 109
Oaxaca & state, Mexico U40+170 100
Ob, R., U.S.S.R. H55+655 62
Obama, Japan C85+355 68
Oban, New Zealand A71-469 112
Oban, Scotland N33+564 41
Obatogamau L., Quebec S88+496 90
Obbia, Somalia J68+054 83
Obeh, Afghanistan H71+345 75
Oberammergau, W. Germany M24+476 48
Oberhausen, W. Germany M49+515 48
Oberlin, Kansas U63+398 94
Oberon, New South Wales C01-337 109
Oberriet, Switzerland M33+473 45
Oberwald, Switzerland M40+465 45
Obi, I. Indonesia D44-016 65
Obidos, Brazil R63-018 105
Obidos, Portugal N55+394 52
Obihiro, Japan C40+428 68
Obo, Cent. Afr. Rep. L20+052 81
Oahe Res., S. Dakota U62+448 88
Obock, F.T.A.I. K10+118 83
Oborona, U.S.S.R. K25+521 61
Oborona, Nicaragua T53+143 101
Obskaya Guba, U.S.S.R. H13+700 62
Ocala, Florida T43+292 97
Ocampo, Mexico U57+229 100
Ocana, Colombia S80+081 104
Ocana, Spain N21+399 52
Occidental, Cord., Colombia T10+050 104
Ocean I., Pacific Ocean A63-012 106
Oceana, W. Virginia T40+377 97
Ocean City, New Jersey S87+393 96
Ocbil Hills, Scotland N22+562 41
Ocland, Romania L28+461 58
Occa, B. de, Dominican Rep. S64+183 101
Oconto, Wisconsin T77+449 91
Ocos, Guatemala U13+145 100
Ocotal, Nicaragua T68+138 101
Ocumare, Venezuela S41+101 104
Oda, Ghana N06+060 80
Oda, Japan D15+352 68
Odate, Japan C54+375 68
Odate, Japan C57+403 68
Odawara, Japan C65+352 68
Odemira, Portugal N52+376 52
Odemis, Turkey L12+382 74
Odense, Denmark M08+554 47
Oder R., Germany M04+527 48
Odessa, Texas U74+318 94
Odessa, Ukraine K86+465 60
Odienné, Ivory Coast N46+096 80
Odorhei, Romania L28+463 58
Odra R., Poland M04+527 48
Odzaka, Congo M02+006 82
Oedelem, Belgium M70+512 44
Oeiras, Brazil Q73-070 105
Oelwein, Iowa U11+426 95
Oetling, New York T03+447 91
Oi, Turkey K27+410 74
Offaly (Ui Failghe), co.,
  Ireland, Rep. N45+533 43
Offenbach, Germany M38+501 48
Ogaki, Japan C67+373 68
Ogallala, Nebraska U70+411 94
Ogden, Utah V42+412 94
Ogdensburg, New York T03+447 91
Ogilvie, Yukon X28+638 88
Ogilvie R., Yukon X00+448 88
Ogoja, Nigeria M38+068 80
Ogoki R., Ontario T70+506 89
Ogr, Sudan L16+120 81
Ogulin, Yugoslavia L89+452 56
Ohakune, New Zealand A27-393 112
Ohau, L., New Zealand A61-442 112
O'Higgins, mt., Chile S80-488 103
Ohio, state, U.S.A. T53+405 91
Ohio R., U.S.A. T68+378 99
Ohrid, Yugoslavia L55+411 58
Ohridsko Jezero, Yugoslavia L56+410 58
Oich L., Scotland N29+571 40
Oignies, Belgium M62+500 44
Oil City, Pennsylvania T43+428 91
Oirot Tura, U.S.S.R. G24+518 62
Oirschot, Netherlands M58+515 44
Oise, dep., France M76+494 54
Oise, R., France M76+490 54
Oita, Japan D20+332 68
Ojinaga, Mexico U87+295 100
Ojiya, Japan C67+373 68
Ojocaliente, Mexico U73+225 100
Ojo de Agua, Argentina S23-294 103
Ojo del Toro, Pico, Cuba T14+200 101
Oka R., U.S.S.R. K16+558 61

33

Palliser B., New Zealand A30-415 112
Palma, Balearic Islands M74+396 53
Palma, Brazil Q74-212 105
Palma, Brazil R16-124 105
Palma, Mozambique K28-110 83
Palma, I., Canary Is. P30+286 80
Palmas, Brazil R42-265 103
Palmas, B., Mexico V28+237 100
Palmas, C., Liberia N46+044 80
Palmas, G. of, Sardinia M39+390 57
Palm Beach, Florida T30+267 97
Palmeira, Brazil R50-279 103
Palmer Land, Antarctica S24-725 27
Palmerston, Ontario T35+439 91
Palmerston, L., Cook Islands Y80-158 106
Palmerston North, N.Z. A26-403 112
Palmerston South, N.Z. A56-454 112
Palmira, Colombia T08+037 104
Palms, Michigan T47+436 91
Palmyra, Syria K41+346 54
Palmyra I., Pacific Ocean Y72+060 106
Palni Hills, India G76+104 70
Palu, Turkey K30+388 74
Palwal, India G76+281 72
Pambon Chan., India G66+092 70
Pamekasan, Indonesia E39-070 65
Pamir, mts., U.S.S.R. H15+374 62
Pamlico Sd., N. Carolina T06+352 97
Pampa, Texas U66+356 94
Pampas, Peru S89-122 104
Pamplona, Spain N10+428 53
Panache L., Ontario T38+462 91
Panagyurishte, Bulgaria L35+425 58
Panaji, Goa, Daman & Diu H07+156 70
Panama & rep.
  Central America T27+090 101
Panama Can., Panama T28+080 89
Panama, G. of, Panama T26+080 101
Panama City, Panama T64+302 97
Panarea, I., Italy M00+386 57
Panay, I., Philippines D75+112 65
Pancevo, Yugoslavia L56+449 58
Panciu, Romania L17+459 58
Pandan, Philippines D77+116 65
Pandharpur, India G40+234 73
Pando, Uruguay R66-347 70
Panevežys, Lithuania L34+558 47
Panfilov, Kazakh. G59+441 62
Panfilovo, U.S.S.R. K12+503 61
Pangala, Congo M02-034 82
Pangbourne, England N07+515 39
Pangkiang, China E41+426 64
Panguitch, Utah V45+378 94
Pania Mutombo, Zaire L36-054 82
Panipat, India G88+177 70
Panja, China F82+400 64
Panjim, See Panaji
Panjnad R., Pakistan H25+290 72
Pannerden, Netherlands M54+519 44
Panruti, India G62+118 70
Pantanaw, Burma F58+169 71
Pantar, I., Indonesia D66-084 65
Pantelleria, I., Medit. Sea M18+368 57
Papa, Hungary L48+472 58 (?)
Papakura, New Zealand A30-371 112
Papantla, Mexico U44+205 100
Papa Stour I., Scotland N10+603 40
Papa Westray, I., Scotland N17+594 40
Papenburg, W. Germany M46+531 44
Papendrecht, Netherlands M62+518 44
Paphos, Cyprus K76+347 76
Paposo, Chile S63-250 103
Pao-an-chow, China E29+403 66
Paochang, China E26+420 66
Pão da Assucar, Brazil Q45-097 105
Pão dos Ferros, Brazil Q49-061 105
Paoking, See Shaoyang
Paola, Italy L84+394 57
Paoli, Indiana U30+386 95
Paoning, See Langchung
Paosham, China F36+252 64
Paoting, China E27+389 64
Pao-tow, China E60+406 64
Papua, G. of, Papua New Guinea
  C30-086 111
Papua New Guinea 111
Papun, Burma F45+181 71
Pará, Brazil R21-014 105
Pará, Brazil R20-010 105
Pará, Brazil R11-172 105
Paracel Is & Reefs,
  S. China Sea E50+165 69
Parachilna, S. Australia C70-311 109
Parachinar, Pakistan H29+339 72
Paracin, Yugoslavia L52+439 58
Paracuru, Brazil Q54-034 105
Parag, Iran H86+255 75
Paragonah, Utah U03+361 99
Paraguá, R., S. America R80-267 103
Paraguari, Paraguay R73-256 103
Paraguay, R., Argent., etc. R80-267 103
Parah, Afghanistan H79+342 75
Parakes, Botswana L48-186 84
Parakou, Benin N74+094 80
Paramaribo, Surinam R62-057 105
Paramoshiri, Peru T17-107 104
Paramushir, Kuril Is. ...
Paraná, Argentina S03-318 103
Paraná, R. Argentina R86-292 103
Paranaíba, Brazil R21-255 103
Paranaíba & R., Brazil R37-197 103
Parang, Philippines D84-059 65
Paranga, Uganda G76+024 83
Parapola I., Greece L39+369 59
Parattah, Tasmania C16-424 109
Parbati R., India G78+235 70
Parbhani, India G79+193 70
Pardubice, Czechoslovakia L84+500 49
Parecis, Brazil R72-140 105

Parecis, Sa. dos, Brazil S10-119 104
Parent, Quebec B10+624 63
Parent, Quebec S88+480 90
Pareora, New Zealand A52-445 112
Pariaguan, Venezuela A52-445 112
Parika, Guyana R81-068 104
Parinari, Peru S87-044 104
Parintins, Brazil R69-025 105
Paris, France M76+488 54
Paris, Illinois T76+396 95
Paris, Kentucky T56+382 97
Paris, Ontario T33+432 91
Paris, Tennessee T80+362 95
Paris, Texas U34+336 95
Parita, B. de, Panama T32+081 101
Pariz, Iran J26+299 75
Park Ra., Colorado V08+400 94
Park Ra., Wyoming V14+413 98
Parker, C., N.-W. Terr. T25+750 89
Parker Dam, Arizona V55+342 98
Parkersburg, W. Virginia T89+393 91
Parkes, New South Wales C11-332 109
Park Falls, Wisconsin U03+459 91
Park Rapids, Minnesota U30+469 93
Parkston, S. Dakota U48+434 93
Parma, Italy M28+448 56
Parmele, N. Carolina T13+358 93
Parnahyba, Brazil Q86-103 105
Parnaíba, Brazil Q71-029 105
Parnu & G., Estonia L33+583 47
Paron, Bhutan G04+274 73
Paro, India G78+249 70
Paros, I., Greece L29+371 59
Parowan, Utah V48+388 94
Parral, Chile S71-361 103
Parral, Mexico V04+269 100
Parramatta, New S. Wales U73+255 109
Parras, Mexico U73+255 100
Parrett R., England N31+453 91
Parry Is., N.-W. Terr. V30+762 88
Parry Sound, Ontario S63+473 73
Parsip, India G30+259 73
Parsnip R., Brit. Columbia W20+556 88
Parsons, Kansas U32+374 95
Parsons, W. Virginia T28+391 96
Partabgarh, India H01+239 70
Partabgarh, India G48+259 73
Partabpur, India G40+234 73
Parthenay, France N01+466 54
Partinico, Sicily M11+381 57
Partridge I., Tibet G20+330 71
Partry Mts., Ireland, Rep. N57+537 42
Pas, The, Manitoba U68+540 88
Pasadena, California V79+341 92
Pasargadae, Iran J42+302 75
Pas-de-Calais, dep., France T81+304 97
Paseagoula & R., Mississippi M76+505 95
Paskuh, Iran H80+276 75
Pasley, C., W. Australia D69-340 110
Pasni, Pakistan H70+252 70
Pasmi, Pakistan M11+381 57
Paso de Indios, Argentina S54-438 103
Paso de los Libres, Argent. R72-297 103
Paso de los Toros, Uruguay S39-326 103
Paso Limay, Argentina S63-405 103
Paso Robles, California W05+356 92
Paspebiac, Quebec S31+481 90
Pasrur, Pakistan H02+322 72
Passamaquoddy B., N.B. S42+451 90
Passau, W. Germany M09+486 48
Passero C., Sicily L89+367 57
Passaic, New Jersey S85+408 96
Passo Fundo, Brazil R44-281 103
Passos, Brazil R10-206 105
Pastaza, Spain N18+404 52
Pastena, Spain R10-206 105
Patagonia, Chile T14+012 104
Patan, India H16+238 70
Patan, Nepal G28+276 73
Patani, India H07+174 70
Pataudi, India G79+283 72
Pataz, Peru T16-076 104
Patchewollock, Victoria C47-354 109
Patea, New Zealand A33-397 112
Paterson, New Jersey S85+409 96
Pathankot, India G86+323 72
Pathankot, India G71+239 73
Pathfinder Res., Wyoming V11+424 93
Pa-tiao, mt., Laos F15+193 69
Patmos, I., Greece L20+373 59
Patna, India G41+207 71
Patna, India G28+256 73
Patos, Brazil Q43-070 105
Patos, L. dos, Brazil R40-314 103
Patquía, Argentina S41-301 103
Patrai, G. of, Greece L49+383 59
Pátrai, Greece L50+383 59
Patras, See Pátrai
Patricio Lynch, I., Chile T02-485 103
Patrocínio, Brazil R12-190 105
Patthalung, Thailand F22+068 69
Patten, Maine S51+460 90
Patterson, Louisiana U08+297 97
Pattukottai, India A12-386 70
Patutahi, New Zealand U69-194 100
Pau, France Q65-094 105
Paul d'Arco, Brazil R26-079 105
Paul, L., N.-W. Territories V30+651 88
Paulista, Brazil Q67-082 105
Paul's Valley, Oklahoma U42-347 95
Paungde, Burma F57+183 71
Pauni, India G62+200 73
Pautask, Sweden L75+648 46
Pavia, Italy M35+452 56
Pávlos, Latvia L35+569 47
Pavlodar, Kazakh. G79+522 62
Pavlograd, Ukraine K55+486 60

Pavlovka, U.S.S.R. K10+519 61
Paylovo, U.S.S.R. K29+504 61
Pavloski, U.S.S.R. K38+558 60
Pawnee City, Nebraska U37+402 95
Paw Paw, Michigan T65+422 91
Pawtucket, Rhode Island S69+419 96
Paxoi, I., Greece L59+392 59
Paxton, Illinois T78+405 95
Payerne, Switzerland M48+468 45
Payne L., Quebec S75+598 89
Payne R., Quebec S70+601 89
Paynesville, Minnesota U29+454 93
Payo Obispo, See Ciudad Chetumal
Paysandu, Uruguay R79-322 103
Payson, Utah V41+401 94
Paz, R., Salvador U00+138 101
Pazardzhik, Bulgaria L34+422 58
Pazaung, Burma F46+190 71
Peace R., Brit. Columbia W20+560 88
Peace River, Alberta V75+560 88
Peak, The, England N11+534 37
Peak Hill, N.S. Wales C10-328 109
Peak Hill, W. Australia V26+384 94
Peale, Mt., Utah V26+384 94
Pearl Harbor, Hawaiian Is. Y45+212 107
Pearsall, Texas U54+290 94
Peary Ld., Greenland Q35+830 26
Pebane, Mozambique K40-168 83
Pebble I., Falkland Islands R88-512 103
Pebo, Cent. Afr. Rep. L68+080 81
Pec, Yugoslavia L58+427 58
Pechora, U.S.S.R. J14+648 62
Pechora, R., U.S.S.R. J47+660 62
Pecos, New Mexico V04+356 94
Pecos R., Texas, etc. U72+310 94
Pecs, Hungary L71+461 58
Pedernales, Venezuela S13+098 104
Pedhoulas, Cyprus K73+350 76
Pedreaul, Panama T44+084 101
Pedro Pt., Sri Lanka G58+198 70
Pedro Juan Caballero, Para. R64-224 103
Pedroll, Brazil Q69-045 105
Pedro Luro, Argentina S16-396 103
Pedrotallagalla, mt., Sri Lanka G56+071 70
Peebinga, S. Australia C54-349 109
Peebles, Scotland N19+556 41
Peekskill, New York S83+413 96
Peel R., Yukon X05+658 88
Peel I., N.-W. S. Wales C38-308 109
Peenemünde, E. Germany M07+541 48
Pe-ra, U.S.S.R. E42+597 63
Peery L., N.-w. S. Wales ...
Peetri, Estonia L25+589 47
Pegasus, B. & New Zealand A41-432 112
Pega Yoma, Burma F55+190 71
Pegnitz, Germany ...
Pegu, Burma F51+173 71
Pegunungan Maoke,
  New Guinea C80-038 65
Pehan, China D52+482 64
Pehpiao, See Peking
Pehuajo, Argentina S19-362 103
Pei Kiang, China E21+400 66
Peipus, L., See Chudskoye Oz.
Peixe, Brazil R21-120 105
Pekan, Malaya F10+036 69
Pekin, Illinois T88+406 91
Peking, China E21+400 66
Pélagos, I., Greece L36+393 59
Pelabuhan, G. ...
Pelée, I., Ontario T46+418 91
Peleng, I., Indonesia D70-014 65
Pelješac, Pen., Yugoslavia L76+430 57
Pelkosenniemi, Finland L15+670 46
Pella, Greece L48+409 59
Pellegrini, Argentina S19-362 103
Pellworm I., W. Germany M38+545 48
Pelly Pt., N.-W. Terr. U66+701 88
Pelly Ra., Yukon W70+612 88
Pelly R., Yukon W83+618 88
Peloncito Ra., Arizona V25+326 94
Peloponisos, Greece L48+370 59
Pelotas, Brazil R45-318 103
Pemba Is., E. Africa K32-052 83
Pelee Is., Medit. Sea M13+355 81
Pembroke, Ontario T13+458 91
Pembroke, Wales N30+517 38
Pembroke, C., Falkland Is. R76-516 103
Peñafiel, Spain N50+412 52
Peñafiel, Portugal N25+413 52
Penalva, Brazil R00-031 105
Penambo Ra., Sarawak E30+030 65
Peña Negra, Sa. de, Spain N37+421 52
Penápolis, Brazil R30-215 105
Penaranda de Bracamonte,
  Spain N31+409 52
Peñarroya, Spain N28+383 52
Penarth, Wales N19+514 38
Peñas, G. de, Chile T00-472 103
Pendembu, Sierra Leone N64+082 80
Pendleton, Oregon V83+457 92
Pend Oreille, L., Idaho V70+480 98
Pennsylvania, state, U.S.A. I25+408 99
Penn Yan, New York S54+441 96
Penobscot B., Maine S53+447 90
Penola, S. Australia C55-374 109
Penong, S. Australia D12-318 110
Penonome, Panama T32+082 101
Penrith, England N17+547 37

Penrith, New South Wales B86-338 109
Pensacola, Florida T73-304 93
Penshurst, Victoria C46-379 109
Pentland Firth, Scotland N20-587 40
Pentland Hills, Scotland N21-558 41
Pentwater, Michigan T68-438 91
Penza, U.S.S.R. K00-532 61
Penzance, England N33-501 38
Penzhinskaya Guba, U.S.S.R. B20+610 63
Peoria, Illinois T88+407 95
Peperga, Netherlands M54+528 44
Pepinster, Belgium M55+506 44
Peqin, Albania L62+411 58
Perak, Malaya E28+054 69
Peralta, Spain S26+485 90
Perce, Quebec S26+485 90
Perdido, Mte., Spain M87+427 53
Perdika, Colombia T04+048 104
Perello, Spain M86+409 53
Perez, Chile S60+260 103
Pergamino, Argentina S04-338 103
Perho, Finland L33+632 46
Peribonca R., Quebec S68+510 90
Perico, Argentina S31-244 103
Périgueux, France M85+452 55
Perija, Sa. de, Venezuela S76+100 104
Perlas, Arch. de las, Pan. T26+084 101
Perlas L., Red Sea K09+127 74
Perm, U.S.S.R. J23+580 61
Pernambuco (Recife), Braz. Q71-042 105
Peristéra, I., Greece L36+392 59
Perm, U.S.S.R. J23+580 61
Péronne, France M72+499 54
Péronnes, Belgium M65+504 44
Perpignan, France M73+427 55
Perranporth, England N31+503 38
Perros, I., S. America 104
Perth, Ontario T08+449 91
Perth, W. Scotland N03+526 37
Peru, Indiana T67+407 104
Peru, rep., S. America C40+424 68
Peruíno, Japan M20+431 56
Perugia, Italy M12-242 105
Peruwelz, Belgium M68+505 44
Pervomaisk, Ukraine K85+481 60
Pervoz, Belgium M61+506 44
Pesaro, Italy M12+439 56
Pescadores Is., See Penghu Is.
Pescara, Italy M05+425 56
Peshchi, Italy L84+419 57
Peshawar, Pakistan H20+340 72
Peshtigo R., Wisconsin T80+455 91
Pesqueira, Brazil Q40-084 105
Pestavka, U.S.S.R. J60+524 61
Petah Tiqva, Israel K61+321 76
Petalioi, G. of, Greece L35+379 59
Petatlan, California W16+383 92
Peterborough, England N03+526 37
Peterborough, Ontario T20+443 91
Peter I. Øy, Antarctica U05-690 27
Peterhead, Scotland N11+575 40
Peterlee, England N08+548 37
Petermann Fd., Greenland S05+810 26
Petermann Pk., Greenland Q00+730 26
Petermann Ra., W. Aust. D35-250 110
Peter Pond L., Sask. V22+558 88
Petersburg, Alaska W75+568 88
Petersburg, Virginia T15-372 97
Peterupe, Latvia L33+573 47
Petit Bois I., Alabama T80+302 95
Petit Francois, Fr. Guiana R44-031 105
Petit Nord Pen., Nfld. R70+509 90
Petiton R., Brit. Columbia W08+598 88
Petitsikapau L., Labrador S40-544 89
Petone, New Zealand A31-412 112
Petorca, Chile S86-321 103
Petoskey, Michigan T60+454 91
Petra, Jordan K65+618 62
Petra Velikogo Zaliv, U.S.S.R. D18+428 63
Petrich, Bulgaria L41+414 58
Petrified Forest Nat. Mon.,
  Arizona V28+348 94
Petrodvorets, U.S.S.R. L82+454 56
Petrolina, Ontario I43+429 91
Petrolina, Brazil Q63-094 105
Petropavlovsk, Kazakh. H35+549 62
Petropavlovsk, U.S.S.R. B36+530 63
Petropolis, Brazil Q80-225 105
Petrovac, Yugoslavia L51+444 58
Petrovsk, U.S.S.R. J22+536 61
Petrovsk, U.S.S.R. E66+513 63
Petrozavodsk, U.S.S.R. K65+618 62
Petsamo, See Pechenga
Petuge, Ireland, Rep. N47+545 42
Petworth, England S71-032 104
Pevsey, Peru S71-032 104
Pewsey, England N11+513 39
Pézenas, France M70+435 55
Pforzheim, W. Germany M38+489 48
Phagwara, India G85+312 72
Phalodi, India H16+270 70
Phan-Rang, S. Vietnam E65+116 69
Phan-Thiet & B. of,
  S. Vietnam E71+110 69
Phaphund, India G63+266 73
Phatthalung, Thailand F29+076 69
Phenix City, Alabama T60+325 97
Phet Buri, Thailand F31+132 69
Philadelphia, Pennsylvania T01+400 91
Philip, S. Dakota D12-318 110
Philippeville, Belgium M63+502 44

34

Rivadavia, Argentina S18-241 103
Rivas, Nicaragua T65+115 101
Rivera, Argentina T65-371 103
Rivera, Uruguay R64-310 103
Riverhead, New York S76+409 91
Rivero, I., Chile S86-456 103
Riverside, New Zealand A67-459 112
Riverside Mt., California V74+340 92
Riverside, New Zealand V57-340 92
Riverton, New York C67-342 109
Riverton, Wyoming V20+430 93
Riviera di Levante, Italy M34+440 54
Riviera di Ponente, Italy M42+438 54
Rivière à Pierre, Quebec S73+470 90
Rivière du Loup, Quebec S57+479 90
Riyadh (Ar Riyāḍ).
Saudi Arabia J80+246 74
Riyaq, Lebanon K54+339 76
Rizaiyeh. See Rezā'īyeh
Rize, Turkey K64+413 74
Rizokarpaso, Cyprus K64+356 76
Rizzuto C., Italy L77+389 57
Roa, Spain N24+417 52
Roane, France M66+461 54
Roanoke, Alabama T62+332 97
Roanoke, Virginia T30+373 97
Roanoke R., N. Carolina T18-366 97
Roaringwater B..
Ireland, Rep. N57+515 43
Roatan I., Honduras T69+164 101
Robat Thana, Pakistan H84+298 70
Robbins I., Tasmania C30-407 109
Robe, S. Australia C62-372 109
Robe, Mt., N. S. Wales C53-316 109
Robe R., Ireland, Rep. N55+536 42
Roberts, Montana V25+454 93
Robertsfors, Sweden L55+642 46
Robertsgani, India G41+247 73
Robertson, Liberia N68+068 80
Robertstown, Ireland, Rep. N41+532 43
Robertstown, S. Australia C66-340 109
Roberval, Quebec S73+485 90
Robinvale, Victoria C43-345 109
Robore, Bolivia R87-183 104
Robson, Mt., B.C. V84+533 88
Robstown, Texas U46+278 94
Roca, la, Spain N40+391 52
Rocha, Uruguay R35-344 103
Rochdale, England N13-536 37
Rochefort, Belgium M59+502 44
Rochefort, France N06+459 54
Rochester, England M87+514 39
Rochester, Michigan T49+427 91
Rochester, Minnesota U15+441 93
Rochester, New Hampshire S66+433 91
Rochester, New York T16+432 91
Rochester, Victoria C32-364 109
Roche-sur-Yon, la, France N09+467 54
Rock Pt., New Zealand A47+409 112
Rock, The, N. S. Wales C18-353 109
Rockall, I. Atlantic Ocean N82+575 34
Rockefeller Plateau, Antarc. X40-800 27
Rockford, Illinois T68+329 97
Rockford, Illinois T85+423 91
Rockhampton, Queensland B86-232 111
Rock Hill, S. Carolina T36+349 97
Rock Island, Illinois U04+415 91
Rockland, Maine S55+441 90
Rockland, Massachusetts S65+421 91
Rockland, Ontario T02+455 91
Rockport, Indiana T72+379 97
Rockport, Missouri U34+404 91
Rock Springs, Wyoming V26+416 93
Rockstone, Guyana R81+058 104
Rockville, Maryland T13+391 96
Rockville City, Iowa U28+424 95
Rockwood, Tennessee T58+358 97
Rocky Mts., N. America V30+550 88
Rockydford, Colorado U82+381 94
Rocky Mount, N. Carolina T16+360 97
Rocky Mt. Nat. Park, Colo. V09+406 98
Rocroi, France M63+499 54
Rodby, Denmark M22+547 47
Rodez, France L12+362 59
Rodhopi, Greece L28+412 58
Rodhos, Greece L14+364 59
Rodhos, I., Greece L12+362 59
Rodney, Mississippi U07+319 97
Rodopi Planina, Bulg.-Greece L36+415 59
Rodosto. See Tekirdağ
Rodriguez, I. Indian Ocean H70-195 77
Roe, N. Ireland N42+551 42
Roebourne, W. Australia E17-208 110
Roermond, Netherlands M54+512 44
Roesbrugge, Belgium M74+509 44
Roeselare, Belgium M71+509 44
Roes Welcome Sound
N.-W. Territories T70+650 89
Roeulx, Belgium M65+505 44
Rogachev, Byelo-Russia L00+531 60
Rogers City, Michigan T53+455 91
Rogersville, New Brunswick S33+468 90
Rogersville, Tennessee T48+364 97
Rogliano, Corsica M33+374 55
Romaine, Italy M15+419 57
Romaine R., Quebec S04+502 90
Romania, S-E. Eur. L29+460 51
Romans, France M60+451 55

Romanshorn, Switzerland M34+476 45
Romanzof, C., Alaska Z10+618 99
Rome, Georgia T61+342 97
Rome, New York T03+432 91
Rome. See Roma
Romerée, Belgium M62+501 44
Romford, England M89+516 39
Romney, W. Virginia T23+393 91
Romney Marsh, England M85+511 39
Romny, Ukraine K69+508 60
Romo, I., Denmark M39+551 47
Romodanovo, U.S.S.R. J48+467 61
Romont, Switzerland M48+467 45
Romsdalshorn, Norway N09+510 39
Romsey, England E81+178 69
Ronda, Spain G89+355 72
Ronda, Spain N31+367 52
Rondeau, Ontario T42+423 91
Rondonia, state, Brazil S31-118 104
Ronge Lac la, Sask. V00+552 88
Rønne, Bornholm, I., Den. M01+551 47
Ronneby, Sweden L88+562 47
Ronse, Belgium M68+507 44
Roosendaal, Netherlands M63+515 44
Roosevelt, Arizona Y65-800 27
Roosevelt Res., Arizona V33+340 98
Rooseveltown, New York S88+450 91
Roosky, Ireland, Rep. N47+538 42
Roper, R., N. Terr., Aust. D00-154 111
Roquefort, France N21+589 40
Rori, India G89+297 72
Roros, Norway M21+626 46
Rorschach, Switzerland M30+464 45
Ros Vatn, Norway M06+658 46
Rosa, Monte, Switz.-Italy M43+459 45
Rosablanche, mt., Switz. M46+461 45
Rosario, Brazil R85-036 104
Rosario, Argentina S04-329 103
Rosario, Chile S60-243 103
Rosario, Mexico V02+263 100
Rosario, Mexico V64+301 100
Rosario, Mexico V05+229 100
Rosario de la Frontera,
Argentina S30-258 103
Rosario Oeste, Brazil R68-148 105
Rosario Tala, Argentina R85-323 103
Rosas, G. of, Spain M71+423 53
Rosas, Spain M70+422 53
Roscommon, Michigan T58+445 91
Roscommon, co.,
Ireland, Rep. N49+536 42
Roscrea, Ireland, Rep. N47+529 43
Rose, I., Samoa Z18-150 106
Roseau, Minnesota U34+488 93
Roseberry, Tasmania C27-418 109
Rosebud, S. Dakota U65+432 93
Roseburg, Oregon W20+432 92
Rosedale, Mississippi U06+338 97
Roseires, Sudan K64+118 81
Rosenheim, W. Germany M17+478 48
Rossberry, Ireland, Rep. N54+516 43
Roseau, I., Ontario T28+452 91
Rossel I., Papua New Guinea B66-114 111
Rosignano Marittamo, Italy M27+433 56
Rosignol, Guyana R76+063 104
Roslavl, U.S.S.R. K73+540 60
Rosport, Luxembourg M51+498 44
Ross, England N16+519 38
Ross, New Zealand A55-429 112
Ross, Tasmania C15-420 109
Ross Ice Shelf, Antarctica Z80-810 27
Ross, I., Antarctica A70-770 27
Ross R., Burma F42+122 71
Ross R., Yukon W70+618 88
Ross Sea, Antarctica Z30-750 27
Rossa, Monte, Italy M35+464 45
Ross & Cromarty, co., See Highland
Rossano, Italy L80+396 57
Rosscarberry, Ireland, Rep. N54-516 43
Rosseau L., Ontario T28+452 91
Rossel I., Papua New Guinea B66-114 111
Rossignol, Belgium M57+497 44
Rossland, Nova Scotia S31+442 90
Rosslare Harb, Ireland, Rep. N78+492 88
Rossland, British Columbia V78+523 43
Rosslyn, Virginia T13-389 96
Rosso, Norway L61+690 46
Rostock, E. Germany M18+541 48
Rostov, U.S.S.R. K34+572 60
Rostov, U.S.S.R. K34-572 60
Roswell, New Mexico U87+334 94
Rosyth, Scotland N21+560 41
Rota, I., Mariana Islands C27+148 106
Rothbury, England N08+534 37
Rothenburg, Germany M29+494 48
Rothes, Scotland N30+558 41
Roti, I., Indonesia D72-108 65
Rotorua, New Zealand A22-381 112
Rotterdam, Netherlands M63+519 44
Rotuma, I., Fiji A17-130 106
Roubaix, France M71+507 54
Rouen, France M84+495 54
Rouge, Estonia L18+577 47
Roussillon, prov. France M74+427 55
Rouveen, Netherlands M53+526 44
Rouyn, Quebec T25+482 91
Roveredo, Italy L26+665 45
Rovaniemi, Finland L44+338 76
Rovigo, Italy M19+451 56
Rovinari, Romania L41+449 58
Rovno, Ukraine L22+506 60
Rowena, New South Wales C07-298 109
Roxburgh, New Zealand A64-457 112
Roxburgh, Scotland N15+556 41
Roxboro, N. Carolina T16+367 97
Royal Canal, Ireland, Rep. N38-534 43

Royale, I., Michigan T84+480 91
Rovan, France N06+456 54
Rozet, Wyoming V02+443 93
Rožňava, Czechoslovakia L57+485 49
Ristichevo, U.S.S.R. K07+523 61
Ruabon, Wales N18+530 38
Ruahine Ra., New Zealand A24-400 112
Ruapehu, Mt., New Zealand A26-393 112
Rubtsovsk, U.S.S.R. G53+513 62
Ruby, Alaska Y30+645 99
Rucava, Latvia L53+561 47
Rudauli, India G49+267 73
Rudbar, Afghanistan H74+301 75
Ruddervoorde, Belgium M71+511 44
Rudkøbing, Denmark M26+549 47
Rudok, Tibet G62+334 70
Rueiba, Sudan L08+156 81
Ruel, Ontario T39+472 91
Ruffec, France M89+460 54
Rufino, Argentina S16-342 103
Rugby, England N08+524 37
Rugby, N. Dakota U68+484 93
Rugeley, England N12+528 37
Rügen, I., E. Germany M10+544 48
Rui Khaf, Iran H89+346 75
Rijiena, Latvia L28+579 47
Ruk, Pakistan H38+278 70
Rukumkot, Nepal G44+286 73
Rukwa L., Tanzania K76-080 83
Rumania. See Romania.
Rumbek, Sudan L02-068 81
Rumburk, Czechoslovakia M03+509 48
Rumford Falls, Maine S63+449 90
Rumilly, France M66+498 44
Rumilies, Belgium M69+506 44
Rum Jungle, N. Terr., Aust. D24-123 110
Rumoi, Japan C50-439 68
Rumonge, Tanzania A52-424 112
Runcorn, England N16+533 37
Rungwa, Tanzania K68-070 83
Rupar, India G81+309 72
Rupbas, India G75+270 73
Rupert, Idaho V54+426 94
Rurrenabaque, Bolivia S45-145 104
Rurutu I., Tubuai Islands X60-250 107
Rusape, Rhodesia K78-186 84
Ruse (Rustchuk), Bulgaria L24+438 58
Rusefa, Jordan K54+330 76
Rusele, Sweden L72+648 46
Rushworth, Victoria C30-366 109
Rusne, R., Lithuania L51+552 47
Russas, Brazil Q48-049 105
Russell, Co., N.-W. Terr. V75+753 88
Russelkonda, India G32+200 71
Russell, Kansas U54+388 95
Russell Pt., N.-W. Terr. V62+729 88
Russellville, Alabama A35-353 112
Russellville, Kentucky T72+368 97
Russian Soc. Federated Soviet
Reps. (Russia), U.S.S.R. 62-63
Russkoye Ustye, U.S.S.R. C07+713 63
Russo, Switzerland M38+462 45
Rustam, Afghanistan H31+371 75
Rustenburg, Virginia T25+372 97
Ruston, Louisiana U16+326 95
Rutba, Iraq K29+329 74
Rutherfordton, N. Carolina T42+353 97
Ruthin, Wales N20+531 38
Rutland, Vermont S78+436 91
Rutland, co., See Leicester & co.
Rutland I., Andaman Is. F74+114 71
Rutland, Netherlands M51+521 44
Ruurlo, Netherlands K30-108 83
Ruwenzori, Mts., Uganda L64+491 49
Ružomberok, Czechoslovakia L00-025 83
Rwanda, Central Africa K32+546 60
Ryazan, U.S.S.R. K30+537 60
Ryazhsk, U.S.S.R. K75+694 62
Rybinsk, U.S.S.R. K37+580 60
Rybinskoye Res., U.S.S.R. K40+586 60
Rye, England N07+507 39
Rye, I. of W., England M86+510 39
Rye Patch Res., Nevada V80+406 92
Rylstone, New South Wales C00-328 109
Rymarov, Czechoslovakia L77+499 49
Rypin, Poland L64+531 49
Ryūkyū Retto, Japan D50+250 64
Rzeszów, Poland L48+501 49
Rzhev, U.S.S.R. K64+563 60

Saanen, Switzerland M22+506 48
Saalfeld, E. Germany M46+465 45
Saarbrücken, W. Germany M48+492 48
Saaremaa I., Estonia L44+584 47
Saarijärvi, Finland L12+682 46
Saarlouis, W. Germany M50+493 48
Saas Grund, Switzerland M42+461 45
Saavedra, Argentina S15-378 103
Saba, Iran J69+308 74
Sabac, Yugoslavia L48+501 49
Sabah (N. Borneo), Borneo 65
Sabalgarh, India G78+262 70
Sabana, Arch. de, Cuba T30+232 101
Sabanalarga, Colombia T00+106 104
Sabancuy, Mexico U06+190 100
Sabará, Brazil S80-387 99
Sable, Latvia L44+570 47
Sabinao, Spain U23+296 95
Sabine and L., Texas U23-296 95
Sabine R., Texas U22+400 95
Sabine Mt. Antarctica A65-720 27
Sable, C., Florida T13-296 99
Sable I., Nova Scotia S33+435 90
Sable I., Nova Scotia S00+439 90
Sables d'Olonne, les, France N10+465 54
Sabrina Coast, Antarctica E45-660 27
Sabzawar (Shindand), Afghan. H77+334 75
Sabzawar, Iran J14+362 75

Sacandaga Res. & R..
New York S85+431 96
Sac City, Iowa U30+424 95
Saedon, Spain N17+405 53
Sachigo R., Ontario U05+546 89
Sachsen-Anhalt, W. Germany M22+520 48
Sackets Harbor, New York T07+439 91
Sackville, New Brunswick S26+459 90
Saco, Maine S63+435 90
Saco, Montana V14+485 93
Sacramento, Brazil R14-199 105
Sacramento, California W09+385 92
Sacramento Mts. New Mex. V03+332 94
Sacramento R., California W12+392 92
Sádaba, Spain N07+423 53
Sadad, Syria K48+343 76
Sada Bandeira, Angola M08-148 82
Sadad, Syria K48+343 76
Saddleback Mt., Maine S63+449 90
Sadhaura, India G77+304 72
Sadij, Iran J07+257 75
Sadiya, India F56+278 71
Sa'diva, Jebel, Saudi Arabia K29-207 74
Sadmarda, Afghanistan H47+356 75
Sado, I., Japan C70+380 68
Sadra, India H13+233 70
Saduan, Saudi Arabia K11+192 74
Saeki, Japan D19+330 68
Safad (Zefat), Israel K57+330 76
Safed Koh Ra., Afghan.-Pak. H26+340 72
Safi, Morocco N56+320 80
Safidabeh, Iran H87+308 75
Safit, Saudi Arabia J53+214 75
Safita, Syria K53+348 76
Safranbolu, Turkey K73+412 74
Saga, Japan D28+332 68
Sagaing, Burma F54+218 71
Sagami B., Japan C64+352 68
Sagar, India G67+238 73
Sagara, Ethiopia K60+058 83
Sagauli, India G31+267 73
Sage Plains, Oregon W06+437 92
Saginaw, Michigan T54+435 91
Saginaw B., Michigan T52+440 91
Sagone, G. de, Corsica M39+421 56
Sagres, Portugal N53+370 52
Sagua la Grande, Cuba T30+228 101
Saguenay R., Quebec S64+483 90
Sagunto, Spain N01+397 53
Sahand, mt., Iran J82+376 74
Sahara Desert, Africa 80-81
Saharanpur, India G74+297 72
Saharien Atlas Mts., Algeria M80+334 80
Sahaswan, India G67+281 73
Sahiadriparvat Ra., India G85+206 70
Sahiwal, Pakistan G14+252 73
Sahnaly, India H11+307 72
Sahuaripa, Mexico U76+200 100
Sahuayo, Mexico V24+288 100
Sahun, Oman N30+423 52
Sahve, France M73+440 55
Sahwal, France S50-472 90
Sahyadri Mts., India H03+150 70
Saibai I., Papua New Guinea C44-095 111
Saida. See Sidon
Saidabad, Iran J26+295 75
Said Bundas, Sudan L32+084 81
Saidpur, India G58+130 70
Saidu, Pakistan H16+348 70
Saigon, S. Vietnam E80+108 69
Saignelégier, Switzerland M48+473 45
Saihut, Yemen, South J53+153 75
Sailana, India F39+491 70
Saimaa Kanal, Finn.-U.S.S.R. L10+610 47
Saimaa L., Finland L12+613 47
St Abb's Hd., Scotland N13+559 41
St Affrique, France M73+440 55
St Agatha, Maine S50+472 90
St Agnes, England M42+450 55
St Albans, England N02+517 39
St Albans, Scotland S79+448 91
St Amour, France S58+477 90
St André, France G58+477 90
St André C., Madagascar K04-164 83
St Andrews, New Brunswick S42+451 90
St Andrews, Scotland N17+563 41
Ste Anne de Beaupré, Quebec S66+474 90
Ste Anne de la Pérnge, Que. S23+096 104
Ste Anne des Monts, Quebec S39+491 90
St Anns Bay, Jamaica T13+185 101
St Anthony, Idaho V41+440 98
St Antonin, Switzerland M31+470 45
St Arnaud, Victoria C41-367 109
St Asaph, Wales N21+532 38
St Augustin, C. de..
Madagascar K10-238 83
St Austell, England T38+299 97
St Austell & B., England N29+503 38
Ste Barthélemy, l., Leeward Is. S17+179 101
St Béat, France M86+429 55
Ste Cécile, Quebec S66+457 91
Ste Catherine, Ontario T25+432 91
St Chamond, France M63+455 54
St Christopher, I. (St Kitts),
Leeward Islands S16+173 101
St Clair, Michigan T45+429 91
St Clair L., Mich.-Ont. T46+425 91
St Clair L., Tasmania C23-421 109
St Cloud, Minnesota U25+456 93
Ste Croix, Switzerland M51+468 45
St Croix, R., Wisconsin U16+457 99

Index

40

Simplon and Pass, Switzerland W42+462 45
Simpson, Fort, N.-W. Terr. W11+614 88
Simpson, C., Alaska Y25+709 88
Simpson Des., Australia C80-254 111
Simpson, I., Chile S83-459 103
Simuna, Estonia L22+590 47
Sinai, pen., Egypt K70+290 81
Sinaloa, state, Mexico V12+250 100
Sinaloa & R., Mexico V20+260 100
Sinamaica, Venezuela S71+110 104
Sinbo, Burma F48+247 71
Sinchang, China D84+295 67
Sin-chow, China E43+385 66
Sind, Pakistan H40+255 70
Sindel, Bulgaria L15+431 58
Sindhuli Garhi, Nepal G25+272 73
Sind Sagar Doab, Pakistan H21+311 72
Sines, Portugal N53+379 52
Singa, Sudan K66+132 81
Singapore & Str., S. Asia F07+012 69
Singaraja, Bali I. Indon. E29-081 65
Singen, W. Germany M38+477 48
Singhbum, India G27+224 73
Singida, Tanzania K62-046 83
Singitic G., Greece L36+402 59
Singkawang, Borneo E66+010 65
Riouw Arch., Indon. F04-006 65
Singleton, New South Wales B83-326 109
Singora. See Songkhla
Singsingisa, China F58+418 64
Singtai, China E33+371 66
Sinho, China E28+375 66
Sinhsien, China E44+384 64
Sinhwa, China E52+277 67
Sining, China F18+363 64
Siniscola, Sardinia M32+406 57
Sinj, Yugoslavia L80+437 56
Sinjar, & Jebel, Iraq K18+364 74
Sinkiang, China K58+320 76
Sin-min-fu, China D74+420 66
Sinnamary, Fr. Guiana R47+053 105
Sinning, China E55+266 67
Sinoe L., Romania L06+446 58
Sinoia, Rhodesia K88-172 84
Sinop, Turkey K58+420 74
Sinton, Texas U44+280 94
Sintra, Portugal N56+388 52
Sinuiju, N. Korea D64+401 64
Sinyang, China E35+322 66
Sion, Switzerland M46+462 45
Sioux City, Iowa U38+426 95
Sioux Falls, S. Dakota U40+435 93
Sioux Lookout, Ontario U11+502 89
Siparia, Trinidad S09+102 104
Sipolilo, Rhodesia K86-166 84
Sipora, I., Indonesia F32-022 65
Siquisique, Venezuela S58+106 104
Sira, India G78+138 70
Sira. See Siros, I.
Siracusa, Sicily M88+371 57
Sirajganj, Bangladesh G01+245 73
Sir Douglas, Mt., Alberta V60+505 88
Sir Edward Pellew Group,
N. Territory, Australia C77-157 111
Siretul, R., Romania L18+462 58
Sirhind, India G81+306 72
Siri, Ethiopia K36+080 83
Sirjan, Iran J28+296 75
Sirma, I., Greece L23+352 59
Sironcha, India G60+188 70
Sironj, India G74+241 73
Siros, I., Greece L30+374 59
Sirsa, India H00+295 72
Sirsi, India H00+146 70
Sirte (Surt), Libya L80+312 81
Sisak, Yugoslavia L82+454 56
Sisaket, Thailand F04+150 69
Sisal, Mexico U00+211 100
Sisi, Botswana L16-218 84
Sisophon, Khmer F12+136 69
Sister I., E. Tasmania C13-397 109
Sister I., W. Tasmania C14-397 109
Sisteron, France M54+442 55
Sitamarhi, India G27+266 73
Sitapur, India G56+275 73
Sitara, Saudi Arabia J83+227 74
Sithonia, Greece L37+401 59
Sitia, Crete L23+352 59
Sitka, Alaska X04+569 88
Sitpur, Pakistan H25+292 72
Sittang, Burma F49+174 71
Sittard, Netherlands M55+510 44
Sitten. See Sion
Sivand, Iran J42+301 75
Sivas, Turkey K48+398 74
Siverek, Turkey K34+378 74
Sivrihisar, Turkey K81+395 74
Sivry, Belgium M65+502 44
Siwa, Egypt L28+292 81
Siwalik Hills, India G73+304 70
Siwan, India G34+262 73
Sixmilebridge, Ireland, Rep. N53+527 43
Sixteen, Montana V36+462 93
Sjælland, Denmark M18+556 47
Själevad, Sweden M06+588 47
Skagafjord, Iceland P28+660 46
Skagen, Denmark M26+577 47
Skagerak, Norway-Denmark M42+573 47
Skagway, Alaska X00+592 88
Skaneateles, L., New York T08+428 90
Skara, Sweden M09+584 47
Skardu, Kashmir G86+353 72
Skarnes, Norway M20+602 47
Skeena R., Brit. Columbia W52+546 88
Skegness, England M88+531 37
Skelleftå, Sweden L66+654 46
Skellefte Alv, Sweden L54+647 46
Skiathos, I., Greece L39+392 59
Skibbereen, Ireland, Rep. N19+546 37
Skien, Norway M32+592 47
Skierniewice, Poland L59+520 49
Skiftet Kihti, Finland L54+600 47
Skiros, I., Greece L32+389 59
Skive, Denmark M36+566 47

Skofja Loka, Yugoslavia M04+462 56
Skopelos, I., Greece L36+391 59
Skopin, U.S.S.R. K33+538 60
Skopje, Yugoslavia L51+420 58
Skövde, Sweden M07+584 47
Skovorodino, U.S.S.R. D67+540 63
Skowhegan, Maine S58+448 90
Skradin, Latvia L85+438 56
Skrunda, Latvia L48+567 47
Skudeshamn, Norway M58+592 47
Skuodas, Lithuania L51+562 47
Skye, I., Scotland N38+574 40
Slamet, mt., Java E66-072 65
Slamannan, New S. Wales C38-320 109
Slane, Ireland, Rep. N39+537 42
Slaney R., Ireland, Rep. N39+524 43
Slapin, L., Scotland N36+571 40
Slatina, Romania L34+444 58
Slatington, Pennsylvania T03+407 96
Slave R., N.-W. Territories V48+604 88
Slaveni, Romania L33+441 58
Slavgorod, U.S.S.R. G70+532 62
Slavonia, Yugoslavia L72+454 56
Slavonski Brod, Yugoslavia L72+452 56
Slavyansk, Ukraine K44+488 60
Slea Hd., Ireland, Rep. N63+521 43
Sleaford, England N02+530 37
Sleat, Sd. of, Scotland N35+571 40
Sleepers, The, N.-W. Terr. T36+572 89
Sledyinge, Belgium M68+511 44
Slide Mt., N.-W. Territories S86+420 91
Siedrecht, Netherlands M61+518 44
Slievanea, Ireland, Rep. N61+522 43
Slieve Anierin, Ireland, Rep. N48+541 42
Slieve Aughty, Mts.,
Ireland, Rep. N51+531 43
Slieve Bernagh, Ireland, Rep.
N51+528 43
Slieve Bloom Mts.,
Ireland, Rep. N54+541 42
Slieve Car, Ireland, Rep. N58+541 42
Slieve Donard, N. Ireland N35+542 42
Slievefelim Mts., Ireland, Rep. N51+531 43
Slieve Gamph Mts.,
Ireland, Rep. N54+541 42
Slieve League, Ireland, Rep. N52+546 42
Slieve Mish, mts., Ireland, Rep. N59+522 43
Slieve Miskish, Ireland, Rep. N60+516 43
Slievemore, Ireland, Rep. N60+540 42
Slievenakilla, Ireland, Rep. N48+541 42
Slievenamon, Ireland, Rep. N45+524 43
Slieve Snaght, Ireland, Rep. N44+552 42
Slieve Tooey, Ireland, Rep. N51+542 42
Sligo B. & co., Ireland, Rep. N51+542 42
Sligo B., Ireland, Rep. N53+543 42
Slite, Sweden L67+577 47
Sliven, Bulgaria L22+427 58
Slobodskoy, U.S.S.R. J58+587 61
Sloka, Latvia L38+569 47
Slonim, Byelo-Russia L28+530 60
Sloten, Netherlands M56+529 44
Slough, England L60+485 49
Slovakia, Czechoslovakia L60+485 49
Slovenia, Yugoslavia M00+459 56
Slovensko, Czechoslovakia L60+488 49
Sluis, Netherlands M67+513 44
Sluiskil, Netherlands M67+513 44
Slunj, Yugoslavia L86+451 56
Slupsk, Poland L78+545 49
Slussfors, Sweden L82+655 46
Slyne Hd., Ireland, Rep. N61+534 43
Slyudyanka, U.S.S.R. F08+516 63
Smethport, Pennsylvania T21+418 96
Smilde, Netherlands M51+530 44
Smiltene, Latvia M55+574 47
Smith, Alberta V54+551 88
Smith B., N.-W. Territories T20+770 89
Smith B., Gt. Bear L.,
N.-W. Territories W15+661 88
Smith I., Quebec T24+606 89
Smith I., South Shetlands S12-630 27
Smithers, British Columbia W42+548 88
Smithfield, N. Carolina T20+355 97
Smithfield, Utah V41+418 94
Smithland, Kentucky T80+371 97
Smiths Falls, Ontario T06+449 91
Smithton, Tasmania C29-409 109
Smoky R., Alberta V78+552 88
Smoky Hill R., Kansas U65+388 98
Smola, Norway M42+634 46
Smolensk, U.S.S.R. K78+548 60
Smoothstone L., Sask. V13+542 88
Smyrna. See Izmir
Snaefell, Isle of Man N27+543 37
Snake, R. & Canyon,
Washington, etc. V83+464 92
Snake R., Yukon W77+657 88
Snares I., New Zealand A81-481 112
Snåsa, Norway M16+642 46
Snåsa Vatn, Norway M18+642 46
Sneek, Netherlands M56+530 44
Sneem, Ireland, Rep. N59+518 43
Snizort, L., Scotland N34+623 40
Snohetta, mt., Norway M34+623 46
Snow Flake, Arizona V31+345 94
Snow Lake, Manitoba U60+548 88
Snowdon, mt., Wales N24+530 38
Snowpk, mt., Wyoming V09+414 98
Snow Water L., Nevada V60+406 94
Snowy Mts., Vict.-N.S.W. C12-366 109
Snowy R., Victoria C11-386 109
Snyder, Texas U66+326 94
Soanzara, Italy L80+403 57
Soave, Switzerland M35+463 45
Sobakin, U.S.S.R. J71+538 61
Soboko, Cent. Afr. Rep. L30-068 81
Sobrado, Brazil R49-055 105
Sobral, Brazil Q62-037 105
Sobrance, Czechoslovakia L47+487 49
Sochi, U.S.S.R. K34+438 62
Social Circle, Georgia T52+336 97
Society Is., Pacific Ocean Y20-150 107
Socorro, Colombia S80+064 104
Socorro, I., Mexico V12+341 94
Socotra, I., Indian Ocean J36+124 83

Soc-trang, S. Vietnam E84+096 69
Sodankylä, Finland L20+674 46
Soda Springs, Idaho V44+426 94
Söderhamn, Sweden L77+604 47
Söderköping, Sweden L82+585 47
Sodiri, Sudan L06+142 81
Sodus, New York T12+432 96
Sodus Pt., New York T12+432 96
Soela (Sülü) Eiln, Indonesia D58-018 65
Soemba (Sumba), I., Indon. E00-100 65
Soembawa (Sumbawa), I.,
Indonesia E10-088 65
Soerabaja, See Surabaya
Soest, W. Germany M41+516 48
Soest, Netherlands M58+522 44
Sofala, Mozambique K62-202 84
Sofala, New South Wales C02-331 109
Sofiya (Sofia), Bulgaria L40+427 58
Sogamosa, Colombia S77+057 104
Søgndal, Norway M52+583 47
Søgne Fd., Norway M54+611 47
Sögüt, Turkey K89+401 74
Sohag, Egypt K80+266 81
Sohagpur, India G51+233 73
Sohan R., Pakistan H16+330 72
Sohar, Oman J20+244 75
Sohawal, India G55+246 73
Sohteb, Yemen, South J79+139 74
Sohna, India G77+283 72
Soignies, Belgium M66+506 44
Soissons, France M70+494 54
Soke, England N02+526 37
Soke, Turkey L16+378 74
Sok Gomba, Tibet F68+320 64
Sok Karmalinsk, U.S.S.R. J45+541 61
Sokki, Chad L04+112 81
Sokode, Togo M84+090 80
Sokol, U.S.S.R. K39+594 60
Sokolo, Mali N36+146 80
Sokoto, Nigeria M58+128 80
Sola Consalina, Italy L87+404 57
Solai, Kenya K52+001 83
Solbad Hall, Austria M21+473 48
Soledad, Venezuela S21+082 104
Soledade, Brazil S55-066 106
Solent, The, England N08+508 39
Solenzara, Corsica M34+418 57
Sol Iletsk, U.S.S.R. J29+511 61
Solimoes (Amazonas), R.,
Brazil S40-020 104
Solingen, W. Germany M48+512 48
Sollefteå, Sweden L76+632 46
Sollum, see Salûm
Solok, Sumatra F25-007 65
Solomon Is., Pacific Ocean B30-060 106
Solomon R., Kansas U59+396 98
Solothurn & canton, Switz. M45+472 45
Solsona, Spain M81+420 53
Solstad, Norway M17+651 46
Solund, I., Norway M60+611 47
Solway, Minnesota U31+475 93
Solway Firth, Eng.-Scot. N22+548 37
Solwezi, Zambia L22-122 82
Soma, Turkey L14+392 74
Somalia, E. Africa K00+050 83
Somanga, Tanzania K56-108 83
Sombor, Yugoslavia L66-458 58
Sombreiro Chan., Nicobar Is. F70+076 71
Sombrerete, Mexico U81+238 100
Sombreiro, I., Leeward Is. S21+187 101
Somcuta Mare, Romania L39+475 49
Someren, Netherlands M56+514 44
Somerset, Kentucky T58+371 97
Somerset, Pennsylvania T24+400 91
Somerset, Queensland C45-108 111
Somerset, co., England N18+510 38
Somerset Res., Vermont S77+430 96
Somerset I., N.-W. Terr. U20+730 89
Somerville, New Jersey S88+405 96
Somerville, Tennessee T86+353 97
Somme, dep., France M76+500 54
Somme, R., France M79+502 54
Sommes, Belgium M58+503 44
Sömmerda, E. Germany M37+463 48
Sonmiani, Pakistan H50+258 70
Sonmiani B., Pakistan H50+476 72
Sonneberg, E. Germany M23+503 48
Sonogno, Switzerland M37+463 45
Sonora, Sardinia M35+400 57
Sonora, Spain N15+418 53
Sonora, state & R., Mexico V38+288 100
Sonoyta, Mexico V47+319 100
Sonpur, India G36+208 71
Sonora, Uruguay R80-336 103
Sonrico, Switzerland M38+464 45
Sonson, Colombia T01+057 104
Soochow, China D86+313 66
Soping. See Yuyu
Sopley, England N11+508 39
Soppero, Sweden L50+681 46
Sopron, Hungary L80+476 56
Sopur, Kashmir H03+343 72
Sora, Italy M08+417 57
Sorata, Bolivia S52-158 104
Sorbas, Spain N11+371 53
Sorell, Tasmania C15-428 109
Sörenberg, Switzerland M42+468 45
Sorfold, Norway L87+675 46
Sorgono, Sardinia M35+400 57
Soria, Spain N15+418 53
Soriano, Uruguay R15-334 103
Sorocaba, Brazil R15-234 105
Soroki, Moldavia L10+482 60
Sorol, U.S.S.R. C55+075 106
Soromesis, Botswana L46-194 84
Soron, India G67+279 73

Sorong, New Guinea D22-008 65
Soroca, Brazil S09+008 104
Soroti, Uganda K68+016 83
Soroya I., Norway L44+705 46
Sorrento, Italy M04+406 57
Sorsele, Sweden L75+655 46
Sortavala, Karelia K86+617 46
Sortavala, state, Aust. 110-111
South Bend, Indiana T68+417 91
South Bend, Washington W23+467 92
Southbridge, Massachusetts S72+422 96
Southbridge, New Zealand A46-438 112
South Boston, Virginia T24+367 97
South Carolina, state, U.S.A. T40+341 99
South China Sea, Asia E60+100 31
South Dakota, state, U.S.A. U78+448 98
South-East C., Tasmania C19-436 109
South-East C., Victoria C22-390 109
Southend-on-Sea, England M86+515 39
Southern Alps, New Zealand A60-436 112
Southern Cross, W. Australia E04-311 110
South Foreland, England M83+511 39
South Georgia, I., Atlant. Oc. Q40-540 27
South Hadley Falls, Mass. S76+422 96
South Haven, Michigan T68+424 91
South Indian L., Manitoba U52+568 88
South Jacksonville, Florida T40+303 97
South Milwaukee, Wisconsin T77+430 91
South Nahanni R.,
N.-W. Territories W40+616 88
South Orkneys, Is., Atlantic
Ocean R00-610 27
South Paris, Maine S63+443 90
South Pittsburg, Tennessee T64+350 97
South Polar Plateau, Antarc. B30-870 27
South Pole, Antarctica 27
Southport, England N18+536 37
Southport, Queensland B70-279 111
South River, New Jersey S87+404 96
South Ronaldsay I., Scot. N18+588 40
South Sandwich Is., Atl. Oc. P80-570 27
South Shetlands Is., Antarc. S00-630 27
South Shields, England N08+550 37
South-West C., Tasmania C23-435 109
South-West Africa, S. Africa L76-250 84
South Yemen, Asia J80+150 74
South Yorkshire, co., Eng. N08+535 37
Souza, Brazil Q49-067 105
Souzel, Portugal N46+389 52
Sovetsk, U.S.S.R. L48+551 47
Sovetsk, U.S.S.R. J66+576 61
Sovetskaya Gavan, U.S.S.R. C57+488 63
Soy, Kenya K58+008 83
Soya & B., Japan C50+454 68
Soya Misaki, Japan C49+455 68
Soyopa, Mexico V26+290 100
Spa, Belgium M55+505 44
Spain, W. Europe N24+400 50
Spalato. See Split
Spalding, S. Australia C78-334 111
Spalding, England L46+371 37
Spanish, Ontario T44+462 91
Spanish Fork, Utah V40+401 94
Spanish Town, Jamaica T12+180 101
Sparks, Nevada V89+395 92
Sparta, Illinois T88+382 95
Sparta, N. Carolina T37+365 97
Sparta, Wisconsin U05+439 91
Sparta (Sparti), Greece L46+371 59
Spartanburg, S. Carolina T42+350 97
Spartivento C., Italy L33+379 57
Spas, U.S.S.R. K11+538 61
Spassk, U.S.S.R. J64+550 61
Spassk, U.S.S.R. D13+447 63
Spencer, Iowa U46+437 93
Spencer, S. Dakota T37+365 97
Spencer G., S. Australia C78-340 111
Sperrin Mts., N. Ireland N42+548 42
Spetsai, I., Greece L41+372 59
Speyer, W. Germany M39+493 48
Spezand, Pakistan H48+299 70
Spezia, La, Italy M31+441 56
Sphinx, Montana V36+452 93
Spilsby, England M89+532 37
Spinazzola, Italy L83+410 57
Springen, Switzerland M38+469 45
Spirit Lake, Iowa U30+434 95
Spitsbergen, Arctic Ocean L40+800 62
Spitsbergen, Vest., Arctic
Ocean L80+790 62
Spittal, Austria M09+468 48
Split, Yugoslavia L81+435 56
Spluit L., Manitoba U38+560 88
Splügen Pass, Switzerland M34+466 45
Splügen Pass, Switzerland-Italy
M30+465 45
Spofford, Texas U62+292 94
Spokane, Washington V75+476 92
Spoleto, Italy M14+428 56
Spontin, Belgium M60+503 44
Sporadhes, Aegean Sea L18+370 59

Tache, L., N.W. Territories W03+642 88
Tacloban, Philippines D60+111 65
Tacna, Peru S62-180 104
Taco, Argentina S20-256 103
Tacoma, Washington W15+473 92
Taconic Mts., N.Y.-Mass. S80+425 96
Tacuarembo, Uruguay R66-317 103
Tadcaster, England N08+539 37
Tadjoura & G. of, F.T.A.I. K12+116 83
Tadoussac, Quebec S58+481 90
Tadzhikskaya, rep., U.S.S.R. H30+390 62
Taegu, Korea D38-358 64
Taejón, Korea D44+363 64
Taf R., Wales N27+518 38
Tafalla, Spain N10+425 53
Taff R., Wales N20+515 38
Tafila, Jordan K56+309 76
Taft, Iran J34+318 75
Taftville, Connecticut S72+415 96
Taganrog & G., U.S.S.R. K36+473 61
Tagish, Yukon W86+602 88
Taga Zong, Bhutan G00+270 71
Tahora, New Zealand A31-390 112
Tahsien, China E75+313 66
Ta Hu, China E43+391 66
Tahta, Egypt K82+268 81
Tahuna, Indonesia D58+037 65
Ta-an, China E17+362 66
Taichow. See Linhai.
Taichung, Taiwan D86+242 67
Taieri, R., New Zealand A58-456 112
Taif, Saudi Arabia K28+211 74
Taihang-shan, China E36+370 66
Taihape, New Zealand A25-396 112
Taiku, China E00+355 66
Taihsien, China E43+391 66
Taima, Saudi Arabia K36+277 74
Tain, Scotland N41+579 40
Taiyuan, China E45+378 66
Taizz, Yemen K06+136 74
Tajo, R., Spain-Portugal N44+397 52
Tajrish, Iran J52+358 75
Tak, Thailand C70+371 68
Takada, Japan D08+348 68
Takahashi, Japan D19+346 68
Takaka, New Zealand A43-409 112
Takamatsu, Japan D06+343 68
Takao. See Kaohsiung.
Takaoka, Japan C78+368 68
Takapuna, New Zealand A31-368 112
Takasaki, Japan C66+363 68
Takaungu, Kenya K30-038 83
Takayetos, mts., Greece L46+370 59
Takayama, Japan C76+362 68
Takefu, Japan C83+358 68
Takhta Bazar, Turkmen H74+360 62
Takhi-Suliaman, Pakistan H30+316 70
Takingeun, Sumatra F49+047 65
Takla, L., British Columbia W35+554 88
Takla Makan, des., Sinkiang,
   China G40-380 30
Takoradi, Ghana N12+050 80
Ta-ku, China E14+389 66
Takuapa, Thailand F40+088 69
Talagang, Pakistan H15+329 70
Talaimannar, Sri Lanka G62+091 70
Talalass Ala Tau, Kirgiz. H20+423 62
Talar Ra., Pakistan H64+254 70
Talara, Peru T38-045 104
Talavera de la Reina, Spain N29+399 52
Talca, Chile S70-354 103
Talcahuano, Chile S79-367 103
Tali, China E61+348 66
Tali, China S63-254 103
Talsi, Latvia L45+572 47
Taltal, Chile S63-254 103
Tamale, Ghana N04+094 80
Tamanrasset, Algeria M58+226 80
Tamaqua, Pennsylvania T06+408 96
Tamar R., England N25+505 38
Tamarite de Litera, Spain M87+419 53
Tamási, Hungary L71+467 49
Tamatave, Madagascar J64-182 83
Tamaulipas, state, Mexico U53+235 100
Tamazula, Chile S69-305 103
Tamba, Rhodesia L02-214 84
Tambach, Kenya K56+006 83
Tambacounda, Senegal N82+138 80
Tambo de Mora, Peru T07-135 104
Tambohorano, Madagascar K06-176 83
Tamboril, Brazil Q63-048 105
Tambov, U.S.S.R. K22-527 61
Tambura, Sudan L14+056 81
Tame, Colombia S71+066 104
Tamel Aiken, Argentina S66-482 103
Tamiahua & L., Mexico U46-212 100
Tamil Nadu, state, India G70-114 70
Tamins, Switzerland M33+468 45
Tamluk, India G12+223 73
Tammisaari (Eknäs), Finland L39+600 47
Tammu, Burma F54+242 71
Tampa, Florida T45+280 97
Tampa B., Florida T46+278 99
Tampere, Finland L37+615 47
Tampico, Mexico U48+222 100
Tamra, Saudi Arabia L23+591 47
Tamtsak Bulak, Mongolia E13+470 64
Tamworth, England N10+526 37
Tamworth, New S. Wales B85-311 109
Tana Fd., Norway L10+707 46
Tana L., New Hebrides A65-195 106
Tana L., Ethiopia K46+118 83
Tana R., Norway L23+698 46
Tanabe, Japan C88+338 68
Tanabu, Japan C52+413 68
Tanaga I., Aleutian Is. Z80+512 99
Tanah Merah, Malaya F17+057 69
Tanahmerah, New Guinea C60-062 65
Tanami, N. Terr., Australia D32-200 110
Tanana, Alaska Y10+652 99
Tanana, R., Alaska X60+635 99
Tananarive (Antananarivo)
   Madagascar J76-190 83
Tancanhuitz, Mexico U54+216 100
Tancheng, China E09+346 66
Tanda, India G44+266 73
Tanda Urmar, India G86+316 72
Tandil, Argentina R85-372 103
Tandou L., New S. Wales C47-326 109
Taneatua, New Zealand A18-380 112
Tanega Shima, Japan D24+306 68
Tanen-taunggyi Mts.,
   Thailand-Burma F42+191 69
Tanga, Tanzania K36-050 83
Tanganyika. See Tanzania.
Tanganyika, L., E. Cent. Afr.
   L00-050 83
Tangermünde, E. Germany M22+606 47
Tangier, (Tanger), Morocco N34+356 80
Tang-shan, China E11+396 66
Tangshan, China E21+344 66
Tangtu, China D63+401 66
Tangu, U.S.S.R. F24+555 63
Tanimbar Kep., Indon. D22-074 65
Tanjungpandan,
   Billiton I., Indonesia E74-027 65
Tanjunperiuk, Java, Indon. E78+060 65
Tanjungredeb, Borneo E16+021 65
Tanjungselor, Borneo E16+028 65
Tank, Pakistan H27-322 72
Tankapirtti, Finland L16+682 46
Tankse, Kashmir G70+340 70
Tännäs, Sweden M14+625 46
Tanta, Egypt K84+308 81
Tantung, China E67+320 66
Tanuf, Oman J17+230 75
Tanzania, E. Africa K60-050 83
Tao, Burma F71+228 71
Taoan, China D73+454 64
Taochow. See Lintan.
Taofu, China F23+310 64
Taormina, Sicily L88+378 57
Taos, New Mexico V04+364 94
Tapa, Estonia L24+592 47
Tapachula, Mexico U13+149 100
Tapah, Malaya F22+042 69
Tapajos, R., Brazil R63-040 105
Tapalque, Argentina S00-362 103
Tapanui, New Zealand A64-459 112
Tapa Shan, China E67+320 66
Tapauá, Brazil S26-057 104
Tapera do Retiro, Brazil S11-099 104
Taplang Dzong, Nepal G14-274 73
Tappahannock, Virginia T11+381 97
Tapti R., India G78+216 70
Tapuaenuku, mt., N.Z. A38-420 112
Taquara, Brazil R80-092 104
Taquari, Brazil R35-297 103
Taquaretinga, Brazil Q36-079 105
Tara, New Zealand A63-040 112
Tara Estonia L24+592 47
Tarabulus esi Sham (Tripoli),
   Lebanon K55+344 76
Taradale, New Zealand A18-395 112
Tarago, New South Wales C02-351 109
Tarahumare, Sa., Mexico V16-280 100
Tarakan, Borneo E14+034 65
Tarakki, Turkey K87+404 74
Taralga, New South Wales C01-344 109
Tarana, New South Wales C01-336 109
Taranaki Bight, N., N.Z. A36-388 112
Taranaki Bight, S., N.Z. A38-397 112
Tarancon, Spain N10+400 52
Taranto, Italy L76+404 57
Taranto, G. di, Italy L77+400 57
Tarapoto, Peru T08-065 104
Taraqua, Brazil S49-002 104
Tarascon, France M80+428 55
Tarasp, Switzerland N41+579 44
Tarauaca, Brazil S65-084 104
Tarawera, New Zealand A20-390 112
Tarazona, Spain N10+419 53
Tarazona de la Mancha, Sp. N12+392 53
Tarbagatai Khrebe., Kazakh. G40+470 62
Tarbat Ness, Scotland H05+567 62
Tarbela, Pakistan R56+526 43
Tarbert, N., N.Z. A36+558 41
Tarbert, Scotland N32+558 41
Tarbert, Scotland N41+579 40
Tarbes, France N00+432 55
Tarboro, N. Carolina T05+359 97
Tarchan, Tibet G52+310 70
Tarcoola, S. Australia D02-307 111
Tarcoon, New South Wales C20-303 109
Tarcutta, New South Wales C14-353 109
Taree, New South Wales B76-320 109
Tärendö, Sweden L44+672 46
Târgovişte, Romania L27+449 58
Târgu Mures, Romania L33+466 58
Târgul Ocna, Romania L20+463 58
Tarija, Bolivia S29-214 104
Tarim, Basin & R., Sinkiang G30+400 30
Tarlac, Philippines D87+156 65
Tarma, Peru T05-114 104
Tarn, dep. & R., France M77+438 55
Tarn, Sweden L88+657 46
Tarn-et-Garonne, dep., Fr. M81+442 55
Tarnobreg, Poland L50+506 49
Tarnow, Poland L54+500 49
Tarnowskie Gory, Poland L67+505 49
Tartna Point, New S. Wales C45-330 109
Tartu, Estonia L19+583 47
Tartus, Syria K55+349 76
Tarum, Iran J26+281 75
Taseko Ls., Brit. Columbia W22+514 88
Tashi Bhup Tso, Tibet G30+322 71
Tashihto, China F82+438 64
Tashkent, Uzbek. H34+415 62
Tashkurghan, Afghanistan H43+367 75
Tash Kurghan, China G86+392 72
Tasil, Syria K54+328 76
Taskan, U.S.S.R. B89+630 63
Tasköprü, Turkey K62+416 74
Tasman B., New Zealand A40-410 112
Tasman Mt., New Zealand A58-435 112
Tasman Mts., New Zealand A45-410 112
Tasman Pen., Tasmania C13-431 109
Tasmania I. & state, Aust. C20-420 111
Tassgong, Bhutan F80+272 71
Tata, Hungary L70+478 49
Tatakoto, Tuamotu Arch X20-175 107
Tatarsk, U.S.S.R. G84+552 62
Tatarskaya, aut. rep., U.S.S.R. J60-553 62
Tatarskiy Proliv, U.S.S.R. C50-500 63
Tathlina, L., N.-W. Terr. V75+604 88
Tating, China E86+271 67
Tatnam C., Manitoba U05+578 89
Tatong, Victoria C24-367 109
Tatranska Lomnica, Czech. L59+491 49
Tatry, mts., Poland-Czech. L60+493 49
Tatu R., Pakistan H43+247 70
Tatu R., China F22+320 64
Tatuby, Brazil R16-232 105
Ta-tung, China E41+401 66
Tatung Ho, China F14-370 64
Tatung, China S06-025 104
Taubate, Brazil R03-230 105
Tauha, Brazil Q62-060 105
Taumarunui, New Zealand A28-388 112
Taumaturgo, Brazil F56-200 71
Taungdwingyi, Burma F48+209 71
Taungyi, Burma F64+189 71
Taungup, Burma F78+276 71
Taunton, England N18+510 38
Taunton, Massachusetts S67+419 96
Taunus, mts., W. Germany M40+503 48
Taupo & L., New Zealand A24-387 112
Tauranga & Harb., N.Z. A23-377 112
Taurus. See Toros.
Tauste, Spain N07+419 53
Tavda, U.S.S.R. H57+581 62
Taverne, Switzerland M36+461 45
Tavistock, England N25+505 38
Tavolara I., Sardinia M32+409 57
Tavoy I., Burma F40+130 71
Tavoy I., Burma L03-396 74
Tavsanli, Turkey L03-396 74
Tawang, India F78+276 71
Tawas City, Michigan T51+443 91
Tawau, Sabah E12+043 65
Tawitawi I., Philippines E00+052 65
Taxco, Mexico U57+184 100
Tay, Firth of & R., Scotland N19+564 41
Tay L., Scotland N25+565 41
Tayabas, Mexico U63+192 100
Tayga, U.S.S.R. G27+558 62
Taylor, Mt., New Mexico V18+352 94
Taylorsville, Alabama T69+345 97
Taylorsville, N. Carolina T37+359 97
Taymyr, Ozero, U.S.S.R. F15+746 63
Tayport, Scotland N17+564 41
Tayside, reg., Scotland N23+567 41
Taytay, Philippines E04+108 65
Tayu, China E34+255 67
Tayung, China N24+342 80
Tazewell, Virginia T39+371 97
Tazovskaya G., U.S.S.R. G85+692 62
Tbilisi, Gruzinskaya, U.S.S.R. K01+418 62
Tchad. See Chad.
Tchaourou, Benin M76+088 80
Tczew, Poland L67+541 49
Te Anau, L., New Zealand A73-452 112
Teano Ra., W. Australia E10-345 110
Teapa, Mexico U18+174 100
Te Aroha, New Zealand A26-376 112
Te Awamutu, New Zealand A28-380 112
Tebessa, Tunisia M43+364 81
Tebingtinggi, Sumatra F44+030 65
Tebulosmta, U.S.S.R. K31+648 61
Tecka & R., Argentina S65-434 103
Tecolutla, Mexico U43+205 100
Tecoripa, Mexico V28+290 100
Tecpan, Mexico U62+172 100
Tecumseh, Michigan T54+420 91
Tedzhen, Turkmen. H87+373 62
Tegerhi, Libya M04+240 81
Tegucigalpa, Honduras T72+141 101
Teheran. See Tehran.
Tehpao, China E80+233 67
Tehran, Iran J52+357 75
Tehri, India G69+304 70
Tehsien, China E22+375 66
Tehuacan, Mexico U44+185 100

Tehuan, Mexico U44+185 100
Tehuantepec, Mexico U32+164 100
Tehuantepec, G. of, Mexico U30+158 100
Tehuantepec, Isth. of, Mex., U28+172 100
Teian. See Anlu
Teifi, R., Wales N26+520 38
Teign, R., England N22+506 38
Teignmouth, England N21+505 38
Teith, R., Scotland N24+561 41
Te Karaka, New Zealand A57-439 112
Tekari, India G31+250 73
Te Kuiti, New Zealand A29-383 112
Tela, Honduras T75+158 101
Tel-Aviv-Yafo, Israel K62+321 76
Telegraph Creek, B.C. W67+581 88
Telford, England N15 + 527 37
Telichie, S. Australia C61-317 109
Telkalakh, Syria K52+347 76
Tel Kochek, Syria K17+370 74
Tell Bise, Syria K49+348 76
Tell Ejine, Syria L68+212 81
Tell el Milh, Israel K60+312 76
Telloapan, Mexico U60+182 100
Tel Or, Israel K56+326 76
Telposiz, U.S.S.R. J05+637 62
Telsen, Argentina S41-424 103
Teluk Cenarawasih, Indon. E89-054 65
Telukbetung, Sumatra, Indon. F16+040 69
Tembeling, Malaya F16+040 69
Temblador, Venezuela S17+090 104
Teme R., England N15+523 37
Temesvar. See Timisoara
Temir, Kazakh. J18+491 62
Temir Tau, U.S.S.R. G16+532 62
Temiscouata, L., Quebec S53+476 90
Temma, Tasmania C31-413 109
Temnikov, U.S.S.R. K10+546 61
Temora, New South Wales C15-345 109
Temosachic, Mexico V15+288 100
Tempe, Arizona V41+334 94
Tempio, Sardinia M35+409 57
Temple, Texas U44+310 95
Templemore, Ireland, Rep. N47+528 43
Temse, Belgium M65+511 44
Temuka, New Zealand A52-440 112
Tenali, India G88+377 72
Tenasserim, Burma F36+120 71
Tenasserim, R., Burma F37+136 71
Tenby, Wales N28+517 38
Ten Degree Chan.,
   Andaman Islands F75+098 71
Tenerife, I., Canary Is. P10+282 80
Ténès, Algeria M84+362 80
Tengchow. See Penglai
Tengiz, Oz., Kazakh. H35+504 62
Tepic, Mexico M08+426 56
Teramo, Italy C43-383 109
Terang, Victoria D05-195 111
Ter Apel, Netherlands M48+529 44
Terban, Jebel, Saudi Arabia K18+197 74
Terborg, Netherlands M52+519 44
Terenceville, Newfoundland R58+477 90
Tenterfield, New S. Wales B78-290 109
Teresina, Brazil Q77-050 105
Teresopolis, Brazil R00+485 63
Terespol, S. Australia C67-331 109
Terewie, S. Australia C40+485 63
Terni, Italy L31+661 46
Terowie, S. Australia C67-331 109
Terpeniya, Zal, U.S.S.R. C40+485 63
Terracina, Italy M01+413 57
Terralba, Sardinia M38+397 57
Terra Nova, Newfoundland R55+485 90
Terra Santa, Brazil R69-019 105
Terrazas, Mexico V17+303 100
Terre Haute, Indiana T74+395 91
Teruel, Spain N07+404 53
Tervola, Finland L31+661 46
Tervuren, Belgium M63+508 44
Teshekpuk, L., Alaska Y20+705 88
Tesin, Mongolia M38+389 57
Tesio, Japan C50+459 68
Teslin, Yukon W76+602 88
Teslin L., Yukon W84+609 88
Teslin R., Yukon W40+134 80
Tessaoua, Niger M40+134 80
Tessenderlo, Belgium M59+511 44
Tete, Mozambique K68-162 84
Teton Ra., Wyoming V36+436 93
Tetouan (Tetuan), Morocco N32+356 80
Tetyukhe, U.S.S.R. See Rudnaya Pristan
Teulada, Sardinia M37+390 57
Teulada C., Sardinia M38+389 57
Teutoburger Wald,
   W. Germany M41+521 48

Index

Index

Trier, Germany M50+497 48
Trieste, Italy M07+457 56
Trikeri Str., Greece L41+390 59
Trikkala, Greece L50+396 59
Trikomo, Cyprus K67+353 76
Trim, Ireland, Rep. N41+536 43
Trincomalee, Sri Lanka G53+086 70
Trinidad, Bolivia S28-148 104
Trinidad, Colorado U87+372 94
Trinidad, Cuba T29+218 97
Trinidad, Uruguay R72-336 103
Trinidad, I., Argentina S12-392 103
Trinidad, I., West Indies S07+105 104
Trinidad I. & B., Newfoundland R50+482 90
Trinity, Texas U32+310 95
Trinity Pen, Antarctica R75-640 27
Trinity R., Texas U30+312 95
Trionto C., Italy L78+396 57
Tripoli (Tarábulus), Lebanon K55+345 76
Tripoli, Greece L46+375 59
Tripolis, Greece L46+375 59
Tripolitania, Libya M00+300 81
Tripura, India F80+240 71
Tristan da Cunha, Atlantic Oc. N76-372 85
Triunfo, Mexico V31+239 100
Trivandrum, India G79+085 70
Trmbesh, Bulgaria L27+434 58
Trn, Bulgaria L44+428 58
Trnava, Czechoslovakia L75+484 49
Trobriand Is.,
 Papua New Guinea B84-086 111
Trogir, Yugoslavia L82+435 56
Trois Pistoles, Quebec S55+481 90
Trois Ponts, Belgium M55+504 44
Trois Rivières, Quebec S76+464 91
Troitsk, U.S.S.R. H81+540 61
Troitsk, U.S.S.R. K07+541 61
Troitsko Pechorsk, U.S.S.R. J23+629 62
Trollhättan, Sweden M16+583 47
Trollheimen, Norway M36+629 46
Tromen, mt., Argentina S60-371 103
Tromsø, Norway L66+697 46
Trondheim & Fd., Norway M28+635 46
Troödos, Cyprus K73+349 76
Troon, Scotland N28+555 41
Tropea, Italy L85+387 57
Troppau. See Opava
Trosa, Sweden L75+589 47
Trossachs, Scotland N26+562 41
Trout Lake, Michigan T60+462 91
Trowbridge, England N35+513 39
Troy, New York S82+427 91
Troy, Turkey L22+400 74
Truk, I., Caroline Is. B82+070 106
Truksum, Tibet G40+300 71
Trumbull, Mt., Arizona V50+364 92
Trundle, New South Wales C15-329 109
Truns, Switzerland M36+467 45
Truro, England N30+502 38
Truro, Nova Scotia S19+454 90
Truro, S. Australia C65-344 109
Truskmore, Ireland, Rep. N50+544 42
Trutnov, Czechoslovakia L85+506 49
Trzebnica, Poland L78+514 49
Tržič, Yugoslavia M04+464 56
Tsabong, Botswana L46-262 84
Tsagan Olom, Mongolia F50+467 64
Tsaratanana, mt., Madagascar J70+148 74
Tsarevo. See Opava
Tschenstochau. See Czestochowa
Tschiertschen, Switzerland M32+468 45
Tselim, Israel K63+313 76
Tsetchow. See Tsincheng
Selinograd, Kazakh H21+512 52
Semah, Israel K56+327 76
Tsenghsien, China E37+233 67
Tses, S.-W. Africa L70-260 84
Tsho Mirari L., Kashmir G70+329 72
Simlyanskoye Vdkhr.,
 U.S.S.R. K12+470 61
Tsinan, China E17+367 66
Tsincheng, China E43+353 66
Tsinchow. See Tienshui
Tsing-chow. China E29+381 66
Tsinghai. See Chinghai
Tsing Hai. See Ching Hai
Tsaochow. See Hotseh
Tsaokiang. China E28+376 66
Tsaritsyn. See Volgograd
Tsaritin. See Volgograd
Tsavo Nat. Park, Kenya K40-028 83
Tsetsen. See Czestochowa
Tsinan, China E17+367 66
Tsingkiang, China E06+336 66
Tsingkiang, China E05+348 66
Tsingtao, China D88+361 66
Tsingtze (Singtze), China E23+294 67
Tsingyuan. See Paoting
Tsinyang, China E37+233 67
Tsingyun, China E20+354 64
Tsining, China E22+284 67
Tsinsien, China E42+351 66
Tsitsihar, China D66+474 64
Tsivory, Madagascar J84-242 83
Tskhinvali, Grazinskaya K07+425 61
Tsu, Japan C81+347 68
Tsugaru Str., Japan C54+416 68
Tsugitak, mt., Taiwan D82+248 65
Tsumeb, S.-W. Africa L37+466 84
Tsunhwa, China E12+403 66
Tsuno, China D81+316 66
Tsunyi, China E76+224 64
Tsuruga, Japan C83+356 68
Tsuruoka, Japan C61+387 68
Tsuyama, Japan D06+350 68
Tsuyama, Japan F20+250 64
Tua, Portugal N45+412 52
Tua, Zaire L80-036 82

Tuakau, New Zealand A30-373 112
Tuam, Ireland, Rep. N53+535 43
Tuamarina, New Zealand A36-414 112
Tuamotu Arch., Pacific Oc. X30-200 107
Tuao, Philippines D82+178 65
Tuapse, U.S.S.R. K36+441 62
Tuatapere, New Zealand A74+461 112
Tubai, I., Society Islands Y10-160 107
Tubarão, Brazil R24-285 103
Tubas, Jordan K58+323 76
Tubbercurry, Ireland, Rep. N52+540 42
Tübingen, Germany M36+485 48
Tubize, Belgium M65+507 44
Tubuai, I., Austral Islands X88-210 107
Tubutama, Mexico V39+308 100
Tucacas, Venezuela S49-108 104
Tuckernuck I., Massachusetts S61+413 96
Tuckerton, New Jersey S86+396 91
Tucson, Arizona V36+322 94
Tucson Ra., Arizona V37+324 94
Tucumcari, New Mexico U82+352 94
Tucunare, Brazil R63-051 105
Tucupita, Venezuela S12+090 104
Tucurui, Brazil R26-038 105
Tudela, Spain N10+421 53
Tufi, Papua New Guinea C04-092 111
Tug, Turkey K16+385 74
Tuguegarao, Philippines D80+176 65
Tugur, U.S.S.R. C79+537 63
Tukums, Latvia L41+569 47
Tula, Mexico U55+200 100
Tula, U.S.S.R. K44+542 60
Tulan, China F38+369 64
Tulancingo, Mexico U50+201 100
Tularosa, New Mexico V06+330 94
Tularosa Basin, New Mexico V09+329 94
Tulcan, Ecuador T16+008 104
Tulcea, Romania L07+452 58
Tulchin, Ukraine L07+487 60
Tulear, Madagascar K08-234 83
Tuli, Rhodesia L04-220 84
Tulkarm, Jordan K60+323 76
Tullahoma, Tennessee T68+353 97
Tullamore, Ireland, Rep. N45+533 43
Tullamore, New S. Wales C15-327 109
Tulle, France M79+453 55
Tullow, Ireland, Rep. N40+528 43
Tulsa, Oklahoma U36+362 95
Tulsk, Ireland, Rep. N49+538 43
Tulua, Colombia T08+041 104
Tulun, U.S.S.R. F27+545 63
Tumaco & Rado de,
 Colombia T22+017 104
Tumany, U.S.S.R. B55+611 63
Tumbarumba, N.S.W. C12-358 109
Tumbes, Peru T33-035 104
Tumit-Guna, China E55+414 66
Tumkur, India G77+132 70
Tumlong, India G08+274 73
Tummel, R., Scotland N24+567 41
Tump, Pakistan H76-260 70
Tumu, Ghana N12+108 80
Tumucumaque, Sa., Brazil R52+018 105
Tumupasa, Bolivia S48-142 104
Tumut & R., New S. Wales C11-354 109
Tunas de Zaza, Cuba T28+216 101
Tunbridge Wells, England M88+511 39
Tuncurry, New South Wales B76-321 109
Tundla, India G85+274 70
Tunduru, Tanzania K46-112 83
Tongan, China D87+329 66
Tungchang. See Liaocheng
Tungchow. See Tali
Tungchwan. See Santai
Tunghai, China E04+346 66
Tungho, China D38+460 64
Tunghwa, China D56+416 64
Tungien, China E65+277 67
Tungkiang, China E37+230 67
Tungkwan, China E59+346 66
Tungkwan, China E65+350 66
Tungliao, China D76+436 64
Tungnan, China. See Suchow
Tungtai, China D87+329 66
Tung Ting Hu, China E45+290 67
Tunguska, R., U.S.S.R. F30+640 63
Tunhwang, China F61+402 64
Tuni, India G44+173 71
Tunis, Tunisia M30+368 81
Tunisia, N. Africa M30+350 81
Tunja, Colombia S81+056 104
Tunnsjo, Norway M10+647 46
Tunuyan & R., Argentina S55-335 103
Tuoy Khaya, U.S.S.R. E51+622 63
Tuparoa, New Zealand A10-379 112
Tupelo, Mississippi T82+343 97
Tupik, U.S.S.R. D76+436 64
Tupinambaranas, I., Brazil R80-034 104
Tupiza, Bolivia S34-213 104
Tupper Lake, New York S87+442 91
Tuquerussu, Brazil R20-102 105
Tuquerres, Colombia T15+010 104
Tura, India F89+255 71
Tura, U.S.S.R. F30+641 63
Turakom, Laos E15+184 69
Turbat-i-Heideri, Iran H86+353 75
Turbat-i-Jam, Iran J06+353 75
Turbo, Colombia T10+081 104
Turda, Romania L37+466 58
Tureia I., Tuamotu Arch. X20-208 107
Turfan, Brazil R02-018 105
Turfan, Sinkiang, China G02+429 64
Turgay, Kazakh H69+499 62
Turgutlu, Turkey L14+385 74
Türi, Estonia L27+588 47
Turin. See Torino
Turkestan, Kazakh, etc. H40+432 62
Turkey, rep., Europe-Asia K78+390 51
Turkmenskaya, rep. U.S.S.R. J10+405 62
Turks Is., Bahamas,The S67+214 101
Turku, Finland L47+604 47
Turnhout, Belgium M60+513 44

Tornoovo, Bulgaria L27+430 58
Turnu Severin, Romania L44+446 58
Turquino, Pico de, Cuba T10+200 101
Turr, Ethiopia K08+064 83
Turrialba, Costa Rica T52+100 101
Turshiz, Iran J10+352 75
Turtkul, Uzbek. H84+415 62
Turtle Mts., N. Dakota U61+490 93
Turukta, U.S.S.R. E30+610 63
Turukhansk, U.S.S.R. G11+657 62
Turun, Iran J20+355 75
Turut, Iran J29+355 75
Turzovka, Czechoslovakia L68+494 49
Tus, Iran J03+366 75
Tuscaloosa, Alabama T76+332 97
Tuscarora Mts., Pa. T17+402 96
Tuscola, Illinois T80+398 91
Tuscumbia, Alabama T76+347 97
Tuxtla, Vol. de, Mexico U15+383 97
Tuxtla Gutierrez, Mexico U18+168 100
Tuy, Spain N52+421 52
Tuyen-Quang, N. Vietnam E89+217 69
Tuy-hoa, S. Vietnam E64+131 69
Tuyun, China E75+263 67
Tuz Gölu, Turkey K70+386 74
Tuzla, Yugoslavia L68+446 58
Tvärän, Sweden L54+656 46
Tverditsa, Bulgaria L26+427 58
Twante, Burma F54+169 71
Tweed, Ontario T14+445 91
Tweed, R., Scotland N13+557 41
Tweedsmuir Hills, Scotland N20+554 41
Tweedsmuir Park, B.C. W35+534 88
Twelve Pins, Ireland, Rep. N59+535 43
Twenty-five de Mayo, Argent. S46-380 103
Twenty-five de Mayo, Argent. S01-354 103
Twin Buttes, Montana V02+486 93
Twin Falls, Idaho V57+425 92
Twofold B., New S. Wales C00-370 109
Two Harbors, Minnesota U10+470 93
Two Mountains, L. of, Que S86+455 91
Two Rivers, Wisconsin T76+442 91
Tyda, U.S.S.R. D52+532 63
Tygda, U.S.S.R. D61+553 63
Tyler, Texas U31+322 98
Tyler, Texas U32+324 95
Tyndall, Mt., New Zealand A55-433 112
Tyne & Wear, co., England N09+550 37
Tynemouth, England N08+550 37
Tynset, Norway M25+623 46
Tyr (Sour), Lebanon K59+330 76
Tyrone, China E18+356 66
Tyrone, China E82+256 67
Tyrone, co., N. Ireland N43+546 42
Tyrrell, L., Victoria C43+354 109
Tyrrhenian Sea, Italy M18+400 57
Tyumen, U.S.S.R. H57+572 62
Tywyn, Wales N24+526 38
Tzechung, China E33+364 66
Tzeya Ho, China E16+356 66
Tzeyun, China E82+256 67

Uanle, Nicaragua T58+138 101
Uau el Chebir, Libya L58+252 81
Uaupés & R., Brazil S42-001 104
Uba, Brazil Q78-211 105
Ubaitaba, Brazil A55-433 112
Ubari, Libya M14+266 81
Uberaba, Brazil R18-197 105
Uberlandia, Brazil R20-190 105
Uberlingen, W. Germany M35+477 48
Ubon Muang, Thailand F01+153 63
Ubsa Nor, Mongolia F73+503 63
Ucayali, R., Peru S88-060 104
Uch, Pakistan H23+293 72
Uchiza, Peru T08-084 104
Uckfield, England M89+510 39
Uddain, Yemen K06+141 74
Udaipur, India H07+246 70
Uddevalla, Scotland N31+579 40
Uddevalla, Sweden M19+584 47
Udd Jaur, Sweden L73+660 46
Uden, Netherlands M56+517 44
Udine, Italy M11+461 56
Udon Thani, Thailand F13+175 69
Udskaya Guba, U.S.S.R. C85+550 63
Udzha, U.S.S.R. E19+717 63
Uelen, U.S.S.R. Z30+660 63
Ueno, Japan C82+348 68
Ufa, U.S.S.R. J24+547 61
Uganda, E. Africa K70+010 83
Ugwashi-Uku, Nigeria M50+062 82
Uhersko Hradiste, Czech. L75+491 49
Ui Failghe. See Offaly
Uinta Mts., Utah V36+408 98
Uist, North, I., Scotland N43+576 40
Uist, South, I., Scotland N43+573 40
Uitenhage, Cape Province L28-338 84
Uitgeest, Netherlands M62+525 44
Ujhani, India G85+230 70
Ujjain, India G85+230 70
Ujpest, Hungary L48+476 49
Ukermark (Uckermark),
 E. Germany M08+532 48
Ukhta, Karelskaya K85+652 62
Ukiah, California W20+391 92
Ukraine, rep., U.S.S.R. L00+490 60
Ulangom, Mongolia F77+500 63
Ulan Ude, U.S.S.R. E74+520 63
Uldecona, Spain M87+406 53
Ulldalla, New S. Wales B87-354 109
Ulapool, Scotland N31+579 40
Ullared, Sweden M14+571 47
Uljung Dico, Sea of Japan D25+376 68
Ulmarra, New South Wales B72-296 109

Ulster, prov.,
 Ireland, Rep.-N. Ire. N48+548 42
Ulster Canal,
 Ireland, Rep.-N. Ire. N42+542 42
Ultima, Victoria C41-355 109
Ulua, Honduras T76+158 101
Ulukisla, Turkey K63+376 74
Ulva, I., Scotland N37+565 41
Ulverstone, England N19+542 37
Ulverston, Tasmania C23-412 109
Ulyanovsk, U.S.S.R. J70+544 61
Ulzen. W. Germany M27+530 48
Uman, Ukraine K88+488 60
Umanak Fd., Greenland R35+710 26
Umarkot, Pakistan H31+253 70
Umbria, reg., Italy M15+429 56
Umea, Sweden L58+638 46
Umm At Rusays, Oman J07+205 75
Umm el Quibain, Saudi Arabia K20+279 74
Umm Kuteira, Sudan L30+146 81
Umm Lej, Saudi Arabia K46+250 74
Umm Qasr, Iraq J73+300 74
Umm Ruwaba, Sudan K84+128 81
Umnak I., Aleutian Is. Z20+529 99
Umtali, Rhodesia K74-188 84
Umtata, Cape Province L08-318 84
Umvuma, Rhodesia K86-194 84
Una, India G82+315 72
Una R., Yugoslavia L80+452 56
Unadilla, New York T02+423 96
Unalakleet, Alaska Y65+637 99
Unalaska, Aleutian Is. Z10+535 99
Uncastillo, Spain N06+424 53
Uncia, Bolivia S39-185 104
Uncompahgre Plat., Colorado V20+385 94
Underhood, Victoria C49-352 109
Undur Khan, Mongolia E57+474 64
Ungarie, New South Wales C18-336 109
Ungava B., Quebec S45+594 89
União, Brazil Q77-045 105
União da Victoria, Brazil R36-262 103
União Marara, Brazil R40+730 26
Unini, Peru S84-106 104
Union, Argentina S35-352 103
Union, Argentina S50-292 103
Union, Missouri U06+384 97
Union, S. Carolina T40+347 97
Union City, Tennessee T85+364 97
Union of Soviet Socialist Republics,
 (U.S.S.R.), Europe-Asia 30-31
Uniontown, Pennsylvania T77+378 97
Unionville, Missouri U18+400 97
Unionville, Nevada V80+404 92
United Arab Emirates,
 S.-W. Asia J35-240 75
United Kingdom of Gt. Britain
 & N. Ire. N.-W. Europe 34
United States of America
 (U.S.A.) 98-99
United States Ra. N.-W. Terr. T30+810 26
Unnao, India G57+265 73
Unst, I., Scotland N05+607 40
Unterwalden, canton, Switz. M41+469 45
Unzha, U.S.S.R. K06+580 61
Uozu, Japan C75+368 68
Upata, Venezuela S15+081 104
Upemba, Zaire L22-086 82
Upernivik, Greenland L52-284 84
Upington, Cape Province T29+396 96
Upolu, I., Samoa Z40-140 106
Upper Marlboro, Maryland T10+388 96
Upper Sandusky, Ohio T50+408 91
Upper Seal L., Quebec S84+558 89
Uppsala, Sweden L74+599 47
Upper Volta, rep., W. Afr. N15+130 80
Ur, Iraq J85+310 74
Urakawa, Japan C43+422 68
Ural, U.S.S.R. J54+508 62
Uralsk, U.S.S.R. J52+513 62
Uralskiye Khrebet, U.S.S.R. J10+535 62
Urana, New South Wales C23-354 109
Uranium City, Saskatchewan V20-598 88
Urapunga, N. Terr., Aust. D03-147 110
Ura Tyube, U.S.S.R. H36+400 62
Urawa, Japan C62+358 68
Urbakh, U.S.S.R. J78+512 61
Urcos, Peru S70-137 104
Urda, U.S.S.R. J75+488 62
Ure R., England N11+543 37
Ures, Mexico V32+292 100
Urfa, Turkey K37+372 74
Urgun, Afghanistan H35+329 75
Uri, canton, Switzerland M38+468 45
Uribe, Colombia S85+031 104
Uribia, Colombia S73+116 104
Urisino, New South Wales C38-297 109
Urnasch, Switzerland M34+473 45
Urtazymsk, U.S.S.R. J07+520 61
Urtuin, Mongolia U72+194 100
Urubamba & R., Peru S74-134 104
Urucara, Brazil R76-024 105
Urucui, Brazil Q64-177 105
Uruguaiana, Brazil R72-297 103
Uruguay, rep., S. America 103
Uruguay, R., Uruguay, etc. R81-334 103
Urumchi, Sinkiang, China G14+437 62
Urussanga, Brazil R26-286 103
Urville, Tg. d., New Guinea C73-015 65
Uryupinsk, U.S.S.R. K18+508 61
Urzhum, U.S.S.R. J60+571 61
Urziceni, Romania L20+446 58
Usak, Turkey L04-387 74
Usakos, S.-W. Africa L86-220 84
Usborne, mt., Falkland Is. R84-516 103
Usedom, E. Germany M06+540 48
Ushant I. See Ouessant, I. d'
Ushirombo, Tanzania K78-034 83
Ush Tobe, U.S.S.R. G69+455 62
Ushuaia, Argentina S50-548 103
Usk, R., Wales N19+518 38
Uska, India G41+272 73

Index

Index

Index

Yithion, Greece L45+368 59
Yitu, China E09+367 66
Yiyang, China E46+287 67
Yocalla, Bolivia S36-192 104
Yochow. See Yoyang
Yogovsk, U.S.S.R. J22+576 61
Yogyakarta, Java E58+079 65
Yoho Park, Brit. Columbia V70+512 88
Yokkaichi, Japan C80+350 68
Yoko, Cameroun M16+056 81
Yokohama, Japan C62+354 68
Yokosuku, Japan C62+352 68
Yokote, Japan C57+393 68
Yola, Nigeria M16+092 81
Yonago, Japan D10-354 68
Yone Zawa, Japan C59-379 68
Yonkers, New York S83+409 96
Yonne, dep., France M69+478 54
York, Alabama T80+325 97
York, England N07+539 37
York, Nebraska U46+408 95
York, Pennsylvania T11+400 96
York, W. Australia E19-319 110
York, C., Greenland S50-760 26
York R., Virginia T10-374 97
York Sd., W. Australia D58-150 110
Yorke Pen., S. Australia C74-346 109
Yorketown, S. Australia C75-350 109
York Factory, Manitoba U16+567 89
Yorkshire, North, co., Eng. N08+542 37
Yorkshire Moors, England N05+544 37
Yorkshire Wolds, England N03+540 37
Yorkton, Saskatchewan U75+511 88
Yorktown, Virginia T09+372 97
York Village, Maine S64+432 90
Yoro, Honduras T71+150 101
Yosemite Nat. Park, Cal. V88+379 92
Yoshkar Ola, U.S.S.R. J72+568 61
Youghal & Harb., Ireland, Rep. N47+519 43
Youghiogheny River Res.,
   Penn. etc. T27+397 96
Youkadouma, Cameroun M00+036 81
Young, New South Wales C10+343 109
Younghusband Pen., S. Aust. C64-360 109
Youngstown, Ohio T34+411 96
Yount Pk., Wyoming V30+440 93
Yoyang, China E40+294 67
Yozgat, Turkey K62+398 74
Ypres (Yeper), Belgium M73+508 44
Ypsilanti, Michigan T52+423 91
Yreka, California W16+417 92
Ysabel, I., Solomon Islands B35-080 106
Yssingeaux, France M65+451 55
Ystad, Sweden M07+555 47
Ytterhogdal, Sweden M01+622 46
Yüanchow. See Ichun
Yüanchow. See Chihkiang
Yüanling, China E58+285 67
Yubalia, S. Australia C58-336 109
Yubi C., Morocco N78+280 80
Yucamani, mt., Peru S60-170 104
Yucatan, state, Mexico T84+208 100
Yucatan Chan., Mex.-Cuba T66+216 101
Yugoslavia (Jugoslavia),
   Cent. Europe L70+440 51
Yuhsien, China E32+398 66
Yuhwan, China D82+282 67
Yukhnov, U.S.S.R. K59+548 60

Yukon Terr., Canada W80+610 88
Yukon, R., Alaska Y60+526 99
Yulin, China E62+383 66
Yuma, Arizona V58+329 98
Yuma, Colorado U76+401 94
Yumen, China F50+410 63
Yungchow. See Lingling
Yungera, Victoria C41-348 109
Yungfu, China E60+250 67
Yungki. See Kirin
Yungkia. See Wenchow
Yungnien, China E31+368 66
Yungning (Nanning), China E70+228 67
Yungning, China F25+277 64
Yungping. See Lulung
Yungshun, China E61+290 67
Yungsin, China E33+270 67
Yungsui, China E63+286 67
Yungtsi, China E59+349 66
Yunhsien, China E54+329 66
Yunsi, China E57+331 66
Yunta, S. Australia C63-326 109
Yurievets, U.S.S.R. K11+574 61
Yurimaguas, Peru T07-059 104
Yurlovka, U.S.S.R. J79+536 61
Yurmysh, U.S.S.R. H70+572 61
Yushu, China F50-332 64
Yütze, China E44+377 66
Yuyang, China E67+288 67
Yuyu, China E46+402 66
Yverdon, Switzerland M50+468 45
Ywathit, Burma F45+192 71
Zaachila, Mexico U41+168 100
Zaandam, Netherlands M61+524 44
Zabid, Yemen K11+141 74
Zabrze, Poland L67+504 49
Zacapa, Guatemala T38+149 100
Zacapoaxtla, Mexico U46+198 100
Zacatecas & state, Mexico U76+228 100
Zadar, Yugoslavia L89+441 56
Zadonsk, U.S.S.R. K36+524 60
Zafarabad, Iran J75+390 74
Zafarwal, Pakistan H01+323 72
Zafra, Spain N38+384 52
Zagazig, Egypt K80+306 81
Zagreb, Yugoslavia L84+458 56
Zahedan, Iran H84+295 75
Zahle, Lebanon K55-338 76
Zahran, Saudi Arabia K06+174 74
Zaidiya, Yemen K12+152 74
Zainsk, U.S.S.R. J47+553 61
Zaire, rep., Cent. Africa L50-050 82
Zaisan, Kazakh. G30+474 62
Zajecar, Yugoslavia L46+439 58
Zakho, Iraq K13+373 74
Zakin, Afghanistan H81+326 75
Zakinthos, I., Greece L56+378 59
Zakroczyn, Poland L55+498 49
Zikros, Crete L22+351 59
Zalau, Romania L42+472 49
Zalew Wislany, Poland L62+544 49
Zalma, Missouri U01+370 97
Zambia, Africa L30-150 84
Zambezi R., S.-E. Africa K52-186 84
Zamboanga, Philippines D77+070 65
Zamora, Ecuador T22-042 104
Zamora, Spain N34+415 52
Zandberg, Netherlands M48+529 44

Zandvoort, Netherlands M63+524 44
Zanesville, Ohio T42+399 91
Zangla, Kashmir G78+336 72
Zanjan, Iran J69+367 74
Zante. See Zakinthos I.
Zanzibar & I., E. Africa K34-062 83
Zapala, Argentina S61-388 103
Zapallar, Argentina R87-265 103
Zapata Pen., Cuba T40+223 101
Zaporozhye, Ukraine K59+479 60
Zara, Turkey K44+399 74
Zara. See Zadar
Zaragoza, Colombia S89+074 104
Zaragoza, Mexico U57+241 100
Zaragoza, Spain N05+416 53
Zaraguro, Ecuador T25-036 104
Zarand, Iran J20+308 75
Zarasai, Lithuania L22+558 47
Zarauz, Spain N13+433 53
Zaraza, Venezuela S32+094 104
Zaria, Nigeria M44+110 80
Zarki, Poland L64+507 49
Zarmiqa, Saudi Arabia J61+250 74
Zarqa, Jordan K53+321 76
Zaruma, Ecuador T28-038 104
Zarzis, Tunisia M35+335 81
Zatec, Czechoslovakia M09+503 48
Zavitinsk, U.S.S.R. D33+500 63
Zawiercie, Poland L63+505 49
Zaysan, Oz., Kazakh. G35+480 62
Zbaszyn, Poland L84+522 49
Zdunska Wola, Poland L66+516 49
Zealand, New Brunswick S41+461 90
Zealand. See Sjaelland
Zebak, Afghanistan H21+364 75
Zebdani, Syria K53+337 76
Zebid Qadhima, Saudi Arabia K35+224 74
Zeebrugge, Belgium M71+513 44
Zeehan, Tasmania C28-419 109
Zeeland, prov., Netherlands M67+515 44
Zeerust, Transvaal L24-256 84
Zegharta, Lebanon K55+344 76
Zeila, Somalia K10+112 83
Zeist, Netherlands M58+521 44
Zeitz, E. Germany M17+510 48
Zelaf, Syria K46+329 76
Zele, Belgium M66+511 44
Zelezna Ruda, Czech. M11+491 48
Zella, Libya L76+284 81
Zelman, U.S.S.R. J84+507 61
Zemio, Cent. Afr. Rep. L30-050 81
Zemun, Yugoslavia L57+448 58
Zenica, Yugoslavia L73+442 58
Zepce, Yugoslavia L72+445 58
Zermatt, Switzerland M43+460 45
Zernez, Switzerland M29+467 45
Zetland (Shetland), Scot. N07+604 40
Zevenbergen, Netherlands M62+516 44
Zeya, U.S.S.R. D47+537 63
Zeyma, Saudi Arabia K29-217 74
Zgierz, Poland L63+519 49
Zgorzelec. See Görlitz.
Zhdanov, Ukraine K44+471 60
Zhigansk, U.S.S.R. D70+667 63
Zhitomir, Ukraine L08+504 60
Zhmerinka, Ukraine L10+490 60
Ziarat, Pakistan H43+304 70
Ziba. See Dhaba.
Zidani Most, Yugoslavia L89+461 56

Ziemupe, Latvia L53+568 47
Zierikzee, Netherlands M66+516 44
Zijpe, Netherlands M66+517 44
Zikhron Ya'aqoy, Israel K60+325 76
Zile, Turkey K54+402 74
Zilfi, Saudi Arabia K02+262 74
Zilina, Czechoslovakia L67+492 49
Zima, U.S.S.R. F18+540 63
Zimapan, Mexico U56+207 100
Zindajan, Afghanistan H79+344 75
Zinder, Niger M36+138 81
Zingst, pen., E. Germany M14+544 48
Zion Nat. Park, Utah V48+374 92
Zira, India H00+310 72
Zirc, Hungary L73+473 49
Ziraquira, Colombia S84+050 104
Zittacuaro, Mexico U63+193 100
Zittau, E. Germany M01+509 48
Zizers, Switzerland M32+469 45
Zlatoust, U.S.S.R. J02+551 61
Zmeinogorsk, U.S.S.R. G47+511 62
Znin, Poland L74+528 49
Znojmo, Czechoslovakia L84+489 49
Zofingen, Switzerland M42+473 45
Zoisa, Tanzania K50-058 83
Zolder, Belgium M58+510 44
Zollino, Italy L71+402 57
Zolotoye, U.S.S.R. J85+508 61
Zomba, Malawi K58-154 83
Zonguldak, Turkey K78+416 74
Zorita, Spain N34+393 52
Zoute, Het, Belgium M70+514 44
Zoutkamp, Netherlands M52+533 44
Zrenjanin, Yugoslavia L58+454 58
Zuara, Libya M18+328 81
Zuevka, U.S.S.R. J55+585 61
Zug & canton, Switzerland M39+472 45
Zuger See, Switzerland M39+471 45
Zuhab, Iran J85+347 74
Zuid Beijerland, Netherlands M64+518 44
Zuider Zee. See IJsselmeer
Zuidland, Netherlands M65+518 44
Zuid Natoena Eiln., Indon. E66+028 65
Zuidwolde, Netherlands M51+527 44
Zuila, Libya L88+262 81
Zukur, Jab., Yemen K13+140 74
Zula, Ethiopia K32-152 83
Zulfikar, Afghanistan H82+356 75
Zumbo, Mozambique K88-156 84
Zumpango, Mexico U54+198 100
Zundert, Netherlands M62+515 44
Zungeru, Nigeria M54+098 80
Zuni, Mt.- New Mexico V18+352 94
Zürich & canton. Switz. M39+474 45
Zürich See, Switzerland M38+472 45
Zurzach, Switzerland M40+476 45
Zutphen, Netherlands M53+522 44
Zwai L., Ethiopia K38+078 83
Zwartsluis, Netherlands M54+526 44
Zweelo, Netherlands M50+528 44
Zweibrücken, W. Germany M47+493 48
Zweisimmen, Switzerland M46+466 45
Zwickau, E. Germany M15+507 48
Zwolen, Poland L51+513 49
Zwolle, Netherlands M53+525 44
Zyrardów, Poland L57+521 49
Zyryanka, U.S.S.R. B85+645 63
Zyryanovsk, Kazakh. G35+498 62
Zyyi, Cyprus K70-347 76

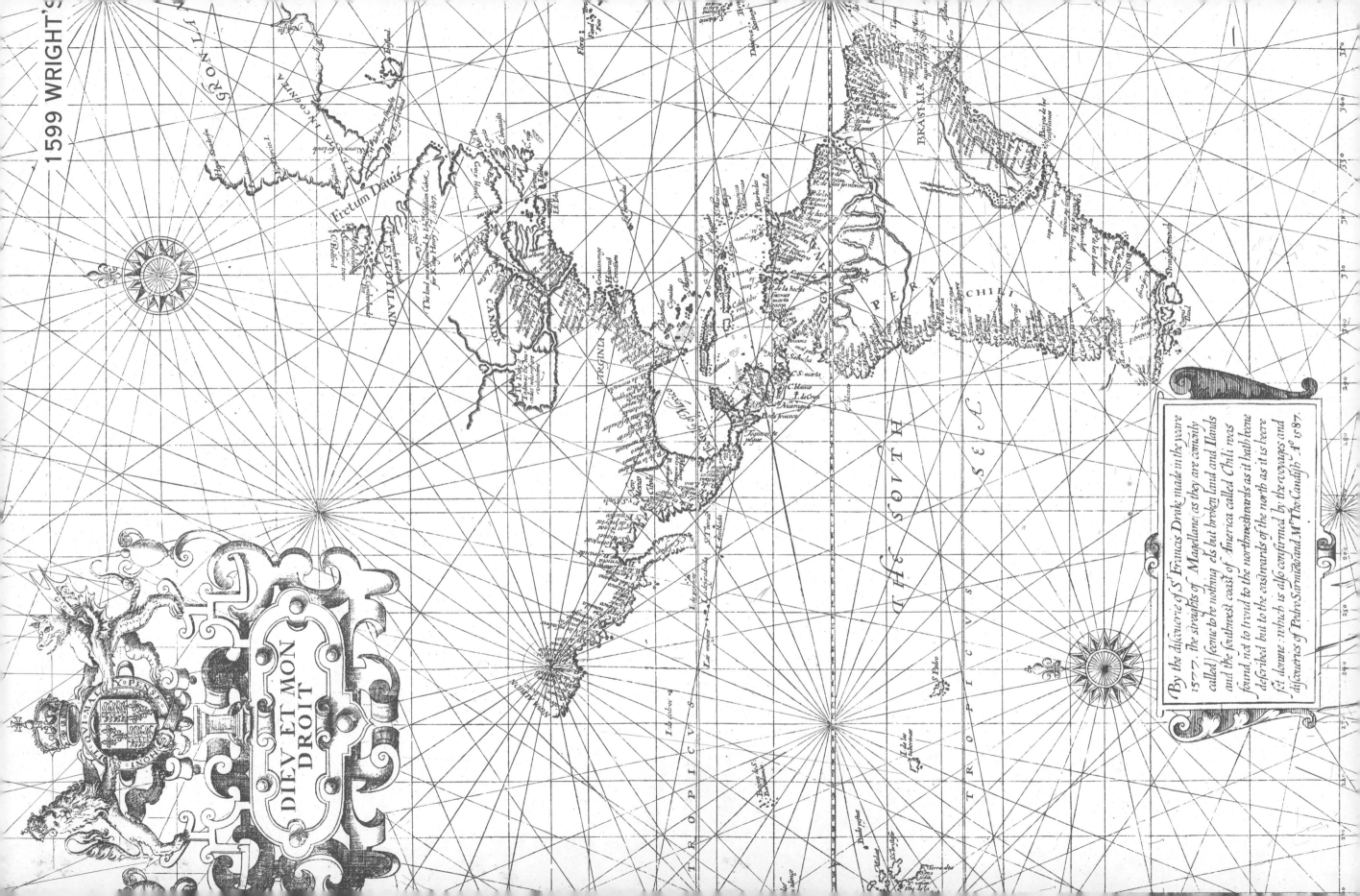

THE SOUTH SEA

By the difcouerie of Sr Francis Drake made in the yeare 1577. The ftreightfs of Magellane, as they are comonly called) feeme to be nothing els but broken land and Ilands and the foulhwest coast of America called Chili was found, not to trend to the northwestwards as it hath beene described but to the eastwards of the north as it is heere fet downe : which is alfo confirmed by the voyages and difcoueries of Pedro Sarmie and Mr Tho:Candish Aᵒ 1587.

DIEV ET MON DROIT

HONY SOIT QVI MAL Y PENSE